Duncan Petersen
Charming Small Hotels
BRITAIN & IRELAND

Duncan Petersen
Charming Small Hotels
BRITAIN & IRELAND

Consultant editor Fiona Duncan

Duncan Petersen

19th edition

Conceived, designed and produced by
Duncan Petersen Publishing Ltd,
Studio G9, 82 Silverthorne Road, London SW8 3HE

Copyright © Duncan Petersen Publishing Ltd 2024, 2018, 2014, 2008, 2004, 2001, 2000, 1999, 1998, 1997, 1996, 1995, 1994, 1993, 1992, 1991, 1990, 1989 and 1988

All rights reserved. No reproduction, copy or transmission of this publication may be made without written permission. No paragraph of this publication may be reproduced, copied or transmitted save with written permission or in accordance with the provisions of the CopyrightAct 1956 (as amended).Any person who does any unauthorized act in relation to this publication may be liable to criminal prosecution and civil claims for damages.

Editorial director Andrew Duncan
Consultant editor Fiona Duncan
Editor Madeleine Sadler
Contributing editors Francesca O'Mahony, Jonathan and Joan Noble, Mike and Jane Hodgson, Geraldine Onslow, Jenny Donath
Cover design Madeleine Sadler
Maps Map Creation Ltd
Photo credits contact hotels for picture credits

A CIP catalogue record for this book is available from the British Library

ISBN 978-1-7396684-2-6

DTP by Duncan Petersen Publishing Ltd
Printed in the EU by Finetone.

Cover photos: The Alice Hawthorn (front), Artist Residence - Cornwall, Cynefin Retreats, Another Place The Lake, Glebe House, The Cartford Inn
Title page: Artist Residence - London

Page 6: Fort Road

Contents

Introduction	6-13
Reporting to the guide	14
Hotel location maps	15-25
Southern England	
The South-West	26-95
The South-East and Channel Islands	96-176
Central England and Wales	
Wales	177-198
Midlands	199-244
East Anglia and Region	245-271
Northern England	
The North-West	272-304
The North-East	305-329
Scotland	
Southern Scotland	330-343
Highlands and Islands	344-372
Ireland	
Northern Ireland	373-375
Irish Republic	376-407
Indexes	
Index of hotel names	408-422
Index of hotel locations	423-429

Introduction

In this introductory section:
Our selection criteria 8

Types of accommodation 9-10

How to find an entry 10

Reporting to the guide 14

Maps 15-25

Welcome to the 19th edition of *Charming Small Hotels Britain & Ireland* – a guide with a long history. It was first published in 1988 by my husband Andrew Duncan, his co-director Mel Petersen and with Chris Gill as the editor. I took over as editor in the mid 1990s and looked after several editions until 2006 when I began writing my hotel column in *The Telegraph*. Since then it has been looked after by Duncan Petersen with myself as consultant editor, giving advice on new entries and which to drop.

The guide's focus on smaller places, usually with four to 12 bedrooms, is especially close to my heart – and to my view on hotel keeping – which is that small is, mostly, beautiful because large places find it hard to create a place with that elusive quality of character and charm, where the guest feels like a person, not just a customer.

I have not been able to visit every single entry in the guide, though most are known to me in some way. Though all the entries are faithful to our idea of a charming small hotel, I do like some better than others; and I have had to trust that the detailed work of updating facts has been done well. Those aside, I believe that the guide is as unique and as valuable as it was when first published in 1988. I hope you agree.

Happy travels - Fiona Duncan

Introduction

This new edition reflects the recent changes in our sector of the hospitality industry. Following the lockdowns in 2020 many places found day-to-day operations difficult. However, we have been delighted to find that the spirit of good hospitality has come through. Many old favourites have held on to their reputations and plenty of enthusiastic newcomers have opened: the indexes highlight more than 70 places new to the guide. We've noticed that many places now offer private self-catering options in the guise of eco-lodges, houses for hire, shepherds huts and glamping. This new edition features some of them, but above all the surge in 'dining pubs' with rooms: they have always been a feature of British hospitality, but since the pandemic many new ones have opened and plenty of established pubs have converted to the formula.

Because of the cost of living increases in recent years we have often mentioned actual prices in the descriptions. This is in addition to the ususal price band information - see page 10.

In all other respects, the guide remains true to the values and qualities that make it unique (see below), and which have won it so many devoted readers. It has sold hundreds of thousands of copies in the U.K., U.S.A. and in five European languages.

Why are we unique?

This is the only independent (no hotel pays for an entry) UK-originated accomodation guide that:

- concentrates on places that have real charm and character;
- is highly selective and fussy about size. Most hotels have fewer than 20 bedrooms; if there are more, the hotel must have the feel of a much smaller place. Time and again we find that a genuinely warm welcome is *much* more likely to be found in a small hotel;
- gives proper emphasis to description – doesn't use irritating symbols;
- is produced by a small company with like-minded reporters.

Above all, the text doesn't read as if it's an advert, paid for by the hotel, which is the case with most other guides. Our reviews are honest: objective, distanced and they mention negatives *and* positives.

Opposite: Fort Road Hotel, Margate

Introduction

So what exactly do we look for?
Our selection criteria

- A peaceful, attractive setting. Obviously, if the entry is in an urban area, we make allowances.
- A building that is handsome, interesting, historic or characterful.
- Adequate space, but on a human scale. We don't go for places that rely too much on grandeur.
- Good taste and imagination in the interior decoration. We reject standardized, chain hotel fixtures, fittings and decorations.
- Bedrooms that look like real bedrooms, not hotel rooms, individually decorated.
- Furnishings and other facilities that are comfortable and well maintained. We like to see interesting antique furniture that is there to be used, not simply revered.
- Proprietors and staff who are dedicated and thoughtful, offering a personal welcome, but who aren't intrusive or overly effusive.
- Interesting food.
- A sympathetic atmosphere; an absence of loud people showing off their money; or the 'corporate feel'.

No fear or favour

To us, taking a payment for appearing in a guide seems to defeat the object of producing a guide. If money has changed hands, you can't write the whole truth about a hotel, and the selection cannot be nearly so interesting. This seems to us to be proved at least in part by the fact that pay guides are so keen to present the illusion of independence: most only admit taking payment in small print inside.

Not many people realize that on the shelves of British bookshops there are many more hotel guides that accept payments for entries than there are independent guides. This guide is one of the few that do not accept any money for an entry.

Just as selective

The guide is still all about places that are more than just a bed for the night. Every time we consider a new hotel, we ask ourselves whether it has that extra special something, regardless of category and facilities, that makes it worth seeking out.

Introduction

Types of accomodation

Despite its title, the guide does not confine itself to places called hotels or places that behave like hotels. On the contrary, we actively look for places that offer a home from home. We include small and medium-sized hotels; pubs; inns; restaurants-with-rooms; guest-houses; bed-and-breakfasts; and a handful of self-catering cottages and apartments which offer food and other services. Some places, usually private homes which take guests, operate on house-party lines, where you are introduced to the other guests, and take meals at a communal table. If you don't like making small talk to strangers, or are part of a romantic twosome that wants to keep itself to itself, this type of establishment may not be for you. On the other hand, if you are interested in meeting people, perhaps as a foreign visitor wanting to get to know the locals, then you'll find it rewarding.

Home from home

Perhaps the most beguiling characteristic of the best places to stay in this guide is the feeling they give of being in a private home – but without the everyday cares and chores of running one. To get this formula right requires a special sort of professionalism: the proprietor has to strike the balance between being relaxed and giving attentive service. Those who experience this 'feel' often turn their backs on all other forms of accommodation – however luxurious.

Our pet dislikes

Small hotels are not automatically wonderful hotels; and the very individuality of small, owner-run hotels, makes them prone to peculiarities that the mass-produced hotel experience avoids. For the benefit of those who run the small hotels of Britain – and those contemplating the plunge – we repeat once more our list of pet hates:

Price too high Prices tend to be higher, like for like, than in France and Italy. This is not always the fault of hotels, but it is disappointing.

Not entirely child-friendly Again, compared with mainland European hotels, children are much more often seen as a nuisance by hoteliers.

'Contemporary-formulaic' decoration Too many hotels think they can appeal simply by putting 'modern' paint on the walls. The more we see of this, the more of a cliche it becomes.

The hushed dining room Owners have a duty to create an atmosphere in which conversation can flow.

Introduction

The ordinary breakfast Even hotels that go to great lengths to prepare special dinners are capable of serving prefabricated orange juice, sliced bread and tea made with tea bags at breakfast.

The schoolteacher mentality If you run a hotel, you should be flexible and accommodating enough to deal with the whims of travellers.

The inexperienced waiter Or waitress. Running a small operation does not excuse the imposition on the paying public of completely untrained (and sometimes ill-suited) staff who can spoil the most beautifully cooked food.

The lumpy old bed Beds have improved much in recent years. There's no excuse for a creaking frame or an old mattress.

The erratic boiler It doesn't often happen, but tepid baths are unforgiveable. Even the cheapest places should regard this as a basic.

Check the price first In this guide we have adopted the system of price bands, rather than giving actual prices. This is because prices were often subject to change after we went to press. Price bands refer to the approximate price of a standard double room (high season rates) with breakfast for two people. Prices for Ireland are quoted in Euros. They are as follows:

£	under £100	€	under 120 euros
££	£100 – £200	€€	120 – 230 euros
£££	£200 – £400	€€€	230 – 460 euros
££££	more than £400	€€€€	more than 460 euros

Always check what is included in the price (for example service, breakfast, afternoon tea) when booking.

How to find an entry

In this guide, the entries are arranged in geographical groups. First, the whole of Britain and Ireland are divided into five major groups, starting with Southern England and working northwards to Scotland; Ireland comes last. Within these major groups, the entries are grouped into smaller regional sub-sections such as the South-West, Wales, the Midlands and the Highlands and Islands – for a full list, see page 5. Within each sub-section, entries are listed alphabetically by nearest town or village; if several occur in or near one town, entries are arranged in alpha order by name of hotel.

Introduction

To find a hotel in a particular area, use the maps following this introduction to locate the appropriate pages.

To locate a specific hotel, whose name you know, or a hotel in a place you know, use the indexes at the back, which list entries both by names and by nearest place name. The name of the county follows the town name in the heading for each entry.

The five main sections of the book (Southern England, Central England, The North, Scotland and Ireland) are introduced by area introductions.

Using the guide

We use three different hotel entry formats in order to give you perspective on the character and quality of the places to stay. Although all are worthy of the guide, some are better than others. The **whole page** entries are the cream of our selection – mainstream charming small hotels that tick all or most of our boxes. **Half pages** shouldn't be overlooked or under-rated. They are also true charming small hotels, some of them good, some excellent. Usually, but no means always, because of their larger size, they don't conform as closely to our criteria as the whole page hotels. They are grouped at the end of each regional section, after the whole page entries. **Section opener** entries are useful back-up entries with small photos and brief descriptions. They are found on the five area introduction pages – see above. Again, don't overlook these: they are great places that have attracted our attention but not quite as faithful to our criteria as whole and half page entries.

So within each region you need to look in three different places to get the whole range of recommendations, and the entire contents are also easily accessible by using the maps on pages 15-25 and the indexes on pages 408-429.

Glebe House

Introduction

How to read an entry

Postal address and other key information.

Places of interest within reach of the hotel.

This sets the hotel in its geographical context and should not be taken as precise instructions as to how to get there; always ask the hotel for directions.

Rooms described as having a bath usually also have a shower; rooms described as having a shower only have a shower.

Essential booking information.

THE NORTH-WEST | NORTHERN ENGLAND

Bowland Bridge, Cumbria

Bowland Bridge, Grange-over-Sands, Cumbria, LA11 6NN

Tel 015395 55549
email hello@hareandhoundslakes.com
website www.hareandhoundslakes.com

Nearby Cartmell Fell, Windermere, Bowness, Kendal, World of Beatrix Potter
Location just off the A5074
Food breakfast, lunch, dinner
Price ££-£££
Rooms 4; doubles with ensuites
Facilities pub, dining room, garden, private parking, snug
Credit cards MC, V
Children welcome
Accessibility pub only
Pets dogs welcome
Closed never
Proprietors Andrew Black and Simon Rayner-Langmead

Hare and Hounds
Village inn

Arriving in Bowland Bridge you could feel you're in a sleepy, lost village. But step into this pub and you'll get a lively buzz. Guests, locals and walkers seem to have a common cause: the wonder of the fells around Lake Windermere (and retreating when the weather turns). The lively atmosphere arises partly from the enthusiasm of American co-owner Andrew Black, whose friendliness and curiosity encourage a sense of community among the guests. Restoring this quintessential country pub is the joint venture of long-time friends and day-dreamers, Andrew and Simon Rayner-Langmead.

With quirky artworks, including a Tracy Emin, the Hare and Hounds has energized this old Cumbrian village, and its reputation is growing. Each of the four bedrooms (delightfully named in the vernacular of Cumbrian Shepherds: Yan (one), Tyan (two), Tethera (three), Methera (four) is a testament to classic country cottages, with a palette of warm and inviting hues of earthy tones and soft, muted greens. The daily menu offers a selection of classic Cumbrian dishes and traditional fare. The pub often hosts residencies for talented chefs, so the menu will change. Breakfast is ordered the night before using a checklist. Fresh milk is put outside your room every morning.

Introduction

City, town or village, and region, in which the hotel is located.

Name of hotel.

Type of establishment.

Description – never vetted by the hotel.

Breakfast is normally included in the price of the room. Other meals, such as afternoon tea, may also be available. 'Room service' refers to food and drink, either snacks or full meals, which can be served in the room

This information is only an indication for wheelchair users. Hotels increasingly offer other ammenities for those with sensory or mobility differences. Always check on suitability with the hotel.

Children
Where children are welcome, there are often special facilities, such as cots, high chairs, baby listening and high teas. Always check whether children are accepted in the dining room.

Pets
Always let the hotel know in advance if you want to bring a pet. Even where pets are accepted, certain restrictions may apply, and a small charge may be levied.

We list the following credit cards:
AE American Express
DC Diners Club
MC Mastercard
V Visa
Most hotels accept many other credit cards.

Introduction

Reporting to the guide

Please write and tell us about your experiences of small hotels, guest houses and inns, whether good or bad, whether listed in this edition or not. As well as hotels in Britain & Ireland, we are interested in hotels in Austria, France, Italy, Spain, Germany and Switzerland.

Readers whose reports prove particularly helpful may be invited to join our Travellers' Panel. Members give us notice of their own travel plans; we suggest hotels that they might inspect, and help with the cost of accommodation.

Write to us:

Editor, *Charming Small Hotels*
Studio G9, 82 Silverthorne Road, Battersea, SW8 3HE.

charmingsmall.hotels@zen.co.uk

Checklist

Please use a separate sheet of paper for each report; include your name, address and telephone number on each report.

Your reports will be received with particular pleasure if they are typed, and if they are organized under the following headings:

- Name of establishment
- Town or village it is in, or nearest
- Full address, including postcode
- Telephone number
- Time and duration of visit
- The building and setting
- The public rooms
- The bedrooms and bathrooms
- Physical comfort (chairs, beds, heat, light, hot water)
- Standards of maintenance and housekeeping
- Atmosphere, welcome and service
- Food
- Value for money

We assume that in writing you have no objections to your views being published unpaid, either verbatim or in an edited version. Names of major outside contributors are acknowledged, at the editor's discretion, in the guide.

Hotel Locations

Hotel location maps

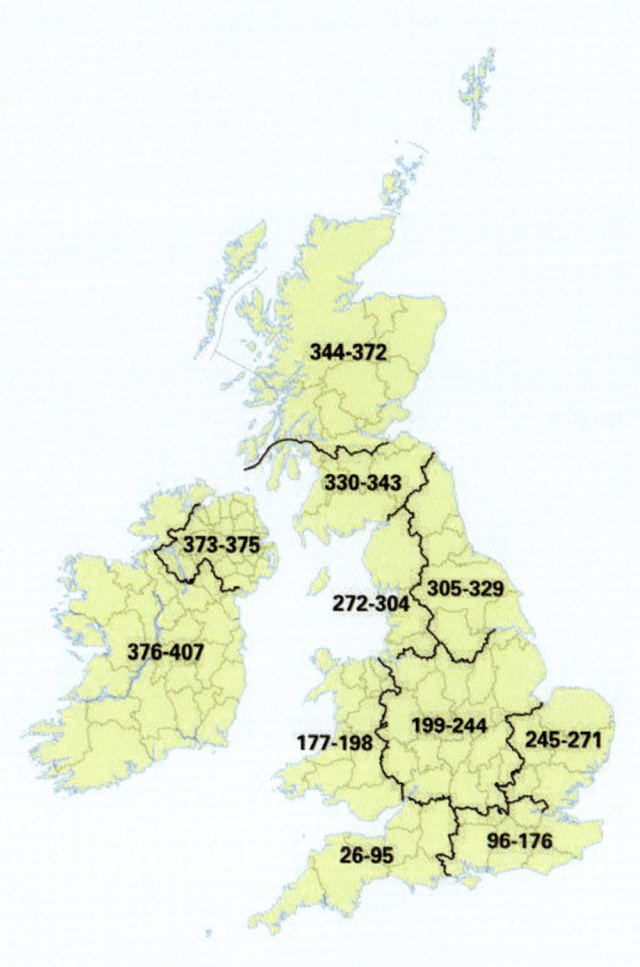

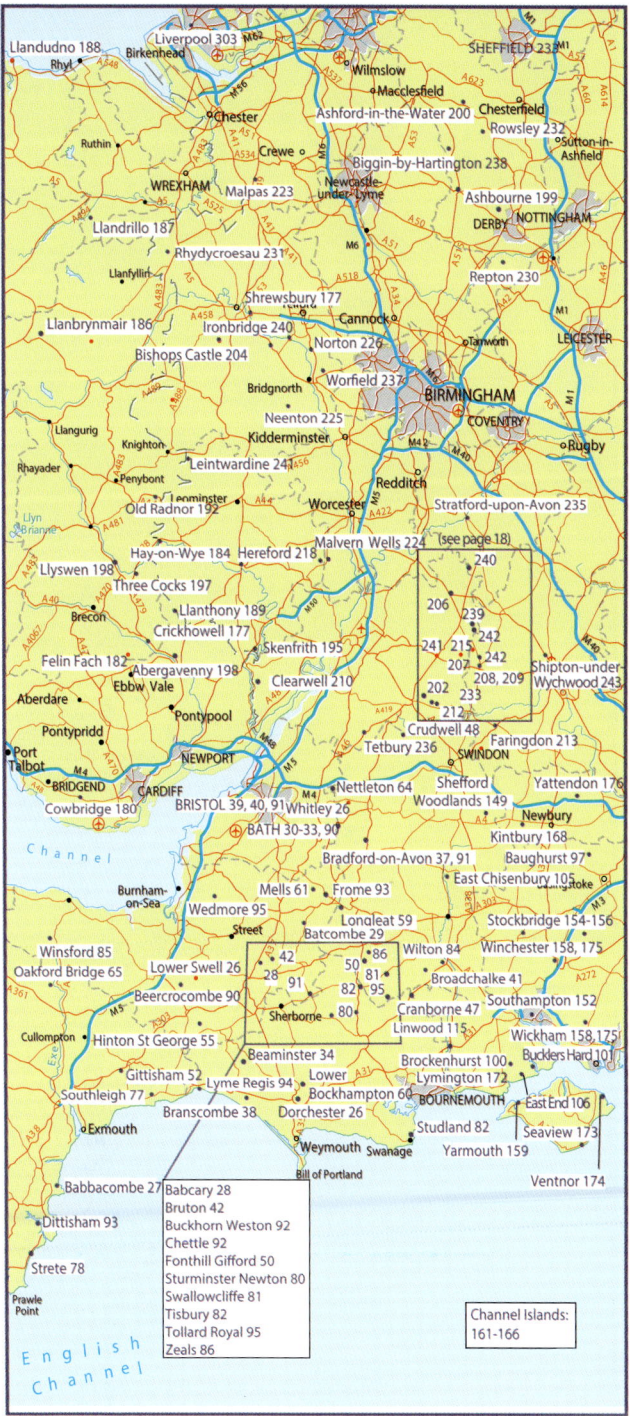

22

THE SOUTH-WEST / SOUTHERN ENGLAND

Area introduction

This first section, covering the whole of Southern England, includes the important summer tourist counties, Devon and Cornwall, with their spectacular coastline and wonderful patchwork countryside, their sunken lanes and timeless villages. Add to them Somerset and Wiltshire, Dorset and south-west Hampshire, and you have what is loosely known as the West Country – what used to be, more or less, the early medieval Kingdom of Wessex. The rest of the section consists of densely populated south-east England – East and West Sussex, Kent, Berkshire and Greater London. Here, as elsewhere, you can scarcely go a mile without discovering somewhere worth seeing: a picturesque village, a Georgian town or a spectacular view. Charming small hotels are thick on the ground. We draw the border dividing southern England from Central England roughly along the M4, or a line linking London in the east with Bristol in the west.

Below are some useful back-up places to try if our main selections are fully booked:

Gidleigh Park
Country house hotel, Chagford
Tel 01647 432367
www.gidleigh.co.uk
Luxury, fine dining.

The Casterbridge
Town guesthouse, Dorchester
Tel 01305 264043
www.casterbridgehotel.co.uk
Relaxed guesthouse offering bed-and-breakfast service.

The Compasses
Village pub, Littley Green
Tel 01245 362308
www.compasseslittleygreen.co.uk
Charming pub-with-rooms in the hamlet of Littley Green.

Chiltern Firehouse
Town house hotel, London
Tel 020 7073 7676
www.chilternfirehouse.com
Luxury hotel with a Michelin starred chef.

Langford Fivehead
Restaurant-with-rooms, Lower Swell
Tel 01460 282020 www.langfordfivehead.co.uk
'Farm to plate' fine dining.

The Scarlet
Coastal hotel, Mawgan Porth
Tel 01637 861800
www.scarlethotel.co.uk
Eco-friendly, adults only hotel.

The Mermaid Inn
Town inn, Rye
Tel 01797 223065
www.mermaidinn.com
Charming inn in pretty Rye, dating back to 1420.

Longueville Manor
Country house hotel, St Saviour Tel 01534 725500
www.longuevillemanor.com
Traditional Relais & Chateaux hotel, high standards.

Hotel du Vin
Town mansion hotel, Tunbridge Wells
Tel 084474 89266
www.hotelduvin.com
Elegant hotel in spa town.

The Pear Tree Inn
Restaurant-with-rooms, Whitley Tel 01225 70940
www.peartreewhitley.co.uk
Formerly owned by Marco Pierre White.

Babbacombe, Devon

Oddicombe Beach Hill,
Babbacombe, South Devon TQ1 3LX

Tel 01803 327110
email enquiries@caryarms.co.uk
website www.caryarms.co.uk

Nearby Babbacombe Bay, Torquay, Torre Abbey, Berry Pomeroy Castle
Location turn onto Babbacombe Downs Road, continue along the Downs with the sea on your left then turn left onto Beach Road.
Food breakfast, lunch, dinner, afternoon tea **Price** ££££ **Rooms** 10 sea-facing rooms and suites at inn; 5 restored fisherman's cottages: TV, hairdryer, tea/coffee facilities. 8 deluxe beach huts/suites; each with terrace, sitting room, wet bar, fire, bathroom **Facilities** residents' sitting room with fire, Yon-Ka Spa, conservatory, bar, dining room, wi-fi
Credit cards MC, V **Children** welcome **Accessibilty** some suitability
Pets some dog friendly cottages and spaces **Closed** never
Proprietor Lana and Peter de Savary

Cary Arms & Spa
Beach inn

Special places need a special effort to reach them. Set beneath the cliffs on the beach at Babbacombe, the Cary Arms' location is spectacular, but its approach, via an alarmingly steep single-track road, is not for the faint hearted. Queen Victoria was equally enchanted 150 years ago, rowing ashore with Prince Albert from the Royal Yacht on several occasions.

The present hotel was built in the late 1880s: a solid, reassuring building with a stone walled, slate floored bar at its core. Here, superior gastropub dishes are served. Try the local Devon beef or Lyme Bay lobster.

There are ten bedrooms and three self-catering cottages, all delightful, with retro red leather bed-heads, pretty wardrobes, sticks of rock on snow white pillows and walls adorned by old posters advertising the delights of Devon and colourful photographs (recalling de Savary's passion) for racing yachts. Since the last edition more beach huts have been added and two suites. Each hut sleeps two, and quirkily combines vintage seaside style with bespoke contemporary art. There is also a spa offering luxury Thalgo treatments.

Chic and secluded doesn't come cheap, but it's worth it. Standard double rooms were £245 as we went to press — including breakfast.

THE SOUTH-WEST / SOUTHERN ENGLAND

Babcary, Somerset

North St, Babcary, Somerton TA11 7ED

Tel 01458 223230
email info@redlionbabcary.co.uk
website info@redlionbabcary.co.uk

Nearby Glastonbury Town & Tor, Stourhead, Hauser & Wirth, Lytes Cary Manor, Montecute House
Location From London or Cornwall A303 access directly off to Babcary 2 half miles, and A37 from Bristol
Food breakfast, lunch, dinner
Price ££-£££
Rooms 6; double, twin, superior or family rooms
Facilities restaurant, bar, pizza shack, private dining room
Credit cards MC, V
Children welcome
Accessibility suitable
Pets dogs welcome
Closed Monday nights and Tuesdays
Proprietors Clare and Charlie Garrad

The Red Lion
Village inn

A versatile dining pub that stands out locally for atmosphere, service and food. The authentic, rustic appeal of the ground floor public areas has been preserved for the 20 years or so that Clare and Charlie Garrard have been owner-managers, but they've developed the exterior by adding a pizza shack and a separate building for parties and functions. The bedrooms in the adjacent Barn have had a fairly recent makeover, using fashionable grey and white as the recurring colour scheme. They're comfortably equipped but standardised.

Charlie has been in the hospitality industry since he started at the bottom, Clare was a model and worked in the fashion industry, so they understand marketplaces. The menu reflects this, in order to appeal to a range of punters: comfort food ie traditional pub dishes sit alongside ambitious restaurant dishes, some priced in the high £20s as we went to press; just one main course was less than £20. The chef had been in place for ten years, a good sign.

Dog owners are encouraged to add a photo of their pet to a gallery of doggy images on a wall - a friendly touch that says Clare and Charlie are good hosts and that this is a proper community hang-out.

Batcombe, Somerset

The Three Horseshoes, Batcombe
BA4 6HE

Tel 01749 326147
email enquiries@thethreehorseshoesbatcombe.co.uk
website www.thethreehorseshoesbatcombe.co.uk

Nearby King Alfred's Tower, Mells Village, Nunney Castle
Location Batcombe, three miles from Bruton
Food breakfast (included), lunch, dinner
Price £££-££££
Rooms 5; all Super King Relyon beds with en suites
Facilities restaurant, bar, WiFi, outdoor seating, private dining room
Credit cards MC, V, AE
Children welcome, cots and some joining room
Accessibility public rooms only
Pets dogs welcome in some rooms, extra charge
Closed never
Proprietors Max Wigram and Margot Henderson

The Three Horseshoes
Country Inn

Imaginative, top-chef food comes to rural Somerset. This is the first venture outside London (opened 2023) of respected New Zealand chef Margot Henderson of the Rochelle Canteen in Shoreditch. Besides overseeing the food here alongside Head chef Nye Smith, she runs a catering business while husband Fergus is the proprietor of St John Restaurant, Smithfield. The short, often-changed menu is a foodie statement in its own right. Duck leg comes with white beans cooked in the juice of a pig's trotter; a bacon chop gets lentils and 'green sauce'; venison sits beside beetroot and horseradish. The wine list is also full of surprises. Prices are friendlier than many a rural dining pub which can't claim a nationally known chef. The bar menu offered fried pig's head and ketchup. Service is unstuffy, swift and knowledgeable.

The rooms are perfect examples of what we look for, more like bedrooms in a private country house than a hotel, very nicely judged and understated. Specially crafted beds are among the most comfortable we've slept in and all five rooms are notably spacious. There are intentionally no radios or TVs, encouraging you to relax and forget the 'real' world.

The garden is another reason to visit: it's the work of Libby Russell of Mazullo Russell Garden Design. This is easily worth a detour of 50 miles, or a weekend away in its own right.

THE SOUTH-WEST   SOUTHERN ENGLAND

Bath, Somerset

1 Crescent Gardens, Upper Bristol Road BA1 2NA

Tel 01225425543
email info@brooksguesthouse.com
website www.brooksguesthouse.com

Nearby The Royal Crescent, Roman Baths, Jane Austen Centre, Royal Victoria Park
Location Bath city centre
Food breakfast, cooked to order; an honesty bar; afternoon tea
Price £-££
Rooms 22, including 4 family rooms
Facilities dining room
Credit cards MC, V
Children welcome
Accessibilty no access
Pets not allowed
Closed never
Proprietor Carla Brooks

Brooks Guesthouse, Bath
Guesthouse

Brooks Guesthouse mixes antique and modern, to create an environment which it hopes will soothe and welcome you after a day in the city.

The 22 bedrooms vary in size and style, but they all share bold wallpaper, sumptuous carpets, and eye-catching, antique details. They're cosy and space is optimised – armchairs by windows, TVs tucked neatly into corners. Comfort is a priority.

The guest living room at the front of the house is warmly decorated and well lit. The absence of hosts may seem strange to some, but it can add to the homely atmosphere – take what you want from the honesty bar and simply leave a note.

The dining room is the only other communal space, and here is where the champion breakfast is offered. The sitting room is not made for guests to sit in all day, fair enough in a city where there's so much to see.

Brooks is located below the Royal Crescent, and close to the Roman Baths.

THE SOUTH-WEST — SOUTHERN ENGLAND

Bath

1 Upper Oldfield Park,
Bath, Avon BA2 3JX

Tel 01225 426336
email info@dorianhouse.co.uk
website www.dorianhouse.co.uk

Nearby Bath centre, The Royal Crescent
Location from Bath, take A367 signposted Shepton Mallet, after 1 minute's drive, take first road on the right; with car parking
Food breakfast
Price £££
Rooms 13 doubles; all with bath or shower, all rooms have TV, phone, hairdryer, wi-fi
Facilities sitting room, dining room, honesty bar; garden
Credit cards MC, V
Children accepted by arrangement
Accessibility access difficult
Pets not accepted
Closed 24th and 25th Dec
Proprietors Tim and Ros Forester

Dorian House
Bed-and-breakfast

Although Bath has a large number of hotels, Dorian House stands out as a place of elegance and charm. Tim Hugh has made the most of this Victorian building built in 1880 of Bath stone, standing on a hill overlooking the city centre – bedrooms have splendid views towards Royal Crescent.

With high ceilings and large windows (including some impressive bay windows), rooms are drenched in light and, with tan, beige and cream tones, have a feeling of airiness. The house retains all of its original features and many rooms have fireplaces and fine antiques. The elegant decoration combines Asian antiques with contemporary pieces and works of art.

The high-quality breakfast is taken in a tastefully decorated Orangery in the Japanese-inspired garden, also with views of the city. The sitting room (with honesty bar) is equally refined. You can't have dinner here, but there are plenty of good restaurants in Bath and Tim provides a book of menus collected from the better restaurants in town.

Since our last edition Dorian House has added a small self-catering shepherd's hut, The City Hut. It's separate from the main building and a cosy choice for single travellers or couples. Like the rest of the hotel, it is efficiently run yet with homely touches.

Bath

Hunstrete House, Hunstrete, Pensford, Bath, BS39 4NS

Tel 01761 490490
email info@thepignearbath.com
website www.thepighotel.com/near-bath

Nearby Hamburger Hill (Bristol Outdoor Pursuits, 0.5m), Bath (6m) with Roman Baths, Royal Crescent, Thermal Bath Spa, Fashion Museum **Location** down a rural road in unspoilt countryside, car park **Food** breakfast, lunch, dinner **Price** ££-££££ **Rooms** 29; doubles and 2 suites; twin bedding, cots and extra beds available in some rooms. All have shower or bath, TV, tea-making facilities; some have larder, drinks, Nespresso machine **Facilities** grounds, kitchen garden, treatment room, lounge, library, restaurant **Credit cards** V, MC, AE **Children** welcome **Accessibility** has an accessible room suitable for a wheelchair **Pets** not accepted **Closed** never **Manager** Sarah Holden

The Pig - near Bath
Country house hotel

This Grade II-listed house, dating back to 1820, stands in the Chew valley, imposing and dignified, surrounded by its own deer park. It became the third of the Pig hotels, a venture conceived by Robin Hutson and David Elton that's now grown into a fully formed family of eight hotels.

The style is rural shabby-chic and it works beautifully: stripped wooden floors, painted timber-panelled walls and velvet curtains create a grand but informal atmosphere. Robin's wife Judy is responsible for the interior design: mismatched rugs and fabrics create a feeling of relaxed glamour, while every object has been chosen with taste and panache. The bedrooms are consistent with the style: comfortable and laid back. They include 'larders' stocked with snacks and large bathrooms. As well as the rooms in the country house, there are four delightful garden rooms and two 'hideaway rooms' in the kitchen garden, with wood-burning stoves and freestanding baths.

The large kitchen garden provides much of the produce used in the kitchen, freshly picked on the day. The flavoursome dishes, using local game such as wild rabbit and duck, are uncomplicated and satisfying. It's hard to find fault here: an all-round good address, where you will feel relaxed and spoiled. See other Pig hotels on pages 52, 79, 100 and 152.

THE SOUTH-WEST — SOUTHERN ENGLAND

Bath

Russell Street, Bath, Somerset BA1 2QF

Tel 01225 447928
email reservations@thequeensberry.co.uk
website www.thequeensberry.co.uk

Nearby Assembly Rooms; Museum of Costume; The Circus.
Location in middle of city, close to main shopping area; paved gardens behind; daytime car parking restricted – but valet parking available
Food breakfast, lunch, dinner
Price £££
Rooms 29, 1 with shower, rest with bath; all rooms have phone, TV, hairdryer
Facilities sitting room, bar, restaurant; courtyard
Credit cards AE, MC, V
Children welcome
Accessiblity lift/elevator
Pets guide dogs only
Closed never
Proprietors Laurence and Helen Beere

The Queensberry
Town house hotel

This Bath hotel is a little large for our purposes, but shouldn't be left out. South African Laurence and Helen Beere bought this discreet, quiet and beautifully decorated haven right in the centre of Bath in 2003. It has the advantage of a lift to all levels, which cuts down on confusion in the maze of stairwells, corridors and different levels resulting from the linking of three buildings.

Despite the small-scale appearance of the hotel, the majority of the bedrooms are surprisingly spacious, and are kitted out to the highest standards of comfort and elegance. Double beds generally mean king-size here, almost guaranteed to give you a good night's sleep, and are made up with lovely cotton sheets. Rooms on the first floor are largest, with armchairs and breakfast tables; bathrooms are lavish, with quality toiletries and proper towels. The rooms have a contemporary feel, while still making use of the original features and antiques.

Downstairs, the principal sitting room is beautifully furnished in muted colours. The award-winning basement restaurant, the Olive Tree, attracts non-residents. Chef Chris Cleghorn had been at the helm for a decade as we went to press and has devised an impressive and cheerful set of tasting menus inspired by the seasons and local produce - book in advance.

Beaminster, Dorset

3 Prout Bridge, Beaminster, Dorset
DT8 3AY

Tel 01308 862200
email enquiries@theollerod.co.uk
website www.theollerod.co.uk

Nearby Mapperton Gardens; Forde Abbey; Abbotsbury Swannery & Sub-Tropical Gardens.
Location on A3066 in centre of town; ample car parking
Food breakfast; lunch; dinner
Price £££
Rooms 13; 7 double, 3 twin, 1 single, 2 family, all with bath or shower; all rooms have phone, TV, wi-fi
Facilities sitting room, bar, restaurant, 2 conservatories; outdoor dining area, walled garden, treatment room
Credit cards AE, MC, V
Children accepted
Accessibility 4 bedrooms with easy access
Pets dogs accepted in selected rooms
Closed never
Proprietors Silvana Bandini and Chris Staines

The Ollerod
Restaurant-with-rooms

Dating from the 13th century, this stone building is reputedly a former clergy house and the oldest building in Beaminster. Whatever its antecedents, it is certainly a venerable and charming building and Silvana Bandini, formerly from The Pig near Bath, has been at the heart of this well-oiled operation since 2018.

Foodie-focused, led by michelin-starred chef Chris Staines, the restaurant has an excellent reputation and presents a seasonal menu, with asian twists. The daily-changing menu reflects its setting in an area blessed with quality local produce: fish, meat and cheese all come from nearby. Wood-fired pizzas are also avaliable. Meals are served in the Georgian panelled dining room or the conservatory, and in the summer, guests can also eat outside under a large 'Gazova', which looks out on to the walled gardens. The works of local artists and artisans are integral to the soul of this place and neighbouring distillerys make their own contributions to the spirits enjoyed in the bar. Silvana's collaboration with the locals continues with the local brand, Lovegrove Essentials, who offer facials and massages.

Bedrooms, with mahogany beds, Frette Italian linen and theatrical wallpaper are all different, as would be expected in a building so full of nooks and crannies – including a priest hole.

THE SOUTH-WEST — SOUTHERN ENGLAND

Beesands, Devon

Beesands, Kingsbridge TQ7 2EN

Tel 01548 580215
email enquiries@thecricketinn.com
website www.thecricketinn.com

Nearby Start Bay Lighthouse, Beach, South West Coastal Path, Slapton Ley Nature Reserve, Great Mattiscombe Sand, Salcome
Location Beesands, There is an unofficial one-way system in Beesands due to the narrow road. Park opposite the hotel for free.
Food breakfast, lunch, dinner
Price ££-£££
Rooms 7; 5 doubles and 2 family suites with walk-in showers, Smart TV, coffee machines
Facilities restaurant, outdoor seating
Credit cards MC, V
Children welcome
Accessibility not suitable
Pets dogs welcome in some spaces
Closed never
Proprietors Nigel and Rachel

The Cricket Inn
Coastal inn

In the heart of historic fishing village of Beesands, directly on the South West Coast Path and on a road that leads to nowhere, nestles a small 19thC inn, frequently dubbed a hidden gem. Offering outstanding sea views and an idyllic setting surrounded by miles of empty beach, it is a great place for walkers. You may find a walk to the Start Bay lighthouse of particular interest, as it takes you to one of the most exposed peninsulas on the English coastline.

Climbing the stairs to the bedrooms opens up stunning views over the sea. You cannot see the ground, so you can almost feel as if you are on a boat. The rooms are neat and cosy: white walls and white wood panelling create a sense of space, especially with plenty of bright light coming in from the windows. Bold splashes of blue, striped and zigzag patterns on the bedding, and fish print pillows will remind you of the sea. You can drift off to sleep listening to the waves.

The restaurant gets crabs, lobsters and scallops direct from the bay, only yards away, caught by a local fisherman. The dining space is appropriately decorated: pillars wrapped in ropes; decorative oars; a large ship model and framed photos on the walls telling the inn's story. A large number of guests recommend the seafood pancake. The restaurant is very popular with the locals and visitors alike, so book in advance.

THE SOUTH-WEST — SOUTHERN ENGLAND

Bigbury-on-Sea, Devon

Folly Hill, Bigbury-on-Sea, Devon
TQ7 4AR

Tel 01548 810240
email info@thehenleyhotel.co.uk
website www.thehenleyhotel.co.uk

Nearby Burgh Island, Avon Estuary.
Location 20 minutes from A38 beyond Bigbury-on-Sea towards sea; ample car parking
Food breakfast, dinner (give 3 days notice)
Price ££-££££
Rooms 5; all double and 3 can be twin, all have bath/shower; all have phone, TV, radio
Facilities conservatory/dining room; garden, private cliff path and steps to beach, beach
Credit cards AE, MC, V
Children over 12 only
Accessibilty not suitable
Pets dogs welcome (£5 per day)
Closed Nov to Mar
Proprietors Martin Scarterfield and Petra Lampe

The Henley
Coastal hotel

Recommended several editions ago by an astute reader who described it as 'the sort of place that I always hope to discover on holiday, and alas, rarely do.'

Originally built as a holiday cottage during Edwardian times, the hotel has a beach-house feel and spectacular views that stretch from the Avon Estuary around to Burgh Island. And if simply looking at the sea isn't enough, you can climb down the private cliff path to a stretch of pristine beach.

Although owner Martyn Scarterfield was a PE and Art teacher in a previous life, he comes from a family hotel in Sidmouth and has been in the trade for many years. Co-owner Petra Lampe brings both charm and a sense of warmth and elegance to the hotel. Together, they create a relaxing atmosphere that is, above all, unpretentious.

Bedrooms are simple, yet comfortable and spacious. The dining room has Lloyd Loom furniture and overlooks the sea. Martyn does the cooking and it can be described as real home cooked food – excellent quality without fancy presentation. The dining menu is limited but often includes fresh, locally caught fish (three days notice required).

A winning combination of great food, beautiful views and friendly owners.

THE SOUTH-WEST SOUTHERN ENGLAND

Bradford-on-Avon, Wiltshire

Newtown, Bradford-on-Avon,
Wiltshire BA15 1NQ

Tel 01225 862230
email priorysteps@clara.co.uk
website www.priorysteps.co.uk

Nearby Barton Tithe Barn; Bath.
Location off A363 on N side of town; in 0.5 acre garden, with car parking
Food breakfast, dinner (to order)
Price ££
Rooms 5 double and twin, all with bath; 3 self-catering apartments
Facilities sitting room, dining room; terrace, garden
Credit cards MC, V
Children accepted
Accessibility not suitable
Pets not accepted
Closed occasionally
Proprietors Carey and Diana Chapman

Priory Steps
Town B&B

High above the lovely little wool town of Bradford-on-Avon, Carey and Diana Chapman's converted row of weavers' cottages look out over the predominantly Georgian houses interspersed with a smattering of Saxon and medieval buildings. Although only a three minute walk from the centre, Priory Steps is not easy to find. It is so discreetly signposted that it looks like a private home – which it is for the Chapmans and their (now grown-up) children. As a result, the pictures and pieces that decorate the house have family connections and the atmosphere is informal and easy-going, especially in the book-lined sitting room.

Each of the bedrooms has a theme – Indian, Chinese and so on. In spite of the cottage architecture, there is nothing cramped about them: they are light and airy, with wonderful views. Beautifully decorated, each is furnished mainly with antiques. Unflashy, lived-in and loved, standards are reliably maintained and there are no concessions to contemporary taste. Three self-catering aparments are also available: plain but spacious. The largest, The Coach House, has a private terrace with impressive views.

Diana is a keen cook and breakfast is served either at a communal table in the elegant dining room or, in good weather, out on the terrace of the garden looking down over the town. You will feel like a house guest in a particularly well-run home.

THE SOUTH-WEST | SOUTHERN ENGLAND

Branscombe, Devon

Branscombe, Devon
EX12 3DJ

Tel 01297 680300
email reception@masonsarms.co.uk
website www.masonsarms.co.uk

Nearby South Devon coastal path; Sidmouth.
Location in village 8 miles (11 km) S of Honiton, off A3052 between Sidmouth and Seaton; with ample car parking
Food breakfast (for residents), lunch, dinner
Price ££-£££
Rooms 28; 7 in the main inn; 15 cottage rooms; 6 above car park
Facilities bar, restaurant; garden
Credit cards MC, V
Children welcome
Accessibility some facilities but access a little difficult
Pets welcome
Closed never
Proprietors St Austell Brewery Company Ltd
Manager David Putt

Masons Arms
Seaside village inn

Branscombe is a picturesque little Devon village, at the end of a winding lane, surrounded by steep, wooded hillsides and overlooking the sea. The National Trust owns most of the land around, and the South Devon Coastal Path passes through it. In other words, this village is a hive of activity, inspiring visits from walkers in winter and beachcomers in summer, many of whom pitch up at the Masons Arms. Welcoming, yes; popular, certainly. It's what a village pub should be, although its success has led to expansion: what was a simple inn, converted from four cottages, now has a restaurant and a bar serving food, a large function room, plus 28 rooms spread out between the main inn, cottage rooms and above the car park.

St Austell Brewery have been at the helm for over a decade and recently refurbished the inn, stiking a tasteful balance between luxury and simpilicity while preserving its hearty character. The refreshed rooms and restaurant are chic and comfortable with a cottagey feel, pretty fabrics, beamed ceilings and sloping floors.

The food is several notches above pub fare, with the restaurant and bar offering the same menu with a wide selection catering for different diets. A map is provided alongside the menu showing the source of the ingredients - a nice touch.

THE SOUTH-WEST | SOUTHERN ENGLAND

Bristol

28 Portland Square, St Paul's,
Bristol BS2 8SA

Tel 0117 4288440
email bristol@artistresidence.co.uk
website
www.artistresidence.co.uk/our-hotels/bristol

Nearby BristolMuseum and Gallery, Bristol Old Town, Clifton Bridge
Location Bristol City centre
Food breakfast, lunch, dinner, bar snacks
Price ££-£££
Rooms 23, including 2 suites, a lookout apartment, doubles and twins. All have wifi, hairdryers, TV.
Facilities bar, events space
Credit cards MC, V
Children welcome
Accessibility some, access to ground floor and a lift although narrow corridors and a few steps throughout
Pets some dog friendly rooms
Closed never
Proprietors Charlotte and Justin Salisbury

Artist Residence Bristol

There is only one interesting central Bristol hotel: the Artist Residence on the corner of Portland Square and Cave Street, minutes' walk from the city centre. (We also feature Brooks, but that's a guesthouse). The other Artist Residences: Brighton, Penzance, London and South Leigh (Oxfordshire) are also in the guide, see pages 68, 99, 119 and 234.

Justin Salisbury and his wife Charlotte (for their story see our review of the Brighton Artist Residence) have hit the spot unerringly here, defying the financial challenges of lockdown to realise their confident vision of shabby-chic comfort. Our reporter (who is the wrong side of 70) immediately felt stimulated and at ease in a place whose core audience is probably 30-50 year olds.

The large town house's varied history adds to the atmosphere: it has been a private residence and a boot factory, but it's comfortable because the basics are right: good beds, sparkling (but some smallish) bathrooms, thorough sound proofing. See the photos to get an idea of Justin's often witty choices of art for the walls.

Two highlights: on the ground floor, the huge downstairs bar/casual dining area. Here you can sit around a table tennis table with drinks, eats and do conversational ping pong, net still in place. Event spaces available.

Bristol

St Nicholas Street, Bristol, BS1 1UB

Tel 01179300066
email info@brooksguesthousebristol.com
website www.brooksguesthousebristol.com

Nearby St Nicholas Market, Wapping Whard,
Location between the Bristol Old City and the City Centre
Food breakfast, cooked to order; an honesty bar; afternoon tea also available when pre-ordered
Price £-££
Rooms 24 including four family rooms; plus four rooftop caravans with en-suites.
Facilities dining room, sitting room, courtyard
Credit cards MC, V
Children welcome
Accessbility lift access, excluding the third floor
Pets not allowed
Closed never
Proprietor Carla Brooks

Brooks House, Bristol
Guesthouse

There are fewer antique touches here than at its sister hotel (Brooks Guesthouse Bath, page 30), and this place mirrors the youth and vibrancy of the city. It's a great base for urban adventuring, or a chic choice for boozy weekends.

Brooks' distinct style is mirrored in the individually styled bedrooms; eye-catching wallpapers and crisp bedding alongside retro statement pieces. The vibrant chrome rooftop 'Rocket' caravans are an alternative choice for sleeping — an exciting and private experience. Leather chairs in the sitting area are complemented by unusual furniture, matching the modern yet eclectic feel of the rest of the house.

This communal area extends out into the courtyard, where you can also enjoy the honesty bar.

The breakfast is award winning, and the perfect fuel for a day in the city. Continental, cooked, and takeaway options are available until 10am, so there is no pressure to rush in the morning.

Broad Chalke, Wiltshire

1 North Street, Broad Chalke,
Salisbury, SPN 5EN

Tel 01722780344
email
hello@queensheadbroadchalke.co.uk
website
www.queensheadbroadchalke.co.uk

Nearby Salisbury Cathedral,
Wardour Castle, Rockbourne
Roman Villa
Location village of Broad Chalke, 7
miles west of Salisbury
Food breakfast, lunch, dinner
Price ££££
Rooms 4; 2 double en-suites and 2
triple en-suites
Facilities dining room, sitting
room, terrace
Credit cards MC, V, AE
Children allowed
Accessibilty enquire when booking
Pets not allowed
Closed never
Proprietors Chickpea Group

The Queens Head
Pub with rooms

In a charming, long, lowish building in a mostly pretty village this place has one of the best pub restaurants we've seen in the Salisbury area. It's a genuine feel-good space.

The welcome is personal and friendly - staff aim to say hello to everyone within three seconds of entering and the menu has more than its share of surprises: how about sweetbread skewers with wild garlic aioli for a starter or chicken Kiev, fennel slaw and fries for a main? A recent guest felt the dining room too dark - but it was a rainy day in November. She also reported a mixed reaction to the food - an unappetising Dahl, but a delicious root vegetable Wellington.

As we went to press there were four rooms in a boxy modern annexe - five more are planned. Once inside, you'll forget the exterior. We liked No 3, smallish but fairly priced at £90 including breakfast.

The Chickpea team started building their group in 2019. The Queen's Head is the newest, opened 2023. See pages 54, 84 and 86. The Dog and Gun, Netheravon, is also worth knowing about but aren't in this edition because the bedrooms weren't finished. The Chickpea formula is youthful, cosy, personal, even playful hospitality and they seem to be getting it right because the food and drink areas buzz and room occupancy is high.

THE SOUTH-WEST — SOUTHERN ENGLAND

Bruton, Somerset

28 High St, Bruton, Somerset BA10 0AE

Tel 01749 814070
email bedrooms@atthechapel.co.uk
/restaurant@atthechapel.co.uk
website atthechapel.co.uk

Nearby Bath, Hauser & Wirth Gallery, Stourhead
Location central Bruton
Food breakfast, lunch, dinner
Price ££
Rooms 8 double, all with wi-fi, TV, safe, tea/coffee facilities
Facilities sitting room, dining room, bar, brasserie, gun lockers
Credit cards AE, MC, V
Children welcome
Accessibility access to the restaurant
Pets not accepted
Closed Christmas Day
Proprietors Catherine Butler & Ahmed Sidki

At the Chapel
Town guesthouse

This handsome 19thC congregational chapel has been brilliantly transformed. Catherine Butler, the inspired owner, along with her partner Ahmed, spent eight years restoring it, and rapidly established it as an indispensable meeting place ("it's the town piazza" a regular tells us) – a hub for the community, just as it was when it was first built.

You wake in a bedroom dominated by floor-to-ceiling stained-glass and stone-framed windows: what an estate agent would call the the wow factor. Freshly-baked croissants are delivered from the in-house bakery to your room at seven each morning. The smell wafts temptingly through the door (handmade by Ahmed, like all the doors, much of the furniture and the stone bread oven in the bakery).

Things just happen here. Sergei Polunin and other Royal Ballet stars have danced here; the night we stayed, there was a showing of local boy Julian Temple's film *London: The Modern Babylon* downstairs in the 'club room' … and on it goes. "People just suggest things," says Catherine. "The building has the right chemistry; I believe it always did."

The restaurant is relaxed but elegant and serves an uncomplicated, trendy menu of brasserie-style fare, alongside sourdough pizza, an extensive juice list and an excellent selection of baked goods in the morning.

Bude, Devon

Summerleaze Crescent, Bude, Devon EX23 8HJ

Tel 01288 389800
email enquiries@thbeachatbude.co.uk
website www.thebeachatbude.co.uk

Nearby Bude heritage centre and museum, the National Coastal Path, surfing and seawater swimming pool available on the beach, Boscastle village, the ruins of King Arthur's Castle in Tintagel **Location** Bude, some car-parking available
Food breakfast, lunch, dinner
Price ££-££££
Rooms 17; all with flat-screen TV, direct-dial telephone, hairdryer, fridge, safe, hospitality tray
Facilities restaurant, bar, terrace, club room, wi-fi **Credit cards** AE, MC
Children accepted, extra bed £30 per night, £50 per night for 5-16 year olds.
Accessibility there is a lift to all floors, and 1 ground-floor room
Closed select dates over Christmas
Manager Will and Susie Daniel

The Beach
Coastal hotel

The Beach can claim to be one of the hottest recent openings on the north Cornwall coast. The old Victorian building has kept its character, with rooms of different shapes and sizes, but a modern feel has been added by thoughtful, contemporary redecoration. Guests especially enjoy the bedrooms, describing them as comfortable and homely. All the rooms are decorated in cool colours – in the New England seaside style – with fashionable design features and accessories, particularly in the bathrooms. It is the combination of the views over Summerleaze Beach and the stylish decoration that make them so appealing – most have views that also extend over the spectacular Cornish scenery surrounding Bude, including the Downs at Efford and the Bude canal.

The adjoining restaurant, Elements, is presided over by head chef Simon Platt with a menu championing seafood and local produce. The menu is unpretentious and good value – crayfish mac 'n' cheese, crab bruschetta as well as pizzas, pasta and steaks. Their bar – popular with locals – has views across Summerleaze beach, and is especially lively during weekends and evenings. If you prefer to eat out, the interesting town of Bude has a medley of local restaurants. This is definitely a place for more than one night's stay.

THE SOUTH-WEST SOUTHERN ENGLAND

Carbis Bay, Cornwall

Boskerris Road, Carbis Bay, St Ives, Cornwall, TN26 2NQ

Tel 01736 795295
email reservations@boskerrishotel.co.uk
website www.boskerris.co.uk

Nearby St Ives, Porthminster beach, Eden Project, Lands End, Minnack Theatre
Location above Carbis Bay beach, on the edge of St Ives
Food breakfast dinner
Price £££-££££ **Rooms** 15; 3 super-king; 4 king; 1 twin; (not ocean view) 3 king, 1 twin. All have hairdryer, TV, nespresso machines
Facilities guest sitting room, bar, outside decked terrace; treatment room, small dining room, breakfast room, garden **Credit cards** all major accepted **Children** 10+
Accessibility Classic Deluxe room is on ground floor, with a walk-in rain shower
Pets not accepted
Closed early Nov-mid March
Owner Catherine Duff and family

Boskerris

Seaside hotel

The relaxed vibe of Cornwall combined with a touch of St Tropez glamour characterizes this small hotel nestled on the Cornish coast. Taking over in 2021, Catherine Duff has preserved the cheerfulness of this place and its breezy Mediterranean atmosphere.

It looked a little drab when we visited in November, but one could easily imagine its magic in summer, when light pours in from the floor-length windows and guests can enjoy a drink on the elegant decked terrace, with panoramic views from St Ives bay towards the Newlyn (Godevry Lighthouse, which inspired Woolf's modernist novel, can be spied in the distance).

After a day in St Ives (a convenient three-minute train journey away) the turquoise sitting room, filled with twinkling music and aromatic smells from their luxury spa, is the perfect bolt-hole.

The rooms (some with sea views) vary in size and comfort, and reflect the calm, continental theme, with white walls offset by colourful headboards, though we felt some of the Classics could do with a bit of a decorative lift.

Their Bits and Bites menu is short, unfussy, but sophisticated. The breakfasts are first rate, with a daily buffet spread and cooked menu including French toast with fried bananas, bacon and syrup.

THE SOUTH-WEST | SOUTHERN ENGLAND

Charlestown, Cornwall

Charlestown Harbour PL25 3NX

Tel 01726 68966
email antonia@antoniaspearls.co.uk
website www.antoniaspearls.co.uk

Nearby Shipwreck Treasure Museum, Lanhydrock House, Cotehele House, Tate St Ives, The Lost Gardens of Heligan, Trevose Golf Club
Location Charlestown Harbour, 5 mins from A390
Food self-catered; breakfast box, food can be ordered
Price ££-££££
Rooms 6 cottages, 1-3 bedrooms each. Washing machine, tumble dryer, iron and ironing board, radio, television, wi-fi
Facilities Spa at home, private sea side garden, Marine Villa has burning fireplaces, sitting room and kitchen
Credit cards MC, V
Children welcome; preschool utensils available, babysitting available
Accessibility access to ground floor only **Pets** not accepted
Closed never

Antonia's Pearls
Self-catering

You can't take a private atmosphere for granted any more on Cornwall's south coast, but in these nicely restored serviced cottages you can really be yourself. They appeal to independent people who find a homely ambience helps them to relax. You can be fully self catering if you wish, but most prefer to pre-order Antonia's food boxes – freshly made home cooked supper dishes, cheese boards and breakfast.

The six cottages nestle at the edge of the green oasis which separates Charlestown and Carlyon Bay. Rooms are bright, with mainly white and brown furniture and quite minimalist decoration – typically pretty ceramics and pictures of the sea. Each has its own private garden and is heated by a wood burner.

The harbour entrance and sandy Charlestown beach are a two-minute walk away, but of course you need a car if you want to explore – or hire a bike in the village. Antonia and David have plenty of expeditions to suggest – historic houses, walks, riding, family fun.

Seaflowers, another charming self-catering place, is quite nearby. As we went to press, it had been imaginatively repurposed as a guesthouse for party bookings, but unlike Antonia's Pearls, does not offer a pre-ordered food service.

THE SOUTH-WEST — SOUTHERN ENGLAND

Coverack, Cornwall

Coverack, Nr Helston, Cornwall, TR12 6TF

Tel 01326 280464
email reception@thebayhotel.co.uk
website www.thebayhotel.co.uk

Nearby Lizard Peninsula, the Eden project, Trebah gardens, Iron-Age fort, open-air theatre, St Michael's Mount, Falmouth, Helston, Penzance, Truro, St Ives
Location M5 Motorway: junction 31 onto A30 into Cornwall, then onto Broads.
Food breakfast, lunch, dinner
Price £££-££££ **Rooms** 13 double and twin; hairdryers, tea and coffee making facilities **Facilities** restaurant, terrace, flatscreen televisions, parking, yoga retreats **Credit cards** MC, V **Children** not under 8
Accessibility some ground floor rooms **Pets** small and medium dogs welcome but not in public rooms; £8 valeting charge per dog per day; pet food arrangeable. **Closed** Dec-Feb
Owners Sanders family
Manager Caroline Beadle

The Bay Hotel
Seaside hotel

Peace and quiet. One visitor remarked that during her whole time here, she saw "no more than fifty people on the entire beach." Nestling in the fishing village of Coverack, the hotel is a second's walk from miles of unspoilt coastline.

Inside, attentive manager Caroline has gone to great lengths to create a peaceful and calming atmosphere. Rooms are decorated in mellow, coastal tones, which perfectly complement the sea views most visitors will have. Some are smallish, but all are well furnished with more than enough storage space. You can really switch off here: none of the rooms have a phone, and the area itself has no mobile reception. There is, however, free wi-fi.

The hotel has a terrace and a superbly decorated conservatory restaurant, which looks out across the sea. Guests should expect to sit down to top food – chef and proprietor Ric House has a reputation for creating excellent dishes. Ingredients are all local, and, of course, all fish is freshly caught. Service is excellent in the restaurant, as it is throughout the rest of the hotel.

As ownership of the hotel has passed between families the friendly spirit of the place, and the welcoming atmosphere crops up continually in guests' comments.

THE SOUTH-WEST — SOUTHERN ENGLAND

Cranborne, Dorset

Cranborne, Wimborne, BH21 5PZ

Tel 01725 551 133
email enquiries@10castlestreet.com
website www.10castlestreet.com

Nearby Cranborne gardens and local walks (500m), Wimborne (11km), Salisbury (27km), Poole beach (27km), Sandbanks beach
Location Cranborne village; ample parking
Food breakfast, lunch, dinner, snacks, afternoon tea, room service
Price £££-££££
Rooms 11; 4 luxury doubles, 5 lovely doubles, 1 snug double, 1 double with separate bathroom; all have TV, wi-fi, tea and coffee making facilities, bath products, robes
Facilities 2 sitting rooms, restaurant with separate dining room for small groups, garden room, large grounds
Credit cards V, MC, DC, AE
Children welcome **Accessibility** not suitable **Pets** well behaved dogs allowed in some rooms (£10); welcome in bar **Closed** Christmas day
Proprietors Gretchen and Alex Boon

10 Castle Street
Country house hotel

Don't be fooled by the humble name: 10 Castle Street is a grand and sumptuous 18th century Queen Anne house. Former family home of the Countess of Lichfield before Alex and Gretchen Boon took up the lease and transformed it into an art-filled restaurant and private members club.

The concept is novel and we think it has potential. On the ground floor the restaurant, drawing room, terrace and bar are open to all; while the first floor with a billiard room, kids' playroom and sitting room is reserved for members. Members have access to discounted room rates, special events, and full use of the spa. Hotel guests become 'passing members' for the time of their stay. This arrangement, and the jovial atmosphere fostered by Alex and Gretchen, makes you feel like you are staying in an old friend's house rather than a hotel.

The eleven bedrooms are furnished with attractive sofas and an eclectic mix of art. The marble-clad bathrooms are lovely, as are the views onto the phenomenal garden.

Enjoy dinner at the restaurant decorated with art from Messum's gallery in London, in the intimate Blue Room or in the Tasting Room, where you can watch your dishes being prepared: each is unique. Head Chef Alex Fullock prepares sophisticated dishes with meat reared on the grounds and hand-picked herbs and vegetables.

THE SOUTH-WEST — SOUTHERN ENGLAND

Crudwell, Wiltshire

Crudwell, Malmesbury
Wiltshire SN16 9EP

Tel 01666 577194
email info@therectoryhotel.com
website www.therectoryhotel.com

Nearby Cotswolds
Location village of Crudwell on the edge of the Cotswolds with parking
Food breakfast, lunch, dinner
Price ££-£££
Rooms 15 doubles, most with bath and shower, radio, TV, skincare products
Facilities bar/sitting room, Victorian walled garden, croquet, outer heated swimming pool
Credit cards AE, MC, V
Children welcome
Accessibility not suitable
Pets dogs accepted (charges apply)
Closed never
Proprietors Alex Payne and Khalil Toukan

The Rectory
Village hotel

A real find: this hotel is as soothing as it is professional. Assured, and stylishly simple, devoid of gimmicks, it's unaffected but excellent. Recently refurbished and reopened in 2017 by its new owners, The Rectory stands on the edge of the Cotswolds in the village of Crudwell. The entrance hall is homely as well as contemporary.

The reception area opens on to a wide, light, flagstoned corridor, with interesting antique maps adorning the walls. Opening off it are a lovely panelled dining room, and elegant Glass House where breakfast can be taken. This leads in to a sophisticated bar serving up cocktails, draft beer and all-day canapes. Guests can head to the elegant and warmly decorated Drawing Room for after dinner drinks, and sometimes a projected film.

The dining room offers a seasonal menu, or if you prefer to eat out, try The Potting Shed Pub (their sister property) in Crudwell village, which produces great pub fare with some interesting twists.

The 15 bedrooms could have been furnished and decorated just for this guide. They are all different, attractive without being fancy, sensibly priced homes from home in which it's a pleasure to spend time.

THE SOUTH-WEST / SOUTHERN ENGLAND

Falmouth, Cornwall

22 Melvill Road, Falmouth, Cornwall, TR11, 4AR

Tel 01326 314466
email info@highcliffefalmouth.com
website www.highcliffefalmouth.com

Nearby 3 beaches in walking distance; Maritime Museum (1km); Pendennis Castle; several gardens 5 min by car; Heligan 1hr, Eden Project 1hr, St Ives 1hr, Penwith **Location** 1 min walk from sea front, 6 min walk from main town **Food** breakfast; picnic baskets on request **Price** £-£££ **Rooms** 8; 3 super-king double (1 can be twin), 3 king-size double; 2 single; all ensuite; all with iPod/iPhone docking station, digital flat TVs, hairdryer, wi-fi, robes, Molton Brown troiletries **Facilities** sitting room, free parking, wi-fi **Credit cards** all except AE **Children** only 8+ allowed **Accessibility** 1 ground floor suite, but no special facilities **Pets** not allowed **Closed** Dec to mid-Jan **Proprietors** Simon and Vanessa Clark

Highcliffe B&B
Contemporary bed-and-breakfast

The 'contemporary' in the title is no misnomer. Nearing its ten year anniversary, Highcliffe constantly regenerates to keep up with its trendy Falmouth clientèle. Every December they shut for upkeep, and every second year Vanessa redecorates almost every room. The general effect is Scandi-chic: white painted walls and floorboards offset by flashes of colour and bespoke lighting. One bedroom we saw, with *Toile du Jouy* wallpaper and a handmade pleated headboard, was about to be upholstered with navy velvet and matching curtains: guests should feel like they're the first to use them. All are kitted out with Molton Brown toiletries, Egyptian cotton bedding and monsoon showers. You'd be hard-pushed to find the same luxury at this price in the area.

The breakfast is as versatile as the interiors, with guests encouraged to cherry pick from the menu. Choices can be adapted to any dietary requirement without fuss, as can their daily specials. The homemade granola even has its own Facebook page, set up by an admiring guest.

For all its trendiness, Highcliffe is a family-run bed-and-breakfast that offers a highly personal experience. Vanessa and Simon go the extra mile to adapt to their guests needs, and advise them on the best of Cornwall.

THE SOUTH-WEST / SOUTHERN ENGLAND

Fonthill Gifford, Wiltshire

Fonthill Gifford, Tisbury, Wiltshire, SP3 6PX

Tel 01747 870385
email info@beckfordarms.com
website www.beckfordarms.com

Nearby Fonthill Estate; Tisbury station (5 minute drive); Rushmore Golf Club
Location just off the Fonthill Estate, near Tisbury
Food breakfast, lunch, dinner
Price ££
Rooms 10; 8 rooms above the pub and 2 private lodges a short walk away, plus the gatehouse; all with own bath or shower and TV
Facilities traditional pub bar, large garden; terrace
Credit cards DC, MC, V
Children welcome except in the lodges
Accessibility only to downstairs rooms
Pets welcome (except in the lodges)
Closed on Christmas day
Proprietors Dan Brod and Charlie Luxton

The Beckford Arms
Country pub

Although a night-time fire threatened to destroy the Beckford Arms a few years ago, owners Charlie Luxton and Dan Brod have taken this event in their stride and used it to create something exceptional. It's a successful hotel hybrid — traditional country pub, restaurant and charming hotel all in one. You can either eat at the bar, where mulled wine and cider are warmed over an open fire during winter, the elegant private dining room, the laid back conservatory, or even the sitting room if you like. The food can't be faulted. Charlie and Dan are hospitality naturals.

After dinner, you can retire to one of their ten small but well-appointed bedrooms, where a range of comforts await you: Siberian goose-down duvets, vintage Welsh blankets and woolly hot-water bottles. We particularly enjoyed the quirky drawings by local artist Zebedee Helm. Outside, the garden rambles towards a professional *boules* court. There are hammocks, a games area for entertaining children, even a dog bath. Nearby, on the Fonthill Estate, are two beautiful private lodges and a newly converted room in the estate's gatehouse. Arrive to a fully-stocked fridge and cook yourself breakfast in the morning, or saunter over to The Beckford for their famous eggs benedict. On summer weekends they have a BBQ, and a woodfired oven serves pizzas.

THE SOUTH-WEST — SOUTHERN ENGLAND

Fowey, Cornwall

28 Fore Street, Fowey, Cornwall
PL23 1AQ

Tel 01726 833302
email info@theoldquayhouse.com
website www.theoldquayhouse.com

Nearby The Eden Project; The Lost Gardens of Heligan; Lanhydrock; coastal walks
Location on main street; no hotel car park but in summer low-cost permits available for car park 800 yards away
Food breakfast, lunch (through the summer), dinner
Price £££
Rooms 11 double, all with shower, some with bath; all have phone, TV, wi-fi
Facilities restaurant, sitting areas, bar, riverfront terrace
Credit Cards AE, DC, MC, V
Children not under 12
Accessibility not suitable
Pets guide dogs only
Closed never
Proprietors Fair Tree Capitol
Manager Martin Nicholas

Old Quay House
Seaside hotel

Location, location, location. This is a long, thin building jutting out over the wonderful Fowey River in the heart of charming Fowey, loved by yachties and the rest, and it is rightly geared around the endless amusement you'll get from the comings and goings on the river, not to mention the prettiness of it all.

You can eat or just sit with a drink on the terrace right over the water watching it all go by, or, when cold, move just inside to a sitting area. Most of the bedrooms have the view, the best being corner rooms and the loft suite. The interior design is cool, uncluttered, contemporary, to attract a core market of 30s-50s: grey paint, pine floors, perspex tables. The long, thin, downstairs combined bar, restaurant and sitting area has recently been redecorated. Food was fairly priced at around £30 for three courses when we visited; the list of wines by the glass has been extended since then.

They aim for a personal welcome and with 11 bedrooms, and the current competent, friendly management, that's a reasonable claim. However, with so many non-residents coming in to eat, it's not especially strong on the private, unique character we appreciate. It's a 'hotel and restaurant' formula, one that can work well, but in different hands might be merely formulaic.

Gittisham, Devon

Gittisham, Honiton, EX14 3AD

Tel 01404 540400
website www.thepighotel.com/at-combe
email info@thepigatcombe.com

Nearby Honiton (1.5m), Allhallows Museum of Lace and Antiquities (2m), Honiton Golf Club (4.5m), South Devon coast (8m), Seaton Wetlands (10m), Exeter (16m)
Location down rural road in unspoilt countryside, car park
Food breakfast, lunch, dinner
Price ££-££££
Rooms 27; king/superking, 1 family room with bunk beds; twin, cots and extra beds available. All have shower or bath; some have larder, drinks, Nespresso machine
Facilities large grounds, kitchen garden, treatment rooms, restaurant, garden folly, sitting room
Credit cards MC, V, AE
Children accepted
Accesibility 1 adapted room
Pets not allowed **Closed** never
Proprietors Fiona Moores

The Pig - at Combe
Country hotel

An excellent addition to The Pig litter is this dreamy Grade I-listed Elizabethan manor surrounded by undulating Devon countryside and grazing horses. Previously the traditional Combe House Hotel, already loved by this guide, it's now also charismatic, says our series editor Fiona Duncan.

Step directly into the wood-panelled, glamorous bar, with shelves of colourful glasses stacked against the windows and a blazing fire. In the dining room, a tall bricked-up window has been revealed, bringing in light and beautiful views. The old garden folly has been transformed into an atmospheric bar and outdoors dining space serving woodfired pizza; the potting sheds are now treatment rooms. The restored kitchen gardens and Victorian greenhouses provide fresh herbs and ingredients for the restaurant's '25-mile' menu.

Judy's design talent is evident in the bedrooms: they are traditional and stylish, with quirky touches and they are conceived for practicality and comfort. One occupies a converted row of stables stalls; many have charming vintage furniture and freestanding baths. The hotel's location just off the A30 makes it easy to reach – although going back to routine after a stay here might not be as easy.

THE SOUTH-WEST — SOUTHERN ENGLAND

Gulworthy, Devon

Gulworthy, Tavistock,
Devon PL19 8JD

Tel 01822 832528
website www.thehornofplenty.co.uk
email info@thehornofplenty.co.uk

Nearby Cotehele House, Dartmoor, Plymouth, The Garden House, Buckland Abbey
Location 3 miles (5 km) W of Tavistock on A390; with ample car parking
Food breakfast, lunch, dinner
Price ££-£££
Rooms 16; 4 in main house, 6 in new original Coach House, 6 in new Coach House; all can be double or twin; all have bath/shower; all rooms have TV, minibar, hairdryer, tea/coffee facilities
Facilities sitting room, bar, restaurant; terrace, garden
Credit cards MC, V
Children welcome
Accessibility 2 suitable bedrooms
Pets ground floor rooms only, extra charge
Closed never
Proprietors Jeremy Vincent

The Horn of Plenty
Country hotel

The Horn of Plenty has been in the guide from the very start. Its stock has continued to rise since a change of ownership in 2022 which involved a major reinvestment. All the rooms are a high standard, including one imaginatively done in mauve: this goes for those in the main house and those in the coach house (the Garden Rooms), overlooking the charming walled garden.

Built in 1830 by the Marquess of Tavistock, the secluded house is approached down a short drive and has a splendid location overlooking the Tamar Valley, a view shared by the bedrooms, some of which have small terraces.

Under head chef Ashley Lewis the menus are constantly changing in tune with seasonal produce and often include fresh local crab, Dartmoor meat and adventurous takes on classic british flavours. Owner Jeremy Vincent plans to carry on making this place a landmark for foodies.

It's not especially cheap, but we reckon you get what you pay for here – a view backed up by a guest we overheard expressing his satisfaction. Competent, friendly manager. Reports welcome.

THE SOUTH-WEST — SOUTHERN ENGLAND

Hindon, Wiltshire

High St, Hindon, Salisbury, Wiltshire, SP3 6DJ

Tel 01747820696
email hello@grosvenorarmshindon.co.uk
website www.grosvenorarmshindon.com

Nearby Fonthill Estate, Wardour Castle, Grovely Woods, Tisbury, Ebble Valley
Location South of the A303
Food breakfast, lunch, dinner
Price ££-£££
Rooms 9; split between the main inn and courtyard rooms
Facilities pub, outdoor seating, Ev charging
Credit cards MC, V
Children welcome
Accessibilty ground floor only
Pets welcome
Closed never
Proprietors Chickpea Group

The Grosvenor Arms
Pub with rooms

A handsome stone building in a village noted for its houses and cottages of harmonious grey-green Chilmark stone, this is one three Chickpea pubs new to the guide, and like the others combines style with atmosphere. The typical Chickpea layout and style works nicely here, with an especially charming 'private dining' area that can seat a party of 15-20 or small parties of 5-10. From the mains menu we chose chickpea pancake, roasted tomatoes, whipped tofu and grilled spring onions - as inventive as it sounds.

Room one, with plenty of space, is a wise choice, reasonably priced at £110 including breakfast as we went to press. Rooms follow the same quite neutral but tasteful decorative style with enough difference in the detailing to make them seem individual. There are no clothes cupboards in Chickpea pubs: you hang your kit on a row of coat hangers on hooks on the wall - fine for a short stay. Chickpea's founders are Ethan and his sister Jordan, only 26 in 2023. Their parents once managed The Pembroke Arms in Wilton. The third member of the team is close friend Tommy, responsible for the design and eclectic art on the walls. Other Chickpea pubs with rooms in this edition are on pages 41, 84 and 86.

Hinton St George, Somerset

High Street, Hinton St George
Somerset, TA17 8SE

Tel 01460 73149
email info@lordpoulettarms.com
website www.lordpoulettarms.com

Nearby local cider makers; Montacute House, Sherborne Castle, Forde Abbey; Jurassic coast, Blackdown Hills.
Location in village street, plenty of free car parking; own small private car park.
Food breakfast (for residents), lunch, dinner
Price ££
Rooms 6; small, medium or large doubles, ensuites except for Room 2 and Room 3 which have bathrooms across the corridor
Facilities bar, garden, boule area
Credit cards all except AE
Accessibility not suitable
Children welcome, Room 6 can be converted to family room
Closed never
Proprietors Beckford Group

The Lord Poulett Arms
Country inn

Taken over by the Beckford Group in 2018, this inn showcases what Dan, Charlie and Matt do best; warming hospitality, comforting food, great wine and charming interiors.

The place has undergone a gentle and stylish refresh and is still a favourite spot for guests and locals. Expect to feel completely at home in rooms with views of the picture-perfect village. There's much attention to detail with rolltop baths, natural Bramley products, and homemade shortbread biscuits.

In the winter, sit by the fireplace, or on warmer days take a seat in the Provencal-style courtyard. The unique garden has a lavender-edged boule piste, where locals play a yearly tournament.

The pub has a main bar stocked with fine local ales, including Beckford's very own, brewed in Somerset. Further dining rooms serve unpretentious food and the talented team is committed to cooking with the abundance of seasonal produce found on its doorstep.

A friendly pub that's got it just right, thanks to a balance of old and new with an emphasis on quality and things that matter. See pages 50, 59 and 61 for other Beckford Group properties.

THE SOUTH-WEST / SOUTHERN ENGLAND

Lewannwick, Cornwall

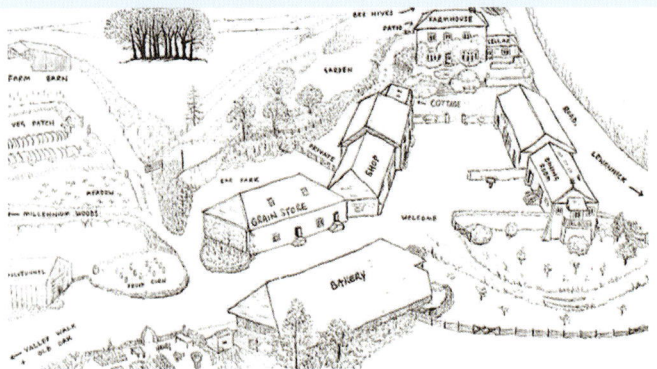

Lewannick, Launceston PL15 7QQ

Tel 01566 782009
email bookings@coombeshead-farm.co.uk
website www.coombeshead-farm.co.uk

Nearby Surfing beach at Polzeath
Location Just off Lewannick Road
Food breakfast, lunch, dinner
Price £££
Rooms 11; 5 in main farm house, 4 in Grain Store and one 2 bed self-catering cottage
Facilities dining room, sitting room, farm
Credit cards MC, V
Children only if whole place rented out
Accessibilty difficult
Pets dogs welcome, not in public rooms
Closed Mondays and Tuesdays
Proprietors Tom Adams and April Bloomfield

Coombeshead Farm
Farm restaurant and rooms

One of three terrific 'farm to fork' places to stay that have joined this new edition. In Italy they're known as *agriturismos*. Our series editor Fiona Duncan, who visited some years back, much enjoyed it, and describes it as the father of the new English *agriturismos*.

Coombeshead really does the concept justice, with a butchery for converting whole animals raised on the farm, a grain store, a bakery, a farm shop and a restaurant. The chefs prepare the whole range of food from the farm (pigs, chickens, sheep, cattle, bees) for the table and do some of the farm work themselves. What's not eaten in the restaurant or sold in the shop finds a market elsewhere.

Jaded city folk can feel they've connected with the land, but people from all walks of life on all budgets seek out the place for its genuine farmhouse food, changing with the seasons, for the lifestyle and perhaps to learn a bit about farming. It's a charming world of its own - see the visual map above - we really like the feeling of being unsure if you're in a B & B, a small hotel, or a farm guesthouse.

As we went to press the rooms started at £150 including breakfast (check), fair enough, and the three-course set dinner or Sunday lunch was a reasonable £45

THE SOUTH-WEST — SOUTHERN ENGLAND

Lewdown, Devon

Lewdown, near Okehampton,
Devon EX20 4PN

Tel 01566 783222
email info@lewtrenchard.co.uk
website www.lewtrenchard.co.uk

Nearby Dartmoor; Tintagel; Exeter; Boscastle.
Location from old A30 at Lewdown, take road signposted Lewtrenchard; in 11-acre grounds with ample car parking
Food breakfast, lunch, dinner, afternoon tea
Price £££–££££
Rooms 14; all double and 8 can be twin, all have bath/shower; all rooms have phone, TV, hairdryer
Facilities drawing room, library bar lounge, restaurant, breakfast room, ballroom; garden, croquet
Credit cards AE, MC, V
Children accepted
Accessibility ramp, 1 wheelchair adapted room, chairlift
Pets accepted
Closed never
Proprietors Murray family

Lewtrenchard Manor
Manor house hotel

Driving east down the narrow road from Lewdown, on the edge of Dartmoor, nothing quite prepares you for the first sight of Lewtrenchard Manor, a magnificent 16thC stone manor house, with some Victorian additions, approached by an avenue of beech trees and set in stunningly beautiful grounds which lead down to a lake studded with swans.

The interior is equally impressive. The massive reception rooms are rich in ornate ceilings, oak panelling, carvings and large open fireplaces. Despite its size, however, the hotel has the warm, hospitable atmosphere of a much humbler building, engendered in great part by its attentive staff. The drawing room invites you to curl up with a good book.

On the first floor, a splendid long gallery, full of family paintings and portraits, leads to the spacious bedrooms, all of which have extensive views through leaded windows and over the Devon countryside.

A former owner of Lewtrenchard was the Reverend Sabine Baring Gould (who wrote, amongst others, the hymn *Onward, Christian Soldiers*). Mercifully, he largely resisted the Victorian habit of embellishing an already beautiful building.

The Murray family, aside from a ten-year hiatus, have been at the helm of this Devonshire gem since 1988.

THE SOUTH-WEST — SOUTHERN ENGLAND

Lifton, Devon

Lifton, Devon, PL16 0AA

Tel 01566 784666
email bookings@thearundell.com
website www.thearundell.com

Nearby Dartmoor; Tintagel; Boscastle; Port Isaac; Exeter.
Location 3 miles (5 km) E of Launceston, just off A30 in Lifton; with ample car parking
Food breakfast, lunch, dinner
Price £££
Rooms 21; singles and doubles available, all ensuite, plus a self-catering cottage that sleeps up to 4 people
Facilities bar, restaurant, library sitting room, games room, drying room; garden, salmon and trout fishing, fishing lake, fly fishing lessons, organised shooting parties
Credit cards AE, DC, MC, V
Children accepted
Accessibility suitable
Pets 8 dog friendly rooms in the Coach House
Closed never
Proprietors Arabella Munro and Simon Village

The Arundell
Fishing inn

A 200-year-old coaching inn, on a site that dates back to Saxon times, which is famous – indeed an institution – for fishing and for food.

Traditional country pursuits are taken seriously here. The Arundell has been one of England's premier fishing hotels for more than half a century but has been given a new lease of life since Arabella Munro and Simon Village took over in 2020.

Anglers have 20 miles of private fishing and a 90-feet-deep lake at their disposal (containing some very large, wily trout). When autumn comes, the fisherman go, shooting parties arrive with spaniels and labradors, and talk at the bar is of high birds and driven snipe. Lifton is surrounded by some of the loveliest countryside in England. Fishing arrangements are flexible – don't be shy if you're a beginner.

Then there's the food, meticulously prepared and beautifully presented, complemented by well chosen wines and attentive, friendly service. From the sitting room you can see the garden and the 250-year-old former cockpit, now a tackle room. There are two rather grand interconnecting dining rooms and a friendly bar. Bedrooms are homely, pretty and fresh. A unique place. For full information on the fishing see www.charmingsmallhotels.co.uk/Britain/Devon/TheArundell

Longleat, Somerset

Longleat, Horninghsam,
Warminster BA12 7LY

Tel 01985 844308
email info@batharmsinn.com
website www.batharmsinn.com

Nearby Longleat Estates, ath, Victoria Art Gallery, Hauser and Wirth, Holurne Museum, Stourhead, Safari
Location in Horningsham village, on-street parking
Food breakfast, lunch, dinner, private dining, snacks
Price ££-£££
Rooms 16 doubles; 6 small, 6 medium, 4 large. All with baths, TV's, radio's and wifi
Facilities pub, private dining room, terrace, garden
Credit cards MC, V, AE
Children welcome
Accessibility ground floor only
Pets dogs welcomein most rooms
Closed never
Proprietors Dan Brod and Charlie Luxton

Bath Arms
Country inn

We have known about this Wiltshire institution for a long time – it was one of the first places our series editor Fiona Duncan reviewed for her Telegraph column. We didn't include it in Charming Small Hotels until now because although good, it wasn't quite individual enough for our selection. Now Dan Brod and Charlie Luxton have taken it over, The Bath Arms has become more of its own man, more than just a bed for the night. Note that there are several Bath Arms in the West Country. This one is near the Longleat tourist attractions in the village of Horningsham. A major feature of the ground floor has long been the public bar, popular with locals, some of whom see it as their patch. Hotel guests will feel OK there, especially if they like cheerful banter and sometimes a bit of noise, but adjacent to it are several sitting and dining areas where you can be more low-key. On a recent visit our reporter thought the small supper dishes were well above average including a huge bowl of chilli and mayonnaise flavoured chips. The bedrooms are all individually decorated in a rural chic style, tasteful with never an overstatement as you would expect from Dan and Charlie.

See their other places: The Beckford Arms, The Lord Poulett Arms and The Talbot Inn at Mells (pages 50, 55 and 61).

THE SOUTH-WEST — SOUTHERN ENGLAND

Lower Bockhampton, Dorchester

Lower Bockhampton, Dorchester, DT2 8PZ

Tel 01305 262382
email enquiries@yalburycottage.com
website www.yalburycottage.com

Nearby Thomas Hardy's birthplace (Upper Bockhampton), 1 mile; Dorchester, 5 miles
Location 3km east of Dorchester, on a single track road. 5 minutes' drive from the A35. **Food** breakfast; Farmers' Market lunch on Sundays; dinner for guests 7 days a week; non-guests Tues - Sat **Price** £-££
Rooms 8 double; 1 can be adapted to take 4 people, 2 can be twin/double; all have tea/coffee facilities, complimentary water, hairdryer, toiletries, TV, wi-fi
Facilities breakfast room, restaurant, lounge, bar **Credit cards** MC, V **Children** welcome **Accessibility** not suitable **Pets** allowed in some rooms with a charge of £8.50 per night (enquire)
Closed 4 weeks from Dec 23rd
Proprietors Ariane and Jamie Jones

Yalbury Cottage
Country hotel

If you love 19thC English literature, then this could be for you. This pretty 17thC thatched cottage is an ideal base for exploring Thomas Hardy's Wessex. He was born a mile away in Higher Bockhampton and set all his fiction in this area.

With eight bedrooms, this is a personal and characterful place to stay. Rooms are tastefully decorated using creams, whites and lilacs. There is also a sitting room for guests' use where pre-dinner drinks and canapes are served by Ariane. The cosy and highly rated restaurant, led by co-owner and chef Jamie Jones, accommodates just 26 people and serves earthy food in hearty portions. On Sundays, a special lunch is prepared using local ingredients purchased from the local Farmer's Market earlier in the day.

If the Thomas Hardy trail is not for you, there is still plenty to do. Dorchester is just two miles away, with its Roman remains and architecture, shops and museums. From there, it's another 15-minute drive to the famous Jurassic Coast (including Chesil Beach), and the popular seaside town of Weymouth.

Mells, Somerset

Mells, Somerset BA11 3PN

Tel 01373 812254
email info@talbotinn.com
website www.talbotinn.com

Nearby Longleat Estate; Shepton Mallet; Wells; Farrington Golf Course
Location the estate village of Mells
Food breakfast, lunch, dinner
Price ££-£££
Rooms 8; all with king- or emperor-sized beds, own bath or shower, Smart TVs, internet radio and wi-fi
Facilities pub bar, coach house grill room, garden, cobbled courtyard, in-room massage
Credit cards DC, MC, V
Children accepted, 1 family room
Accessibility 1 ground floor suite
Pets welcome
Closed never
Proprietors Dan Brod, Charlie Luxton and Matthew Greenlees

The Talbot Inn
Country inn

Our series editor Fiona Duncan visited this off-the-beaten track inn again recently and rated it highly. Owners Charlie and Dan, proprietors of the Beckford Arms (see page 50) bought the lease from the present Earl of Asquith and Oxford and reopened in 2013. Their new venture is up there with the Beckford Arms because they know how to combine style, value for money and character.

The Talbot gets a head start with the charm of its location, the pretty Somerset village of Mells, and this is reinforced as you approach through the unevenly surfaced, cobbled courtyard. Inside there is a choice of cosy dining areas, a sitting room across the courtyard in a barn dating from the 1500s, and the Grill Room housed in the old coach house. The speciality here is meat and fish cooked over an open fire. When it's busy at weekends the atmosphere is bustling and jolly.

There are eight stylish but unpretentious bedrooms which are very fairly priced. We especially like spacious no 6: relax in a deep freestanding bath, have a rain shower or chill out in the sitting room with two sofas. Witness the sawn logs stacked in the fireplace, the woolly hot water bottle covers and pegs with hangars doing the work of wardrobes. The rest of the rooms offer the same value.

THE SOUTH-WEST — SOUTHERN ENGLAND

Milton Abbot, Devon

Milton Abbot, Tavistock, Devon
PL19 0PQ

Tel 01822 870000
email hotelendsleigh@thepolizzicollection.com
website www.hotelendsleigh.com

Nearby Tavistock market, Tamar Valley, Plymouth historic dockyards, Exeter cathedral
Location 15 minutes from Tavistock down mile long drive in own extensive grounds; ample car parking
Food breakfast, lunch and dinner
Price ££££
Rooms 18; all have bath and shower; all have phone, TV, WIFI
Facilities dining room, sitting room, garden, terrace, library, helipad, use of local country club (swimming, gym, spa) **Credit Cards** AE, MC, V
Children accepted
Accessibility good access, 1 ground floor suite with private garden
Pets accepted, dog beds provided
Closed never
Proprietors Olga Polizzi

Hotel Endsleigh
Country house hotel

Endsleigh, on the edge of Dartmoor, and a sister of Olga Polizzi's Tresanton in Cornwall (page 75) and The Star at Alfriston, was one of the most talked about new British hotels when it opened eight years ago. Our reporter found it 'effortlessly elegant and – crucially – unpretentious, unlike many of its try-hard, oh-so-hip rivals.'

It's down a mile-long private drive in 'one of the loveliest locations I've seen in over 20 years of writing about hotels'. The sixth Duke of Bedford built the 18-bedroom fishing and shooting lodge as a retreat, in the cottage *orné* style. The gardens are by Humphry Repton.

Olga Polizzi has decorated it in her cool, inimitable style, but the spirit of the old house remains intact – old pull-down maps of Devon in the hall, the family crests in the dining room, the floor made of sheeps' knuckles on the veranda. Bedrooms are lovely: stylish and unfussy, with original baths and basins and a welcome lack of puzzling Spend time pouring over the absorbing collection of books in the library. Apart from that, there's little to do, other than to fish, walk or picnic in the grounds, a fantasy of dells and grottoes.

A discerning regular guest reports that standards here were solidly maintained on a visit in late 2023. Prices, as you might expect, are high.

THE SOUTH-WEST — SOUTHERN ENGLAND

Mousehole, Cornwall

The Parade, Mousehole, Penzance, Cornwall TR19 6PR

Tel 01736 731222
email bookings@oldcoastguardhotel.co.uk
website www.oldcoastguardhotel.co.uk

Nearby by the sea; 1 hour away from Newquay
Location situated above the harbour wall of Mousehole; St Clement's Isle in front
Food breakfast buffet, lunch, dinner
Price ££-£££
Rooms 15 double and twin; all rooms have bathroom with either shower or bath, Roberts Radio, books, tea and coffee facilities, most have sea views and some have a balcony. **Facilities** sub-tropical garden, seating area, dining room, bar, private access to beach **Credit cards** DC, MC, V **Children** welcome, under 5's free of charge **Accessibility** not suitable **Pets** welcome **Closed** Christmas day and 1 week a year, usually in January **Proprietors** Edmund and Charles Inkin

The Old Coastguard
Seaside hotel

Not everyone likes the style of the Inkins' hotels, writes our series editor, Fiona Duncan, but if you agree with the *Charming Small Hotel Guide* attitude that a jar of fresh flowers and a stylish old radio are as good as a large flat screen TV in the bedroom, then you'll get the point of The Old Coastguard.

It was a boring Victorian seaside hotel until its recent makeover, but the Inkins have avoided formulaic designer dodges to bring it up to date. They have spent money instead on the basics — the beds are soundly comfortable, there are thick towels, and properly served, not over-ambitious food.

The downstairs sitting area is the hotel's ace card: full of sunlight. You relax on deep armchairs and sofas looking out over the harbour and sea through a wall of big windows that capitalise on a view that will keep you stationary for hours.

The 14 bedrooms are gradually being made over to Charlie Inkin's taste for tongue-and-groove panelling behind the beds, mustard yellow paint and striped curtains in greens and blues. We like bedrooms 1, 2 and 3 the best, and 5 with its bath facing the sea. See the Inkins' other hotels: Gurnard's Head and The Felin Fach Griffin Inn on pages 87 and 182.

THE SOUTH-WEST — SOUTHERN ENGLAND

Nettleton, Wiltshire

Nettleton Shrub, Nettleton, near Chippenham, Wiltshire SN14 7NJ

Tel 01249 782286
email caroncooper@fossefarmhouse.com
website www.fossefarmhouse.com

Nearby Castle Combe; Cotswolds.
Location in countryside off B4039, 6 miles (9.5 km) NW of Chippenham, in 1.5 acres of garden with car parking
Food breakfast, lunch, dinner
Price £££
Rooms 2 doubles in main house, whole property including 3 rental cottages sleep up to 20
Facilities sitting room, dining room, tea room; terrace, garden
Credit cards MC, V
Children welcome
Accessibility The Garden House
Pets dogs welcome in most rooms, extra charge
Closed never **Proprietor** Caron Cooper

Fosse Farmhouse
Country bed-and-breakfast

Former cookery presenter Caron Cooper presides over a small corner of France in the Wiltshire countryside. She has decorated Fosse Farmhouse with style, bringing together English vintage and French brocante. Antiques, including many French pieces, fill the house and the adjoining cottages.

Popular for group getaways are the three self-catering cottages, The Dovecote, The Garden House and the converted Stables. All follow the style of the main building and can be hired individually or as a group.

Some more recent renovations mean the bedrooms in the main house feel homely and Caron has added some charming detail to each, with the bathrooms being finished to a high standard.

While Fosse Farmhouse claims it is only a bed-and-breakfast, two and three course dinners are available if booked in advance. Caron's food blends French with English influences. You might get rack of lamb with a mint and port wine sauce or chicken basquaise; dessert might be sticky toffee pudding or crème brûlée.

THE SOUTH-WEST | SOUTHERN ENGLAND

Oakford Bridge, Devon

Oakford Bridge, Near Bampton,
Devon
EX16 9HZ

Tel 01189 842244
website www.thebarkhouse.co.uk

Nearby Exmoor, Knightshayes House, Marwood and Rosemoor gardens
Location on A396 near Bampton
Food breakfast, lunch, dinner, picnic baskets on request
Price ££
Rooms 7; 4 double with bath or shower; 1 double and 1 twin in self-catering cottages.
Facilities dining room, sitting room, garden, bar, croquet
Credit cards Cash only
Children welcome
Accessibility limited
Pets dogs welcome
Closed never
Proprietors Hillbroke Hotles

The Bark House
Guesthouse

Tucked away in the beautiful Exe Valley, this delightful guest-house is about 200 years old and was originally used to store bark for tanning. It's everyone's idea of a Devon cottage, particularly in spring when the facade is smothered by a magnificent old wistaria. By day, you can explore the woodland paths and gardens behind the house and, opposite the building, a sitting area provides a sunny spot for afternoon tea. By night, the tiny hamlet of Oakford Bridge sparkles in the velvet-black valley while the only sounds are the trickling of a small cascade in the garden and the burbling River Exe.

Just before this new edition Alistair Kameen handed over Bark House to new owners, who are continuing to run it as a guest-house along much the same lines. Inside, the cosy and intimate sitting room, with an open fire, is the perfect place to relax and anticipate dinner. The new owners describe the food as more traditional than Alistair's cooking, and dinner might be a starter of potted salmon, roast shoulder of lamb, and a choice of home-made pavlovas and puddings.

The bedrooms reflect the essential simplicity of Bark House but we anticipate a renovation soon.

THE SOUTH-WEST — SOUTHERN ENGLAND

Padstow, Cornwall

16/18 High Street, Padstow,
Cornwall, PL28 8BB

Tel 01841 532093
email info@paul-ainsworth.co.uk
website www.paul-ainsworth.co.uk

Nearby Paul Ainsworth at no.6, Camel Estuary, Rock, Polzeath
Location Padstow's High Street (a quiet residential street in Old Town)
Food breakfast, Paul Ainsworth at Number 6 down the road, for dining
Price ££££
Rooms 6 suites; all come with TV, wi-fi, mini bar, Car Rosa products
Facilities parking, 'honesty larder', electric car on hand
Credit cards all major
Children only 16+ allowed
Accessibility not suitable
Pets not allowed
Closed 24 -26 Dec; restaurant closed in Jan (dates vary yearly)
Proprietors Paul Ainsworth

Padstow Townhouse
Town guesthouse

We're usually wary of chefs-turned-hoteliers: bedrooms rarely live up to the food. Paul Ainsworth has bucked this trend by a mile with his five-bedroom guesthouse, set up to compliment his Michelin-starred restaurant. When you dig a little deeper this isn't surprising: he and his sister Michelle, with whom he runs it, grew up in a B&B. The attention to detail is noticeable from the moment you walk in the door – literally: the welcome mat is changed three times daily to read 'Morning/Afternoon/Evening'. Their 'honesty pantry' brims with delicious treats guests can pile into wicker baskets and take to their rooms. Michelle is kindness itself, bringing beef and seaweed pasties on arrival, and a flask of hot chocolate after dinner.

The rooms (named after ingredients in Paul's Fairground dessert) have been decorated by Paul's wife, Emma (it's a proper family affair) with the designer Eve Cullen-Cornes. They are simultaneously decadent and cocooning: ours (Honeycomb) had a bold black and gold scheme, and wrought-iron bed made by local craftsmen. They're well-equipped with Smart TVs (Apple ones for films) and voluminous baths and showers. Breakfast is as expected from a top chef, served in Rojano's – which guests are transported to in the hotel's electric car. Ainsworth style, you want for nothing.

THE SOUTH-WEST — SOUTHERN ENGLAND

Padstow, Cornwall

The Seafood Restaurant & St Petroc's Hotel
Restaurant-with-rooms

Riverside, Padstow,
Cornwall PL28 8BY

Tel 01841 532700
email reservations@rickstein.com
website www.rickstein.com

Nearby surfing beaches; Trevose Head **Location** in village centre, 4 miles (6 km) NW off A39 between Wadebridge and St Columb; various car parks in Padstow; parking included for some rooms.
Food breakfast (included), lunch, dinner **Price** £££
Rooms 36 doubles, (some can be twins) in 3 different buildings, most with bath, some with shower; all rooms have phone, TV, hairdryer; some have minibar **Facilities** Seafood Restaurant: bar, conservatory, terrace; St Petroc's: Ruby's Bar next door, garden **Credit cards** MC, V **Children** welcome in St Petroc's Hotel and the Café, over 3 in The Seafood Restaurant
Accessibility some **Pets** welcome with dog sitting available **Closed** Christmas; restaurants closed on 1st May **Proprietors** Rick and Jill Stein

Rick Stein's Padstow empire has grown exponentially in recent years to include nine different places to stay, at varying prices, as well as seven places to eat/drink: his flagship Seafood Restaurant, the Bistro in St Petroc's Hotel, Rick Stein's Cafe, Stein's Fish & Chips, The Cornish Arms, The Seafood Bar and Ruby's Bar. If you are intent on eating at the quayside Seafood Restaurant (superb seafood, straight from the fishing boats, served in a lively dining room) then the bedrooms above make the best choice for a night's stay. They are spacious and understated; a couple of them offer superb estuary views. What the place lacks in public rooms, it makes up for in laid-back atmosphere and its prime position on the quay. St Edmund's House, behind the restaurant, has six new pricey suites. Less expensive, but no less tasteful, are the rooms in St Petroc's Hotel just up the hill, a little removed from the bustle of the quayside. This is an attractive white-painted building with views across the older parts of town and the estuary. The place exudes a friendly ambience, not least in the Bistro, where a short, very reasonably priced menu serving seafood and meat. There are three attractive rooms above the Café in Middle Street, and self-catering properties just outside of Padstow in Trevone.

Penzance, Cornwall

20 Chapel Street, Penzance,
Cornwall TR18 4AW

Tel 01736 365 664
email
penzance@artistresidence.co.uk
website www.artistresidencecornwall.co.uk

Nearby St Michael's Mount, Lands End, St Ives, Minack Theatre & Porthcurno Beach, Tate St Ives, Eden Project (48 miles) Newquay Airport (41 miles)
Location historic Chapel Street in Penzance's old quarter
Food breakfast, lunch, dinner
Rooms 22; 19 in main hotel, and a 3-bed cottage; all have wi-fi, hairdryer, TV **Facilities** restaurant, beer garden, bar/sitting room
Credit cards AE, DC, MC , V
Children welcome
Accessibility no special facilities
Pets accepted in 2 ground floor rooms, enquire
Closed Jan
Proprietors Charlotte and Justin Salisbury

Artist Residence Penzance **Town hotel**

It was no surprise when a new Artist Residence popped up on Cornwall's creative west coast, choosing ramshackle Penzance over picture-perfect St Ives. Loyalists to the brand won't be disappointed by the hotel's artful rusticity and olde worlde charm, complete with wood-burning stoves, stacks of logs, distressed leather armchairs, and candle lanterns peppering its cosy interior. They'll also find something new in its laid back Cornish atmosphere – the staff are young, local and extremely friendly.

We admire the flexibility here: there are double, house-decorated and artist rooms, and a cottage was added in 2016 sleeping up to six people. The original 'arty' rooms were decorated by British painters and a vibrant art collection injects pops of colour into the spaces. Our loft suite, The Look Out, had the feel of a Parisian garret: slanted walls with exposed beams, a freestanding copper bath, and its own balcony terrace, with views across Penzance. Bedrooms come with an irresistible minibar, stocked with pork scratchings, chocolate-covered honeycomb and Cornish ale, while the informal restaurant downstairs serves hearty smokehouse classics such as ribs and beer-can chicken (though the vegetarian dishes could do with a bit of a lift). In summer, they fire up a barbecue in the beer garden.

THE SOUTH-WEST — SOUTHERN ENGLAND

Penzance, Cornwall

Chapel House, Chapel Street,
Penzance, Cornwall TR18 4AW

Tel 07810020617 / 01736362024
email hello@chapelhousepz.co.uk
website chapelhousepz.co.uk

Nearby St Michael's Mount, Lands End, St Ives, Minack Theatre & Porthcurno Beach, Tate St Ives, Eden Project (48 miles) Newquay Airport (41 miles)
Location historic Chapel Street, in the old quarter of Penzance
Food breakfast, dinner 3 times weekly (by arrangement), Sunday brunch, cake available at all times
Rooms 6 double; all have en suite, waterfall showers, sea views, iPad dock with local info & room service
Facilities sitting room, kitchen, garden, terrace, boot room, spa
Credit cards all major
Children welcome
Accessibility no special facilities
Pets well behaved dogs allowed
Closed never
Proprietor Susan Stuart

Chapel House
Town bed-and-breakfast

Former accountant Susan Stuart has transformed this elegant Georgian townhouse with great aplomb, marrying original features and antique pieces with the clean lines of Cornish modernism. Her personal service goes well beyond the remit of a 'bed-and-breakfast'. In the kitchen-basement she whips up exquisite breakfasts for her guests every morning, along with three mid-week meals (by arrangement).

There's a perennial supply of home-made cake and tea, as well as stacks of wellies, wax jackets and winter-warmers for ill-equipped townies. In summer, guests breakfast in the garden, or have a g+t on the terrace – staying here is like being in a house party: relaxed and unregimented.

The six bedrooms (all with sea views) each have unique individual features: bespoke oak bed frames (the four-poster in Room 3 is particularly striking), two Hepworth-esque oval bathtubs, a wood burning stove – and a glass roof/window in Room 6, with panoramic views across Penzance (the more modern loft rooms build up into the rafters). Each is kitted with an iPad – the fount of Susan's local knowledge and a conduit to room service through her FaceTime.

New in 2023 was an on-site sauna, hot tub and spa. It is worth enquiring about the wellness package; guided sea swimming, local walking tours, meditation sessions and massages included.

THE SOUTH-WEST — SOUTHERN ENGLAND

Rock, Cornwall

Rock, Wadebridge, Cornwall
PL27 6LA

Tel 01208 863394
email info@enodoc-hotel.co.uk
website www.enodoc-hotel.co.uk

Nearby Polzeath 2 miles; Padstow (by ferry).
Location overlooking the Camel Estuary, bordering St Enodoc golf course in Rock, 2 miles off B3314 from Wadebridge; car park
Food breakfast, lunch, dinner
Price ££££
Rooms 20; 16 double, all with bath/shower, 4 suites; all rooms have phone, TV, radio, hairdryer, fan
Facilities sitting room, library, dining room, bar, billiard room, sauna; outdoor heated swimming pool
Credit cards AE, DC, MC, V
Children welcome
Accessibility some suitability
Pets some dog friendly rooms
Closed mid Jan to mid Feb
Manager Lucy and James Strachan

St Enodoc
Seaside hotel

Well-heeled British families have flocked to Rock for their bucket-and-spade holidays for generations, but stylish hotels were thin on the ground hereabouts – until, that is, the emergence in 1998 of the old-established St Enodoc Hotel from a change of ownership and total makeover.

The imposing building is typical of the area: no beauty, but solid and purposeful, with pebbledash walls and slate roof.

Weathered delabole slate floors, quirky fabrics and 20thC Cornish paintings make up their decorative scheme, combined with clean lines and easy-going comfort. Bedrooms, with bright colours and original artwork on the wall, feel like bedrooms rather than hotel rooms, with marvellous views across the Camel Estuary.

There are two restaurants: The Karrek for an elegantly presented tasting menu; and the more relaxed, but still impressive Brasserie. Guy Owen, former Idle Rocks chef, focusses on relaxed, healthy ingredients,. He buys the freshest market fish and for produce he relies heavily on the nearby Strachan family farm.

There are panoramic views from the restaurants, and a wide terrace for outdoor eating.

THE SOUTH-WEST — SOUTHERN ENGLAND

Rosevine, South Cornwall

Rosevine, near Portscatho,
South Cornwall, TR2 5EW

Tel 01872 580644
email info@driftwoodhotel.co.uk
website www.driftwoodhotel.co.uk

Nearby Eden Project, Tate Gallery, the gardens of Heligan, Glendurgan and Trebah
Location in countryside just off A3078, S of Truro; ample parking for cars and boats
Food breakfast, dinner
Price ££££
Rooms 14 double and 1 twin, 3 with bath, 1 with shower; rest with bath and shower, cabin with double and twin; all rooms have phone, TV, hairdryer **Facilities** sitting room, drawing room, TV room, dining room, bar; garden, beach
Credit cards AE, MC, V
Children welcome
Accessibility difficult
Pets not accepted
Closed mid Dec to beginning of Feb
Proprietors Paul and Fiona Robinson

Driftwood Hotel
Coastal hotel

'Situated on seven glorious acres of Cornwall's finest heritage coastline,' says the brochure – and Driftwood does indeed provide all you could want on a seaside break. It's a clapboarded converted family house that has been refurbished and renovated into a stylish yet comfortable haven by interior designer Fiona and husband Paul. All fourteen bedrooms, including the cabin overlooking the beach, have a clean, fresh style that helps maximise the space, as do the cosy sitting and drawing rooms.

Those who love seafood will be happiest here, but the rest of the food is good too. The menu, overseen by Chef Paul Green, is concentrated on well prepared dishes with fresh local ingredients. The Michelin-starred restaurant has spectacular views of the rugged Cornish coastline. For children there is a TV room with computer games and video library. If you fancy getting out and about there are numerous small pubs and restaurants nearby St Mawes; or hampers can be made up for lazing on the beach.

All around Driftwood there are varied activities that suit different tastes. Great walks and gardens such as Trelissick, the Eden Project, within a short drive; for art lovers, the Tate Gallery at St Ives; or for the energetic, watersports, riding, tennis and golf.

THE SOUTH-WEST — SOUTHERN ENGLAND

St Austell, Cornwall

Boscundle, St Austell, Cornwall
PL25 3RL

Tel 01726 813557
email hello@boscundlemanor.com
website www.boscundlemanor.com

Nearby Eden Project, Heligan Gardens, Lanhydrock House
Location 2.5 miles (4 km) E of St Austell, close to A390; in 5 acre woodland gardens; ample car parking
Food breakfast, dinner
Price £££
Rooms 12; 4 standard suites, 1 excecutive suite, 4 cosy suites, 4 superior, 1 single; all rooms have shower, bath or both. 1 on-site self-catering
Facilities sitting room, bar, restaurant; heated indoor pool; hot tub; spa treatment room; garden, croquet, woodland walks
Credit cards MC, V
Children not overnight
Accessibility difficult
Pets dogs in selected rooms
Closed never
Proprietors Jason and Louise

Boscundle Manor
Country house hotel

Chic and relaxed, this charming wistaria-draped hotel (which has been a mainstay in the guide for many years) came under the new, youthful ownership of local hospitality power-couple Jason and Louise early in 2020. Perhaps not the luckiest time to take over a new hotel venture. But, they have triumphed with a full-scale update: new furniture, modern artworks and refreshing the previously tired architure with fresh wood panelling and many coats of paint.

The kitchen, serves a casual breakfast and dinner menu. The options: burgers, sandwiches and a few larger plates are flavourful, hearty dishes and incorporate quality Cornish products whenever available. Early morning sunlight brings the Breakfast Room to life where the green and yellow walls lead into the garden. In the summer months meals and cocktails are served on the terrace and patio.

Bedrooms are uncomplicated and calm with modern, quality furniture, fittings. Some are more spacious than others and the onsite self catering is a good option for longer stays.

The grounds include five acres of terraced gardens and woodland, with several pleasant walks through the woods, ponds and old tin mine remains.

THE SOUTH-WEST — SOUTHERN ENGLAND

St Hilary, Cornwall

St Hilary, Penzance, Cornwall
TR20 9BZ

Tel 01736 740262
email hello@ennys.co.uk
website www.ennys.co.uk

Nearby Lands End; Penzance; Lizard peninsula; St Michael's Mount; St Ives
Location in gardens with car parking; from B3280 from Marazion turn left into Trewhella Lane, between St Hilary and Relubbus
Food cottages are self-catering with welcome tea, luxury suites come with welcome breakfast hamper **Price** ££
Rooms 3 cottages and 2 luxury suites. All double with TV, sitting room, kitchen/kitchenette, all with shower/bath **Facilities** heated swimming pool. grass tennis court (May-Sept); conservatory with sofas, books and local information; laundry room, free parking **Credit cards** MC, V
Accessibility difficult
Pets not accepted **Closed** Part closed Jan-March
Proprietors Nick and Karen

Ennys
Self-catering cottages

This is a beautiful, creeper-clad 17thC Cornish manor house at the end of a long tree-lined drive in little St Hilary, a few miles from Penzance. The sheltered gardens include a swimming pool and a grass tennis court. The fields stretch down to the River Hayle, along which you can walk and picnic.

Since our last edition, energetic couple Nick and Karen have taken over the properties. With a large, growing family themselves they are busy on all fronts, but manage to give guests a personal welcome.

The two family suites are in an adjacent converted stone barn, near the three cottages. Each is its own microcosm, with kitchen facilities, sitting rooms and televisions — perfect for families or couples seeking seclusion and intimacy. The real draw is the impressive facilities on the Georgian estate: a grass tennis court and heated swimming pool spread across luscious grounds. Guests are welcomed with a complimentary hamper, and there's a wealth of restaurants nearby. A peaceful oasis from which to explore Cornwall.

THE SOUTH-WEST — SOUTHERN ENGLAND

St Mawes, Cornwall

Harbourside, St Mawes, Cornwall, TR2 5AN

Tel 01326 270270
email reservations@stmawes.com
website www.idlerocks.com

Nearby St. Mawes, Trelissick, Glendurgan, Heligan and Trebah gardens; Truro; Eden Project
Location follow signs for the castle which will bring you down to the harbour side, allocated spaces in St Mawes Public Car Park
Food breakfast, lunch, dinner; afternoon tea, children's high tea at 5.30pm **Price** ££££
Rooms 19; 4 in separate annexe, all ensuite, with underfloor heating, some family rooms
Facilities bar, lounge, terrace, children's room, baby listening
Credit cards all major
Children welcome **Accessibility** annexe has some disabled access
Pets 2 dog-friendly room in the annexe
Closed 2 weeks in Jan
Proprietors Karen & David Richards

Idle Rocks
Seaside hotel

No surf here on the beautiful Roseland Peninsula, but there's 'harbour jumping' from St Mawes' harbour wall instead – a long-established St Mawes pastime at high tide. "We bet our friends to do it, and give the money to charity," says David Richards, owner of The Idle Rocks.

This is one of those seaside hotels so close to the water you can hear the waves from your bedroom window: magical. With 20 nigh-on faultless (though not large) bedrooms, kids' playroom, elegant dining room and stone-walled terrace where chilled music plays.

As this hotel enters its second decade of Richards ownership it continues to attract an increasingly sophisticated clientèle. Everything is fresh, new and of the highest quality, predominantly white but liberally splashed with vibrant pattern and colour.

The food has also been edging toward Michelin standard. The menu is correctly pitched to reflect the ambience and location. focussing on fresh Cornish produce, locally sourced — served in a relaxed setting. Their Sunday lunch comes especially recommended.

THE SOUTH-WEST SOUTHERN ENGLAND

St Mawes, Cornwall

St Mawes, Cornwall
TR2 5DR

Tel 0132 270055
email info@tresanton.com
website www.tresanton.com

Nearby Trelissick, Glendurgan, Heligan and Trebah gardens; Truro; Eden Project; National Maritime Museum.
Location in town, just below castle, 14 miles (22 km) S of Truro; car parking
Food breakfast, lunch, dinner; room service **Price** ££££
Rooms 30; 26 double and twin, 4 suites, all with bath; all rooms have phone, TV, hairdryer, free wi-fi
Facilities sitting room, dining room, bar, cinema, terraces; 8-metre yacht, beach club, EV charging
Credit cards AE, MC, V
Children welcome
Accessibility not suitable
Pets accepted in 4 rooms **Closed** 2 weeks in Jan
Proprietor Olga Polizzi

Tresanton
Seaside town hotel

It's easy to drive past the hotel, as it has no obvious entrance, particularly for cars. Look closer and you will see a discreet sign and some steps next to a pair of white-painted garages. Within seconds someone will appear to welcome you, take your luggage and park your car. This is not any old seaside hotel. Tresanton was opened in the summer of 1998, and it is now well established as the West Country hotel for chic townies who prefer not to forego sophistication at the seaside. Yet St Mawes is a happy-go-lucky holiday village, full in summer of chirpy families, bucket and spade in hand, and the two must rub along together. A whitewashed former sailing club and a cluster of cottages on the sea front make up the hotel, which was well known back in the 1960s, but had long lost its glamour before Olga Polizzi came across it. She set about redesigning it in minimalist, elegant style, using restful, muted tones of oatmeal and flax, accentuated by blues, greens, browns or yellows. Bedrooms are a study in understated luxury and have stunning sea views. The warm and comfortable sitting room and bar are more traditional. The food is also gaining many plaudits.

Guests have reported noise disturbance from wedding parties. We don't know if this has been addressed, but considering the prices charged it could be something to ask about before booking.

THE SOUTH-WEST — SOUTHERN ENGLAND

St Minver, Cornwall

Trewornan Bridge, St Minver,
Wadebridge, Cornwall. PL27 6EX

Tel 01208 812359
email info@trewornanmanor.co.uk
website www.trewornanmanor.co.uk

Nearby Rock, Polzeath,
Wadebridge, Padstow
Location set in 25 acres of land. Off
the B3314. Ample parking.
Food breakfast
Price ££-££££
Rooms 7 double; all with emperor
size beds, large en suites, TVs, hospitality tray with homemade biscuits,
bathrobes, wi-fi
Facilities sitting room with honesty
bar, breakfast room, 8 acres mature
garden **Credit cards** all major
Children not allowed
Accessibility not suitable
Pets not allowed
Closed never
Proprietor Paul and Lesley
Stapleton

Trewornan
Country bed-and-breakfast

Paul and Lesley have perfected the romantic 'getaway', marrying the romance of their 13thC Grade II-listed manor house with supreme comfort and stylishness. Perched in 8 acres of well-tended garden (and 25 acres of farmland) Trewornan has the feeling of intimate seclusion, whilst being a ten-minute drive from the north coast heavyweights of Rock, Port Isaac and Padstow. The decoration is plush, without obliterating original features: crushed velvet furnishings sit alongside arched portals and a flagstone hall. The five guest bedrooms are superb, with Emperor beds, upholstered headboards and views across the garden (our room, Porthilly, was especially luxuriant, with a huge bathroom).

At breakfast guests are greeted by a regal spread, including cooked dishes whipped up by Paul's mother. Paul is a the perfect host: quietly efficient without being overbearing, and always on hand for insider advice. Small touches combine to make guests feel special, from jars of sweets in bedrooms to the well-stocked honesty bar in the sumptuous living room.

The couple have plans to convert a study into a second living room, and add two bedrooms to the outbuilding – further cultivating a sense of privacy and relaxation (which drives their no child, no pet policy).

THE SOUTH-WEST — SOUTHERN ENGLAND

Southleigh, Devon

Glebe House, Southleigh, Colyton, Devon EX24 6SD

Tel 01404871276
email bookings@glebehousedevon.co.uk
website www.glebehousedevon.co.uk

Nearby Jurassic Coast, Shute woods, Branscombe, Lyme Regis, Beer Beach, Axe Valley
Location outside Southleigh village
Food breakfast, lunch, dinner
Price ££-££££
Rooms 7; doubles, including a self contained cabin and an annexe
Facilities 3 dining rooms, sitting room, garden room, outdoor swimming pool, tennis court
Credit cards MC, V
Children welcome, extra charge for camp beds and cots
Accessibilty ground floor only
Pets two dog friendly rooms
Closed never
Proprietors Olive and Hugo Guest

Glebe House
Guesthouse and restaurant

Everything's about slow living here. There's a vegetable garden, a swimming pool and a tennis court; several farm animals call this home. The agritourism theme surfaces everywhere – vines grow on the outside walls; a wood burner awaits you in the hall plus the smell of fresh bread.

In 2020, Olive and Hugo quit city life to transform Hugo's childhood home into a farm-style guesthouse. The house has seven cosy bedrooms decorated with a mix of family antiques and designer touches.

Officially a farm or smallholding, but with none of the hard grind, it radiates a homely, perhaps Bohemian feel. Take a closer look at the paintings and decoration crafted by local artists, many by Olive herself.

Breakfast is included and supper can be (pre-ordered). Most of the produce for the simple but delicious dishes, such as pies and vegetable lasagne, comes from the kitchen garden. Hugo cooks a more sophisticated dinner Thursday to Sunday – choices include tagliarini with monkfish ragu and roast chicken.

Explore with one of Olive's illustrated local walks booklets, and return for courses in bread, pasta, and salami making or art classes.

With considerable cool the Guests balance high standards of food, and housekeeping with the laid-back atmosphere of a well-run home from home.

THE SOUTH-WEST / SOUTHERN ENGLAND

Strete, Devon

Totnes Road, Strete, Dartmouth, Devon TQ6 0RU

Tel 01803 770364
email info@stretebarton.co.uk
website www.stretebarton.co.uk

Nearby Slapton Ley, Slapton Beach, South West Coast Path, Blackpool Sands, Greenway (NT), Coleton Fishacre (NT), Salcombe, Dartmouth, boating, golf
Location access from A38 and A384, see website for full details
Food breakfast; 2 restaurants serving lunch and dinner within a minute's walk
Price ££-£££
Rooms 5 double and 1 cottage suite, with flat-screen television, fresh flowers, hairdryer, magazine selection **Facilities** drawing room, dining room, garden, massage treatments available
Children 8 years and over
Accessibility not suitable
Pets not allowed
Closed rarely
Proprietor/Manager Stuart Litster & Kevin Hooper

Strete Barton House
Country bed-and-breakfast

Nestling in the peaceful coastal village of Strete, this smart B&B within reach of award-winning beaches and the Slapton Ley Nature Reserve will appeal to nature lovers with a taste for luxury.

The refurbished 16thC manor house has five smart bedrooms in a variety of eye-catching styles, with sea views, king-sized sleigh beds and flat-screen TVs. There's additional accommodation in the Cottage Suite, with its log-burning stove and inglenook fireplace. On arrival, the welcoming hosts will offer you a hot drink and a slice of home-made cake.

Strete is in the hilly area of south Devon known as the South Hams, with great walking and cycling, to give an extra dimension to the coastal scenery. If the weather's poor, book a massage appointment with the qualified therapist.

They make a serious effort with the buffet breakfast here, served in a pleasant room overlooking the large gardens. There's no lunch or dinner, but the hosts can recommend local restaurants.

According to one recent visitor, 'hosts Stuart and Kevin deserve the highest of praise', while another termed Strete Barton 'one of the most beautifully appointed guesthouses we have ever stayed in'.

THE SOUTH-WEST — SOUTHERN ENGLAND

Studland, Dorset

Manor House, Manor Road, Studland, Swanage, BH19 3AU

Tel 01929 450288
email reservations@thepighotel.com
website https://www.thepighotel.com/on-the-beach/

Nearby Studland to Swanage trail, Studland Sea School, Studland Beach and Nature Reserve, Studland Stables, Shell Bay, Durlston Park, Corfe Castle, Bournemouth Beach. **Location** just outside the village of Studland; car parking **Food** breakfast, lunch, dinner **Price** ££-££££ **Rooms** 27; king, super-king and twin bedrooms; 2 shepherd huts and 2 dovecotes; twin bedding, cots and extra beds available in some rooms. All have shower or bath; some have larder and Nespresso machine **Facilities** restaurant, bar, sitting room, spa, terrace, garden **Credit cards** V, AE, MC **Children** welcome **Accessibility** ground floor and part of the gardens **Pets** guide dogs only **Closed** never **Hotel Director** Tara Crabb

The Pig - on the beach
Coastal hotel

A quirky fantasy with gargoyles and an overlapping stone roof, this manor house might remind of you of the witch's gingerbread house in Hansel and Gretel, says our series editor Fiona Duncan. With its yellow exterior and terrific position overlooking Studland Bay, you are likely to fall for its enchantment from the moment you see it. Taken over in 2014 by Robin Hutson and David Elton of the Pig hotels, it is relaxing outside and cosy inside.

Once the holiday home of a historic landed family, it retains an eccentric atmosphere, with antiques, curios, chandaliers and vintage finds. It's been extended to include a new wing, and 23 spacious rooms have been refurbished – while preserving period features and reclaimed floorboards. In one bedroom you will find Portuguese carved woodwork, while in another a four-poster bed. The bedrooms are exceptionally well-stocked, with excellent bathrooms. There is also a terrace with dramatic views over Old Harry Rocks, to be enjoyed in summer.

As in all The Pig hotels, the restaurant is decorated with herbs and edible flowers, a reminder that the kitchen garden provides plenty of the fresh ingredients picked and used daily. The focus is on fresh fish, which, like breakfast, is superb. See other Pig hotels on pages 32, 52, 100 and 152

THE SOUTH-WEST — SOUTHERN ENGLAND

Sturminster Newton, Dorset

Hazelbury Bryan Road, Sturminster Newton, Dorset DT10 2AF

Tel 01258 472507
email book@plumbermanor.co.uk
website www.plumbermanor.co.uk

Nearby Thomas Hardy country; Shaftesbury; Sherborne.
Location 2 miles (3 km) SW of Sturminster Newton; private car parking
Food breakfast, lunch, dinner
Price ££-£££
Rooms 16; 14 double, all with bath, 2 small doubles with bath; all rooms have phone, TV, tea/coffee facilities with shortbread, hairdryer
Facilities dining room, sitting room, bar; garden, croquet, tennis court, shooting parties
Credit cards AE, DC, MC, V
Children welcome
Accessibility 2 adapted courtyard rooms, dining room and hotel facilities are wheelchair accessible
Pets by arrangement, £10 **Closed** Feb **Proprietors** Alison and Richard Prideaux-Brune

Plumber Manor
Manor house hotel

This is a handsome Jacobean manor house, 'modernized' in the early 20th century, that has been in the Prideaux-Brune family for well over 300 years. Since 1973 brothers Richard and Brian have been running it as an elegant but relaxed restaurant with comfortable bedrooms. Richard Prideaux-Brune is much in evidence front-of-house, as is his brother Tim. Together with Brian, who is responsible for the highly-regarded food, they draw in restaurant customers from far and wide – expect plenty of bustle on Friday and Saturday evenings, and non-residents in the dining room.

The brothers, alongside Richard's wife Alison, make charming hosts, and have created a very relaxed and welcoming atmosphere. Old family portraits hang in the house; labradors lounge in the bar; the decoration is homely and comfortable rather than smart. The large bar area might detract from the feeling of a family home, but it helps the Prideaux-Brunes' operation in a practical way (shooting parties are a feature in winter).

Bedrooms are divided between those in the main house (which lead off a gallery hung with portraits) and those in a converted stone barn and courtyard building which overlook the extensive gardens and stream. All are spacious and comfortable.

THE SOUTH-WEST — SOUTHERN ENGLAND

Swallowcliffe, Wiltshire

Swallowcliffe Salisbury. Wiltshire
SP3 5PA

Tel 01747 870211
email hello@royaloakswallowcliffe.com
website www.royaloakswallowcliffe.com

Nearby walking routes, Cranborne Chase, Shaftesbury hill top market town, Wilton House, Salisbury Cathedral, Stonehenge, Bath **Location** Swallowcliffe, car park available **Food** breakfast, lunch, dinner, tea, snacks, informal room service **Price** ££ **Rooms** 6; 3 doubles, 2 doubles or twins, 1 double with sofa bed. 2 rooms can be connected. All have hairdryer, radio alarms, tea and coffee making facilities, wi-fi **Facilities** garden, dining room, oak room, lounge area, pub **Credit cards** V, MC **Children** welcome; cots, z-beds and games available **Accessibility** lift (1 king room and 1 twin room) **Pets** 1 room suitable, £10 fee **Closed** Christmas Day **Proprietor** James May **Landlord** Chris Bryett

The Royal Oak
Village inn

In 2015 this traditional village inn rose like a phoenix from the ashes thanks to the efforts of its locals after the place had been neglected. Renovations were made, but when the lockdowns arrived in 2020 further investment was needed. One of the pub's regulars, TV presenter James May, swooped in. It survived the pandemic and is now running nicely, with the spirit of the 19thC inn preserved.

The traditional thatched-roof exterior belies a modern, stylish interior. The bar and restaurant areas on the ground floor combine low ceilings and an open hearth fireplace with Matthew Burt's custom-made furniture and contemporary landscape paintings. There is an oak and glass garden extension, which impresses with its lightness and simplicity. Upstairs, six individually designed bedrooms are extremely peaceful thanks to the pub's location in a quiet village street, with its back to the valley. They are comfortable, with huge beds and luxurious duvets and toiletries. Two rooms also have freestanding baths.

The imaginative take on pub food, with a focus on local produce, is popular among residents and visitors. You might find slow roast pork belly, smoked haddock and homemade baked beans among the choices, but the menu changes often. For breakfast, expect freshly baked bread, seasonal fruit and scrambled eggs.

THE SOUTH-WEST — SOUTHERN ENGLAND

Tisbury, Wiltshire

West Hatch, Tisbury, Wiltshire SP3 6PA

Tel 01747 870 444
email info@pythousekitchengarden.co.uk
website www.pythousekitchengarden.co.uk

Nearby Tisbury, Salisbury, Old Wardour Castle, Stone Henge
Location on a small country lane betwen villages of Tisbury and Semley
Food breakfast, lunch, dinner, fire cooking, Sunday roast **Price** ££
Rooms glamping village; 6 bell-tents and 1 shepherds hut, with comfy beds, fresh linen, kitchenette, breakfast/cocktail bar, WCs **Facilities** restaurant, terrace, walled garden, bar, glamping. Can be rented out for private parties and weddings **Credit cards** all major
Children welcome
Accessibility no special facilities
Closed Glamping season is Mar-Oct; restaurant open all year round
Proprietor Sophia and Piers

Pythouse Kitchen Garden Glamping

An unconventional place not much known outside its neighbourhood. The charm is in the way the huge conservatory dining room – a masterpiece of shabby-chic interior decoration – interfaces with the huge 18thC walled garden. Out of sight behind a hedge at the bottom are the six comfortable, heated bell tents, set up for 'glamping': comfortable beds, fresh linen, a large covered dining area, breakfast bar, kitchenette, smart WCs and hot showers, open from March to October.

The tenting comes into its own in summer, of course, when in fine weather the terrace will be your sitting room. If you want to be indoors, hang out in the homely coffee shop area with its nicely displayed homemade cakes and biscuits.

The seasonal menus offer simple, traditional British kitchen garden food, cooked inside on the stove or outside over a beechwood fire pit. Order from The Garden Board to sample whatever chef Darren Broom has sourced from the garden that morning.

The fire pit is a major feature, with meat and fish expertly and deliciously cooked or smoked. The whole set-up artfully satisfies city dwellers' nostalgia for the good life and its home-grown trappings – every area of paint deliberately left peeling, every painted (or unpainted) chair – contributes something.

THE SOUTH-WEST | SOUTHERN ENGLAND

Wareham, Dorset

Church Green, Wareham,
Dorset BH20 4ND

Tel 01929 551666
email reservations@theprioryhotel.co.uk
website www.theprioryhotel.co.uk

Nearby Poole Harbour; Swanage; Lulworth Cove.
Location in town near market square; in 4.5 acre gardens with ample car parking
Food breakfast, lunch, dinner
Price ££££
Rooms 17; 13 double, 5 suites, all have bath/shower; all rooms have phone, TV, hairdryer, minibar
Facilities drawing room, bar, restaurant; terrace, garden, croquet, pontoon, organised golf outings, Electric Car Charging **Credit cards** DC, MC, V **Children** accepted over 8 in restaurant, over 14 in hotel
Accessibility facilities available in restaurant, difficult in hotel **Pets** guide dogs only
Closed never
Proprietor Jeremy Turner

The Priory
Country town hotel

Hidden behind the church, this 16thC Priory is the perfect retreat for anyone who appreciates a sense of history, as well as peace, comfort and good food. It has been run for almost five decades by the Turner family, and is currently under the guiding hand of a new generation. Visiting as we went to press our series editor Fiona Duncan found it as appealing as ever, with the old-fashioned atmposhere intact and long-serving courteous staff giving a timeless feel.

The bedrooms are all that should be expected from a 16thC priory: beams, sloping ceilings and floors, as well as being supremely comfortable and well-equipped with books and attractive toiletries in the bathrooms. To keep up with the demand for rooms the boathouse has been converted to provide four extra bedrooms, or rather suites, equipped with luxury baths and French windows opening on to the River Frome. Indeed, it's possible to arrive by boat to The Priory: moorings are available and, after a quick walk through the stunning gardens you can relax with a pre-dinner drink on the terrace. The food is richly sastisfying, with a mainland European flavour emanating from the menu.

THE SOUTH-WEST | SOUTHERN ENGLAND

Wilton, Wiltshire

Minster St, Wilton, Salisbury
SP2 0BH

Tel 01722743328
email hello@pembrokearms.co.uk
website www.pembrokearms.co.uk

Nearby Stonehenge, Pepperbox Hill, Longford Castle, Breamore House, Salisbury Cathedral
Location west of Salisbury
Food breakfast (included), lunch, dinner, pizza
Price ££-£££
Rooms 9; 1 twin, smal and standard doubles, triples and family-sized ensuites
Facilities dining room, pub, courtyard,
Credit cards MC, V
Children welcome
Accessibility to ground floor only
Pets dogs welcome
Closed never
Proprietors The Chickpea Group

Pembroke Arms
Town inn

Our series editor Fiona Duncan describes it as a landmark Georgian building opposite the entrance to Wilton House, one of Inigo Jones's most famous houses, seat of the Herbert family, Earls of Pembroke. The building has had several uses, among them a tax office and a Second World War officers' mess and is now part of the Chickpea mini-group.

The interior's theme is Victorian: 19thC prints, brass rails hung with short cafestyle curtains; heavily embossed wallpaper. A solidly attractive 18thC staircase climbs to the Georgian blue Assembly Room on the first floor, popular for functions.

The bedrooms are often wittily decorated following Victorian and Georgian themes with plenty of charming quirks such as plays on their names – 'Florence' works especially well. We particularly enjoyed The Orangery – small but with lovely colours (tangerine William Morris style wallpaper and an apricot silk bed throw); and Queen's Bedchamber with its gold and cream colour scheme.

Back downstairs for a drink after dinner – relax in the sitting room, an authentic replica of an 18thC print room, or in the bar, which like the dining room is dark but atmospheric. The food is well above what you'd expect.

Winsford, Somerset

THE SOUTH-WEST | SOUTHERN ENGLAND

Winsford, Exmoor National Park, Somerset TA24 7JE

Tel 01643 851455
email enquiries@royaloakexmoor.co.uk
website www.royaloakexmoor.co.uk

Nearby Exmoor Pony Centre; Dunster Castle; Tarr Steps; Caracatus Stone; Stone Age Burial Site **Location** in centre of village on B road, 1.5miles from junction with A396, ample parking in hotel car park and on street
Food breakfast, lunch, dinner
Price ££
Rooms 12; 6 doubles under the thatch (5 with four poster beds), 2 twins, 2 doubles in annexe; all rooms have bath/shower, telephone, TV, hairdryers, tea/coffee making facilities **Facilities** residents lounge, dining room, bar, wi-fi, garden
Credit Cards all major **Children** welcome **Accessibility** possible to annexe rooms **Pets** accepted in bar and some of the bedrooms **Closed** 1st-8th Feb **Proprietors** Mark & Sally Bradley

The Royal Oak
Village inn

This Exmoor institution has been improving steadily since the Bradleys took over a few years ago. Locals popping in for a drink feel relaxed because their custom is valued and they have their own bar area. Hotel guests have a peaceful refuge at the far end of the building – a large sitting room replete with Victorian-style deep-buttoned chairs and sofas. Along with the rest of the public areas and bedrooms, it's conservatively rather than imaginatively decorated – 30 and 40-somethings won't like it as much as their parents – but it's appropriate to Exmoor.

There's room in the dining area for the shooting parties not to swamp the regular guests. Several menus, including a family one, and a long wine list, offer the wide choice needed to satisfy these different groups. We liked the chunky, brown-stained tongue-and-groove panelling throughout the ground floor – quite smart and pleasing because it pulls it all together in an unpretentious way. Ceilings are low, beams are everywhere and because of the thatch overhang, the ground floor is darkish. We also liked the spacious bedrooms, with conventional repro and antique furnishings and adequate, plain white bathrooms. No 4, at £140, is especially roomy. No 3, the smallest, is roomy by comparison with what other similar places offer for £120.

THE SOUTH-WEST | SOUTHERN ENGLAND

Zeals, Wilstshire

New Rd, Zeals, Warminster,
BA12 6NJ

Tel 01747 840404
email hello@bellandcrown.com
website www.bellandcrown.com

Nearby Longleat safari, Salisbury Cathedral, Stonehenge, Stourhead House & Gardens
Location North of the A303
Food breakfast, lunch, dinner and pizza
Price ££-£££
Rooms 6 double en-suites
Facilities bar, outdoor seating
Credit cards MC, V
Children welcome
Accessibilty ground floor only
Pets not allowed in rooms
Closed never
Proprietors Chickpea Group

The Bell and Crown
Pub with rooms

Cosy, friendly, stylish in its way and a useful stopover for the West Country, this is one of five pubs with rooms currently in the new Chickpea mini collection. We're wary of hotel groups because their properties can be samey, but that's not true here. The open-plan layout allows three groups to co-exist: thirsty locals; diners from the neighbourhood; and passing travellers. There's a core area around the bar where all can mingle but which is mainly for locals and could get lively and crowded; a second bigger, table-filled zone is less busy, loosely separated by partitions; and finally a calm restaurant area.

The decorative style could be called country-chic: a step up from rough and rustic, it relies on good looking period country furniture. The menu typically has six starters and six mains which change often, unique to the pub, plus a section named Pub Bangers. Imaginative starters on our visit included crab rarebit; mains handmade tagliatelle, violet artichoke, spinach and garlic; and the Pub Bangers English Rose veal liver. We liked rooms 3 and 4: 3 is smallish and good value at £90 as we went to press; 4 is ideal for a family of three. Zeals is a nothing-special west Wiltshire village but the Bell and Crown gives it a lift. For other Chickpea pubs with rooms, see pages 41, 54 and 84.

THE SOUTH-WEST SOUTHERN ENGLAND

Zennor, Cornwall

Treen, Zennor, Cornwall
TR26 3DE

Tel 01736 796928
email enquiries@gurnardshead.co.uk
website www.gurnardshead.co.uk

Nearby Tate Galley at St Ives; South West Coast Path; Trengwainton
Location on the B3306 between St Ives and Land's End; ample car parking
Food breakfast, lunch, dinner
Price £££
Rooms 7; 4 double, 3 twin, some with a bath and all with shower; all with phone, Roberts Radio and hairdryer.
Facilities bar, dining room; garden
Credit cards MC, V
Children welcome
Accessibility no special facilities
Pets dogs welcome
Closed Christmas day and 1 week in early Dec
Proprietors Charles and Edmund Inkin; they also own The Old Coastguard (page 63) and Felin Fach Griffin (page 182) in Wales

The Gurnard's Head
Seaside inn

An early 17thC coaching inn near Zennor, standing like a beacon on the windswept coastal road that runs between St Ives and Land's End. Brothers Charles and Edmund Inkin's motto is 'the simple things in life done well' and they reckon on applying this to all aspects of The Gunard's Head, as also to their other establishments.

The stunning location and views of the Atlantic make this inn popular with walkers, tourists and city dwellers looking for tranquility, although the sounds and smells from the neighbouring farm may not be for urban-outdoor types. The bedrooms are simple and tastefully decorated, with handmade beds and good linen. Each room is lined with old books and local pictures and maps – you might be staying with friends.

With the Atlantic 500 metres away, locally caught fish is a highlight of the seasonal menu. The lunch menus suit most guests, from the hungry walker to those who want to settle in for a fixed-price menu with a carafe of wine. In the evening, the menu is short and delicious, changing daily according to what suppliers bring through the back door. Drink from a choice of well-chosen and affordable wines or local real ales and cider.

St Mary's, Isles of Scilly

St Mary's, Isles of Scilly,
TR21 0TA

Tel 01720 422317
email info@star-castle.co.uk
website www.star-castle.co.uk

Nearby other Scilly islands including Tresco; bird watching; swimming with seals
Location in own grounds
Food breakfast, lunch, dinner
Price ££-£££
Rooms 38 (8 in castle, 30 Guard House rooms); 4 singles with shower, 34 double or twin with bath and shower; all rooms have phone, TV
Facilities sitting room, bar, 2 restaurants, tennis, indoor swimming pool
Credit Cards AE, MC, V
Children accepted
Accessibility difficult, but some ground level rooms
Pets accepted
Closed 3 days before Christmas, 4 weeks after New Year
Proprietor James Francis

Star Castle Hotel
Island hotel

There's only a handful of upmarket hotels in the Scillies, some of which strive to appeal to the mainland's chic set. They tend to lack heart, but this one decidedly does not. The welcome begins at the airport, or ferry, where James – who has now taken over the hotel from his father, Robert – or the hotel's driver comes to meet guests.

Castles often make dismal hotels, but this one, inside its walls in the shape of an eight-pointed star, has something of the charm and intimacy of a Cotswold cottage. As well as the cosy bar, first floor sitting room and ground floor, stone-walled dining room, there are eight charming bedrooms in the castle itself. In 2017 the rooms were redecorated with new licks of paint, curtains and some new bathrooms fitted.

Each morning at breakfast, James enquires from his guests what they feel like doing, arranging boat trips and providing packed lunches and maps for walkers. Many regulars simply say they are "going with Tim", a hugely popular local boatman who takes guests on trips to the off-islands.

The spacious bedrooms in the annexe have also been overhauled. An exotic garden is growing up between the two wings to detract from their somewhat Butlinesque appearance. We could not fault the food, and there's an interesting personal wine list. This is not a chic hotel, but a very good one.

THE SOUTH-WEST | **SOUTHERN ENGLAND**

Tresco, Isles of Scilly

Tresco Estate, Isles of Scilly,
TR24 0QQ

Tel 01720 422849
email contactus@tresco.co.uk
website www.tresco.co.uk

Nearby Tresco's sub-tropical Abbey Garden; boat trips to other Scilly Isles; ferry to Bryher.
Location Tresco island.
Food breakfast, lunch, dinner
Price very variable, see website
Rooms 16; 7 self-catering, 9 self-catering with hotel services (eg daily clean), for 2-10 people. See website for details of individual cottages
Facilities restaurants and pubs (eg New Inn in New Grimsby), swimming pool, gym, spa, bike hire, golf buggies **Credit cards** DC, MC, V
Children welcome
Accessibility no special access (golf buggies available for people with reduced mobility)
Pets not accepted
Closed Never
Proprietor Tresco Estate

Sea Garden Cottages
Self-catering cottages

The whole of Tresco is in effect a multi-faceted holiday destination, unique in Britain. The Island Hotel has disappeared, to leave a mix of timeshare and rental accommodation dotted all over the island. The Sea Garden Cottages – built from sympathetic wood and stone – comprise seven self-catering cottages and nine cottages that have certain hotel facilities as part of the package.

Our cottage suite was faultless: comfortable, well-equipped kitchen and garden, seaside-fresh decoration. It also had some interesting modern art, much of it from the collection of Tresco's proprietors, Robert and Lucy Dorrien-Smith.

There's an indoor pool and tennis court by the cottages. Guests can also eat in the stylish restaurant at the Flying Boat Club at New Grimsby or in the new restaurant, The Ruin. This shares the same electrifying sea views as the rooms, and does tasty food – although we preferred the surf'n'turf at The New Inn at New Grimsby, its menu was tantalising and made choosing difficult.

Accommodation on Tresco is expensive. However, it's a no-car, protected environment and under blue skies the archipelago dances in the sunlight. If you want the full hotel experience think about Hell Bay Hotel (www.hellbay.co.uk), on Bryher, also owned by the Dorrien-Smiths.

THE SOUTH-WEST — SOUTHERN ENGLAND

Bath

32 Broad Street
BA1 5LP

Tel 01225 330190
email reception.broadstreettownhouse@butcombepubs.com
website www.butcombe.com/broad-street-townhouse-bath/
Food breakfast and lunch in cafe, dinner in Pig and Fiddle
Price ££ **Closed** never
Proprietors Butcombe

Broadstreet Townhouse
City hotel

Smartly revamped by Butcombe Brewery in 2019 to create a Regency ambience worthy of its centre-of-Bath location. The 11 bedrooms over three stories are all individual, stylish and comfortable with plenty of space and stimulating artworks echoing the beiges, greys and pale blues of the colour schemes. Downstairs is an informal bar-café offering food, coffee and cocktails - settle down after a day's sightseeing in one of the enticing shabby-chic seating niches with a street view to watch the world go by. It manages to be glamorous and quite homely, and although part of a large and growing chain of Butcombe properties, you are not especially aware of the corporation behind it. Next door is a lively Butcombe pub, The Pig & Fiddle.

Beercrocombe, Somerset

Hatch Beauchamp, Taunton, Somerset TA3 6AF

Tel 01823481883
email info@frog-street.co.uk
website www.frog-street.co.uk
Food self-catering
Price £££
Closed never
Proprietors Louise and David

Frog Street Farmhouse
Self-catering

This longhouse dates back to the 15th century and can be found at the end of a lane in deepest Somerset. The house has considerable character and warmth with views across farmland, cider apple orchards and the pretty garden. They are all spacious and comfortable, with white duvets and antique furniture. The bathrooms are modern, and guests have exclusive access to a spa, hot tub and outdoor kitchen.

Since the last edition, the place has changed from B&B to a fully-self catering six-bed farmhouse. We still think it's a useful address as the atmosphere is unique for a privately hired space: friendly, restful and unpretentious, helped by relaxed and welcoming hosts Louise and David.

THE SOUTH-WEST — SOUTHERN ENGLAND

Bradford-on-Avon

Trowbridge Road, Bradford-on-Avon
BA15 1UH

Tel 01225864750
email stay@widbrookgrange.co.uk
website www.widbrookgrange.co.uk
Food breakfast, lunch, dinner
Price £££-££££
Closed never
Proprietors Charlotte and Nick Dent

Widbrook Grange
Town house hotel

Relaxed-family friendly-quirky is the formula of this relative place set in open country up a drive in spreading grounds. Our first impressions were of relaxation and homeyness – lived in, genuine, and though there are quirky elements, it's not contrived.

The main dining room has pleasing distressed chairs in different styles and there's a second conservatory dining room where dog owners eat. The food is ambitious and fairly priced. A gin bar, manned on our visit by friendly Attila, is a cosy den with a helpful menu to help you make your choice from the 150 dizzying alternatives.

Several steps up from the B & B it once was, but without the pretensions of a posh country house hotel. A valuable niche, and staying here is a great way of doing Bath.

Bristol

The Sugar House,
Narrow Lewins Mead,
Bristol, Avon BS1 2NU

Tel 0117 9255577
email theteam@hotelduvin.com
website www.hotelduvin.com
Food breakfast, lunch, dinner
Price £££
Closed never
Proprietors Frasers Hospitality

Hotel du Vin
Town house hotel

Converted from a collection of derelict 18thC sugar warehouses, the hotel's gracious Queen Anne frontage belies the wizardry behind. This is probably still one of the more interesting and stylish place to stay in Bristol. Open brickwork, painted girders and sweeping stairs with a curving steel bannister combine industrial elements with contemporary style to great effect.

The huge bedrooms contain custom-made beds, alongside equally huge bathrooms with showers and free-standing baths. The aptly-named Sugar Bar has white-washed walls, wood flooring and rugs that contribute to the unhurried, plantation house feel.

THE SOUTH-WEST — SOUTHERN ENGLAND

Buckhorn Weston, Dorset

Church Hill, Buckhorn Weston,
Gillingham, Dorset SP8 5HS

Tel 01963 370028
email thestapletonarms@gmail.com
website www.thestapletonarms.co.uk
Food breakfast, lunch, dinner
Price ££
Closed Mondays and Tuesdays
Proprietors Jo and Phil Sellars

The Stapleton Arms
Pub with rooms

In deepest Dorset lies this new-wave village inn, the type you might describe as 'urban-chic with a country twist'. With pillared portico and elegant proportions, it looks more like a gentleman's residence than a long-established hostelry. Step inside, and the scene is contemporary: open-plan, leather sofas and chunky tables.

The bedrooms are great, especially for the price: airy and well-proportioned. We had a lovely bathroom, with large, free-standing tub and generous toiletries.

Dinner, on our last visit, prior to the hiring of new head chef Phil, was a little disappointing. We are interested to hear if the service and food has improved. When the place is humming, as it often is, it makes a great stop-off en route to the West Country.

Chettle, Dorest

Chettle, near Blandford Forum,
Dorset, DT11 8DB

Tel 07774 353010
email info@chettlelodge.co.uk
website www.chettlelodge.co.uk
Food self-catering
Price ££
Closed Feb
Proprietors Alice Favre

Chettle Lodge
Country house for hire

Chettle is one of those rare estate villages that has hardly changed in the 150 years it has been in the benign ownership of one family, who live in the fine Queen Anne manor house. Part of the building dates back 400 years, but it was much altered in Victorian times when it was tricked out with a galleried hall; a richly carved oak Jacobean fireplace was also installed in one of the reception rooms (the other is Regency style) with bookcases to match.

Upstairs, the elegant proportions of the rooms have been left intact, and bedrooms are just right: comfortable and in good taste,. several of the bathrooms have Victorian roll-top baths.

The eight-bed property and grounds are now private hire only.

THE SOUTH-WEST / SOUTHERN ENGLAND

Dittisham, Devon

Old Coombe Manor Farm,
Dittisham, Devon Q6 OJA

Tel 01803 722398
email info@fingals.co.uk
website www.fingals.co.uk
Food self-catering
Price ££-££££
Closed Never
Proprietors Richard and Sheila Johnston

Fingals
Self-catering

Fingals is different, and those who love it will really love it – which sums up why we remain enthusiastic about this manor farmhouse in a secluded valley close to the River Dart. The 17thC house, with Queen Anne front additions, has plenty of charm. Inside, new and old furniture, pine and oak blend stylishly.

Some years ago the number of rooms was reduced to six self-catering properties for families. It's country house party appeal suits large family gatherings – the owners frequently host parties that sleep up to 30 across all generations.

Fingals is a laid-back place with a laid-back yet thoroughly professional proprietor.

Frome, Somerset

Babington, near Frome,
Somerset BA11 3RW

Tel 01373 812266
email reception@babingtonhouse.co.uk
website www.babingtonhouse.co.uk
Food breakfast, lunch, dinner, room service **Price** ££££
Closed never
Proprietors Nick Jones

Babington House
Country house hotel

Babington was the idea of Nick Jones, owner of the trendy Soho Club in London, and bought as a country retreat for club members. In practice anyone can stay here, although it might be better if you were young, or at least young at heart. Having said that, everyone is made to feel welcome, in a laid-back yet professional, atmosphere. It's a contemporary hotel set in an elegant country house that offers metropolitan and unpretentious luxury. Bedrooms are wonderful, with huge bottles of complimentary lotions in the bathrooms. You can have any number of beauty treatments in the Cowshed, where there is also an indoor pool and a gym. Small children are kept occupied in the well-equipped crêche.

THE SOUTH-WEST — SOUTHERN ENGLAND

Lyme Regis

The Alexandra Hotel, Pound Street
Lyme Regis Dorset DT7 3HZ

Tel 01297 442010
email info@hotelalexandra.co.uk
website
www.hotelalexandra.co.uk
Food breakfast, lunch, dinner, afternoon tea **Price** ££
Closed never
Proprietors The Haskins Family

The Alexandra
Country house hotel

Despite its 25 rooms, this seaside hotel has caught our attention because it feels smallish, and is owner managed with a relaxed atmosphere. Service is personal but not intrusive. Above all, we can't resist the five-star location. From the garden you get grandstand views over Lyme Regis and across Lyme Bay – an ideal base for exploring the Jurassic Coast.

The individually designed bedrooms are colourful and bright, enhanced by big windows that bring in plenty of natural light. Botanical prints and seaside themed knick-knacks are scattered throughout, bringing a relaxed and playful energy to the historic building.

There's no need for a car here, in fact, you can get to the beach without even having to cross the road.

Newquay, Cornwall

Fistral Beach, Newquay, Cornwall
TR7 1EW

Tel 01637 872211
email
reception@headlandhotel.co.uk
website
www.headlandhotel.co.uk/accommodation/cottages **Food** breakfast, lunch, dinner **Price** £££-££££
Closed never
Proprietors Mr and Mrs Armstrong

The Headland Cottages
Self-catering cottages

Talk about a Victorian pile. The Headland Hotel's outward appearance is so frightening it was the setting for the 1990 film adaptation of Roald Dahl's *The Witches*.

The 39 one- to three-bedroom self-catering cottages make an attractive alternative to staying at the hotel – indeed any hotel – with all the benefits of hotel facilities close by. They are built in Cornish village style with rough stone and granite walls. Ours was airy and freshly painted in seaside colours, and had an excellent kitchen and gas log fire too.

You can mix self-catering with meals in the hotel. The Headland also has a fully equipped spa (pictured), to which cottage guests have full access. The cottages, food and spa are worth seeking out.

THE SOUTH-WEST — SOUTHERN ENGLAND

Tollard Royal, Salisbury

Tollard Royal, Wiltshire SP5 5PS

Tel 01725 516207
email kingjohninn@butcombepubs.com
website www.butcombe.com/the-king-john-inn-wiltshire
Food breakfast, lunch, dinner
Price ££-££££
Closed never
Proprietor Butcombe Pubs

King John Inn
Country inn

At weekends the King John is jammed with urban couples, though locals come here too – it has a strong feel of village pub turned weekend hang-out. There is a charming 'outdoor kitchen', with a cosmopolitan seafood bar under a Victorian-style pavilion. In the evening, don't be surprised to find a lively throng on the terrace outside, keeping warm from the wood-burning braziers.

Upstairs are the five bedrooms (there are also three in a converted coach house). Ours had a bay window dressed in a beautiful woven fabric and a great feeling of space. The bathroom was a little dark, but had both free-standing bath and shower.

We thought the pork and mustard pies good pub fare, and the snails, crab on toast and fish from Poole Harbour better than expected.

Wedmore, Somerset

Cheddar Road, Wedmore, Somerset BS28 4EQ

Tel 01934 710337
email info@theswanwedmore.com
website www.theswanwedmore.com
Food breakfast, lunch, dinner, afternoon tea, snacks, Sunday lunch
Price ££ **Closed** Christmas Day drinks only **Proprietor** Stay Original Co.

The Swan
Country inn

Another dead-beat country pub restored and converted eight years ago into a comfortable up-to-date haven. Owner Rob Greacen has kept faith with the place's inherited country pub ambience by going for wooden floors, log burners and a choice of real ales. The food, served all day, is hearty country fare – chef Tom Blake was at Hugh Fearnley-Whittingstall's River Cottage. Rare-breed pork is a speciality.

The bedrooms are striking: quality beds and linen, some charming furniture and interesting auction room finds here and there.

Alton (Lower Froyle), Hampshire

Lower Froyle, Alton, Hampshire
GU34 4NA

Tel 01420 23261
email
anchorinn@butcombepubs.com
website www.butcombe.com/the-anchor-inn-hampshire

Nearby Hampshire
Location 1.8 miles from Bentley, just off the A31
Food breakfast, lunch, dinner
Price £££
Rooms 5; all with shower
Facilities 2 bar areas, dining room, private dining rooms, courtyard
Credit cards AE, DC, MC, V
Children welcome
Accessibility dining rooms only
Pets dogs allowed in the bedrooms and bar area
Closed never
Proprietors Butcombe Pubs

The Anchor Inn
Country Inn

As a pleasant place to stay, it works well. You might even ask yourself, why spend more in a hotel when you can stay just as comfortably here? Our room felt spacious, with French doors on to a balcony rising to a high apex, and room for a sofa and table. All the extras of a fully-fledged hotel are in place: a choice of teas and coffees; Bush radio; antique-style sleigh bed; Egyptian cotton linen. The decoration is fashionable yet full of character, with oriental carpets on sisal, pale sage walls covered in pictures and shelves of books. A number of classic English touches help achieve the pleasant effect of staying in a country house rather than a hotel: fabrics in tweed patterns, eccentric *objets d'art*, pewter goblets and mochaware can be found in the bedrooms and dining room – which is illuminated by particularly cosy lighting.

The night we stayed we were chilly in the wood-panelled dining room, but that was probably a one off. We got used to the low beams in the bar and kept our heads, but it's good sport watching new arrivals lose theirs. The food is properly English and enjoyable. Breakfast is excellent, and the staff friendly.

The Anchor is owned by Butcombe Brewery. Other Butcombe pubs-with-rooms are on pages 90, 109 and 115.

THE SOUTH-EAST

SOUTHERN ENGLAND

Baughurst, Hampshire

Baughurst Road, Baughurst,
Hampshire RG26 5LP

Tel 0118 9820110
email hello@thewellingtonarms.com
website
www.thewellingtonarms.com

Nearby Highclere Castle, The Vyne, Silchester Roman Wall, Bishopswood Golf Course, Sandford Springs Golf Club
Location on Baughurst Road, leading south from Baughurst
Food breakfast, lunch, dinner
Price £££-££££
Rooms 4 doubles; all with shower, heated floors, wi-fi, TV and mini bar
Facilities bar, restaurant, large garden **Credit cards** DC, MC, V
Children welcome
Accessibility wheelchair possible
Pets dogs welcome
Closed First two weeks of Jan
Proprietor Jason King and Simon Page

The Wellington Arms
Pub restaurant-with-rooms

Our series editor, Fiona Duncan, writes: 'The Wellington Arms is a dining pub with four rooms so immaculate that even in plutocratic north Hampshire, it stands out like a supermodel in a street market – oak furniture, Hungarian goose down bedding and slate flagstones with underfloor heating are just some of the features that set it apart. Over two decades partners Simon and Aussie born Jason have gently expanded this pretty former shooting lodge into something that looks, feels and is quite special.

Just an hour's drive from central London yet set in peaceful countryside, it ticks all the boxes for urbanites seeking rural idyll; immaculate, fulsome flower- and vegetable gardens, which the owners and kitchen staff tend themselves; orchards; they even keep rescue hens – not to mention the beehives, flock of Jacob sheep and Tamworth pigs. They have tea cosies knitted by Simon's mum from their own sheep, and fabric hens dangling from the room keys. Jason's cooking takes pub dining to its highest level: home made, locally sourced and tasty, with a state of the art cheese soufflé. After lunch, take the footpath from the door of the Wellington Arms, which leads through woods and fields, or perhaps head for Watership Down, site of Richard Adams's famous book of the same name.

THE SOUTH-EAST — SOUTHERN ENGLAND

Bepton, West Sussex

Bepton, Nr Midhurst,
West Sussex GU29 0JB

Tel 01730-819020/819000
email reservations@parkhousehotel.com
website www.parkhousehotel.com

Nearby Petworth; Goodwood; Cowdray Park Polo Club; Chichester. **Location** on the B2226 in the village of Bepton; ample car-parking **Food** breakfast, lunch, dinner; room service **Price** ££-£££ **Rooms** 21 double: 12 in main house, 6 in South Downs Cottage, 2 in Polo Cottage and 1 in Bay Tree Cottage. All have tea, coffee, wi-fi, TV, radio, bathrobes, hairdryer, room service **Facilities** dining, drawing room, conservatory, bar; gardens, outdoor swimming pool, two grass tennis courts, croquet lawn, bowls green, golf, spa **Credit cards** MC, V **Children** welcome **Accessibility** adapted ground-floor bedroom, South Down Cottage has lift, spa has lift **Pets** by arrangement **Closed** never **Proprietor** Seamus O'Brien

Park House and Spa
Country hotel

Park House has been in the O'Brien family for four generations, and has always retained the atmosphere of a private country house thanks first to the careful attention of Ioné O'Brien and now to Seamus. A 16thC farmhouse with Victorian additions with its cream-painted roughcast walls, at first it looks rather suburban.

Inside, however, the elegant public rooms strike a very different note. The honesty bar, festooned with mementoes and photographs of polo players (Cowdray Park is close at hand) is admirably well-stocked, while the drawing room, particularly appealing at night, gleams with polished parquet floor, velvet-backed alcoves filled with books and china, yellow walls, and table lamps which cast a golden glow.

Bedrooms are traditional. The Polo is perhaps the best cottage, adjacent to the main house with entrance to a private garden. The dinner menu has been expanded (it used to be quite limited) and features traditional English food. Dinner might include lamb rump with aubergine and puy lentils, followed by pistachio, chocolate and rasberry soufflé.

The extensive facilities include the likes of grass tennis courts and golf, as well as the Park House Spa – a luxurious area with an indoor pool, gym and fitness suite, saunas, steam rooms and a Jacuzzi.

THE SOUTH-EAST / SOUTHERN ENGLAND

Brighton

33 Regency Square, Brighton, BN1 2GG

Tel 01273 324 302
email brighton@artistresidence.co.uk
website www.artistresidence-brighton.co.uk

Nearby beach, Brighton Pier, The Royal Pavilion, The Lanes, Brighton Dome, Brighton Wheel, Komedia, train station. **Location** in historic Regency Square **Food** breakfast and snacks **Price** £-££££ **Rooms** 24; 17 double; 5 twin or triple, one suite, one bunk room (for groups of up to four sharing, 4 built in single bunk beds); 3 apartments next door. All rooms have TV, hairdryer, tea and coffee making facilities **Facilities** ping pong, cocktail bar, breakfast room/art gallery, sitting room, meeting room, event space **Credit cards** AE, DC, MC, V **Children** welcome **Accessibility** no special access **Pets** selection of dog-friendly rooms **Closed** never
Proprietor Charlotte and Justin Salisbury

Artist Residence, Brighton **Town hotel**

When 20-year-old Justin Salisbury quit university in 2008 to help his injured mother run her ailing guesthouse, he made a call to arms to local artists on gumtree: to decorate in return for free board. Thus Artist Residence – now five branches strong – was born. Their flagship in Brighton has also expanded over the years, acquiring the house next door. The nine original 'Arty' rooms are supplemented by 15 rooms, done up in their 'House' style – a mixture of rustic shabby-chic and faux-industrial.

We stayed in the art-themed No. 4, muraled with a fantasy cityscape, and hung with photographs by an artist called Bonnie & Clyde. The fairly basic bathrooms and bedrooms in these rooms are elevated by the wacky and creative surroundings – perfect for its trendy Brighton setting.

The relaxed cafe serves breakfast and snacks to guests and laptop-wielding locals alike. Later in day the lights dim as the place evolves into a popular cocktail hour.

The hotel's original concept may whiff of gimmick but our series editor, Fiona Duncan, calls this is the real deal. It may be 'funky' but it certainly isn't naff. On top of this, the staff are charming.

THE SOUTH-EAST | SOUTHERN ENGLAND

Brockenhurst, Hampshire

Beaulieu Road, Brockenhurst,
Hampshire SO42 7QL

Tel 01590 622354
email
info@thepighotel.com
website www.pighotel.com

Nearby Beaulieu National Motor Museum, Bucklers Hard; Lymington; New Forest wildlife centres. **Location** in own extensive grounds, in the heart of the New Forest, close to Brockenhurst; ample private car-parking **Food** breakfast, lunch, afternoon snack menu, dinner **Price** ££–£££ **Rooms** 29; rooms, suites and outdoor cabins available. **Facilities** restaurant, lounge, bar, spa treatments, vegetable garden, guided walks, cycling, tennis courts, pigsty with pigs **Credit cards** AE, DC, MC, V **Children** welcome **Accessibility** wheelchair access to ground floor rooms and garden **Pets** guide dogs only **Closed** never **Hotel Director** Chris Drodge

The Pig
Country house hotel

In its earlier incarnations, we thought of this place as a benchmark for the sort of establishment we didn't want in the guide – it was one of hundreds of nothing-special country house hotels. But when Robin Hutson, creator of the Hotel du Vin chain and one of Britain's most inspired hoteliers, practised his magic on the place it was transformed

Robin's wife Judy did the interior. It's quite a contrast to the controlled, Georgian exterior: a set piece of shabby-chic with touches of anarchy. The conservatory-dining room is the big draw: an imaginative, light-filled space with a wonderful tiled floor, pots of herbs on wooden boxes lining the outside windows and on every table. Over the corridor in the drawing room shabby-chic reasserts itself emphatically. The floor boards are distressed, and 'damaged' plasterwork on the walls reveals areas of brickwork beneath – only it's not damaged, it's *trompe l'oeil*. The bedrooms are truly comfortable.

Don't leave without a stroll through the walled kitchen garden, where they grow some of what's eaten in the dining room.

See also The Pig - near Bath, The Pig - at Combe, The Pig - on the Beach and The Pig - in the Wall (pages 32, 52, 79 and 152).

THE SOUTH-EAST

SOUTHERN ENGLAND

Bucklers Hard, Hampshire

Bucklers Hard, Beaulieu,
Hampshire SO42 7XB

Tel 01590 616253
email
enquiries@themasterbuilders.co.uk
website
www.themasterbuilders.co.uk

Nearby New Forest; Beaulieu; Lymington.
Location overlooking Beaulieu river at Bucklers Hard, 2 miles (3 km) SE of Beaulieu, 9 miles (14 km) SE of Lyndhurst; ample car parking
Food breakfast, lunch, dinner
Price £££ **Rooms** 26 double, 18 can be twin; all rooms have phone, TV, hairdryer, wi-fi, tea/coffee facilities, complimentary Godminster vodka
Facilities sitting room, Riverview restaurant, yachtsman's bar; terrace, garden, pontoon available
Credit cards MC, V **Children** welcome **Accessibility** difficult
Pets 7 dog-friendly rooms
Closed never
Proprietors Hillbrooke Hotels

The Master Builder's
Riverside hotel

The location of this hotel really is special, and historic, at the bottom end of a row of 18thC shipwrights' cottages, looking down on to the Beaulieu River. It contains a bar that's popular with visiting yachtsmen, and nearby is a maritime museum.

When Hillbrooke Hotels took over some years ago they carried out a much-needed overhaul. The bedrooms in the main building have a quirky character, combined with luxury. The 18thC house was lumbered some years back with an unsympathetic modern annexe, the Henry Adams Wing. Since our last edition this has been refurbished, offering Posh Classic Rooms decorated with a coastal feel. While these were always comfortable and attractive, they now have more character.

The reception area is sophisticated, and the newly refurbished Riverview restaurant is designed to reflect a forest, and streamlined to creative intimate dining settings. The former Yachtsman's Bar has had a successful revamp and been renamed Henry's. There is a large outdoor eating area, again with great views of the Beaulieu River, which comes into its own in summer when the barbecue operates.

Hillbrooke Hotels specialise in hotels and inns on country estates. In this edition of the guide we also feature The William Cecil, Stamford, page 244.

THE SOUTH-EAST — SOUTHERN ENGLAND

Camber, East Sussex

New Lydd Road, Camber, Rye, East Sussex TN31 7RB

Tel 01797 225 057
email reservations@thegallivant.co.uk
website www.thegallivant.com

Nearby Camber Sands, Romney Salt Marshes, Dungeness, Rye. **Location** 90 minutes from central London, 5 minutes from Rye, car park opposite **Food** breakfast, lunch, dinner **Price** £££–££££
Rooms 20 doubles; 4 Luxury Garden Rooms, 3 Baby Hampton Rooms, 2 Deck Rooms and 1 Snug Cain. All rooms have wi-fi, telephone, flat-screen television, hairdryer, tea and coffee and Bramley toiletries
Facilities 2 function rooms, Beach Hut spa treatment room, coastal garden and shingle courtyard, yoga studio, vineyard tours
Credit cards MC, V **Children** welcome **Accessibility** access possible and all rooms are ground floor **Pets** dogs welcome **Closed** never
Proprietor Harry Cragoe

The Gallivant Hotel
Beach hotel

The Gallivant started in the Sixties as the Blue Dolphin Motel, when no doubt it saw its fair share of gallivants and their girls. It's still identifiable on the outside as being inspired by the California coast motel, but it's also buzzy, inexpensive and in a great location: Camber Sands is over the road, and Rye is five minutes by car.

The sunny restaurant, with bleached wood bar, simple tables and chairs, has a Scandi/New England feel, and the food is spot on – with ingredients sourced within 15 miles of the hotel. On a predominantly piscatorial menu, we enjoyed a pungent fish soup and salt-marsh lamb, with a creamy buttermilk panna cotta. The wine list has a lovely array of local sparkling varieties from which to choose. The bedrooms are compact, with beach shack-style furniture, taupe walls and curtains incorporating quirky retro touches, with an eye to The Hamptons, the expensive residential enclave on Long Island, near New York city. All bedrooms come with King or Super-King Hypnos mattresses, along with plump goose-down bedding. An onsite yoga studio offers favourable rates for guests with friendly instructors. A recent partnership with local winery Gusbourne Estate now offer residents exclusive vineyard tours and tastings. See also the Gallivant Littlestone Beach, page 116.

Cuckfield, West Sussex

Ockenden Lane, Cuckfield,
West Sussex RH17 5LD

Tel 01444 416111
email reservations@ockenden-manor.co.uk
website www.hshotels.co.uk

Nearby Nyman's; Sissinghurst; Wakehurst Place; Gatwick; Brighton.
Location 2 miles (3 km) W of Haywards Heath close to middle of village, ample car parking
Food breakfast, lunch, afternoon tea, dinner
Price £££
Rooms 28; 26 double, 2 single, all with bath; all rooms have phone, TV, hairdryer
Facilities sitting room, bar, dining room; terrace, garden, spa
Credit cards AE, DC, MC, V
Children welcome
Accessibility access possible in a couple of rooms (enquire before)
Pets not accepted **Closed** never
Proprietors Miranda Carminger

Ockenden Manor
Manor house hotel

Anne Goodman made many changes for the better here after taking over this attractive 16th/17thC manor house. Now her daughter Miranda owns the hotel, and continues to keep up her high standards.

Bedrooms are spacious and individual (and crammed with giveaways); a superb master suite with sombre panelling relies on reds and greens to give a feeling of brightness. Several of the bathrooms are notably spacious, and they are well-equipped. The main sitting room, though lavishly furnished, has a personal feel. Staff are friendly and obliging. (A notice in the hotel states that whatever a hotel's character and charm, it is only as good as its staff.)

Dinner, which is served in the dining room with sweeping views towards the Souths Down National Park, is another highlight. The menu, devised by Head CHef Stephen Crane, is based on local produce, with vegetables and herbs from the garden.

Although Ockenden Manor is popular with business people, it is a human, comfortable hotel. 'Hidden away behind trees and a high wall; quiet; good value', says a reporter.

East Chilington, East Sussex

Chapel Lane, East Chiltington,
Lewes BN7 3BA

Tel 01273890400
email hello@thejollysportsman.com
website www.thejollysportsman.com

Nearby South Downs National Park, Lewes Castle, Plumpton Village, 8 miles from the beach
Location nearest train station is Plumpton
Food breakfast, lunch, dinner
Price ££-£££
Rooms 4; 3 doubles and 1 suite
Facilities dining room, sitting room, terrace, sun terrace, garden, live music
Credit cards MC, V
Children welcome
Accessibility access to ground floor only
Pets dogs welcome
Closed never
Proprietor Chris Colville

The Jolly Sportsman
Country pub and B&B

Hidden in the South Downs National Park, the Jolly Sportsman is a warm and homely country pub with a sense of slow living. There are just four adequately sized yet comfortable bedrooms and a terrace for great views of the countryside.

We found the team's dedication to maintaining a low carbon footprint especially impressive. They have adapted age-old cooking techniques, such as cooking over a wood fire, as well as baking their own bread. Working closely with local suppliers means the team can offer fresh fish from the coast and seasonal dishes such as fermented pearl barley risotto. A complimentary wine list featuring over forty wines accompanies lunch and dinner, served in a pub surrounded by vineyards. In the winter food is served inside, but in the warmer months you can eat in the garden. The garden bar is open every Friday and on weekends. Sip a refreshing Montenegro Spritz or order Jersey rock oysters. We especially enjoyed the easy-going atmosphere of the garden, with its wild flowers and hedging.

If you are staying a couple of days and wondering what to do, try the East Chiltington Circular Walk or the Hassocks to East Chiltington Walk. We see it as not just a great bed and breakfast, but a weekend destination in its own right with well above average food.

East Chisenbury, Wiltshire

East Chisenbury, Pewsey, Wiltshire
SN9 6AQ

Tel 01980 671124
email redlion@eastchisenbury.com
website www.eastchisenbury.com

Nearby Area of Outstanding Natural Beauty; Salisbury Cathederal & Magna Carta; Stonehenge; Longleat House & Gardens; Safari Park; Avebury; White Horse Trail. **Location** East Chisenbury village
Food lunch and dinner **Price** £££
Rooms 5 doubles, all rooms have riverside views & private decking, wi-fi, TV, tea & coffee, outdoor weather kit, organic handmade toiletries
Facilities dining room, pub, bar, garden, private fishing
Credit cards MC, V **Children** welcome in pub **Accessibility** 1 room with wheelchair access **Pets** dogs welcome in pub and 3 dog friendly rooms **Closed** one week in Jan
Proprietors Brittany & Guy Manning

Red Lion Freehouse
Village inn

The Red Lion is a quintessential English village pub – *à la mode* – with a Michelin star and five glamourous bedrooms. The delightful chef/patron, Guy Manning, runs the pub with his equally charming and hard-working wife and general manager, Brittany.

There's everything you could wish for in a thatched pub: a log burner, beams, blackboards and assorted wooden tables and chairs. However, we missed comfy sofas – their absence made it feel static.

The food was superb for an inn, but perhaps quite expensive compared with other similar establishments. But the care that Guy and his close-knit team put into what is essentially home cooking is of the highest order. The rich and gamey menu features dishes such as Huntsham Farm jambonette served with celeriac purée, Sandridge Farm bacon and Bourguignon garnish – Guy doesn't hold back on flavour.

The five bedrooms are in a converted bungalow, Troutbeck, along the lane. They are a bit glitzy: silvery furniture and fake fur throws, but the standard is high, and they are an exhilarating contrast to the inn. Thoughtful extras include a well-stocked minibar; a list of items you may have forgotten, which Brittany can then provide for you; and especially the views of the Hampshire Avon, running through the garden.

East End, Hampshire

Lymington Road, Hampshire SO41 5SY

Tel 01590 626223
email info@eastendarms.co.uk
website www.eastendarms.co.uk

Nearby Exbury Gardens, Cowes, New Forest, Buckler's Hard, Motor Museum, Beaulieu.
Location on Lymington Road, half way between Beaulieu and Lymington, close to Solent shore
Food breakfast, lunch, dinner (not Sunday night)
Price ££
Rooms 5 double/twin, all have bath/shower, all with TV, wi-fi, gun safe, tea/coffee facilities
Facilities bar, restaurant, terrace
Credit cards DC, MC, V
Children accepted
Accessibility only to ground floor
Pets dogs in bar but not restaurant or bedrooms
Closed 3-6 o'clock Monday to Friday
Proprietor John Illsley

East End Arms
Country inn

An honest, affordable base on the southern edge of the New Forest in a backwater between Beaulieu and Lymington. It's part of the renaissance since 2005 in New Forest places to stay, joining the quite recently refurbished Master Builder's (page 101) and The Pig (page 100).

When owner John Illsley (the former bass guitarist of Dire Straits) bought the pub in the mid 1990s he got a letter from the regulars: 'Hands off our bar' – they wouldn't even let him repair the hole in the ceiling. Most new owners of old pubs would have turned the whole of the lower floor into a gastropub eating area, but Illsley had the sense to keep the old public bar intact. If you want posh food turn left after the front door; if you want a plain, bare floored room, with coal in the grate and murmuring locals, real ale and a chatty bar maid, turn right.

Upstairs, John's wife Steph has created five truly charming bedrooms: crisp sheets, king-sized beds, OKA furniture, Mulberry fabrics, walls decorated with John's paintings. The result is a country pub that is an up to date, comfortable place to stay yet retains its integrity and sense of identity. The food is mostly reliable, sometimes imaginative, above average for the price.

THE SOUTH-EAST SOUTHERN ENGLAND

East Grinstead, West Sussex

Vowels Lane, near East Grinstead, West Sussex RH19 4LJ

Tel 01342 810567
email info@gravetyemanor.co.uk
website www.gravetyemanor.co.uk

Nearby Wakehurst; Nyman's Gardens; Glyndebourne
Location 4.5 miles (7 km) SW of East Grinstead by B2110 at Gravetye; in 35 acre grounds with ample car parking
Food breakfast (for residents), lunch, dinner, room service **Price** £££
Rooms 17; 16 double, 1 single, all with bath; all rooms have phone, TV, hairdryer, bluetooth speaker on request, wi-fi; 8 rooms have air conditioning
Facilities 2 sitting rooms, bar, dining room; terrace, garden, croquet
Credit cards AE, MC, V **Children** welcome over 7 **Accessibility** ramp access but no adapted rooms
Pets not accepted (1 mile from kennel) **Closed** never
Proprietors Jeremy and Elizabeth Hosking

Gravetye Manor Hotel & Restaurant Country hotel

The country house hotel, now so much a part of the tourist scene in Britain, scarcely existed when Peter Herbert opened the doors of this serene Elizabethan house over 50 years ago. This place is still flourishing thanks to the Hoskings, whose standards remain consistently high. Service achieves the elusive aim of attentiveness without intrusion, while the food can still claim to be among the best in the county. A recent visitor, who had known the hotel for 30 years, remained as impressed as ever: 'A sleek operation that doesn't compromise.' However, another commented on 'lots of wealthy-looking people in sunglasses and strange-looking jogging suits'.

The pioneering gardener William Robinson lived in the house for half a century until his death in 1935. Great care is taken to maintain the various gardens he created; Robinson was also responsible for many features of the house as it is seen today – the mellow oak panelling and grand fireplaces in the calm, gracious sitting rooms, for example. Bedrooms – all immaculate – vary in size from the adequate to the enormous, and prices range accordingly.

THE SOUTH-EAST

SOUTHERN ENGLAND

East Hoathly, East Sussex

East Hoathly, Sussex BN8 6EL

Tel 01825 840216
email stay@oldwhyly.co.uk
website www.oldwhyly.co.uk

Nearby Glyndebourne, Charleston Farm House, East Sussex National Golf Course, Batemans.
Location just off A22 S of Uckfield on road to Halland, ample car parking
Food breakfast, dinner
Price ££
Rooms 4 double with bath, 1 with shower
Facilities sitting room, dining room; terrace, garden, croquet, hard top tennis court, heated swimming pool, lake, walking paths
Credit cards not accepted
Children welcome
Accessibility difficult
Pets by arrangement
Closed never
Proprietor Sarah Burgoyne

Old Whyly
Country house guesthouse

Driving up to Old Whyly in the springtime is magical; owner Sarah Burgoyne has planted 4,000 tulip bulbs and at the right season, the lawn is ablaze with colour. Set in 40-acre grounds, with a duck-dotted lake, well-maintained gardens and walks that take in the nearby 600-acre stud farm, this Grade II listed 18thC manor has an enviable setting

Once you cross the well-gravelled drive and climb the front steps, you will be welcomed in Sarah's (and her dog, Noodles) antique-filled home. The impressive family painting collection lines the walls, including a full-length portrait of Sarah herself. The sitting room has a roaring fire with inviting furniture – perfect for admiring the china collection or just reading a book. Bedrooms are spacious and comfortable. However, one of the best reasons to stay at Old Whyly is the food. Sarah, a passionate cook who trained in Paris, prepares excellent dishes and, although many of her customers tend to eat at Glyndebourne, Sarah is more than happy to provide dinner.

Breakfast includes honey from Sarah's bees kept in the orchard and eggs from the hens that wander about on the lawn.

East Lavant, West Sussex

Pook Lane, East Lavant, West Sussex PO18 0AX

Tel 01243 527434
email royaloaklavant@butcombepubs.com
website www.butcombe.com/the-royal-oak-inn-west-sussex

Nearby Chichester, Littlehampton.
Location turn off A3 at Milford Junction onto the A286 via Haslemere and Midhurst. On entering Lavant take the left turn signposted East Lavant. Royal Oak is just past hump-back bridge
Food breakfast, lunch, dinner
Price ££-£££
Rooms 6 doubles, all have bath/shower. 2 additional self-catering cottages
Facilities bar, restaurant, terrace, garden **Credit cards** AE, MC, V
Children welcome
Accessibility not suitable
Pets allowed in bar area, restaurant and a couple of the rooms
Closed never
Proprietor Butcombe Pubs

The Royal Oak
Country inn

The Royal Oak is in beautiful Goodwood country just two miles from Chichester. With a widespread reputation for its food – the restaurant serves a combination of French, Mediterranean and New English cuisine with wines to match – the Inn is always busy at night, and a stay in one of six well-appointed rooms makes for an encapsulating short break.

Each room is lavishly furnished and with all mod-cons, including flat-screen TVs. The exposed beams and brick work offer a pleasant old-and-new style we particularly like about the Butcombe Pubs (see pages 90, 95 and 115).

Rooms in the Sussex Barn and Deluxe Flint Cottage however, just a few short steps from your dinner table, are universally acclaimed. A touch small, perhaps, but greatly prepared and provided for and with every angle and idea covered (including cots for children and complimentary morning papers for those with a little more time on their hands). Staff are always on hand and obliging and the buffet breakfast is top-notch.

East Lavant is in prime position for visiting the South Downs and this place is a more-than-comfortable place to stay while exploring.

Egerton, Kent

The Street, Egerton, Kent, TN27 9DJ

Tel 01233 756599
email info@thegeorgeategerton.com
website
www.thegeorgeategerton.co.uk

Nearby Leeds Castle (7.3 m), Biddenden Vineyards (9.8 m), The Granary Spa (5.9 m) and Woodside spa (6.9 m). Chart Hills Golf Club (7.4 m)
Location halfway between Maidstone and Ashford in the idyllic village of Egerton
Food breakfast, lunch, dinner & bar menu, Pizza menu available from spring-autumn
Price ££ Rooms 3; 2 large doubles, 1 double/twin; 2 have shower/bath, 1 has shower only; all rooms come with coffee/tea, TV, wi-fi
Facilities bar, live music
Credit cards V, D, VD, M
Children welcome
Accessibility not suitable
Pets no access (dogs allowed in bar)
Closed never

The George at Egerton
Village inn

Since our last edtion this place has been taken over by a local aviation enthusiast, the owner of Aero Legends. Its white weatherboard exterior has all the traditional features you'd expect from an inn dating back to 1576, when it was built using timbers from sailing ships (the name refers to an ancient barrow in a nearby field). Inside it's been given a contemporary makeover, with Farrow & Ball paintwork in chalky blues and creams. These are artfully combined with more rustic features, such as stone floors, antler chandeliers and two open fires in the cosy bar area – which still bears the signatures of American and Canadian airmen who frequented The George when they were stationed nearby during the Second World War.

There are three comfortable and attractive bedrooms upstairs (our only quibble was with the somewhat cramped bathrooms). They're ideal bolt-holes from which to explore Egerton: that rare breed of village that still exudes a thriving sense community spirit. It's dominated by the 13thC ragstone church at its centre, with a network of small lanes leading out of the village, offering stunning views of the Weald of Kent and Ashford Valley.

Aero Legends offers flying experience in Spitfires, fighter jets and other small aircraft.

THE SOUTH-EAST
SOUTHERN ENGLAND

Emsworth, Hampshire

47 South Street, Emsworth,
Hampshire PO10 7EG

Tel 01243 375592
email info@36onthequay.co.uk
website www.36onthequay.co.uk

Nearby Hayling Island, Portsmouth, Chichester, South Downs National Park, Portsmouth ferries 10 minutes
Location Emsworth is on A259 between Havant and Chichester
Food breakfast, lunch, dinner
Price £££-££££
Rooms 7; 5 doubles with bath/shower; rooms have TV, phone, tea/coffee facilities, iPod docking station, wi-fi
Facilities restaurant, bar
Credit cards DC, MC, V
Children accepted
Accessibility restaurant only
Pets dogs accepted in the cottages
Closed 2 weeks in Jan, one week in May and 1 week in Oct/Nov
Proprietors Raymon and Karen Farthing

36 on the Quay
Village restaurant-with-rooms

Chef Ramon Farthing got his Michelin star in 1997, but Restaurant 36 on the Quay only became a place to stay recently. He and wife Karen (front of house) developed the accommodation cautiously, achieving five doubles plus two cottages over several years.

In fact the operation feels like a wise balance of form with content. The food, served in an appropriately smart (but not flashy or unrelaxing) dining room overlooking Emsworth Quay and Bay, is consistently delicious and imaginative. Ramon's training was French classical, he migrated to modern British and has now added a Scandinavian influence – fresh, clean flavours, ingredients that speak out. One pudding, peanut parfait, could be unique.

The reasonably priced, comfortable rooms have quirky corners (the house is listed). Saffron is an apartment with kitchenette, useful for a family; Nutmeg has a great harbour view; Vanilla, the top room, has a lovely bay window seat, again with the harbour view. Neutral, off whites and variations on vanilla predominate.

There's nothing like this in the area – the waterfront location is charming and endlessly interesting. It would make a great weekend break, or a spoiling stopover before an early ferry from Portsmouth.

THE SOUTH-EAST — SOUTHERN ENGLAND

Fletching, East Sussex

Fletching, near Uckfield,
East Sussex TN22 3SS

Tel 01825 722890
email griffininn@youngs.co.uk
website www.thegriffininn.co.uk

Nearby Sheffield Park; Glyndebourne; Ashdown Forest.
Location in village 1 mile (1.5 km) E of A275; with car parking
Food breakfast, lunch, dinner
Price ££
Rooms 12 double and 1 twin, 6 with bath, 7 with shower; all have wi-fi, TV, hairdryer
Facilities bars, restaurant, bar billiards; terrace, patio, garden
Credit cards AE, DC, MC, V
Children welcome
Accessibility 2 ground floor rooms
Pets accepted in bar, but not in bedrooms or restaurant
Closed never
Manager Joel Dos Santos

The Griffin Inn
Village inn

On our latest visit to the Griffin Inn, the pub was packed, the dining room was almost full and the kitchen was bustling.

This 16thC village inn maintains its winning combination of good food (it can claim to be Britain's first gastro-pub) and pretty bedrooms with beams, low ceilings and four-poster beds. Everything is a bit uneven, quaint, on a small scale – but endearing rather than cramped. Beds are inviting and bathrooms are in an attractive Victorian style, with funky porthole mirrors and plenty of natural light.

The pub has more beams, panelling, open fires and hunting prints, while the old public bar has been turned into the 'Club Bar', with a sofa and a woodburner. Good food is always at hand either in the pub or in the restaurant, which uses fresh seasonal ingredients and local organic vegetables. Both menus change daily. The wine list has over 100 wines, many of which are priced at under £25 per bottle. You can take your drink out to the garden overlooking Sheffield Park and enjoy live jazz at the weekends. In summer, there's a full-scale BBQ serving Modern European dishes.

The recently retired Pullen family were the soul of this place but it's now in new ownership. Feedback especially welcome.

THE SOUTH-EAST SOUTHERN ENGLAND

Haslemere, Surrey

High Street, Haslemere, Surrey,
GU27 2JY

Tel 01428771027
email
reservations@variouseateries.co.uk
website www.coppaclub.co.uk/the-georgianhaslemere

Nearby Surrey Hills, Grayshott Pottery, National Trust sites
Location West Surrey, near the A3.
Food breakfast, lunch, dinner, bar snacks
Price ££-£££
Rooms 13; 2 double with bathroom and 1 suite with bathroom
Facilities dining room, sitting room, terrace, bar and 'summer house'
Credit cards MC, V, Amex
Children not under 16
Accessibilty One ground floor room
Pets dogs welcome, not in public rooms
Closed never
Proprietors Coppa Club

The Georgian
Town hotel

This newcomer gets a page because of stimulating ground floor public spaces combining work and relaxation. The Coppa Clubs were founded in 2014 by Hugh Osmond, an entrepreneur who wanted to create practical work spaces where people could get out of the house to work yet also hang out in a stylish, comfortable environment.

There were 12 Coppas as we went to press with more on the way, mostly, like The Georgian, in the home counties, some in hotels, some stand alone.

The central bar-restaurant area on The Georgian's ground floor is lively and light with floor-to-ceiling external glass walls for an indoor-outdoor atmosphere. Spreading out each side are smaller work spaces: one with a work table in a bay window, another on a long worktop. An attractive private function area has a fine row of coach-house style doors. There's fast wifi and you can stay here as long as you wish, ordering or not ordering food and drink, no pressure. Come here for a work-away-from-home day and do a business lunch. Or just work.

The garden is pleasant but shady and overlooked. Bedrooms are smart and comfortable but no more or less than hotel rooms, each following the same layout and colour scheme.

THE SOUTH-EAST — SOUTHERN ENGLAND

Horsham, West Sussex

Brighton Road, Lower Beeding, Horsham, RH13 6PP

Tel 08718733363
email stay@leonardsleegardens.co.uk
website www.leonardsleegardens.co.uk

Nearby Leonardslee Estate, Horsham, Mannings Heath Wine Estate
Location Off the A281. Nearest station train is Horsham.
Food breakfast, lunch, dinner, afternoon tea
Price £££-££££
Rooms 10; king-sized classic, super-classic and superior roomsand 1 suite with bathroom
Facilities dining room, lounge, art gallery and sculpture park
Credit cards MC, V, AE
Children welcome
Acccessibilty some access
Pets dogs welcome, not in public rooms
Closed never

Leonardslee House
Country Hotel

At first sight, this 2020 opening appears to be an off-piste selection: a luxurious, upmarket conventional country house hotel in a West Sussex mansion. But as soon as you enter the forecourt from the car park you realize that it's something different: a meeting of hotel, outstanding garden and a sculpture park.

The whole is much more than the sum of its parts, worth a detour - a unique experience. Common and rare trees and shrubs work their calming effect as you stroll the twisting paths. Stop and absorb the diverse and imaginative sculptures which are sometimes in keeping, sometimes in contrast with nature.

Inside the front door is a tiled atrium-hall where a self-playing piano tinkles easy listening - the keys responding to unseen fingers. Full afternoon tea is served some days, a popular event in combination with a garden visit.

The style and furnishings of the ground floor is more hotel than private house. The nine bedrooms upstairs are smart and individually designed. If you're young and in search of a relaxed low-key vibe, perhaps not for you, but for culturally engaged folk, middle aged and upwards, not on a budget, this will be memorable.

THE SOUTH-EAST
SOUTHERN ENGLAND

Linwood, Hampshire

Linwood, Ringwood, Hampshire
BH24 3QY

Tel 01425473973
email
highcornerinn@butcombepubs.com
website www.butcombe.com

Nearby Bolderwood Deer
Sanctuary, Blashford Lakes,
Beaulieu National Motor Museum,
Moors Valley Country Park and
Forest, Lulworth Castle
Location 20 minute drive from
Ringwood
Food breakfast, lunch, dinner
Price ££-£££
Rooms 7; standard doubles, king-sized double and 1 suite for 3 guests.
Facilities dining room, outside dining, stables, private function room
Credit cards MC, V
Children welcome
Accessibility limited
Pets dogs welcome
Closed never
Proprietors Butcombe, Will and
Hannah Ollason

High Corner Inn
Country inn

Can anywhere beat this location and approach? It's down a gravel track leading off a single track road in an especially beautiful part of the western edge of the New Forest with unspoiled lowland heath and woodland stretching to the horizon. Lost in the woods amongst herds of pigs and ponies, this inn has been here as long as locals can remember, but its reincarnation as a Butcombe pub with rooms is recent.

We're wary of anywhere that's part of a chain, but High Corner Inn is its own man. Butcombe Brewery branding is all around but not annoying. The seven bedrooms in an outhouse are smart and comfortable, and charmingly individual with earthy colour schemes.

The public ground floor spreads through multiple seating and dining areas, done out in traditional inn style with some genuine period furniture here and there, all quite brown, like the bedrooms. There's a huge outside drinking and eating area with pub-style bench-tables seating up to 300 which can be very busy in summer - maybe too busy. Food is pub classics done well.

Value for money can't be faulted - a charming double can start as low as £130. Deals at specific times can offer a room for £100 plus £50 towards the drinks and food bill.

It's genuinely dog friendly and if you have a horse, bring it - there are stables and this is God's own riding country.

THE SOUTH-EAST | SOUTHERN ENGLAND

Littlestone, Kent

Coast Road, Littlestone,
New Romney, Kent TN28 8QY

Tel 01797 364747
email
reservations@thegallivant.co.uk
website www.thegallivant.com

Nearby Rye; Dungeness
Lighthouse; Sandwich.
Location in New Romney, take
Station Road to sea front, turn left,
and follow hotel signs for 1 mile; car
parking
Food breakfast, lunch, dinner
Price £££-££££
Rooms 10 double and twin, all with
bath or shower
Facilities sitting room, dining room,
look-out room, tea room, terrace,
garden, croquet, yoga studio boules,
beach adjacent to golf course
Credit cards AE, MC, V
Children welcome
Accessibility difficult
Pets dogs welcome **Closed** never
Proprietors Harry Cragoe

The Gallivant Littlestone Beach

Seaside hotel

The approach through sprawling Littlestone is unpromising, particularly in the dark when you don't know where you're heading. But this dignified 1920s house, built by Clough Williams Ellis for American columnist Hedda Hopper, has a superb position between the sea and Romney Marsh. Clinton and Lisa Lovell sold it in 2023 to Harry Cragoe. He renamed it The Gallivant Littlestone Beach before undertaking extensive updates before reopening in early 2024. Expect striking, modern interiors and a sense of calm.

An upstairs 'look-out' room has the feel of a beach house, with piles of towels for swimming, wicker chairs and decorative sea shells. Bedrooms have creamy cottons, fresh white bedlinen, bright checks, and antiques. Those on the first floor have full-length windows allowing uninterrupted views out to sea. Reports please.

For a great local expedition, see *Walks for Mind and Spirit* available from www.duncanpetersenltd.square.site

THE SOUTH-EAST — SOUTHERN ENGLAND

London, SW1

41 Buckingham Palace Rd, London
SW1W 0PS

Tel 020 7300 0041
email book41@rchmail.com
website www.41hotel.com

Nearby Victoria station, Sloane Square, Belgravia, Tate Britain, Houses of Parliament, Buckingham Palace, London Eye, Oxford St
Location a short walk from Victoria Train Station
Food breakfast, lunch, dinner, snacks
Price ££££
Rooms 33; 30 doubles and 3 suites; all have wi-fi, TV, air conditioning, baths or shower
Facilities restaurant, cocktail bar, sitting room, private dining room, roof terrace
Credit cards AE, DC, MC, V
Children welcome, although there is a 'smart-casual' dress code
Accessiblity no special facilities
Pets with notice
Closed never
Proprietors Beatrice Tollman

Hotel 41

City hotel

Victoria is the southern buffer zone between the river and ultra-posh Belgravia, so this place is chic and exclusive but not stratospherically so.

The location in busy Buckingham Palace Road, minutes on foot from Victoria Station, chimes with this - five out of ten. It stands next to its sister hotel, The Ruben, a conventional, large city hotel. Perhaps the bedrooms stand out most: set pieces of chic urban style using black and white colour schemes, mahogany panelling and chrome. There are 50, but the place feels smaller.

As we went to press weekend prices even in low season were more than £2,400 for a double room. On weekdays a single could start at over £400, not cheap but to be expected.

It's a 'residents only' hotel, which enables its calm, exclusive atmosphere - the public may not drop in for coffee or a drink at the bar. The calm atmosphere is the main reason it has a page but to be honest, we're not sure about it, having been denied access for a look-around when we dropped by anonymously. Reports welcome.

THE SOUTH-EAST | SOUTHERN ENGLAND

London, SW18

499 Old York Road, Wandsworth
SW18 1TF

Tel 020 8870 2537
email alma@youngs.co.uk
website www.almawandsworth,com

Nearby Wandsworth Common, Wimbledon Common, Battersea Park, Kew Gardens
Location Waterloo 15 minutes by train, on-street parking available
Food breakfast, lunch, dinner
Price ££-£££
Rooms 23; 13 doubles, 3 double/twin, 6 twin; all have bath/shower, with TV, phone, tea/coffee facilities, hairdryer, ironing board
Facilities bar, restaurant, wi-fi, luggage storage, working space
Credit cards AE, MC, V
Children accepted
Accessibility 2 easy access rooms
Pets not accepted
Closed never
Proprietors Young's

The Alma
City restaurant-with-rooms

Built in 1866 and named to commemorate the Crimean Battle of Alma in 1854, shiny green tiles and a domed roof mark this place out as an example of the London pub boom of the 19th century.

Young's, the brewer landlord, who took over some years ago, turned four pokey ground-floor rooms into one impressive one, with a circular bar in the centre. A fine white plasterwork frieze was revealed during conversion, as were the solid mahogany staircase, woodwork and *fin de siècle* mosaics.

Despite claiming to be 'a friendly, local pub' on its website, The Alma is more than that now, with a restaurant as well, adjacent to the bar. You'll find all sorts: chaps in pinstripes propping up the bar, blokes in overalls arguing on the pavement after watching the football on a screen. Food is served in the dining room by busy waitresses from a kitchen open to view and a country-style pine table that doubles as a work station. Bar and dining spaces interact well; in either room everyone is happy.

The 23 bedrooms are well equipped, with armchairs, desks and the latest technology. The decoration is lively, and some have floor to ceiling windows. A laidback option for those who don't want the prices or chic formality of central London.

THE SOUTH-EAST

SOUTHERN ENGLAND

London, SW1

52 Cambridge Street, Pimlico, London, SW1V 4QQ

Tel 0203 019 8610
email london@artistresidence.co.uk
website www.artistresidencelondon.co.uk

Nearby Victoria station, Sloane Square, Belgravia, Tate Britain, Houses of Parliament, Big Ben, London Eye, Oxford St
Location a quiet road in Pimlico, 5 mins from Victoria Train Station
Food breakfast, lunch, dinner, snacks **Price** £££-££££
Rooms 10; 7 double, 1 double/twin, 2 suites; all have wi-fi, TV, radio, air conditioning, mini fridge, tea and coffee making facilities, safe, shower; largest rooms have baths **Facilities** restaurant, cocktail bar, sitting room, private dining room
Credit cards AE, DC, MC, V
Children welcome **Accessiblity** no special facilities
Pets some dog friendly rooms
Closed never
Proprietors Justin and Charlotte Salisbury

Artist Residence London City hotel

This Georgian townhouse, once a run-down pub, is a lively addition to our London section. Like its AR siblings (see pages 39, 68, 99 and 234) it has been characterfully converted into a stylish but relaxing place. Rooms and suites are split across three floors and vary in size, but make the most of their Georgian dimensions: even the smallest rooms have been thoughtfully designed. The modern-rustic style, with exposed brick, distressed leather and wooden floorboards, is low key, but only in comparison to its more extrovert sister hotels and we like the bathrooms, with their retro tiles and modern fittings.

The popular bistro-style restaurant serves seasonal British produce. After dinner, relax in a comfy chair in front of an open fire in the Club Room. Adjoining is a room with a ping-pong table that can also be used for meetings or private dining.

In the basement is the trendy cocktail lounge where 'mixologists' serve drinks infused with celery and foamed with egg-whites. It's snug, dimly lit and decorated with iconographic prints and modern-retro furniture. Very well located for a London hotel: on a quiet street five minutes walk from Victoria station.

THE SOUTH-EAST
SOUTHERN ENGLAND

London, E1

12 Folgate Street, Spitalfields,
London, E1 6BX

Tel 020 7377 4390
email
reservations@battylangleys.co.uk
website www.battylangleys.com

Nearby Dennis Severs' House,
Christ Church, East End/West End
of London **Location** in heart of
Spitalfields, located on site of
Medieval priory St Mary Spital; now
a residential area thronged with bars
and restaurants **Food** breakfast-in-
bed, 24 hr room service
Price ££££
Rooms 29; 28 double, 1 single; 7
with sofa-beds to accomodate chil-
dren or extra adult; 2 suites and 1
deluxe with access to private terrace
Facilities 3 sitting rooms, books,
honesty bar, courtyard garden area
Credit Cards V, MC, AE, Debit
Accessibility 1 specially adapted
room for wheelchair access, lift
Pets not allowed **Closed** never
Chief Executive Caroline Conaty

Batty Langley's
City hotel

The third hotel, and period-passion-proj-
ect, of Douglas Blain and Peter McKay
(see Hazlitts, page 132 and The Rookery,
page 140), Batty's was spun out lovingly over
five years, before quietly opening almost ten
years ago. Georgian-themed with all the
trimmings, everything – from the carved
wooden bedsteads to the housekeeping
trolleys – has been faithfully sourced, or
recreated by an army of local artisans. The
result is an explosion of deep-wine hues,
sumptuous damasks and gilded stucco –
with characterful portraits and *objets d'art* at
every turn.

Not that Batty's takes itself too seriously.
Taking their cue from Georgian wit, visual
riffs abound: mirrors that fold away to reveal
TVs, toilet-cum-thrones – even secret
rooms. The 29 regal bedrooms are named
after historic Spitalfield residents, with espe-
cial preference for 'tarts and thieves'.

Batty's may be grand but it's also homely,
and eminently private. Because they eschew
mass-marketing (preferring word-of-mouth)
you'll often have the sitting room to yourself,
along with its well-stocked honesty bar. An
indulgent breakfast in bed is almost manda-
tory, while the charming staff are on-call 24
hours a day for room service. The hotel is
filled with 3,500 antique books that are play-
fully moved about between rooms – an apt
expression of a hotel bent on storytelling.

THE SOUTH-EAST | SOUTHERN ENGLAND

London, SW3

33 Beaufort Gardens, London
SW3 1PP

Tel 020 7584 5252
email reservations@thebeaufort.co.uk
website www.thebeaufort.co.uk

Nearby Harrods; Victoria and Albert Museum.
Location off Brompton Road, just W of Harrods; pay and display parking in street
Food breakfast; room service
Price ££££
Rooms 29; 18 double and twin, 7 suites and 4 single, all with bath or shower; all rooms have phone, TV, Sky, air-conditioning, hairdryer; wi-fi
Facilities sitting room, bar
Credit cards AE, DC, MC, V
Children accepted
Accessibility difficult
Pets not accepted
Closed never

The Beaufort
City bed-and-breakfast

Three Harrods doormen in a row gave our inspector unerring directions for the hundred-yard walk to The Beaufort, part of a Victorian terrace overlooking a quiet Knightsbridge cul-de-sac. This is still one of the few hotels in the world which surprises you with what doesn't appear later on your bill. Feel like a bottle of water? No charge. Soft drink? Cream tea? The answer's still no charge.

All the rooms are different, some decorated in muted pastels, others following in the cheerful footsteps of the public areas. For those who need added protection from the English weather, there are also chocolates, shortbread and umbrellas. And then there are the flowers. Plenty of them. Many are real, but most are hanging on the walls as part of the enormous collection of English floral watercolours.

Noted for the friendliness of its staff, the Beaufort has many faithful regulars.

THE SOUTH-EAST | SOUTHERN ENGLAND

London, SW12

77 Bedford Hill, London SW12 9HD

Tel 020 3976 8007
email info@thebedford.com
website www.thebedford.com

Nearby Balham Tube, Tooting Common, Clapham Common, Battersea Park, Central London
Location off Brompton Road, just W of Harrods; pay and display parking in street
Food breakfast, lunch, dinner, pizza's on Fridays and Saturdays
Price £-££
Rooms 15; doubles, kings and suoer kings. All with Hypnos beds, rain showers or bathtubs, TV's, nespresso machines, black out blinds and safes
Facilities 5 different bars, live music
Credit cards AE, DC, MC, V
Children accepted
Accessibility difficult
Pets not accepted

The Bedford
City pub-with-rooms

Outside, this looks nothing like a charming small hotel and the location is underwhelming, but step inside and you'll quickly see why it's in the guide. At times, for example a weekday mid afternoon, the huge ground floor bar and dining areas, including a traditional mantlepiece and fire, can (for a city pub) be almost serene - flickering candles, gentle music, chilled atmosphere.

However: on Friday and Saturday nights it transforms into a nightclub. The noisy party fun includes comedy acts and live music in an impressive circular auditorium. Many people staying Friday and Saturday nights are there for the ride, falling into bed at 2 am when the music stops. But ear plugs are provided in every bedroom and if you're a good sleeper, adept at mentally blocking out noise, then you might go to bed at 10 or 11 and get some rest.

The bedrooms are individually designed, colourful, sometimes whacky, with large, super-comfortable Hypnos beds.

Intrinsic to The Bedford's off-beat charm is that on occasions your room could cost less than £100 a night. Central London is half an hour away, including the short walk to Balham overground station. See also pages 139 and 142 for other interesting places in the Three Cheers mini chain.

THE SOUTH-EAST | SOUTHERN ENGLAND

London, TW10

61-63 Petersham Road, Richmond
Upon Thames, London TW10 6UT

Tel 020 8940 0902
email be@binghamriverhouse.com
website
www.binghamriverhouse.com

Nearby Thames, Hampton Court Palace, Royal Botanic Gardens at Kew, Syon House, Ham House
Location 20 mins from Heathrow on A307, 8 min walk from Richmond station
Food breakfast, lunch, afternoon tea, dinner
Price ££££
Rooms 15 double and twin; air-conditioning, TV, radio, iPod dock, wi-fi, shower
Facilities dining room, 2 conference rooms, bar
Credit cards AE, DC, MC, V
Children welcome
Accessibility lift access to event rooms, access to restaurant
Pets guide dogs only
Closed never
Proprietor Samantha Trinder

Bingham Riverhouse
Riverside restaurant-with-rooms

Here's a good example of an 'amateur' London hotel keeper competing with the 'professionals' – ie corporate hotel groups – and being every bit as good if not better.

The Bingham is slick and glamorous, and could be, almost, part of a hotel group: its contemporary, interior designed look is one you often see. It seemed, at first glance, 'professional' rather than 'amateur'. But you soon realize that it isn't: because of the warmth of the staff; the pristine way the place is kept; and the cohesive atmosphere which makes people feel at home.

In 1984, the Trinders bought the two Georgian town houses and turned them into a B&B. In 2001, their daughter Samantha joined and turned it into what it is today – a lovely place to dine and stay.

When we visited the rooms were soothing, spotless and well equipped, with comfortable beds, if a bit dull. They've since been refurbished, and we'd be interested to hear reports. You wake to the river at the end of the garden, with the towpath and rowing boats beyond. A balcony runs the length of the restaurant – this is a subtly opulent room that is successful by anyone's standards.

As we went to press the new restaurant was about to open with a menu devised by South African chef Vanessa Marx - reports please.

THE SOUTH-EAST — SOUTHERN ENGLAND

London, SW3

22 Basil Street, London SW3 1AT

Tel 020 7589 5171
email reservations@capitalhotel.co.uk
website www.capitalhotel.co.uk

Nearby Harrods, Harvey Nichols, Sloane Street, Brompton Arcade, Hyde Park, South Kensington Museums **Location** Knightsbridge, close to Harrods and Harvey Nichols **Food** breakfast, lunch, dinner, afternoon tea **Price** ££££ **Rooms** 49; 8 suites and 7 doubles. All rooms have air-conditioning, radio, television, TV, emails and films on demand, hairdryer, mini-bar **Facilities** Restaurant, Bar, 2 function rooms, wi-fi, laundry/dry cleaning, international newspapers, cot, babysitting, private car-parking, 24 hour room service, health club and gym **Credit cards** all major **Children** welcome **Accessibility** not suitable **Pets** guide dogs **Closed** never **Proprietor** Warwick Hotels **Manager** Kate Levin

The Capital
City hotel

A firm favourite of our series editor Fiona Duncan, The Capital's outstanding reputation has been long established and remains unfaltering. Opened in 1971, it remains faithful to its original concept, to be a family-run hotel in the busy and popular heart of Knightsbridge. Guests can be near Harrods, Harvey Nichols and Hyde Park and get relief from the bustle back within the hotel's luxurious, comfortable atmosphere.

Staff are notoriously brilliant: Clive, the head concierge, can claim to be London's finest, and always goes beyond expectations. He will even take guests jogging around Hyde Park. Likewise in the cosy bar, César the barman holds cocktail master classes for guests, promising a wonderfully fun evening. Chris Prow runs the Michelin-starred The Restaurant at the Capital, serving international dishes, bar snacks and à la carte menus.

In each bedroom the decoration is typically English, with tasteful colour schemes and traditional furniture. Luxury, handmade mattresses and Egyptian cotton sheets add to the comfort.

Bathrooms are marble and beautiful, with the attention to detail of bathrobes and toiletries that we like.

London, SE5

Camberwell Church Street,
London SE5 8TR

Tel 020 7703 5984
email info@churchstreethotel.com
website www.churchstreethotel.com

Location in busy high street near Camberwell Green; parking in nearby residential street with permits (£5) from reception.
Nearby South London Gallery, Oval cricket ground, clubs, London Eye 20 minutes by bus, also County Hall (Saatchi Gallery); leisure centres
Food breakfast, dinner
Price ££
Rooms 28; 18 double, 9 single, 1 triple; all rooms have own bathroom except 3 doubles and 5 singles which have shared bathroom; all rooms have TV, hairdryer; most have flat-screen TV, air-con **Facilities** breakfast 24-hour room-bar, with honesty bar; tapas restaurant
Cards AE, MC, V **Accessibility** not suitable **Children** welcome; under six, free in parents' room **Closed** never **Proprietors** Jose and Mel Raido

Church Street Hotel
City hotel

The conventional name and restrained exterior give no hint of what's inside. In reception, a gold painted altar for the desk; colourful ikons on the walls; French tiles on the floor. Swirly patterned carpets lead you upstairs; lurid religious paintings hang in the passages; custom-made brown bedroom doors have iron studs. The signals are a little confusing, but hip-60s-Latin-American with a contemporary twist more or less sums it up. Your bedroom is likely to burst with colour: our reporter's was cobalt blue with a comfortable hand-made wrought-iron bed, painted crucifixes in high alcoves and hand-painted Mexican tiles in the bathroom.

Spanish-Greek brothers José and Mel Raido created this place, wanting to do something refreshing and affordable – and they have. Their success is borne out by the generally youthful, cool crowd from all over the world that you'll meet in the walnut-panelled breakfast room/bar. The Angels and Gypsies restaurant, downstairs, is a delight. It's tapas, done well – fine local ingredients; relaxed and highly-skilled staff. A cocktail bar called 'Communion' has recently opened in the basement.

Located in noisy, multi-cultural Camberwell, just along from the Green, but Oval tube, with fast access to the centre, is just around the corner. Nothing like this anywhere else in Britain.

THE SOUTH-EAST — SOUTHERN ENGLAND

London, Kew Green

8 Kew Green, Richmond
TW9 3BH

Tel 02089401208
email coachandhorses@youngs.co.uk
website www.coachhotelkew.co.uk

Nearby Kew Gardens, River Thames, Heathrow Airport, Twickenham, Central London
Location just off the A205 south of Kew Bridge
Food breakfast, lunch, dinner
Price ££-£££
Rooms 31; 2 double with bathroom and 1 suite with bathroom
Facilities indoor and outdoor dining, sitting room, patio, car parking
Credit cards MC, V
Children welcome
Accessibility some access
Pets dog friendly rooms available
Closed never
Proprietors Young's

Coach and Horses
Pub with rooms

Sitting in the corner of Kew Green, amidst bookshops and cafes, the location of this Inn, for London, is great. Alan, the manager since 2017, has transformed the pub along with its 31 rooms into a welcoming hub for the local community as well as international guests.

Thoughtful hampers greet you in the boutique rooms whose windows look across Kew Green or the garden. The rooms are spacious and follow a common decorative formula rather than strike out for their own identity. In tribute to local Kew Gardens a floral theme runs through the public spaces with botanical patterns on cushions, tapestries and illustrations on most surfaces. We especially enjoyed the green patio where food is also served.

The menu is mostly a refreshing change to the run-of-the-mill pub food, relying on seasonal British produce, such as Nut Bourne tomatoes, Norfolk rhubarb, and ethically sourced fish. An extensive drinks list includes herbaceous themed cocktails

The pub is popular for weddings and sports fans who come to watch big games on a choice of screens, but Alan and his team ensure that noise levels are reasonable. This is part of the Young's brewery collection of pubs, but overall it's got individuality and style, which is why we welcome it to the guide for the first time.

THE SOUTH-EAST
SOUTHERN ENGLAND

London, W9

2 Warrington Crescent, Little Venice, London W9 1ER

Tel 020 7286 1052
email reservations@colonnadehotel.co.uk
website www.colonnadehotel.co.uk

Nearby Little Venice.
Location 1-minute walk from Warwick Avenue tube, 3 car parking spaces in garage, £15 per night, must be pre-booked
Food breakfast, lunch, dinner, 24 hr room service, brunch, afternoon tea
Price £££
Rooms 43; 35 double, 5 twin, 3 single, most with shower, some with bath; all rooms have TV, stereo, phone, minibar, safe, hairdryer, trouser press, iron
Facilities sitting room, restaurant with terrace, bar
Credit cards AE, DC, MC, V
Children welcome
Accessibility not suitable
Pets guide dogs only
Closed never
Manager Dev Nandy

The Colonnade
City hotel

Set in Little Venice, with its canals and bridges, The Colonnade manages to overcome the trappings of a large hotel to provide a private place to stay. The building itself occupies two Victorian town houses that were built in 1865 as private residences. In the late 1800s, it was used as a girls' school and, in the early 1900s, it became a maternity hospital. Alan Turing, creator of the first computer and the man who solved the Enigma code, was born here, and you'll find a suite named after him. When the building later became a hotel, Sigmund Freud stayed here while waiting for his house in Hampstead to be finished. In his suite, a bed sits in a gallery above a sitting room with enormous floor-to-ceiling windows. In the JFK Suite, you can sleep in the four-poster bed built for President Kennedy's state visit in 1962. The rest of the bedrooms are done out in three smart colour schemes: black and gold, green and gold or red and gold. In the sitting room, comfy sofas, attractive stripy chairs, an open coal fire and complimentary sherry, port and lollipops offset the strange artificial topiary.

In the lower ground floor, the achingly hip bar and restaurant, Banu, serves European and Persian fare.

THE SOUTH-EAST — SOUTHERN ENGLAND

London, WC2

10 Monmouth Street, London
WC2H 9HB

Tel 020 7806 1000
email covent@firmdale.com
website www.firmdale.com

Nearby Covent Garden; Royal Opera House; West End theatres.
Location in fairly quiet street between Shaftesbury Avenue and St Martin's Lane; metered parking or public car park nearby
Food breakfast, lunch, dinner; room service
Price ££££ **Rooms** 58; 52 double and twin, 6 suites; 6 single, all with bath; all rooms have phone, TV, video, air-conditioning, minibar, hairdryer **Facilities** drawing room, restaurant, bar, library, work-out room, beauty treatment room, screening room, meeting rooms
Credit cards AE, MC, V **Children** accepted **Accessibility** possible, lift/elevator
Pets not accepted **Closed** never
Proprietors Tim and Kit Kemp

Covent Garden Hotel
City hotel

The group of seductive London hotels owned by Tim and Kit Kemp includes eight sprinkled across London and two in New York. They began with Dorset Square and then opened several more hotels and town house hotels, before becoming more expansive, now with 11 hotels across London and New York, but without losing any of their previous assurance.

Monmouth Street is an attractive and quiet cobbled street ideally placed for theatre and boutique shopping. The building was formerly a French hospital, which Tim and Kit (she is the Design Director responsible for all the decoration) have transformed into a hotel that at once feels glamorous, yet welcoming and not in the least intimidating. A stunning drawing room and library stretches across the first floor, with a well-stocked honesty bar at one end, where guests can help themselves. On the ground floor is Brasserie Max bar and restaurant, serving tasty, simply cooked dishes, or there's a well-balanced room service menu.

Bedrooms have been individually designed, although each possesses a matching fabric-covered mannequin, and they all have superb granite bathrooms. One bedroom has a memorable four-poster bed. The cosy attic rooms are also delightful.

THE SOUTH-EAST
SOUTHERN ENGLAND

London, SW19

9 Camp Road, Wimbledon Common, London SW19 4UN

Tel 020 8619 1300
email reservations@foxand-grapeswimbledon.co.uk
website www.foxandgrapeswimbledon.co.uk

Nearby Wimbledon village, central London
Location Camp Road, short drive from Wimbledon train and underground station
Food breakfast, lunch, dinner
Price ££
Rooms 3 doubles, all have bath/shower, all with TV and tea/coffee facilities
Facilities restaurant, wi-fi
Credit cards AE, DC, MC, V
Children accepted but no extra beds for children over 2
Accessibility possible to restaurant and pub, but not to rooms
Pets not accepted in bedrooms
Closed never
Proprietor Jolly Fine Pubs

Fox and Grapes
Restaurant-with-rooms

It's not a bad idea, staying in this modest pub on Wimbledon Common instead of an expensive central hotel. Kensington is 40 minutes away, yet the feel of the Fox and Grapes is that of a country inn, especially at weekends, when it is jammed with muddy dogs and their owners.

Or rather, according to *les frères français*, the Bosis, who started the place, an English version of something peculiarly French – a *bouchon* – a neighbourhood bar where the food is hearty, and the owner is key.

Chef Director Paul Merrett oversees a menu of robust dishes that echo meat-heavy *bouchon* fare. Quality cuts of steak, braised ox cheek – eaten at plain deal tables quickly laid with cutlery when you are ready to begin.

The building itself is unusual – one huge room, a beamed village-hall-style extension, with a stylish bar and a kitchen open to view. The atmosphere is certainly convivial (though noisy when busy).

The bedrooms are quite well decorated and equipped, but small, with nowhere to put a sponge bag in our tiny bathroom. Breakfast is taken in the pub, somewhat desolate in the early morning and smelling of beer. Nevertheless, the Fox and Grapes is *très sympa*, as the French say.

THE SOUTH-EAST — SOUTHERN ENGLAND

London, SW1

35-39 St George's Drive, Pimlico
SW1V 4DG

Tel 020 7834 1438
email
reception@georgianhousehotel.co.uk
website
www.georgianhousehotel.co.uk

Nearby Victoria Line Tube, Tate Britain, Theatres, Victoria Coach Station, River Thames, Battersea Park
Location Pimlico, Central London
Food breakfast, lunch, afternoon tea, bar snacks, dinner
Price ££-£££
Rooms 63; standard doubles and 'wizard chambers'
Facilities dining room, sitting room,
Credit cards MC, V
Children welcome
Accessibility 1 ground floor room
Pets enquire
Closed never
Proprietor Serena von der Heyde

Georgian House Hotel
City hotel

In a central area of London saturated with places to stay, Georgian House Hotel has something different to offer. Just ten minutes from Victoria station, at first glance it has the same smart but rather uninteresting look of some of its neighbours. But venture in a little further, through a hidden door with a snake-shaped copper door handle and descend a narrow staircase into a shadowy, candlelit hallway to find the Wizard Chambers: a selection of magical themed rooms decked out with stone walls, wooden bunk beds and various magical props. It sounds gimmicky, and it is, but not in a bad way. It's all a bit of fun: long, velvety curtains are draped over the bedframes; piles of spell books stacked on the side tables. Potion making classes and a magic-themed afternoon tea are available on weekends. The detailed design of the rooms is impressive. They're actually quite beautiful, managing to avoid tackiness. It's not for everyone, but for witches and wizards definitely worth a visit. For those not so magically-inclined, the hotel is just as suitable for a stopover in London, with plenty of regular rooms that are clean, comfortable, and well decorated. In fact, unless you go looking for the magical chambers downstairs, you wouldn't even know they were there.

THE SOUTH-EAST | SOUTHERN ENGLAND

London, SW7

190 Queen's Gate, London
SW7 5EX

Tel 020 7584 6601
email reservations@gorehotel.com
website www.gorehotel.com

Nearby Kensington Gardens; Hyde Park; Royal Albert Hall; Harrods.
Location on Queen's Gate; metered parking and public car park nearby
Food breakfast, lunch, dinner
Price ££££
Rooms 50; 44 double, 6 single or twin, all with bath or shower; all rooms have phone, TV, minibar, hairdryer, safe, wi-fi, 24 hr concierge
Facilities library/sitting room, bar, restaurant
Credit cards AE, MC, V
Children welcome
Accessibility possible, lift/elevator
Pets not accepted
Closed never
Proprietor Star Hotels

The Gore
City hotel

In 1990 the team who opened Hazlitt's (see page 132) bought this Victorian town house (long established as a hotel) set in a wide tree-lined street near Kensington Gardens and Hyde Park, and gave it the Hazlitt treatment: bedrooms furnished with period antiques, walls enlivened with pictures, and they recruited a young and friendly staff, trained to give efficient but informal service. It's since been taken over by Starhotels, but the smart Victorian interiors remain in tact.

It has character by the bucketload: walls whose every square inch is covered with prints and oil paintings; bedrooms furnished with antiques, each with its own style – a gallery in one room, Judy Garland's bed in another. There is also an impressive dossier in each room describing what to do locally – 'put together with verve and a feel for what the guest might really want'. The panelled bar on the ground floor is a popular rendezvous for non-residents as well as guests. Across the hallway is their restaurant, 190 Queen's Gate, headed by Michelin-starred chef Daniel Galmiche. which offers lighthearted French dishes with a British twist. The place is stylish, with rosewood panels and red chairs.

Reports on the new management are welcome.

THE SOUTH-EAST — SOUTHERN ENGLAND

London, W1

6 Frith Street, Soho Square, London
W1D 3JA

Tel 020 7434 1771
email reservations@hazlitts.co.uk
website www.hazlittshotel.com

Nearby Oxford Street; Piccadilly Circus; Covent Garden; theatres.
Location in Soho, between Oxford Street and Shaftesbury Avenue; public car parks nearby
Food breakfast; room service
Price ££££
Rooms 30; 24 doubles, 3 suites, 3 singles; all with bath; all rooms have phone, TV, hairdryer, safe, minibars, air-conditioning and wi-fi.
Facilities sitting room, library with honesty bar, meeting room
Credit cards AE, DC, MC, V
Children welcome
Accessibility not suitable
Pets not accepted
Closed never
Proprietors Edward and Douglas Blain

Hazlitt's
City hotel

There is no quarter of central London with more character than Soho; and there are few places to stay with more character than Hazlitt's, formed from three Georgian terraced houses off Soho Square. The sloping, creaking floorboards have been retained (it can be an uphill walk to your bed), and the rooms decorated with suitable antiques, busts and prints. Restoration work has revealed original fireplaces and Georgian panelling that's 300 years old. The bedrooms, named after some of the people who visited or stayed in the house where the eponymous essayist himself lived, are delightfully different from most London hotel rooms, some with intricately carved wood headboards, others with delightful four-posters, all with free-standing bath tubs and Victorian fittings in the bathrooms.

As befits an establishment with such literary connections, Hazlitt's is particularly popular with visiting authors, who leave signed copies of their works when they depart. Sadly, the dresser in the little sitting room in which they are kept is now locked to protect the books, which had a habit of going missing. Continental breakfast is served in the bedrooms, as well as light dishes such as pasta and filled baguettes. A hotel for people who like their comforts authentic, yet stylish.

THE SOUTH-EAST | SOUTHERN ENGLAND

London, W4

162-166 Chiswick High Road,
London
W4 1PR

Tel 020 8742 1717
email reservations.highroad@soho-house.com
website www.highroadhouse.co.uk

Nearby Hampton Court Palace, Twickenham, Richmond, Kew Gardens
Location on Chiswick High Rd (A315) with no parking but hotel can feed your meter. Nearest tube Turnham Green
Food breakfast, lunch, dinner, room service **Price** £££
Rooms 14; 13 standard doubles, 1 superior; all have showers, superior has bath; all rooms have phone TV, wi-fi, phone, hairdryer **Facilities** dining room, bar, games room, tv room, brasserie **Credit cards** AE, DC, MC, V **Children** welcome
Accessibility 1 adapted room
Pets not accepted
Closed never
Proprietor Nick Jones

High Road House
City hotel

You can hope that a hotel owned by Nick Jones (proprietor of Soho House and Babington House) is going to be interesting and this doesn't disappoint. The decoration is city chic but doesn't feel cold: the colours bring the place to life and add an air of cosiness. The bar and dining room are buzzy, with masses of light and are not so cramped that you think that your next door neighbour can hear your thoughts. The food is traditional English with French twists, but nothing too pretentious.

Downstairs in the basement is a fantastic space painted in grey-blue with retro furniture which can be a nightclub; a place for meetings; a place for private sports parties (big plasma screen); a children's activity area or a place for chilling out and playing pool or mini football.

The bedrooms are, as you would expect, very cool (maybe a bit too white) with comfy beds, delicious Cowshed toiletries in the bathrooms and very quiet. All the windows are triple glazed, which is just as well as there is a very busy yet fun, trendy road outside.

This a great hotel for all ages; and it is especially popular with mothers and children – activities for the latter are supervised by minders on Sundays, while parents have some time off.

THE SOUTH-EAST | SOUTHERN ENGLAND

London, W5

55 Hanger Lane, London
W5 3HL

Tel 020 8991 4450
email info@hotel55-london.com
website www.hotel55-london.com

Nearby Heathrow (20 mins), Ealing Common, Central London (20 mins), North Ealing Tube
Location on A406 Hanger Lane, parking for 5 cars, ample space behind hotel in NCP
Food breakfast, lunch, dinner
Price £-£££
Rooms 29 (inc. 3 suites); all double, all with shower, 5 with bath and shower; all rooms have phone, TV, hairdryer, air-con, wi-fi, safe, tea/coffee facilities
Facilities restaurant, bar lounge, bar, garden, garden room
Credit cards AE, MC, V
Children welcome (in a few rooms extra beds are provided)
Accessibility 2 suitable rooms
Pets not accepted
Closed never
Proprietor Sanjay Tohani

Hotel 55
City hotel

This young hotel is well placed for Heathrow: the Piccadilly line (North Ealing) is right behind the hotel, and takes you in without a change.

Tiberius, the charming and helpful manager, greets you as you step through the automatic doors. Straight through the ground floor and you are in the chic bar area, with walls clad in leather, low seating and a plasma screen. But the real joy of this place is the garden room leading on to a landscaped garden – rare in London. It's surprisingly quiet, considering the hotel is on a busy road and the tube is so close. You can have your continental breakfast in the garden room, read the papers or have a light lunch. The restaurant is now operated by Royal Shezan and the menu has been devised by Indian chef 'KK' Anand of The Cinnamon Club.

The bedrooms and bathrooms are small, but nicely done, and with some interesting furniture in the bigger ones. They too are refreshingly quiet (double glazing); the ones overlooking the garden are particularly peaceful. If climbing stairs is an effort, (there's no lift) then flop on to the orthopaedic mattress (in every room) while sipping your environmentally friendly water. This is Ealing's only halal-friendly hotel.

THE SOUTH-EAST | SOUTHERN ENGLAND

London, W2

8 Pembridge Gardens, London
W2 4DU

Tel 020 792 6688
email reservations@thelaslett.co.uk
website www.living-rooms.co.uk/the-laslett

Nearby Hyde Park, Notting Hill, Portobello Road, Central Line, Kensington, The Electric Cinema, Notting Hill Arts Club
Location a short walk from Notting Hill tube station
Food Breakfast, Lunch, Dinner
Price ££££ **Rooms** 12; 8 std/exec doubles, 3 deluxe, 1 suite; all with bath and shower; all rooms have phone, flat screen TV, wi-fi, digital radio, minibar, Nespresso machine, safe, air-con **Facilities** meeting rooms, spa, Henderson Bar and Grill, winter terrace **Credit cards** AE, DC, MC, V **Children** welcome
Accessibility has 1 ground floor room and lift/elevator **Pets** accepted by arrangement
Closed restaurant only, Sun lunch and dinner
Proprietor Living Rooms group

The Laslett
City hotel

It's all about Notting Hill. The name is a nod to Rhaune Laslett, founder of the Notting Hill Carnival. Notting Hill tube station is a minute's walk. Close by are local landmarks The Electric Cinema and Portobello Road Market. Even the atmosphere is Notting Hill: contemporary-cool but friendly, with staff, casually dressed, ready to swap jokes with guests. The ground floor reception, Henderson Bar and Kitchen plus dining area and sitting room are peaceful, even intimate for a city centre hotel, spread the length of the hotel's frontage, which takes up two neighbouring houses on Pembridge Gardens, a mainly residential street. Outside there's a charming street-side sitting area with awning and overhead heaters, used even in winter - blankets and hot water bottles provided.

The bedrooms, some on the ground floor, come in a variety of sizes and configurations, some split level. Non-commital grey is the dominant colour scheme, design and layout not differing much room to room. Rear-facing rooms look across backs of adjacent terraces or roofscapes. As we went to press an entry-level single room could be as low as £258, suites £469. Quite a new addition to the small London hotel scene (opened 2015), it succeeds in its aim of being a home from home.

THE SOUTH-EAST   SOUTHERN ENGLAND

London, SW1

135-137 Ebury Street, London, SW1W 9QU

Tel 020 7730 8191
email info@limetreehotel.co.uk
website www.limetreehotel.co.uk

Nearby Victoria Station, Buckingham Palace, Westminster Abbey, Houses of Parliament, Natural History Museum, Harrods, all within one mile
Location on a residential road in south Belgravia, surrounded by restaurants, cafés and boutiques
Food breakfast
Price ££-££££
Rooms 26; 12 doubles, 4 twins, 3 triples, 6 singles; all have bathrooms, wi-fi, widescreen TV, garden
Facilities breakfast room, small sitting room, garden
Credit cards MC, V
Children aged 5 and above
Accessibility not suitable
Pets not suitable
Closed never
Proprietors Charlotte and Matthew Goodsall

Lime Tree Hotel
City hotel

Our series editor Fiona Duncan investigated Lime Tree Hotel on a hunch, enticed in by its pretty Georgian façade and overflowing window boxes. What she found was a hotel with a personal, relaxed atmosphere combined with fantastic value – a rarity in London.

The secret to Matt and Charlotte's success? Matt puts it down to zero hotel experience, which has helped them avoid the pitfalls towards becoming an impersonal engine, joining OTAs and bringing in PRs who hike up the prices. Instead they've run it in their own independent style, and as a result have enjoyed 100 per cent occupancy most of the year.

In 2020 all the rooms were updated, and the facilities have been improved along with a new guest sitting room. All bedrooms have luxury beds, draped with Osborne & Little, or Cole & Son curtains. They can be on the small side and only three have baths, but all are priced accordingly.

The hotel has a countrified feel, with homely touches such as painted furniture and breakfast options chalked on a board in the kitchen. Matt and Charlotte have also launched a café-style restaurant, The Buttery, which serves locals and guests knock-out breakfasts followed by a laid-back all-day-menu of light meals, savoury treats and cakes. There is an option for outdoor dining in the peaceful walled garden.

THE SOUTH-EAST SOUTHERN ENGLAND

London, SW1

37 Pimlico Road, London SW1W 8NE

Tel 020 7881 9844
email reservations@theorange.co.uk
website www.theorange.co.uk

Nearby Victoria station, Ranelagh Gardens, Kings Road, Saatchi Gallery, Tate Britain
Location Pimlico Road, walking distance from Sloane Square station and Belgravia, Victoria station short drive away
Food breakfast, lunch, dinner
Price ££-££££
Rooms 4 doubles, all have bath/shower, all have air-conditioning, wi-fi, iPod docking station, TV
Facilities restaurant, bar
Credit cards all major
Children accepted
Accessibility not suitable
Pets not accepted
Closed never
Proprietor Cubitt House

The Orange
City pub-with-rooms

This place was once evidently a public house, and the ground-floor bar still acts as a meeting and drinking spot for locals, albeit noisy, well-heeled ones – it stands opposite Daylesford Organics, on Pimlico Road. They love its wooden floors, country furniture and shabby-chic atmosphere and decoration. However, as a pub with rooms there aren't many guest facilities, and as we went to press a standard room was £205 – not dissimilar to rates of fully-fledged hotels, but without the same level of comfort.

Of the four rooms, two are compact, two a decent size. The best is Pimlico, charming with original floorboards, lofty ceiling criss-crossed with rafters and pine panelling. There was a desk, a whitewashed wardrobe and a bedside radio. When we visited in January 2024 the hotel was about to undergo a major renovation to be completed March 2024 - reports welcome.

There are tables on the first floor and downstairs. The starter of smoked salmon tartare was enjoyable, as was the main course of slow-cooked beef cheeks. Breakfast was beautifully presented, but is not included in the room rate. Despite these reservations, The Orange makes a useful, informal London stopover.

THE SOUTH-EAST — SOUTHERN ENGLAND

London, W1

50 Great Cumberland Place, Marble Arch, London W1H 7FD

Tel 0207 724 4700
email info@theprinceakatokilondon.com
website www.theprinceakatokilondon.com

Nearby Hyde Park, Oxford Street, the City
Location north-east corner of Hyde Park, short walk from Marble Arch
Food breakfast, lunch, 24 hour room service
Price ££££
Rooms 82; all have bath/shower, with TV, wi-fi, internet radio, Nespresso machine
Facilities restaurant, bar and lounge, 3 conference rooms
Credit Cards all major
Children welcome
Accessibility ground floor rooms
Pets welcome
Closed never
Proprietor A.B Hotels

The Prince Akatoki
City hotel

With 82 bedrooms The Prince Akatoki, formerly the Arch, is significantly larger than we usuallly feature, but it feels intimate. A two-minute walk from Marble Arch tube, the lovely Georgian townhouse has been transformed into a quiet haven for guests who want to be in the centre of town. The strong Japanese aesthetics make for a luxurious, but minimalistic atmosphere – ideal for those who want to feel relaxed in their surroundings.

The striking bedrooms are more designed than homely, but with welcome extras such as complimentary soft drinks, Nespresso machines and bedside digital radios. We liked the elegance and calm of the rooms and suites with simple wooden furniture and bright natural tones.

The hotel's cleverest concept is the cocktail lounge that flows into a zinc-topped bar area and on into a dining space with an open-to-view kitchen. This is the heart of the operation, and you can dine and breakfast anywhere you like in these three areas. Dishes are well-executed. The Malt Bar and TOKii restaurant offer an ambitious menu drawing on classic Japanese flavours presented theatrically.

Akatoki means sunrise and rejuvination.

London, W12

217 Uxbridge Road
W12 9DH

Tel 02087494466
email info@princessvictoria.co.uk
website www.princessvictoria.co.uk

Nearby Hammersmith Apollo, Chiswick House and Gardens, Central London (15 minutes on the tube), Holland Park, Portobello Road
Location Shepherds Bush
Food lunch and dinner
Price ££-£££
Rooms 5; super king, kings and twin beds. All with en-suites, nespresso machines and black-out blinds
Facilities pub and dining space, courtroom garden
Credit cards MC, V
Children welcome
Accessibility not suitable
Pets dogs welcome in public areas, not bedrooms
Closed never
Proprietors Three Cheers Pub Co.

The Princess Victoria
Pub with rooms

The Princess Victoria is a project of the Three Cheers Pub Co. As with their other small hotels, the emphasis is on providing the finest British produce, award-winning ales, fine wines and unpretentious hospitality. The property was built as a gin palace in 1829 and while the recent renovations have seen it transform into a pub-with-rooms, the owners have strived to keep its history alive.

The horseshoe bar serves over 100 artisan and big name gins and the five new bedrooms that were installed in June 2018 are individually designed with bespoke gin-inspired artwork and named after a classic gin cocktail.

Food is pub classics with some sophisticated twists, sourcing ingredients from small producers across the British Isles: the chicken and pork is free range, the beef is aged in-house, and the fish is sourced sustainably from English day boats off the south coast. Breakfast can be served in your room Monday to Friday. On Saturdays and Sundays it's served downstairs.

THE SOUTH-EAST | SOUTHERN ENGLAND

London, EC1

Peter's Lane, Cowcross Street,
London EC1M 6DS

Tel 020 7336 0931
email reservations@rookery.co.uk
website www.rookeryhotel.com

Nearby The City; St Paul's; Smithfield; Farringdon tube station.
Location in pedestrian street in Clerkenwell, near Smithfield and City; parking in nearby public car park
Food breakfast, 24 hour room service **Price** ££££
Rooms 33; 27 double, 3 single, 3 suite, all with bath; all rooms have phone, TV, minibar, hairdryer, safe, wi-fi
Facilities conservatory, honesty bar; terrace
Credit cards AE, DC, MC, V
Children accepted
Accessibility 2 bedrooms on ground floor **Pets** not accepted
Closed never
Proprietors Peter McKay and Douglas Blaine

The Rookery
City hotel

Opened by the owners of the imaginative Hazlitt's (see page 132), this homely little hotel full of old curiosities and flights of fancy is in a traffic-free alleyway among the restaurants of fashionable Clerkenwell. Created from a row of converted listed Georgian cottages, it is packed with character and 'time-warp' detail: wood panelling; period shutters; open fires; flagged floors; even a special creaky sound put into the treads of the new stairs to make them seem old. Pretty bedrooms have little half-shutters, Egyptian cotton sheets, summer and winter duvets. Minibars and 'workstations' are discreetly hidden behind antique doors. Bathrooms are delightful, with Victorian fittings, exposed copper pipes and wainscotting. One suite, on two floors, has a rococo French bed, attendant blackamoor and an Edwardian bathing machine; an electronically controlled panel shuts off the upper floor for business meetings.

A conservatory, with open fire and leather chairs, serves as a day room, opening on to a tiny terrace garden. Breakfast, continental, is on trays: fresh orange juice, coffee and croissants prepared and baked by the hotel's own pâtissier. We visited recently and enjoyed the vaguely Dickensian atmosphere as much as ever. Try nearby Luca restaurant on St John Street – good Italian food.

THE SOUTH-EAST — SOUTHERN ENGLAND

London, SW3

9-11 Sydney Street, London, SW3 6PU

Tel 020 7376 7711
email info@sydneyhousechelsea.co.uk
website www.sydneyhousechelsea.com

Nearby Harrods, Victoria & Albert Museum, Natural History Museum
Location between Fulham Road and Kings Road; no parking but two NCP car parks nearby (corner of Sydney St & Kings Road, Sloane Avenue) **Food** breakfast, 24 hour room service (limited after 10pm)
Price ££££
Rooms 21 double, plus 'room at the top'; all have shower, 11 have baths. All have telephone, flat-screen TV, hairdryer, combination safe and internet access **Facilities** sitting room, bar, breakfast room **Credit cards** AE, DC, MC, V
Children welcome **Accessibility** not suitable **Pets** not accepted **Closed** never **Proprietor** Andrew Brownsword

Sydney House Chelsea
City guesthouse

On a handsome residential street, announced only by a subtle nameplate, Sydney House could be a private residence — clearly a draw for its many regular guests, some of whom stay weekly while in London on business.

Andrew Brownsword, owner of Gidleigh Park and The Bath Priory, bought this elegant grade II listed Georgian town house in 2002, totally refurbishing it. Original features are found alongside sophisticated, modern decoration and furnishings. Neutral colours dominate the reception/sitting area, where a large palm, modern tapestries and matching cushions in the suede-covered chairs add splashes of colour.

Bedrooms are smart and fresh, with clean, light bathrooms. The 'room at the top', set on the fifth floor, is perhaps surprisingly small, but leads out on to its own generously-sized private terrace, with wooden table and chairs and an area heater — so you can take in the impressive views over London year-round.

The staff at Sydney House are immaculately presented, professional and courteous but seemed to be feeling the strain of too many visitors. We wondered whether the high volume of guests might take its toll on the interior, or on the service. Reports welcome.

THE SOUTH-EAST | SOUTHERN ENGLAND

London, SE11

185 Kennington Lane, Kennington Cross, SE11 4EZ

Tel 020 7735 1061
email info@thetommyfield.co.uk
website www.thetommyfield.com

Nearby Kennington, Kia Oval, Vauxhall, Elephant & Castle, Imperial War Museum, Waterloo
Location on main road Kennington Lane 5 min walk from Kennington tube
Food breakfast (weekends only), lunch, dinner
Price ££-£££
Rooms 6; all double, all have bath and/or shower, wi-fi, satellite TV, fan, hairdryer, safe, fridge, Nespresso machine
Facilities pub/restaurant, private function room
Credit cards MC, V
Accessibility no special facilities
Pets accepted in pub
Closed never
Proprietors Three Cheers Pubs Co.

The Tommyfield
City pub-with-rooms

We like The Tommyfield because it's different. Part of the Three Cheers Pubs co. south London mini-chain, it's been refashioned as a pub-with-rooms. The ground floor pub has a trendy modern-rustic look: exposed brick, tiled walls and copper light fittings. There's no reception, so the welcome can be hit-or-miss, especially if the place is busy. Once you've checked in, you can come and go as you please as the rooms have a separate entrance. The pub itself draws a young, local crowd in the evenings that enjoy the quiz and comedy nights. The food is unpretentious and good value: pies, burgers, fish and chips, and specials. On our recent visit we ordered grilled lamb chops with couscous and were pleasantly surprised.

The six rooms, spread over the two upper floors, continue the shabby-chic style of downstairs: painted white brick walls are offset by colourful furnishings and bold prints. Bathrooms are well-proportioned and well-stocked: ours had a huge walk-in shower, with enough space for two, and a warm slate floor. Beds are huge and comfortable, and though The Tommyfield is on a main road, we weren't disturbed by noise. Unfortunately, breakfast is only served at the weekend, but porridge-pots, fruit and juices are provided in the room.

THE SOUTH-EAST | SOUTHERN ENGLAND

London, EC1

St Johns Square, 86-88 Clerkenwell Road, London, EC1M 5RJ

Tel 020 7324 4444
email info@thezetter.com
website www.thezetter.com

Nearby Farringdon tube, Barbican, Old Spitalfields Market, Liverpool St Station **Location** Location: off A5201 Clerkenwell road; NCP parking around the corner (residents at hotel get discount) **Food** breakfast, lunch, dinner **Price** £££-££££ **Rooms** 59; all doubles with shower; all rooms have phone, TV, hairdryers, safe, air-con, wifi, Penguin paperbacks, hot-water bottles in knitted tea cosies, colourful mood lighting; rooms on 5th floor have tea/coffee facilities
Facilities restaurant, sitting room, terrace with tables, 2 board rooms with private kitchen **Credit cards** MC, V **Children** accepted **Accessibility** 2 rooms **Pets** not accepted **Closed** never
Manager Altan Buyukgiray

The Zetter
City hotel

This is one of the new breed of eco-friendly hotels gaining popularity in London. Water is pumped from its own bore hole, supplying the rooms and air-conditioning. When it gets too hot, the skylights in the glass atrium pop open for ventilation; the room keys control the lights, so no energy is wasted when you leave.

The bar, restaurant and terrace are all done out in kitsch, retro style which manages, thankfully, not to be garish. The restaurant is wonderfully light thanks to the floor-to-ceiling windows. The simple and well-balanced menu allows the high-quality ingredients to shine. In keeping with The Zetter's sustainable ethos, the produce is seasonal and sourced fom local suppliers.

The bedrooms are stacked over five storeys, clustered around the central atrium: quite a dizzying sight from the ground floor. Each room is individually designed in a quirky retro style, with splashes of colour from bedspreads and rugs. The colours might not be to everyone's taste: neon pinks, greens and blues – but they are all of a fairish size and peaceful, with homey touches such as Penguin paperbacks and hot water bottles in hand-knitted cosies. The seven roof-top suites have great views from their private balconies.

Margate, Kent

18 Fort Road, Margate, Kent, CT9 1HF

Tel 01843661313
email reception@fortroadhotel.com
website www.fortroadhotel/com

Nearby Margate Beach, Turner Contemporary, Margate Old Town
Location on Fort Road, a short walk from the train station.
Food breakfast, lunch, tea and cake, dinner
Price ££-£££
Rooms 14; 1 suite, 13 doubles
Facilities dining room, bar and cinema space, terrace
Credit cards MC, V, Amex
Children yes
Accessibilty 1 adapted room
Pets enquire
Closed never
Proprietors Matthew Slotover and Tom Gidley

Fort Road Hotel
Seaside hotel

Since opening in 2022 This place has quickly anchored itself in Margate's evolving and stylish community. After being forgotten and overlooked for many years, its new owners Matthew Slotover and Tom Gidley alongside Gabriel Chipperfield have turned the building into a breezy, unpretentious choice for a seaside retreat. Echoes of the trio's art-world roots reverberate throughout.

The rooms (some with sea views) are gently individual but uniform in their lightly coloured walls, warm wooden floors and mid-century modern furniture. A relaxed, but chic, consistency in design extends to the art, appliances and fittings. Nothing is fussy or overdone, including the spacious bathrooms. The building's original stairwell is warmly coloured and decorated with memorabilia of Margate's history as a fishing port and seaside resort.

The menu changes daily with an emphasis on locally grown produce with a choice of tasty big and small plates.

The charm of this hotel is in its community ethos, its artworks, seasonal ingredients and its thoughtfulness as a regeneration project. Even the seaweed in the hand soaps had been harvested from Margate's beach. With a lively roster of events, the bar is popular with Margate's creative locals. A roof terrace, exclusively for hotel guests, provides a more private (and probably windswept) moment with extensive views over the town and out to sea.

THE SOUTH-EAST

SOUTHERN ENGLAND

Margate, Kent

31 Hawley Square, Margate, Kent
CT9 1PH

Tel 01843 225166
email
info@thereadingroomsmargate.co.uk
website www.thereadingroomsmargate.co.uk

Nearby Shell Grotto, Powell Cotton Museum, Turner Contemporary Art Centre, outdoor activites
Location Hawley Square in Margate old town, 5 minutes from beach and Old Town Quarter
Food breakfast
Price £££
Rooms 2; both double with bathtubs
Facilities room service
Credit cards all major, not AE
Children not accepted
Accessibility no lift
Pets not accepted
Closed Christmas and Boxing Day
Proprietors Louise Oldfield and Liam Nabb

The Reading Rooms
Town bed-and-breakfast

There are two big reasons to make a special visit to Margate: the new Turner Contemporary Art Centre, and this luxury B&B on a Georgian square five minutes from the seafront, with restricted views to the sea from some of the rooms. It's a little unconventional: each of the two large rooms occupies its own floor, and there is no guest sitting room or dining room, so your room, though large, is your world. Breakfast is delivered to the bedroom – and is unusually good. Bathrooms are huge and glitteringly luxurious.

There's no lift – rooms on the top floors mean climbing the staircase, but the hosts will offer to carry your bags. As we went to press, rooms cost from £170 a night (occasionally lower), which might seem high for a place with no facilities except the rooms. But you'll be happy to pay this if you are, for example, a sophisticated metropolitan type who values quality, style and bespoke service, and the privacy that comes with no possibility of interacting with other guests. The rooms are beautiful and gracious, one with floor-to-ceiling windows.

THE SOUTH-EAST — SOUTHERN ENGLAND

Old Windsor, Berkshire

10 Crimp Hill, Old Windsor,
Windsor SL4 2QY

Tel 01753851470
email reservations@lochandtyne.com
website www.lochandtyne.com

Nearby Windsor Castle, The Savill Garden, Legoland, Thorpe Park
Location Old Windsor
Food breakfast, lunch, dinner
Price ££££
Rooms 2; 1 suite, 1 double
Facilities bar, restaurant, beer garden
Credit cards MC, V, AE
Children welcome
Accessibilty access to ground floor only **Pets** dogs welcome in restaurant only
Closed never
Proprietor Adam Handling

The Loch and The Tyne
Pub with rooms

This is Scottish Chef Adam Handling's first venture outside London, a delightfully intimate pub-with-rooms. The focus is classic and simple British dishes, but with added refinement, luxury and sustainability. The Loch and Tyne? Adam once worked in Newcastle, on the Tyne. Loch is a reference, of course, to his Scottish roots.

The rooms have been designed with the same principles in mind, but never sacrificing comfort. The carefully put-together suite uses texture and soothing shades of green to generate rustic sophistication. The brass fittings and freestanding bathtub are nice touches.

Of course, the food is the main attraction. With a changing menu, a lauded Sunday dinner, and gastro 'packages', there is no lack of variety — there are plenty of opportunities to satiate your taste buds. To dial up your culinary experience, private dining is available, and comes with a personal chef.

This isn't a traditional pub-with-rooms, although the beer garden and Tudor façade may fool you: it's a heightened experience.

The name? Adam once worked in Newcastle, on the Tyne. Loch is reference to his Scottish roots.

Rye, East Sussex

98 High Street, Rye, East Sussex
TN31 7JT

Tel 01797 222114
email stay@thegeorgeinrye.com
website www.thegeorgeinrye.com

Nearby Camber Sands, Rye Harbour Nature Reserve, Great Dixter Gardens, Bodiam castle, Hastings Old Town, Sissinghurst castle gardens
Location off A259 in centre of town; use public car park 5 mins walk away.
Food breakfast, lunch, dinner
Price ££££
Rooms 34; 6 Queen; 11 Superior; 11 Luxury and 6 junior suites; all have copper bath and power shower, TV, hairdryer, wi-fi
Facilities ballroom, restaurant, private dining room, bar; courtyard garden
Credit cards MC, V
Children accepted
Accessibility difficult, no lift
Pets not accepted
Closed never
Proprietors Alex and Katie Clarke

The George in Rye
Town hotel

The George is a Rye institution enjoying a new life. Back in 2005 it was bought by Katie Clarke and her husband Alex. They lived with swirly carpets and partition walls for a year "to get the feel of the place" then attacked, closing for eight months and reopening with stunning results. A fire in 2019 presented a similar challenge for the Clarkes, yet again they have excelled.

At one end of the entrance hall, panelled walls and a huge hearth create a cosy sitting area, while the other side shows the hotel's contemporary face. By contrast, the sprawling bar at the back is somehow less inviting – the panelled 'Dragon Bar' perhaps has a better ambience for pre-dinner drinks.

Katie, a set designer, is responsible for the 34 delicious bedrooms, designing much of the furniture herself. A warren of stairs and corridors leads to the rooms, each different, demonstrating her confident eye for colour, and theatrically stylish wallpapers.

The George Grill's food is memorable. If the 2003 Pinot Noir from Sandhurst Vineyard in Kent is on the winelist, try it. They're making every effort to provide quality at affordable prices here – long may it last.

THE SOUTH-EAST — SOUTHERN ENGLAND

Rye, East Sussex

Mermaid Street, Rye, East Sussex
TN31 7ET

Tel 01797 222828
email stay@jeakeshouse.com
website www.jeakeshouse.com

Nearby Great Dixter; Ellen Terry Museum, 1066 country.
Location in centre of Rye; private car parking nearby (3 minute walk)
Food breakfast
Price ££
Rooms 11; 8 double and twin, 2 family rooms, 1 suite; 9 rooms with bath, 1 with private bath across hall; all rooms have TV, phone, wi-fi
Facilities dining room, sitting room, bar, wi-fi
Credit cards MC, V
Children accepted over 8
Accessibility difficult
Pets by arrangement
Closed never
Proprietor Jenny Hadfield

Jeake's House
Town house bed-and-breakfast

This splendid 16thC house – or rather three houses turned into one – has been lovingly restored to make a delightful small hotel: a verdict confirmed by many readers, who return time after time. It is the domain of Jenny Hadfield, who used to be an operatic soprano, and although the place is essentially a charming small hotel, she has lent it a certain theatrical quality. Originally built as a wool store in 1689, it later became a Baptist school and, the home of American writer Conrad Potter Aiken.

The beamed bedrooms, which come in various shapes and sizes, overlook either the old roof-tops of Rye or Romney Marsh. Bedsteads are either brass or mahogany (some are four-poster), bedspreads lace, furniture antique. There are plenty of thoughtful extras in the rooms. Downstairs, a galleried ex-chapel makes the grandest of breakfast rooms. A roaring fire greets guests on cold mornings, and Jenny will serve you either a traditional breakfast or a vegetarian alternative. There is a comfortable parlour with a piano and a bar, with books and pictures lining the walls. 'Situated on the street in Rye (the cobbled Mermaid Street) within walking distance of all the sights,' says our reporter. It will suit older readers. As we went to press is was unclear how long Jeake's House would remain open.

Shefford Woodlands, Berkshire

Ermin Street, Shefford Woodlands, Hungerford. RG17 7AA

Tel 01488 648284
email pheasant@youngs.co.uk
website www.thepheasant-inn.co.uk

Nearby Wickham House (4km), Hungerford (6km), North Wessex Downs (9km), Marlborough (21km), Highclere Castle (22km), Avebury Stone Circles (31km)
Location less than 1km north of M4 in small village, with own car park
Food breakfast, lunch, dinner, snacks, room service **Price** ££
Rooms 14; cosy, boutique, boutique twin and bigger boutique some with Juliette balconies. All have en suite bathroom, free wi-fi, flatscreen TV, tea and coffee making facilities
Facilities sitting room, dining room, bar, laundry
Credit cards MC, V
Children welcome, cots available **Accessibility** not suitable **Pets** allowed **Closed** never **Proprietor** Young's

The Pheasant Inn
Village inn

Sophisticated, intimate and affordable: The Pheasant Inn is the perfect weekend bolt-hole, says our series editor Fiona Duncan. An old sheep drover's inn surrounded by the unspoiled countryside of the Berkshire Downs, it has uninterrupted views and a feeling of wonderful seclusion, while being only minutes from the M4.

Landlord Lewis has maintained the interior style and heart left by Jack Greenall who had refurbished the inn with the help of interior designer Flora Soames. The result is stylish and cosy down to the last detail. The bar and restaurant have a rustic feel, with red leather banquette benches and wooden tables.

In the 14 immaculate bedrooms upstairs and on the ground floor the beds stand out for their comfort and quality with luxurious fabric headboards and attractive toppers. The bathrooms, while on the small side, are marble-clad with top-quality products.

The kitchen is packed every night, catering to guests and locals alike with his highly superior pub grub. We enjoyed the Scotch eggs and salt-baked saddle of lamb – flavoursome and unpretentious cooking. The atmosphere in the restaurant is animated, but there are also comfy corners for quiet dining.

THE SOUTH-EAST — SOUTHERN ENGLAND

Sidlesham, West Sussex

Mill Lane, Sidlesham
West Sussex, PO20 7NB

Tel 01243 641233
email enquiries@crab-lobster.co.uk
website www.crab-lobster.co.uk

Nearby Chichester, Selsey Bill, Bosham, Pagham harbour walk and nature reserve
Location on B1245 south of Chichester
Food breakfast, lunch, dinner
Price £££-££££
Rooms 4 double; 1 with shower only, 3 with bath; 2-bed self-catering cottage
Facilities bar, dining room, terrace, garden; internet connection
Credit cards AE, MC, V
Children accepted
Accessibility restaurant only
Pets not accepted
Closed never
Proprietor Sam and Janet Bakose

The Crab and Lobster
Restaurant-with-rooms

The landscape surrounding The Crab and Lobster is enchanting: salt marsh and woodland interlaced with watery creeks stretching across Pagham Harbour to the distant sea. Despite its spanking new interior, this 350-year-old building offers, with its slate floors, cream painted or bare brick walls and open fire, sophisticated charm.

There are four attractive bedrooms – all stylishly decorated with pastel or beige walls, and fresh flowers – in the main building, plus a delightful two-bedroom cottage for self-catering next door. We stayed in a deluxe room under the eaves, a cosy hideaway with binoculars for a closer look at that wonderful view – a thoughtful touch. The elegant bathroom had a velvet *chaise longue* (great touch), but was lacking in shelf space.

The Crab and Lobster is a stylish waterside hideaway, with slate floors, exposed brick walls and an open fire in the dining room and bar downstairs, and what's more the food is excellent. Dinner was a great success: local crab from Selsey and lobster, superbly dressed, plus a wild sea bass that had been brought to the door that day by a local fisherman, and a bottle of Sancerre – perfect. The Halfway Bridge in nearby Petworth is under the same ownership.

THE SOUTH-EAST
SOUTHERN ENGLAND

Sissinghurst, Kent

The Street, Sissinghurst, Kent, TN17 2JG

Tel 01580 720200
email fresh@themilkhouse.co.uk
website www.themilkhouse.co.uk

Nearby Sissinghurst Castle & Gardens, Hole Park Gardens, Great Dixter, Pashley Manor Gardens. Scotney Castle, Hever Castle, Bodiam Castle. Vineyards: Chapel Down, Herbert Hall, Biddenden, **Location** Near Staplehurst station; Channel tunnel & Dover within an hour's drive; Gatwick 1 hr away **Food** breakfast, lunch, dinner, pizza available from spring-autumn **Price** ££ **Rooms** 4: 1 large double; 1 family room (sleeps 4); 1 double; 1 twin/double. All have bath and/or shower, flat-screen TV, hairdryer, kettle, iron & ironing board on request, cot on request **Facilities** wi-fi, beer garden, parking on site, bar & dining areas **Credit cards** all major **Children** welcome **Accessibility** not suitable **Pets** dogs in bar only **Closed** never **Proprietors** Dane & Sarah

The Milk House
Village Inn

Contemporary inn The Milk House opened its doors in 2013. Set within a traditional 16thC hall, the open-plan pub interior has been given quite a contemporary redecoration, with a creamy green-and-white colour scheme, faux bookcase wallpaper and a wicker bar at its centre. It's sophisticated and inviting, if perhaps a touch modish and lacking in character. The place draws in hordes of locals at all times of day, who congregate around the bar or come in to sample the menu of chef (and owner) Dane Allchorne. Both the Dining and Classic menu offer fresh British fare (from pan-fried John Dory to beer battered cod), uncomplicated but well done. Service from the young (mainly local) staff is swift and cheerful.

The dairy theme is carried through to the bedrooms (named Dairy, Byre, Buttery and Churn), helped along by milky colour palettes and country furniture. Our series editor Fiona Duncan much enjoyed her stay here, reclining in an expansive four-poster bed, opposite an original brick fireplace Some noise carries through from the high-street, but it is not insistent.

This is a useful address for exploring Bodium Castle and Kent Weald, and considering what's on offer it's good value, with rooms running from £140-£180.

THE SOUTH-EAST — SOUTHERN ENGLAND

Southampton

8 Western Esplanade, Southampton, Hampshire SO14 2AZ

Tel 0845 0779494
email reservations@thepighotel.com
website www.pighotel.com

Nearby Southampton Docks, historic Southampton, museums, high street is within walking distance.
Location within Southampton's historic medieval walls, near cruise terminal and city centre. Private car park in hotel.
Food breakfast, lunch, snacks, dinner at Deli-bar
Price £££
Rooms 12; most with shower only, 3 with bath, some rooms have larders full of snacks and drinks, TV
Facilities deli, wi-fi throughout
Credit cards AE, DC, MC, V
Children welcome, cot and additional bed available
Accessibility ground floor room available
Pets guide dogs only
Closed never
Hotel Director Faye Stone

The Pig - in the wall
Town house hotel

The Pig in the wall was opened more than a decade ago by the same team that created The Pig at Brockenhurst (page 100). Its description – a 'Boutique B&B' – might tempt you to suspect it's a triumph of form over content – but it's not.

They've made this pleasing Georgian house in the medieval walls of Southampton near Town Quay feel as if it's always been a happy place to stay. You step off the wide pavement through the front door straight into the downstairs public space – a long sitting room, bar and bistro dining area. It smells pleasantly of wood smoke and herbs, which are grown in pots as table decorations and for the kitchen. At both ends are log fires with guests relaxing in chairs upholstered in smart fabrics that could be in your home. Warm, friendly, relaxed.

Simply decorated connecting corridors lead to the bedrooms. The cheapest room is artfully shoehorned into the attic. Mid-price and superior rooms are spacious enough – perhaps not especially so, but this is a town house. Colours are soothing browns, whites, greys with splashes of purple velvet. See other Pig hotels on pages 32, 52 and 79.

THE SOUTH-EAST   SOUTHERN ENGLAND

St Leonards-on-Sea, East Sussex

9 Eversfield Place,
St-Leonards-on-Sea, East Sussex
TN37 6BY

Tel 01424 460109
email info@zanzibarhotel.co.uk
website www.zanzibarhotel.co.uk

Nearby Hastings old town, Hastings Fort
Location on seafront near Warrior Square, just off A21; underground secure parking 2 mins from hotel - a limited amount so book in advance.
Food breakfast; all room rates include a champagne breakfast
Price £££
Rooms 8 double, all with shower/bath; all rooms have flatscreen TV with freeview, hairdryer, iron, tea and coffee making facilities, fridge with milk/water
Facilities cafe, sitting room, garden, honesty bar
Credit cards DC, MC, V, Amex
Children no children under 5
Accessibility difficult **Pets** small dogs only, with a fee **Closed** never
Proprietor Max O'Rourke

Zanzibar House
Seaside town house hotel

The somewhat run-down seaside town of St Leonards-on-Sea is not overwhelmed with hotels worth writing about, but this stylish and relaxed place stands out. Zanzibar occupies a Victorian seafront town house which has been restored and modernised by its enthusiastic and hands-on owner, Max O'Rourke. On arrival, along with your complimentary glass of champagne you are given a parking permit, a key, and advice on where to go if you want to explore. The ethos here is very much 'make yourself at home', though the friendly staff are always on hand.

Zanzibar's eight rooms are individually themed around a region of the world and the decoration and furniture subtly reflect this, adding a unique character to each without going over the top. Every bathroom has a special feature – in 'Antarctica' where our inspector stayed, it was a combined shower/sauna. Breakfast is ordered the previous evening and delivered hot to your room, or the grand salon. Choices include kippers, poached eggs, smoked salmon and a 'full English' – all fresh and delicious.

Max says: "the best thing about Hastings and St Leonards is that there isn't that much to do", and the steady stream of (mostly) Londoners coming to Zanzibar for a refreshingly calm, relaxing break, seem to agree.

Stockbridge, Hampshire

31 High Street, Stockbridge,
Hampshire SO20 6EY

Tel 01264 810833
website www.thegreyhoundon-thetest.co.uk

Nearby Mottisfont Abbey, Winchester Cathedral, Salisbury Cathedral, Stonehenge, New Forest, Beaulieu Motor Museum
Location on village High Street in Stockbridge, ample car-parking at rear of building
Food breakfast, lunch, dinner
Price ££-£££

Rooms 10; 6 doubles 3 can be twin, 1 single, all have bath/shower, all with TV, tea/coffee facilities
Facilities restaurant, pub, honesty bar, fly fishing
Credit Cards all major
Children accepted
Accessibility no special access
Pets well-behaved dogs welcome
Closed Christmas day and Boxing Day
Proprietor Lucy Townsend and Alex Lewis

The Greyhound
Country inn

An atmospheric Hampshire pub run by Lucy Townsend, who used to be at The Peat Spade and The Anchor at Lower Froyle (page 95). She bought it in 2011 with an investment partner, and recent business endeavours have seen her establish a catering comapny and an investment in the Hoxton Bakehouse who supply the Inn with fresh bread and cakes. Friendly manager Zak is all hands-on.

The eight first-floor rooms are better than similar country offerings in the area at the same price. They are all different styles, enhanced by painted panelling in Farrow & Ball colours; upholstered bedheads; pretty fabrics; chaises longues; country furniture, big mirrors and colourful paintings. In ours, there wasn't much room for a laptop, and we would have liked fuller information on what to do and see in the area. Six of the rooms have a shower only, but at £110 as we went to press, in the heart of plutocratic Hampshire, they are fair value.

Downstairs, the dining room, with OKA chairs at rustic tables set with prettily coloured glassware, offers top-end pub fare. The Test is right at the back – ask about fishing deals, and barbecues in the fishing hut.

THE SOUTH-EAST — SOUTHERN ENGLAND

Stockbridge, Hampshire

High Street, Stockbridge
SO20 6EU

Tel 01264810606
email info@thegrosvenorstockbridge.com
website www.thegrosvenorstockbridge.com

Nearby Mottisfont Abbey, Longstock Water Garden, Highclere Castle, Danebury hillfort, Stockbridge Marches
Location just off the A39 in the village of Allerford
Food breakfast, lunch, afternoon tea, dinner, packed lunches on request
Price ££-£££
Rooms 3; 2 double with bathroom and 1 suite with bathroom
Facilities dining room, sitting room, courtyard, dry cleaning
Credit cards MC, V
Children welcome, family rooms
Accessibility ground floor only
Pets dogs welcome
Closed never
Proprietor Simon Henderson

The Grosvenor
Hotel

The handsome town of Stockbridge, in the Test Valley, has been a fly fishing Mecca for the past 200 years. For anyone keen to have a go, whether you're an old hand or a newbie, The Grosvenor Hotel provides everything you need, including fish-and-stay deals plus fishing guides.

When our series editor, Fiona Duncan, visited she thought the freshly refurbished hotel was just what the town needed. The rooms strike a fine balance between traditional and contemporary with unique fabrics, thoughtful lighting and attention to detail. Thanks to the hard work of deisgner Lottie Keith, it mostly has the comforatble feel of a private house.

The elegant furnishings extend to the restaurant and bar. The second dining room, a former market hall, features a gorgeous *verre églomisé* (gilded glass) mirror at one end. The restaurant boasts a seasonal menu and offers a rich selection of seafood and local fare includes lobster from Brixham and mussels from Exmouth. However, the crowing jewel is the courtyard. Completely enclosed and with views of 15thC St Peter's Church, it feels a world away from the bustling high street.

Under its previous owner, the Grosvenor was unremarkable. Now, with Simon Henderson at the helm, the 30-room hotel has the feel of a much smaller and more distinctive place.

THE SOUTH-EAST — SOUTHERN ENGLAND

Stockbridge, Hampshire

Village Street, Longstock,
Stockbridge, Hampshire SO20 6DR

Tel 01264 810612
email info@peatspadeinn.co.uk
website www.peatspadeinn.co.uk

Nearby Stockbridge, Romsey, Winchester, Test Valley fishing and fisheries
Location in sleepy village centre with off road car parking
Food breakfast, lunch, dinner
Price ££
Rooms 8 doubles, 2 can be twin, all with bath shower; all rooms have phone, TV, hairdryer, wi-fi, minibar, nespresso machine
Facilities bar, dining room, courtyard, terrace, in-house sporting agents
Credit cards MC, V
Children over 10
Accessibility difficult
Pets accepted in twin room
Closed never
Proprietor The Upham Group
Manager Shelley Diaf

The Peat Spade
Village inn

'A charming mix of traditional and new, rustic and efficient' says a reporter.

The bar-dining area is one long room, and is rustic-smart. It has warm green walls, which continue into The Rod Room, which opens on to the garden. The decoration in here is more faithful to its status as a fishing inn, and features cane fly rods, mounted trout, reels, gilt-framed mirrors, period shooting and fishing prints. There are clean white napkins on scrubbed pine tables; the food OK – ambitious but given the prices perhaps in some respects not quite there. The Mayfly Mess upstairs accommodates private lunch and dinner parties.

Our reporter's room – restful browns and greens and wide oak floor boards in the bathroom, excellent cotton sheets on a thoroughly comfortable bed – homely, comfortable. Ask about their fishing weekends for novices and experts, individuals and companies. Ghillies and tutors to order.

West Hoathly, West Sussex

Queen's Square, West Hoathly, West Sussex RH19 4PP

Tel 01342 810369
email thecatinn@googlemail.com
website www.catinn.co.uk

Nearby The Priest House, Standen, Penshurst, Hever Castle, Bluebell Railway, golf courses, wine tasting, walking
Location West Hoathly village, parking at the inn and in the village
Food breakfast, lunch, dinner
Price £££
Rooms 4 doubles, all have bath/shower and TV, wi-fi, tea/coffee facilities
Facilities pub, dining room
Credit cards MC, V
Children over 7 in pub, no special rooms
Accessibility pub only
Pets dogs welcome in guest rooms
Closed never
Proprietor Andrew Russell

The Cat Inn
Village freehouse

Andrew Russell, formerly general manager of nearby Gravetye Manor, took on this formerly run-down pub some years ago. His management skills, concentrated on a more compact operation, are achieving almost everything we look for. Combining a traditional public bar with more formal dining areas has worked here because (except for the Snug) dining and drinking areas are well separated. Of the dining areas, we especially like the Well Room, with a (deep) original well in the floor, protected by a glass lid. The Snug is an alcove just off the bar area for those who want to be close to the action in the bar. If you don't want to eat from the three-course menu in the restaurant, then you can have one dish (generous helpings) in the bar area. Head chef Max Leonard, produces simple English pub-grub at its best and the extensive wine list features interesting English wines. Go to your bedroom and you find it instantly comfortable, unflashy but pretty. Back downstairs, we noticed how he has cleverly combined airy and cosy dining areas, and made an old-fashioned bar with huge inglenook fireplace work alongside other, gently upmarket modern features. This country inn has plenty of admirers including our series editor Fiona Duncan who says, 'it's her new favourite pub in Britain.'

THE SOUTH-EAST — SOUTHERN ENGLAND

Winchester, Hampshire

14 Southgate Street, Winchester, Hampshire SO23 9EF

Tel 01962896329
website www.hotelduvin.com

Nearby Cathedral; Venta Roman Museum; Winchester College.
Location in the town centre, a minute's walk from the cathedral; limited car-parking onsite
Food breakfast, lunch, dinner; room service
Price £££
Rooms 24; 23 double and twin, 1 suite, all with bath; all rooms have phone, TV, minibar, hairdryer
Facilities sitting room, dining room/breakfast room, private dining room, bar, wine-tasting cellar; garden, boules, laundry
Credit cards AE, DC, MC, V
Children welcome
Accessibility 1 garden room
Pets some dog friendly rooms
Closed never
Manager Hazel Galloway

Hotel du Vin
City hotel

There is still an alluring buzz in the air at this stylish, affordable Georgian town house, once the flagship of the Hotel du Vin mini-chain – even though it's now been taken over by Malmaison, a large hotel group. This was the original Hotel du Vin and it's got panache. The wood-floored, hop-garlanded Bistro sets the tone: staffed by a charming bunch of mainly youngsters, it has the intimate, slightly chaotic yet professional air of the genuine article. Start with a bucket of champagne in the voluptuous mirrored and muralled bar, then choose a bottle from the inventive, kindly priced wine list to go with the inventive, sunny, Modern French food.

The bedrooms and bathrooms are every bit as appealing, with fresh Egyptian cotton bedlinen, capacious baths and huge showers. For maximum quiet, ask for a Garden Room, or splash out on one of the principal suites (see top picture), with hardwood floors, roll-top baths and panoramic floor-to-ceiling windows. Breakfast in Bed' is available as part of the room service.

We also recommend the Hotel du Vins in Bristol (page 91) and Brighton (page 167). There are also Hotels du Vin in Harrogate and Tunbridge Wells (pages 272 and 26) and 19 in total – see www.hotelduvin.com.

Yarmouth, Isle of Wight

Quay Street, Yarmouth, Isle of Wight PO41 0PE

Tel 01983 760331
email info@thegeorge.co.uk
website www.thegeorge.co.uk

Nearby Yarmouth Castle (adjacent); Newport 12 miles; ferry terminal.
Location in town, close to ferry port overlooking Solent; long stay car park 3-min walk
Food breakfast, lunch, dinner; room service
Price £££
Rooms 17; 13 double and twin, 2 suites, 2 single, all with bath; all rooms have phone, TV, hairdryer, many with sea or harbour views. 2 self catering for 6 or 14
Facilities sitting room, restaurant, brasserie; garden, private beach, 36 ft motor yacht available for charter
Credit cards AE, MC, V
Children welcome
Accessibility 1 adapted room
Pets welcome in some rooms
Closed never
Proprietors Felix Spooner

The George
Seaside town hotel

In many ways the George is a perfect hotel: an atmospheric building in the centre of a breezy and historic harbour town, with welcoming rooms, a buzzing brasserie with tables spilling across the waterfront garden, and a quieter, more formal restaurant where good, inventive food is served. A former governor's residence, the property has been restored and renovated with sympathy. A panelled and elegantly proportioned hall sets the scene, leading to a cosy wood-panelled sitting room with thick velvet drapes at the windows, an amusing mid-Victorian evocation of the George above the fireplace and a roaring log fire in winter. Across the hall is anelegant fine dining restaurant, and beyond the central stairs, the Conservatory and garden, where you can dine by the waters edge in fine weather.

Upstairs, the bedrooms are all inviting and all different: one has a four-poster; another is a light and pretty corner room; two have wonderful teak-decked balconies with views across the Solent. 'It's a sheer pleasure,' writes a satisfied reader, 'to hop on the ferry at Lymington, alight at Yarmouth, and settle in to the George for two or three days.'

Young local Felix Spooner bought the hotel in mid 2023 following our most recent visit. Reports welcome.

THE SOUTH-EAST — CHANNEL ISLANDS

Braye, Alderney

Braye Street, Alderney, GY9 3XT

Tel 0800 2800550
email holiday@brayebeach.com
website www.brayebeach.com

Nearby St Anne's Church, 'The Cathedral of the Channel Islands', Mannez Lighthouse at Quesnard Point.
Location Alderney island
Food breakfast, lunch, dinner
Price ££
Rooms 27; all with wi-fi, bathrobes, refrigerator, flat screen television, choice of classic films on in-room box office, hairdryer, complimentary decanter of sherry, tea and coffee making facilities, personal safe, fresh seasonal fruit on arrival
Facilities free wi-fi throughout, cinema, renovated bar, private dining room, restaurant
Credit cards AE, MC, V
Children welcome
Accessibility 1 specially adapted room
Pets dogs in bar but not in rooms
Closed never
Managers Katey and Scott McDonald

Braye Beach
Beach hotel

Now owned by Hand Picked Hotels and managed by the very capable Scott and Katey McDonald, much needed renovation has breathed new life into Braye Beach Hotel. Thoughtfully and tastefully redesigned, it is a welcome retreat for guests, and a great base from which to explore the little island of Alderney.

The old public areas have been opened up to create a big open space, including an award-winning restaurant and bar. Outside, the wraparound terrace gives plenty of outdoor seating, and allows you to follow the sun. There's a little cinema for rainy days.

The bedrooms are comfortable and cosy, and exceptional value for money. Bright patterned covers and cushions give a homely, welcome feel and offset neutral walls and furniture. There are rooms with views and rooms without, but the ones with views on to the beach are the best, and are available on a first come first serve basis. However, our reporter did comment that the windows needed cleaning – sea salt spray obscured the view – but this was after a storm and we are assured that they are normally cleaned regularly.

Deserted and charming, Braye Beach itself is ideal. Located on the edge of the beach, the hotel has great views across the bay and beyond the harbour.

THE SOUTH-EAST | CHANNEL ISLANDS

Castel, Guernsey

Kings Mills, Castel, Guernsey GY5 7JT

Tel (01481) 257996
email info@fleurdujardin.com
website www.fleurdujardin.com

Nearby Vazon and Richmond beaches for surfing and sea fishing trips.
Location Castel
Food breakfast, lunch, dinner
Prices ££-£££
Rooms 11; all rooms have phone, TV, hairdryer
Facilities restaurant, bar, health suite; outdoor solar-heated swimming pool, car and bike hire
Credit cards all major
Children welcome
Accessibility not suitable
Pets allowed in the 2 Garden Rooms
Closed never
Proprietors Ian and Amanda Walker

Fleur du Jardin
Village hotel

A voluptuous bouquet of flowers greets you in reception, teetering on a table next to a vintage suitcase. Thus, the tone is set for Fleur du Jardin – it is a quirky, eccentric and comfortable place that welcomes all guests as if they are returning travellers.

Throughout the hotel we were met with jokey signs ('duck or grouse' over a low ceiling), beautiful furniture and lovely decoration in each room – a mixture of natural elegance and seaside charm. Owners Ian and Amanda Walker are keen to combine design influences seen on their own travels around the world, as well as ensuring Fleur du Jardin's Guernsey heritage.

The award-winning restaurant is charming and homely, and uses as much locally bred beef, pork and fresh fish as possible. Real effort has been spent on thoughtful decoration – a dainty vase of fresh flowers is placed on each table – making the dining room one of the most charming and relaxing places to be in the whole hotel. The adjoining bar is also award-winning, and has a changing selection of real ales.

The bedrooms are spacious and charming, decorated in a seaside theme. Big white lampshades, fluffy bedding and rustic walls make them feel cosy and peaceful.

Herm

Herm, VIA Guernsey GY1 3HR

Tel 01481 750000
email reservations@herm.com
website www.herm.com

Nearby Shell Beach (200 yds/180 m); wildlife: puffins, dolphins and seals; coastal walks.
Location Herm Island
Food breakfast, lunch, dinner
Prices ££-££££
Rooms 40; 18 in cottages, some on ground floor
Facilities 3 sitting rooms, 2 restaurants, 2 bars, conference room; garden, tennis, croquet, heated swimming pool; beach
Credit cards DC, MC, V
Children welcome; over 9 only in restaurant for dinner
Accessibility not suitable
Pets dogs accepted in 1 room
Closed Nov to Mar
Proprietors John and Julia Singer

The White House
Island hotel

Herm is 'an enchanting, self-sufficient time warp' says Fiona Duncan, our series editor. Its sole hotel, The White House, is like a step back in time. There are no televisions, clocks or telephones in the hotel, as they have been deemed inappropriate to the atmosphere of the island – Herm is car-free. You will hear the occasional tractor or the piping of oyster-catchers but not much else.

The hotel has a great sea view, and is in a prime location. When the tide goes out over nearby Shell Beach, it really goes out, leaving a vast and fascinating waterless expanse of sand. Coastal walks in this area are lovely. If visiting from May to July keep an eye out for puffins.

The interior of the hotel has an attractive staircase and light, spacious rooms. There's a beautiful conservatory with a swimming pool surrounded by palms.

The rooms are bright and breezy, with views either across the island or the sea. The sunsets are almost always spectacular.

THE SOUTH-EAST | CHANNEL ISLANDS

Clifden, St Aubin

Clifden 1, Mont Les Vaux, St Aubin
JE3 8AF

Tel 01534 741350
email clifden@hotmail.co.uk
website
www.jerseyyurtholidays.com

Nearby St. Aubin village: bank, post office, supermarket, beauticians, taxi hire, bike hire, art and craft shops, restaurants; the Railway Walk, beaches
Location situated on terraced cotils, overlooking St Aubin's bay
Food self-catering – condiments available to buy **Price ££ Rooms** 3 yurts, 1 double bed, 2 with king sized beds, all with wood-burning stove, BBQ, picnic table, sunloungers
Facilities bathroom has 3 showers – one for each yurt – a toilet and 2 wash basins; hairdryer and natural toiletries available, books, games and toys to borrow, hot tub
Credit cards not accepted **Children** welcome **Accessibility** not suitable **Pets** not accepted **Closed** never
Managers Cath and Andy Mesch

Clifden Yurts
Beach yurts

These yurts are one of many local visitor attractions that show how wrong it is to think of the Channel Islands as old-fashioned.

Set into the hill opposite St Aubin the three luxury yurts bring hotel comfort to lovers of the outdoors. The circular tents are comfortable and cosy, with double beds, furniture and a log-burning stove for chilly nights. Each one, and its fittings, is designed to be eco-friendly, making the whole experience as 'green' as possible.

Matching their names, Ship Ahoy, Forest Green and Harbour Retreat, the yurts are kitted out with vintage and home-made accessories. Decorations such as hand-made lavender bags adorn the walls, apple crates become bedside tables, ladders are turned into towel rails and potato boxes make quirky mirror frames.

The lavatory and shower block is thoughtfully designed, and gleaming clean, as is the communal kitchen 'The Lookout', which has home-grown ingredients to purchase, and a panoramic window with views of the sea. There is an eco-friendly but romantic hot tub installed at the top of the site, again with views over St Aubin.

Many guests are often avid walkers and cyclists, as Clifden is situated perfectly for exploring Jersey's amazing coastline.

THE SOUTH-EAST   CHANNEL ISLANDS

St Brelade, Jersey

Le Boulevard, St Aubin's Harbour,
St Brelade, Jersey JE3 8AB

Tel 01534 741585
email
wakeup@harbourviewjersey.com
website
www.harbourviewjersey.com

Nearby Railway Walk to Corbiere Lighthouse; airport (10 mins); St Helier (15 mins).
Location overlooking St Aubins Harbour; 10 minute drive from airport **Food** breakfast, lunch, dinner
Prices £-££
Rooms 16; 12 double/twin, 2 singles, 2 suites for up to 5; all rooms have central heating, satellite TV, hairdryer, most have harbour views
Facilities breakfast room, wi-fi; sun terrace
Credit cards AE, DC, MC, V
Children accepted (half price for under 10s)
Accessibility one suitable annex
Pets well-behaved dogs
Closed never
Proprietor Kelly Keadell

Harbour View
Harbourside guesthouse

Modest prices, plus the view of St Aubin's Harbour basin and, beyond, the expansive bay, combine to make this possibly Jersey's most charming budget place. From the long, thin garden out front, you can watch the rise and fall of the tide and the comings and goings of the boats. The garden is eclectically – perhaps eccentrically – planted and furnished by owner Kelly, who is not just a people-person, but a bit of a character. Through an unassuming entrance you find a similarly unassuming reception area, which is unlike any hotel, B&B or anything else we can think of. The formerly uninviting staircase and hallway is now lovely and bright after a refurbishment. These lead to the bedrooms. They offer fair space and comfort for the price charged, with cheery stripped bedspreads.

Adjacent is the Muddy Duck restaurant where the focus is on flavour. Chris the chef works hard to be imaginative with his bistro-style food and the place was buzzing when we visited. One jolly celebration continued with squeals of laughter until some time after eleven – not a problem for residents, we were assured, because diners are always eased out before midnight. Of course, this place comes into its own during warm summer weather, when you can loll in the garden.

THE SOUTH-EAST — CHANNEL ISLANDS

St Brelade, Jersey

La Neuve Route, St Brelade, Jersey
JE3 8BS

Tel 01534 741426
email office@lehaulemanor.com
website www.lahaulemanor.com

Nearby La Lande d'Ouest; Portelet Common; St Catherine's Wood; Jersey War Tunnels.
Location St Aubin's Bay, close to airport and Elizabeth ferry terminal
Food breakfast
Prices ££-£££
Rooms 16; all rooms have TV, hairdryer, wi-fi, most have views; 2 self-catering apartment
Facilities outdoor swimming pool, Jacuzzi, hot tub
Credit cards AE, MC, V
Children accepted
Accessibility no special facilities
Pets not accepted
Closed never

La Haule Manor
Village manor hotel

A grand, sturdy exterior combined with a romantic, stylish interior gives La Haule its special charm. Overlooking St Aubin's Bay and Fort and originally dating back to the early 15th century, it was restored once in 1796 and again a few years ago. The owners have succeeded in combining the traditional manor with typically French style and decoration. The mood is romantic and relaxing, and, unsurprisingly, La Haule is popular with honeymooners.

The spacious bedrooms have high ceilings and are decorated in neutral colours, with ornate vintage furniture. We liked the mirrors in the bathrooms, the elegant baths and the impressive chandeliers. All bedrooms are different and most have sea views. The recently refurbished dining room is modern, with an award-winning breakfast bar that caters to all appetites.

There's a lovely, lush sunken garden, where guests can play games or just relax and enjoy the view. A peaceful, spacious place.

THE SOUTH-EAST CHANNEL ISLANDS

St Peter Port, Guernsey

Fermain Lane, St. Peter Port, Guernsey GY1 1ZZ

Tel 0800 316 0314
email reservations@fermainvalley.com
website www.fermainvalley.com

Nearby St. Peter Port.
Location close to St Peter Port town centre, Guernsey
Food three restaurants (The Rock Garden Steakhouse, Ocean Bar & Grill, Buho) serving breakfast, lunch, dinner
Price £££-££££
Rooms 43; all with free wi-fi, bathrobes, refrigerator, flat screen TV, hairdryer, personal safe
Facilities computer room with internet access, indoor heated swimming pool and sauna, poolside terrace, cinema with 3D, 2 lounges, 2 restaurants, gardens
Credit cards all major
Children welcome
Accessibility lifts, 1 fully-equipped room **Pets** not accepted
Closed never
Proprietors Hand Picked Hotels

Fermain Valley
Seaside town hotel

It's larger than our preferred size, but Fermain Valley's focus on individuality and unique design give it charm and originality. Situated high over popular Fermain Bay, its views over the surrounding Channel Islands and, on clear days, as far as France, are spectacular.

Recent new owners, Hand Picked Hotels, helmed by Julia Hands have kept the neutral modern style and ambience of the place. However, it is the thoughtful little touches that we like the most, such as fresh flowers and fruit in the bedrooms to make you feel at home. Bedrooms are all individually designed, many with sea or garden views, and thoughtful touches such as matching headboard cushions or curtain covers and chunky bedspreads give a lovely greeting. The treehouse rooms are our favourite.

Its three restaurants, private cinema and indoor swimming pool/sauna have all helped this place to achieve its four stars, but we especially value the hard work that goes into providing a calm and relaxing atmosphere. One guest commented that it was a 'relaxed atmosphere for such a plush place'.

The hotel is proud of its landscaped gardens, winning the Floral Guernsey Horticultural Award for Horticultural Excellence.

THE SOUTH-EAST — SOUTHERN ENGLAND

Bray, Berkshire

The Waterside Inn
Riverside restaurant-with-rooms

The world-famous cuisine of Michel Roux is the thing at this elegant Thames-side restaurant, these days run by Michel's son Alain – so much so that people tend to overlook the existence of 11 superb bedrooms upstairs and in cottages nearby. They are individually designed, in a French style, feminine and elegant rather than glitzy. Midweek package prices for a room and dinner are, relatively speaking, value for money, given the quality. This is a half-page entry only because super-luxury dining is a little, but only a little, outside our usual territory. It would be easy to fill several pages describing the charm, the service, and of course the sublime food.

Ferry Road, Bray, Berkshire SL6 2AT

Tel 01628 620691
email reservations@waterside-inn.co.uk **website** www.waterside-inn.co.uk **Food** lunch, dinner
Price £££ **Closed** Monday, Tuesday; from 26th Dec for 4 weeks
Proprietor Alain Roux (Chef Patron)

Brighton, East Sussex

Hotel du Vin
Town hotel

Down a narrow cobbled street, tucked back from the seafront, a collection of part-gothic-styled buildings make up this member of the stylish du Vin micro-chain. In the main building, bizarre gargoyles watch over a double-height hall and a heavily carved staircase. Through glass windows and doors, you can see the Bistro, done out in wine-related pictures, floor-to-ceiling windows and bunches of dried hops. Bedrooms facing the central courtyard have chalky blue-green wood siding, a beach-house style, and inside, are decorated in soft blue and sand tones. In the bathrooms, scroll top baths are mounted in driftwood and old railway sleepers.

Ship Street, Brighton, East Sussex BN1 1AD

Tel 01273 718588
email reception.brighton@hotelduvin.com
website www.hotelduvin.com/locations/brighton **Food** breakfast, lunch, dinner **Price** £££
Closed never
Manager Joe Carter

THE SOUTH-EAST

SOUTHERN ENGLAND

Faversham, Kent

Wartling, Herstmonceux, East Sussex BN27 1RY

Tel 01323 832590
email accom@wartlingplace.co.uk
website www.wartlingplace.co.uk
Food breakfast, dinner by prior arrangement
Price ££ **Closed** never
Proprietors Barry and Rowena Gittoes

Wartling Place Country House **Country guesthouse**

Rowena and Barry Gittoes run their upmarket B&B in a substantial former four-bedroom rectory – room for guests and hosts to be separate – guests have the first floor, and their own drawing room and dining room, and there's a 3-acre garden. There is also a cottage with two extra rooms. Tasteful country house decoration and furnishing, including some genuine antiques. This is solid, unflashy quality, with personal but not intrusive attention, backed by 17 years of experience as we went to press. Wartling is a small, peaceful village on the edge of the Pevensey Levels nature reserve and there's much else of interest nearby – this is '1066 country'.

Kintbury, Berkshire

53 Station Road, Kintbury, Berkshire RG17 9UT

Tel 01488 658263
email dundasarms@butcombepubs.com
website www.butcombe.com/the-dundas-arms-berkshire
Food breakfast, snack lunch, dinner
Price ££ **Closed** never
Proprietors Butcombe Pubs

The Dundas Arms
Village inn

At first, we were underwhelmed by our awkwardly shaped room, its sombre furnishings and clock that told the wrong time. In the cramped bathroom, the basin was so shallow that water bounced off the porcelain and on to the floor. But next morning we were charmed by the sunshine on our private terrace bordering the river.

Much of the emphasis is on the food, served in two comfortable dining rooms, but it's still the quirky original bar that acts as the focal point – this is an upgraded pub that can still bring in the locals. The Dundas Arms is not perfect, but the team is cheerful, and its heart is definitely in the right place. Since our last visit an extensive refurbishment and change of ownership have occured, which will no doubt enhance the place – reports welcome.

THE SOUTH-EAST

London, SW7

11 Cadogan Gardens, Chelsea, London, SW7 2RJ

Tel 020 7730 7000
email reception@11cadogangardens.com
website 11cadogangardens.com
Food breakfast, lunch, dinner, afternoon tea **Price** ££££ **Closed** never
Proprietors Cadogan Estate Management Iconic Luxury Hotels

11 Cadogan Gardens
City hotel

Our series editor Fiona Duncan was initially thrown by the dark and sultry interior of 11 Cadogan Gardens, seemingly out of step with its homely Chelsea address. However, its glossy opulence – all shadowy lighting and black wood pannelling – began to grow on her, while the impeccable service from William, and legendary concierge Richie was Chelsea through and through.

Where other top hotels standardize bedrooms, these are all individual: both stately and homely, with beautiful marble bathrooms. Downstairs you'll find the Mirror Room – a genius concoction of gilt-and-glass – as well as their glossy bar. The restaurant, Tartufo, is a welcome surprise of cream hues and natural light, serving delicious Italian food.

London, SW6

247 New Kings Road SW6 4XG

Tel 020 7731 7313
email info@aragonhousesw6.com
website www.aragonhousesw6.com
Food breakfast, lunch, dinner
Price ££-£££ **Closed** never
Management City Pub Group

Aragon House
City hotel

Built on the site of Catherine of Aragon's dower house and perched in a corner of Parsons Green this place is full of energy. The staff are busy, but relaxed and the atmosphere is cheerful. A striped staircase, quirky artworks and a lively bar with eclectic cocktails infuse an element of playfulness which sets it apart from other options in the city. The location helps too. The staff are young, relaxed and friendly. The menu offers smart pub classics, roast dinners and in the Green Room, oysters. The bedrooms vary in size but are all comfortable and homely, with contemporary touches and interesting artworks. Some, particularly those facing the road, can be noisy.

THE SOUTH-EAST — SOUTHERN ENGLAND

London, BR1

6 Court St, Bromley BR1 1AN

Tel 020 75845533
email reservations.thefranklin@starhotels.com
website www.bramahotels.com
Food breakfast, lunch, dinner all in adjacent resaurant
Price £-££ **Closed** never
Management Alasdair Willson

Brama
City hotel

What could be a dreary-commuter hotel is surprisingly vibrant, helped by Art Deco touches throughout, injecting an unusual sense of glamour to what was formerly Bromley's Old Town Hall. The place effortlessly marries historical charm with contemporary convenience. The location, good for both Victoria and Gatwick Airport, makes it ideal for both business and leisure travellers.

Contactless check-in is on ofer, but we prefer the alternative - being greeted by manager Alasdair Willson. Like the staff in the attached bar-restaurant he is friendly, helpful and attentive. Remote working space nearby.

London, E1

40 Commercial St, London E1 6LP

Tel 020 7247 5371
email bookings@theculpeper.com
website www.theculpeper.com
Food breakfast, lunch, dinner, bar snacks **Price** ££-£££
Closed never
General Manager Lewis

Culpeper
Pub-with-rooms

On one of the East End's busiest thoroughfares, this is not for those seeking a calm place to stay. Downstairs, a vibrant crowd hangs out at a communal table in one part of the bar while elsewhere commuters gather at the end of the day to sip herbal infused cocktails.

The bedrooms have a clear design vision - exposed plaster is trendy here. This laid-back approach to painting walls is purely an aesthetic decision and all the rooms are a nice blend of restored Victorian fireplaces, natural materials, contemporary and comfortable furnishing and plenty of plants.

Upstairs there is a rooftop garden with a greenhouse, where light lunches and drinks can be enjoyed with high-rise office buildings, church spires and ever-moving cranes all around.

London, SW3

24 Egerton Gardens, Knightsbridge, SW3 2DB

Tel 020 75845533
email reservations.thefranklin@starhotels.com
website www.starhotelscollezione.com
Food breakfast, lunch, dinner
Price ££££ **Closed** never
Management Star Hotels

The Franklin
City hotel

Contemporary designer-chic in Knightsbridge. The sign at the entrance is discreet, presenting it (almost) as a private house. It's owned by an Italian hotel group whose mission is to bring Italian hospitality and design standards to London hotels. Redesigned in 2016 by Anouska Hempel, creator of Blakes in South Kensington, the style could only be hers, says our series editor Fiona Duncan: sophisticated, urban, innovatative and international, you'll find mirrored surfaces and moody lighting (perhaps a little dark for some).

The regular bedrooms are small – if you want space you have to pay for a suite. The restaurant is for residents only, so feels private, and serves a mixture of sophisticated and simple dishes – Italian cooking at its best, directed by a Michelin starred chef.

London, SW5

26-28 Trebovir Road, London SW5 9NJ

Tel 020 7370 0991
email info@mayflowerhotel.co.uk
website www.themayflowerhotel.co.uk
Food breakfast **Price** ££-££££
Closed never
Manager Shelley DiMeglio

The Mayflower Hotel
City hotel

Trudging past the dire Earl's Court budget hotels en route to The Mayflower, you will feel relief at the sight of its smart, freshly painted façade. No disappointment, either, once inside: to the left, an airy bar/sitting room; to the right, a spacious, calm, sophisticated reception area.

Our room was tiny, but perfectly formed. In a clever move that makes this budget address feel both hip and characterful, the rooms have been enlivened with Oriental artefacts, carved wooden cupboards and mirrored bedheads, silk cushions and velvet bedspreads, plus attractive wooden blinds and sweeping curtains.

The Mayflower stands out like an Aladdin's lamp in a junk shop amongst budget central London hotels.

THE SOUTH-EAST — SOUTHERN ENGLAND

Lymington, Hampshire

Stanwell House
Town hotel

On Lymington's attractive High Street, an Italianate stone-flagged courtyard stretches the length of this building, affording inviting views from the street of a glass-roofed sitting room; on one side of the entrance is a country clothing shop, on the other a seafood restaurant in 17thC style.

With new owners, Calum and Mary Maclean, the hotel has a divisive new look and feel. Since taking over in 2021 they've redesigned the 27 bedrooms and three places to dine – Samphire restaurant, the Salt Bar and The Orangery.

The bedrooms in the main house are theatrical. Dramatic walls, rich hangings and piles of colourful cushions vie for attention. The place attracts a youngish clientèle.

14-15 High Street, Lymington, Hampshire, SO41 9AA

Tel 01590 677123 **email** enquiries@stanwellhousehotel.com
website www.stanwellhousehotel.com
Food breakfast, brunch, lunch, afternoon tea, dinner **Price** £££ **Closed** never **Proprietors** Calum and Mary Maclean

Pangbourne, Hampshire

The Elephant
Restaurant-with-rooms

The 22 bedrooms at the Elephant are each decorated in an individual style which adheres to an oriental theme. Ours was a superior room with décor resembling a cruise ship.

Downstairs they take their food and drink seriously. The restaurant's main dish is steak, cooked on an open fire grill in the dining room, so you can watch the chef prepare your meal. The bar's main focus has shifted to gin over the last year. When we visited, they were planning to add another four gins to the menu, which will take the total to 56. The hotel hosts gin tastings where different brands come in to talk about their gins. They also have a pizza oven in the garden which is used after the tastings and weddings. Parking is limited but there is an adjacent car park which is free between 6 pm and 8 am.

Church Rd, Pangbourne, Reading RG8 7AR

Tel 0118 984 2244
website www.elephanthotel.co.uk
Food breakfast, lunch, dinner, pizza's
Prices ££-£££
Closed never
Proprietors Bluebelt Hospitality

THE SOUTH-EAST — SOUTHERN ENGLAND

Petworth, West Sussex

Petworth, West Sussex GU28 0JF

Tel 01798 342346
email info@old-station.co.uk
website www.old-station.co.uk
Food breakfast (included), cream tea
Prices ££-£££
Closed Christmas
Manager Jennie Hudson

The Old Railway Station **Bed-and-breakfast**

If you've ever dreamed about stepping back in time and taking a great rail journey, now you can do just that – in West Sussex. The Old Railway Station provides unique accommodation in either the original Petworth Railway Station building or in a historic Pullman carriage.

The station building, Grade II listed, is impressive and welcoming. The former waiting-room now contains the breakfast room and sitting-room, and has vaulted ceilings and original ticket office windows

Bedrooms and bathrooms are narrow, but very long. Original furnishings, marquetry in the walls and antique luggage and clocks all add to the charm.

Inside the main building the bedrooms are spacious and well-fitted out.

Seaview, Isle of Wight

High Street, Seaview, Isle of Wight
PO34 5EX

Tel 01983 612711
email reception@seaviewhotel.co.uk
website www.seaviewhotel.co.uk
Food breakfast, lunch, dinner; room service **Price** ££
Closed Christmas day
Proprietor Martin Gardener

Seaview Hotel
Seaside hotel

If you like breezy, old-fashioned English seaside resorts, you will love sailing-mad Seaview. When Brian Gardener bought this hotel in 2003 he had it completely redecorated and refurbished – adding a further seven rooms and greatly improving the disabled facilities. Bedrooms are a class act with clean nautical lines and soothing colour schemes.

Martin and Robin Gardener now run the place. The hotel's restaurant has been taken over by Liam Hayes, who's earned a Michelin Bib Gourmand for his creative and affordable menu (£28 for 3 courses). Alternatively, guests can eat more traditional pub food in one of their two public bars, or sit out on their terrace.

THE SOUTH-EAST — SOUTHERN ENGLAND

Totford, Hampshire

The Woolpack
Village inn

It stands in the smallest hamlet in Hampshire, possibly in England, in the Candover Valley. Built around 1880, the Grade I-listed brick-and-flint building is simple but full of character.

Inside, it's as appealing as outside, with room for armchairs and a pool table in the spacious bar. Next to it is a dining room with a raised open fire. Or you can choose to eat in the extension that cleverly encases the exterior walls of the pub and is designed to look like stables.

The rooms, found at the back of the inn in converted outbuildings, could be improved. In ours, Snipe, the exposed brick-and-flint walls also included swathes of ugly concrete and the furniture was basic.

Totford, near Northington, Alresford, Hampshire SO24 9TJ

Tel 01962 734184
email info@thewoolpackinn.co.uk
website www.thewoolpackinn.co.uk
Food breakfast, lunch, dinner; bar snacks, picnic hampers, Sunday lunch **Price** £££ **Closed** evening of Christmas Day **Proprietor** Andrew Cooper

Ventnor, Isle of Wight

The Hambrough Hotel
Restaurant-with-rooms

Ventnor is a pretty Victorian cliff-top town with winter gardens, an esplanade, a sandy beach and a shack selling crab and lobster. The Hambrough stands between the High Street and the seafront, overlooking the Cascade Gardens and the harbour. It has seven spacious bedrooms, a restaurant and a bar. It doesn't aim to do too much, but what it does, it hopes to do well and, by and large, it succeeds.

The restaurant continues to make waves locally and the five-course, tasting menu comes with well-chosen wines. A serious kitchen opens off an all-white dining room.

Our inspector had absolute quiet in her spacious room. Her only quibbles: the service lacked warmth; and the overall feel is stylish rather than characterful.

Hambrough Road, Ventnor, Isle of Wight, PO38 1SQ

Tel 01983 856333
email info@thehambrough.com
website www.thehambrough.com
Food breakfast, lunch, dinner
Price £££-££££ **Closed** never
Manager Suzanne Wright

Wickham, Hampshire

The Square, Wickham, Hampshire
PO17 5JG

Tel 01329 835870
email info@quobpark.com
website
www.quobpark/estate-and-hotel
Food breakfast, lunch, dinner
Prices ££-£££ **Closed** never
Proprietor Quob Park Estate

The Old House
Village hotel

The Old House, part of Quob Park Estate possesses much that we look for: an interesting setting – at a corner of the main square of one of the finest villages in Hampshire; a superb building; a delightful garden; an immaculately kept interior; an intimate bar; and attractive dining rooms, created from the original timber-framed outhouse and stables.

Bedrooms vary – some palatial, others with magnificent beams, many with original features, one or two rather cramped – but again a mood of civilized comfort prevails. Times are changing for the Old House, and it has changed hands several times in recent years. The restaurant has been reopened, with a separate wine bar while the hotel's decoration and ambience have happily stayed largely the same – and so, it seems, does the warmth of welcome.

Winchester, Hampshire

75 Kingsgate Street, Winchester,
Hampshire SO23 9PE

Tel 01962 853834
email wykehamarms@fullers.co.uk
website www.wykehamarmswinchester.co.uk
Food breakfast, lunch, dinner
Price ££
Closed never
Proprietors Fullers

The Wykeham Arms
Town pub-with-rooms

'Enormously charming; tons of personality,' confirms our latest reporter. Tucked away in the oldest part of the city, with Winchester College yards away and the Cathedral close by, this is a well-frequented pub, and it's first-rate: 250 years old with two bars furnished with old school desks. Quirky character runs to the bedrooms, which are small and low-ceilinged, but each furnished in its own style, and accommodating all the usual facilities.

Breakfast is served downstairs in the restaurant with Windsor chairs and a fine collection of silver tankards. Hearty food at lunch time and an *à la carte* menu in the evenings; real ales and an impressive list of around 100 wines, changed regularly.

THE SOUTH-EAST　　　SOUTHERN ENGLAND

Winkfield, Berkshire

The Winning Post
Country inn

During the week, this pub attracts people on business, but the majority of people drinking at the bar or dining are to do with the worlds of polo and racing – this is polo heartland, with major polo clubs and Ascot racecourse close at hand.

From the outside, the pub looks like a modest cottage but its interior is surprisingly spacious, cosy and characterful. Bedrooms are in a purpose-built nineties addition at the back of the building, and need to be more alluring to justify their price. Happily, there are plans to renovate these these next year.

Staff are friendly and local. Food arrived swiftly and was a cut above the norm for such a place. Cooked breakfast (continental is included in the room price) is an extra £4.

Winkfield Street, Winkfield, Windsor, Berkshire SL4 4SW

Tel 01344 882242
email info@winningpostwinkfield.co.uk
website www.winningpostwinkfield.co.uk **Food** breakfast, light lunch, lunch, dinner **Price** £££
Closed never
Proprietor Upham Pub Brewery

Yattendon, Berkshire

The Royal Oak
Village hotel

The Royal Oak is easy to find in the centre of the village of Yattendon.

Lest you mistake it for a mere pub, the sign on the front of this cottagey, mellow red-brick inn announces Hotel and Restaurant. Certainly, the Royal Oak is no longer a common-or-garden local (as it was when Oliver Cromwell reportedly ate there). Its two dining areas have a style and elegance not usually associated with ale and darts. But there is still a small bar where residents and non-residents alike can enjoy a choice of real ales and sample the Royals Oak's own gin, Slim Gin.

Bedrooms are prettily decorated and equipped with every conceivable extra. Another attraction is the walled garden, full of colour and a delight during the summer.

The Square, Yattendon, Berkshire RG18 0UF

Tel 01635 201325
email info@royaloakyattendon.com
website www.royaloakyattendon.co.uk
Food breakfast, lunch, dinner
Price ££
Closed New Year's Day (evening of)
Proprietors Gubb Inns

CENTRAL ENGLAND AND WALES

Area introduction

The ancient kingdom of Wales, the Midlands industrial heartland and the mostly flat counties of Cambridgeshire, Norfolk and Suffolk are the main ingredients of s section. It also includes the fashionable counties of Gloucestershire and xfordshire, and the home counties to the west and north of London uckinghamshire, Hertfordshire, Essex and so on). Wales and East Anglia have always en important tourist regions, as are Oxfordshire and Gloucestershire because ey contain Oxford and the Cotswolds. But imaginative tourist developments in dland industrial cities (for example, Birmingham) and historic centres such as nbridge Gorge in Shropshire now also means that the Midlands, far from being urist deserts, are increasingly important. Our selection of special places to stay in of these has grown accordingly since the last edition.

Below are some useful back-up places to try if our main selections are fully booked:

ales

The Bear Hotel
Country hotel, Crickhowell
Tel 01873 810408
www.bearhotel.co.uk
Comfortable hotel in the heart of the Brecon Beacons.

Fairyhill
Restaurant-with-rooms, Reynoldston Tel 01792 391468 www.fairyhill.co.uk
Peaceful retreat with award-winning restaurant.

gland

The Riverside Inn
Country inn, Cound
Tel 01952 510900
www.theriversideinn.net
Charming inn with great views of the River Severn.

Barnsdale Lodge
Farmhouse hotel, Exton
Tel 01572 724678
www.barnsdalelodge.co.uk
Extended farmhouse on the shore of Rutland Water.

The Feathers
Town hotel, Godwick
Tel 01328 701948
www.godwickhall.co.uk
Country house with The Great Barn for events.

Old Swan & Minster Mill
Town hotel, Minster Lovell Tel 01993 774441 www.oldswanandminster-mill.co.uk Traditional and contemporary rooms.

Lion and Pheasant
Townhouse hotel, Shrewsbury
Tel 01743 770345
www.lionandpheasant.co.uk
Historic inn.

The Linden
Restaurant-with-rooms, Stansted Tel 01279 813003
www.the linden.co.uk
Smart, trendy restaurant and stylish rooms.

The Tawny
Country hotel, Stoke-on-Trent
Tel 01538787664
www.thetawny.co.uk
Eco-retreats and lucury hotel in 70 acres of Consall Estate.

Bontnewydd, Gwynedd

Bontnewydd, Caernarfon, Gwynedd
LL54 7YF

Tel 01286 830214
email info@plasdinas.co.uk
website www.plasdinas.co.uk

Nearby Caernarfon Castle; Portmeirion; Welsh Highland Railway; Snowdon.
Location 2.5 miles from Caernarfon, ample parking
Food breakfast, dinner
Price £££-££££
Rooms 10; 1 suite, 9 ensuite double/twin.
Facilities restaurant, private dining room, sitting room, bar, gardens
Credit cards MC, V
Children 12+
Accessibility 1 ground-floor room
Pets 2 dog friendly rooms available
Closed never
Proprietors Annie Bickerton and Daniel Perks

Plas Dinas
Country house hotel

It could be a little over-awing but this elegant, mainly Regency gentleman's house (though parts date back 400 years) is a place where you can be yourself. Annie and Daniel have transformed the place over the last few years through major reinvestment since they took over on the eve of lockdown, skillfully combining indulgent luxury with a relaxed ambience that makes guests feel at home.

The drawing room and atmospheric Gunroom restaurant (private dining available for small groups) with its royal memorabilia are the highlights of the downstairs public spaces. Gaining entry to the Michelin Guide in 2022, the restaurant combines excellent service with an ambitious seasonal menu that changes every month. Bedrooms are mostly spacious, some are decorated in traditional country house style, others modern 'boutique' with bold wallpapers that make a statement. All combine characterful antiques with contemporary facilities. Each has been given the sort of individual thought we look for, including the amusingly masculine Major Room, featuring an original WWI King's Royal Rifles jacket hidden away in the wardrobe.

The house, down a 500-m drive, has views over 15 acres of grounds and unspoiled countryside to the Menai Strait.

WALES

CENTRAL ENGLAND AND WALES

Brechfa, Carmarthenshire

Brechfa, Carmarthenshire
SA32 7RA

Tel 01267 202332
email info@wales-country-hotel.co.uk **website** www.wales-country-hotel.co.uk

Nearby Brecon Beacons, National Botanical Gardens of Wales; National Trust Dinfewr Park and Castle, Abergalsney Gardens.
Location 10 miles (16 km) NE of Carmarthen, on B4310, in village; with ample car parking
Food breakfast, dinner
Price ££ Rooms 6; 3 superior super king-size double, 3 twin, all with bath and shower; all rooms have TV, hairdryer, tea and coffee facilities.
Facilities sitting room, dining room, breakfast room, bar/reception; garden, electric car charging
Credit cards MC, V, Amex
Children welcome over 10
Accessibility not suitable
Pets welcome in some rooms
Closed rarely
Proprietors Gill Brown and David Hart

Ty Mawr
Country hotel

Firmly at right angles to the main street of this tiny village on the fringe of Brechfa Forest, and by the River Marlais, Ty Mawr has a pretty garden and fine views of the surrounding wooded hillsides. The interior of this cream-coloured cotttage has oak beams, stone walls and tiled floors that proclaim the building's three and a bit centuries' tenure of this glorious spot.

The public rooms are cosy and cheerful and include an immaculate bar with smart pine fittings, and a comfy sitting room with an open log fire. The long slate-floored restaurant looks out on to the garden and, candle-lit in the evenings, is where the chef's skill in the kitchen shows in earnest: fresh, usually Welsh, ingredients are assembled without undue fuss but with plenty of imagination. The wines are well-chosen and offered at eminently reasonable prices.

Upstairs, the bedrooms are bright, comfortable and pleasantly rustic, and breakfast in the morning answers to appetites ranging from the merely peckish to the downright ravenous. The flowers in the garden tubs are quite impressive, but it's worth remembering that the National Botanical Garden of Wales is nearby.

It was bought in 2022 by Gill and David - reports welcome.

WALES

CENTRAL ENGLAND AND WALES

Cowbridge

High Street, Cowbridge CF71 7AF

Tel 01446 774 814
email enquiries@bearhotel.com
website townandcountrycollective.co.uk

Location off A487 in centre of town on the quay; with ample car parking
Food breakfast, lunch, dinner
Price ££-£££
Rooms 33; four poster double, executive double, standard double, self-catering apartments
Facilities Cellar's restaurant, lounge bar, grill bar, courtyard, St Quentin's suite, georgian ballroom
Credit cards all major suppliers
Children welcome
Accessibility 1 room is adapted
Pets Dogs welcome, £25 per dog per stay
Closed never
Proprietors The Hitchcocks

The Bear
Village hotel

One of a mini-chain of local places owned and managed hands-on by the Hitchcock brothers Julian and Mark, as well as Julien's son Freddie. We're pleased to welcome The Bear to into our new edition because although similar to many a country town ex-coaching inn with stone floors, panelling and pleasingly creaky floorboards it stands out for genuine character, reasonable comfort, well above average food and fair prices. Our reporter described lorry noise from the main street outside starting at around 6 am but this can be avoided by asking for a room on the other side of the corridor.

The ground-floor public area divides into four different spaces – public bar, residents' bar, informal dining area/bar and a more formal dining area – tactfully allowing public and residents either to mingle or separate.

The menu is unpretentiously imaginative. Among the nibbles and small plates are delicious cauliflower tempura with thick soy sauce; red snapper and chorizo Spanish style fishcakes; and a scrambled duck egg and pancetta-topped bagel. Mains include French trimmed chicken with rosemary and merlot reduction and monkfish wrapped in Parma ham plus ratatouille and basil pesto.

WALES

Eglwysfach, Powys

Eglwysfach, Machynlleth, Powys
SY20 8TA

Tel 01654 781209
email info@ynyshir.co.uk
website www.ynyshir.co.uk

Nearby Llyfnant valley;
Aberystwyth.
Location 11 miles (18 km) NE of
Aberystwyth, just off A487; ample
car parking
Food breakfast, lunch, dinner
Price ££££
Rooms 10; 6 in main house, 4
ground floor outside; all with bath
and shower, phone, TV, hairdryer,
tea and coffee trays; garden rooms
have log burners and balconies
Facilities Michelin-starred restaurant, bar, large gardens
Credit cards AE, DC, MC, V
Children 12+ accepted
Accessibility 1 ground-floor room
Pets not allowed
Closed 23 Dec-8 Jan
Proprietors John and Jenny Talbot,
Gareth Ward (chef patron)
Manager Amelia Eriksson

Ynyshir Hall
Restaurant with rooms

Moody, modern and full of drama the Ynyshir makes no compromises with its creative and culinary vision.

Now resolutely a restaurant-with-rooms instead of a country house hotel, with a full-scale refurbishment in 2017 to prove it. Head Chef Gareth Ward, has achieved an avalanche of success since he came to helm in 2013, swiftly earning a Michelin star, and becoming Chef Patron in 2016.

It still has ten well-appointed scandi-style guest rooms. Each is individually decorated and stylishly furnished with contemporary touches, whilst being cosy and comfortable, with king-size beds, excellent bathrooms and extensive views across the Cumbrian mountains.

The main event, however, is the food, served in their intimate, dark-walled, restaurant with 26 covers and a chef's table seating six. Gareth serves what he calls, in his Northern parlance, 'Alternative British Snap' – sourced from the Welsh larder and British Isles, with Japanese influences: an exemplary crossover is his use of Welsh Wagyu Beef. The four to five hours spent sampling the 19-course tasting menu, will not be time wasted.

The breakfast is elaborate, as you'd expect from a top chef, with home-cured salmon, cream cheese, sourdough crumpets and home-soaked muesli.

WALES

CENTRAL ENGLAND AND WALES

Felin Fach, Powys

Felin Fach, Brecon, Powys
LD3 0UB

Tel 01874 620111
email
enquiries@felinfachgriffin.co.uk
website www.eatdrinksleep.ltd.uk

Nearby Hay Bluff; Pen y Fan;
Brecon Beacons and Black
Mountains; Brecon; Hay-on-Wye;
Llangorse Lake (sailing and wind-
surfing).
Location edge of village with off-
road car parking
Food breakfast, lunch, dinner
Price ££-£££
Rooms 8; double and twin; all rooms
have bath, phone, and Roberts Radios
Facilities bar, dining area; grassed
outdoor drinks area, croquet
Credit cards MC, V
Children accepted, travel cots avail-
able
Accessibility wheelchair access
Pets accepted
Closed Christmas Day and 1 week a
year, usually in Jan
Proprietors Charles and Edmund
Inkin

The Felin Fach Griffin
Country inn

The location is uninteresting, beside a busy-ish road, and you might think this is any old Welsh pub. But there's a clue it may be something different: the exterior is painted a mellow ochre, the colour seen all over Tuscany. Inside, you'll be struck by the layout: right by the bar is a pair of squashy leather sofas where you flop with the papers. A log fire is raised above floor level, radiating heat in two directions, into the bar and the adjacent dining room. Tongue-and-groove panelling is painted a brilliant blue.

Nooks and crannies are filled with books: we spied *Debrett* and *Who's Who*. Upstairs are seven fresh, but perhaps boxy bedrooms with homey decoration, again using bright colours. One has a four-poster bed and another extra beds for children.

The food remains distinctly above average for the price. Home-made soda bread arrives on a simple wooden board. There's a large choice of interesting wines by the glass, including prosecco. The Griffin can claim to be Wales's original gastropub. Off the main dining room there's another smaller one with two tables seating eight (great for a party) in front of the AGA, where the day's fresh stocks simmer.

The Inkins also run The Gurnard's Head (page 86) and The Old Coastguard (page 63).

Ganllwyd, Gwynedd

Ganllwyd, Dolgellau, Snowdonia,
Gwynedd LL40 2HP

Tel 01341 440273
email info@dolly-hotel.co.uk
website www.dolly-hotel.co.uk

Nearby Cymer Abbey; Snowdonia; Lake Vyrnwy. **Location** in countryside, on A470 5 miles (8 km) N of Dolgellau; ample car-parking
Food breakfast, lunch by arrangement, dinner **Price** ££
Rooms 10; 9 double, 1 single, all with bath; all rooms have phone, TV, hairdrier
Facilities sitting room, dining room, breakfast room, conservatory bar; garden, fishing **Credit cards** AE, DC, MC, V
Children welcome over 8
Accessibility not suitable
Pets accepted in 2 bedrooms
Closed Nov to Mar
Proprietors Alan and Julie Pulman

Plas Domelynllyn Hall
Country hotel

Alan and Julie Pulman, who took over the hotel ten years ago, run it with considerable style. Parts of it are more than half a millennium old but there was still work going on when we visited. It sits in on its own terrace above Ganllwyd, near Dolgellau, taking in the beautiful views across the valley, and, in the principally Victorian interior, antiques mingle equally comfortably with more modern furnishings to create a warm, friendly atmosphere. China and crystal twinkle on all sides.

The drawing room is elegant but the Old Hall Restaurant – the oldest part of the house, with stone walls and slate floors – is obviously where the team gets down to real business. Visitors mention the quality and choice of breakfast, served in The Shelley Room which dates back to the ninth century and has stained glass windows. Locally sourced meats are used for their dinner menu of 'British classics', and there are homemade pâtés and sausages on offer.

Bedrooms are named after local rivers and individually furnished and decorated. There is excellent walking from the door and all guests have access to that essential room in a Welsh hotel – the drying room. This a passionately non-smoking hotel.

Hay-on-Wye, Hereford

3 Sheepcote Bungalows, Hereford
HR3 5HU

Tel 07841 645238
email relax@cynefinretreats.com
website www.cynefinretreats.com

Nearby Hay-on-Wye, Hereford, The Cider Museum, River Wye, Black Mountains **Location** just off the B4350, first left South of Whitney Bridge
Food 'finish at home' food boxes can be delivered from the local deli
Price ££££
Rooms 4 luxe pods and 3 luxe lodges. All have cooking facilities
Facilities Private hot tub and firepit outside
Credit cards All major
Children Welcome. cot and high chairs be arrangement. Sofa bedding for children under 10 (£20 charge)
Accessibility not suitable
Pets £30 charge for bringing a dog
Closed never
Proprietors Lorna Felgate

Cynefin Retreats
Self-catering lodges

Recommended by trusted reporters, Cynefin Retreats offers something unique: Scandinavian self-catering eco-lodges and pods with great views over the hills and forest. Private terraces with hot tubs and fire pits offer a private moment with the landscape. The buildings, with large windows, are all sustainably powered, well insulated, wooden clad and warmed with central heating and cosy wood burners.

Besides being a peaceful retreat for couples, this is also good for families. Children can explore forest dens and use playground equipment tucked away in the woodlands. The lodges have well-stocked games cupboards for rainy days.

Although no food is served, there are tea and coffee facilities, an honesty shop and nearby Hay Deli can deliver hampers of food if pre-ordered. Hands-on owner Lorna can also help you book nearby pubs and recommend restaurants.

A short walk away is Hay-on-Wye with its cafes, bookshops, annual literary festival and a market on Thursdays. The Black Mountains are a short drive.

Lampeter, Ceredigion

The Falcondale Country House Estate, Falcondale Drive, Ceredigion SA48 7RX

Tel 01570422910
email info@thefalcondale.co.uk
website www.thefalcondale.co.uk

Nearby Cardigan Bay, Cambrian Mountains
Location 5 minute drive from Lampeter. On Sat nav use postcode SA48 7SB
Food breakfast, lunch, dinner
Price ££-£££
Rooms 17; 12 doubles, two suites, two four-posters
Facilities beauty treatments; restaurants; 14 acres of private gardens
Credit cards MC, V
Children allowed
Accessibility one accessible bedroom
Pets welcome
Closed never
Proprietors Lisa and Chris Hutton

The Falcondale
Hotel and spa

This quietly impressive hotel appears as a spot on the landscape within the context of its acres of private gardens and the wider Teifi Valley — but it is a stronghold. The Falcondale is about luxury relaxation, and encouraging guests to explore the Welsh countryside and its own 14 acres of landscaping.

You can get your boots muddy walking the Heritage coastline, and then return to the warmth in time for your spa session.

Bright, airy and extremely spacious, the bedrooms are grand yet functional. Most have views of the gardens or the valley as their centrepiece, but four-poster beds may compete. Each room has individuality, completed with a trademark flourish; they have strong but subtle character.

The rest of the house consists of a sitting room, a heated conservatory, the outdoor terrace, two restaurants and a spa. It's where you'll want to be when not exploring the outdoors. The open fire is of course a favourite spot. The Falcondale estate has been around for some 400 years, and a certain timelessness is mirrored in the hotel itself.

Guests gush about the welcoming staff and the fantastic views, neither of which we believe will change any time soon.

WALES

CENTRAL ENGLAND AND WALES

Llanbrynmair, Powys

Llanbrynmair, Powys SY19 7DY

Tel 07941722980
email richard@barlingsbarn.co.uk
website www.barlingsbarn.co.uk

Nearby Snowdonia; Aberdovey beach
Location 2 miles (3 km) NE of Llanbrynmair at end of private lane off road to Pandy; with ample car parking
Food self-catering
Price ££-£££
Rooms barn sleeps between 14-16 people
Facilities garden, indoor swimming pool - heated all year round, 20 acres of bluebell wood - a Plantation of Ancient Woodland, garden, BBQ, campfire, sauna, squash court, table-tennis, badminton, Sky TV, wi-fi and piano in the Wanws
Credit cards not accepted
Children welcome
Accessibility 2 ground-floor rooms
Pets accepted by arrangement
Closed never
Proprietors Richard

Barlings Barn
Self-catering barns

The only sounds to disturb the peace in this corner of Powys come from the sheep on the surrounding hillsides, and from the nearby brook. Barlings Barn is a rural idyll in Llanbrynmair, in the heart of Wales, with a garden full of roses and honeysuckle: a picturesque setting for the outdoor activities, such as walking, bird-watching, fishing and golf, that you can enjoy in the surrounding Powys countryside.

Established in 1984, it is the perfect peace of the place that keeps it in the guide despite the move a few years ago towards a self-catering set-up. Home-made cakes await your arrival in the secluded barns adjacent to the farmhouse, one with an oak-beamed stone fireplace and wood-burning stove.

Since first featuring in the guide they have expanded from 2 to 22 acres with the purchase of beautiful surrounding woodland. They've also added an all-year-round heated pool, and a sunny new dining room with views over the valley to accomodate large parties of up to 28. The barns are well-equipped with range cookers, fridges, dishwashers, microwaves and barbecues. Though it's basically self-catering, the local caterer can deliver food to the door, and even provide waitresses to serve and wash up if you're feeling spoilt. There's a colourful market every Wednesday in Machynlleth.

WALES

Llandrillo, Denbighshire

Llandrillo, near Corwen,
Denbighshire LL21 0ST

Tel 01490 440264
email info@tyddynllan.co.uk
website www.tyddynllan.co.uk

Nearby Bala Lake and Railway; Snowdonia.
Location 5 miles (8 km) SW of Corwen off B4401; with ample car parking
Food breakfast, lunch, dinner
Price ££££ (half board)
Rooms 12 double and twin, 10 with bath, 2 with shower; all rooms have phone, TV, radio, plus ground floor suite
Facilities sitting room, bar, restaurant; croquet, fishing
Credit cards MC, V, Amex
Children welcome
Accessibility 1 suite suitable
Pets accepted in bedrooms by arrangement **Closed** 2 weeks in Jan
Proprietors Bryan and Susan Webb

Tyddyn Llan
Restaurant-with-rooms

A firm favourite with readers since our first edition, this Georgian stone house near Llandrillo is decorated with elegant flair, period antiques and fine paintings, creating a serene ambience. Tyddyn Llan is very much a home, despite the number of guests it can accommodate. There is a major extension to the building, cleverly complementary to the original, using slate, stone and cast-iron.

A reader writes: 'No intrusive reception desk; spacious sitting rooms furnished with style; dining room shows great flair; bedrooms well equipped with original pieces of furniture; small but modern and very pleasing bathrooms; peaceful, comfortable stay, warm atmosphere provided by attentive hosts'. When Fiona Duncan, our series editor, visited a few years ago, she felt that Bryan deserved a Michelin star 'for his instinctive cooking' and we were delighted to hear that he was awarded one not long after, in 2011.

Bryan and his wife Susan offer diners with a new angle on Welsh country house food with inventive and well-planned small menus using quality local ingredients, plus an impressive wine list.

The place is surrounded by large, beautiful grounds.

Llandudno, Conwy

Promenade, 17 North Parade,
Llandudno, Conwy LL30 2LP

Tel 01492 860330
email sales@osbornehouse.co.uk
website www.osbornehouse.co.uk

Nearby dry ski slope; Conwy Castle; Bodnant Gardens; Snowdonia
Location on seafront opposite pier and promenade gardens; off-road car parking
Food breakfast (in room), lunch, dinner
Price £££
Rooms 7 suites (1 family room), all with phone, bath, walk-in shower, TV, fridge, wi-fi
Facilities bar, 'bistro' restaurant, cafe area, sitting area in reception, terrace
Credit cards AE, DC, MC, V
Children welcome, but no children's menu
Accessibility a ramp
Pets not accepted
Closed one week at Christmas
Proprietors Maddocks family

Osborne House
Town hotel

There's virtually no mobile signal in the charmingly old-fashioned resort of Llandudno, but that's part of its appeal. Between the unspoilt beaches and the backdrop of mountains, life goes at a gentle pace. Summer here means strolling along the Promenade with an ice-cream cornet, pausing to watch Punch and Judy. In a plum position on the Prom, Osborne House fits its surroundings perfectly.

The Maddocks family have lavished attention on it. The public rooms are glamorous enough, but it's the seven gorgeous suites, six with sea views and private parking spaces, that really impress, and are kindly priced considering the wealth of antiques, pictures and porcelain in each one, and the marble bathrooms with splendid roll top baths. Some might find it all a bit over the top, certainly very Victorian, but downstairs the public spaces have plenty of modern touches including a sleek bar with two large plasma TV screens competing for attention. 'The Café,' a bistro-café, reckons on serving good food in a rather grand Victorian surroundings, but in an informal style – no set hours, okay to have just one course, and eat at the bar, a table or on a sofa.

WALES

CENTRAL ENGLAND AND WALES

Llanthony, Gwent

Llanthony, Abergavenny, Gwent
NP7 7NN

Tel 01873 890487
website
www.llanthonyprioryhotel.co.uk

Nearby Offa's Dyke; Brecon Beacons; Hay-on-Wye.
Location off A465 from Abergavenny to Hereford, take mountain road heading N at Llanvihangel Crucorney; with ample car parking
Food breakfast (included), lunch, dinner
Price ££
Rooms 7 double and twin, no en-suites. Showers on first floor
Facilities dining room, bar; garden
Credit cards accepted
Children children under 10 unable to stay in tower rooms
Accessibility not possible
Pets not accepted
Closed Nov-May only open on weekends, but fully open 27th Dec-New Year
Proprietor Geoffrey Neil

Llanthony Priory
Country inn

Far into the Black Mountains, on the west bank of the Afon Honddu and overlooked by Offa's Dyke to the east, Llanthony Priory lies high and remote in the Vale of Ewyas. The most spectacular approach is southwards from the sloping streets and busy bookshops of Hay-on-Wye.

One of the earliest Augustinian houses in Britain, it was endowed by the de Lacy family, but by the time of Henry VIII's dissolution of the monasteries had fallen into disuse. The Prior's quarters survived amongst the ruins and are now used as the hotel. Gothic horror enthusiasts will be delighted not only by the setting but also when they learn that the highest of the bedrooms can only be reached by climbing more than 60 spiral steps up into the south tower.

This is not a hotel for the fastidious or the faint-hearted: it is a long way from anywhere and much used by walkers attracted to the stunning country that surrounds it. Its isolation – not to mention lack of wi-fi and signal – is suited to those willing to switch off and relax, unharassed by the bleating of their mobile phone. The chance to sleep in this unique piece of history (with a four-poster and half-tester available) and to wake up to the view from the tower also comes with a very modest price tag.

CENTRAL ENGLAND AND WALES

WALES

Nant Gwynant, Gwynedd

Nant Gwynant, Gwynedd, LL55 4NT

Tel 01286 870211
website www.pyg.co.uk

Nearby Bodnant Gardens; Caernarfon, Beaumaris and Harlech Castles; Isle of Anglesey; Blackrock Sands. **Location** take the A5 to Holyhead, as you enter Capel Curig, turn left on to the A4086. 4 miles (6 km) on the hotel is on a T junction with the lake in front of it
Food breakfast, lunch, dinner, tea
Price £ **Rooms** 18 double and twin, 1 single; 7 premium rooms with private bathroom, 5 public bathrooms
Facilities sitting room, dining room, smoke room, bar, sauna, natural swimming pool, games room, beer garden, lake
Credit cards MC, V **Children** welcome **Disabled** 1 ground-floor room **Pets** by arrangement **Closed** midweek during Nov to Dec; Jan to 2nd week of Mar
Proprietors Nick and Rupert Pullee

Pen-y-Gwryd Hotel
Climbing hostel

A pilgrimage place for climbers: this is the home of British Mountaineering, where Edmund Hillary and his team set up their training base before the assault on Everest in 1953. Still in the same friendly family after 65 years, the charming old coach inn, set high in the desolate heart of Snowdonia, is just the sort of place you dream of returning to after a day outdoors: simple, unsophisticated, warm and welcoming, with good plain home cooking, including wickedly calorific puddings (dinner is £25 per head).

In keeping with the purpose of the place the bedrooms are simple with no frills, not all of them have private bathrooms, but they all have fluffy towels and warm embroidered bedding and linen; the best room is in the annexe and has a grand four-poster bed. One of the bathrooms houses a vintage Victorian bath that looks deep and inviting. For the less intrepid walkers there is still plenty to see in the vicinity, as it is littered with castles and gardens.

After a hard day on the hill you can soak your aching muscles in the natural pool in the garden or unwind in the sauna. For children (or playful adults) there is a games room with a dart board and table tennis.

WALES

Narberth, Pembrokeshire

Molleston, Narberth,
Pembrokeshire SA67 8BX

Tel 01834 860915
email
reservations@grovenarbeth.co.uk
website
www.thegrove-narberth.co.uk

Nearby walks through Cannaston Wood to the Blackpool Mill; Stackpole Estate Coastal Walk; Tenby; St David's; Porthgain; the Blue Lagooon; galleries; craft shops **Location** Narbeth with shops, restaurants and boutiques, close to the beautiful Preseli Hills **Food** breakfast, lunch, dinner **Price** £££ **Rooms** 25: 13 in the main house, 4 in The Longhouse; 2 in Poyer's Cottage and 6 in Herb Cottage **Facilities** restaurant, sitting room, bar, kitchen garden **Credit cards** all major **Children** welcome **Accessibility** suitable **Pets** 6 dog friendly rooms **Closed** never **Proprietors** Neil and Zoe Kedward

Grove of Narberth
Country hotel and restaurant

Neil and Zoe Kedward acquired this place as a wreck and after nine months of blood, sweat and tears – they worked on a shoestring – got a beautiful result. The former somewhat quirky mansion is now a unique boutique hotel and restaurant that gets a big vote of confidence from our series editor, Fiona Duncan. Its magic worked on her as soon as she arrived. The exterior is unusual, with two facades: one tall and Georgian, painted brilliant white, the other with gables and Arts and Crafts elements that also crop up inside.

She could not fault her bedroom. The rooms are spread out across the main house, two cottages and an old long house. Each room is distinct in design, pairing neutral tones with unique local crafts.

In The Fernery, under chef Douglas Balish, an inventive tasting menu of is served Wednesday through Saturday. Dishes focus on seasonal and local produce, with vegetarian and vegan options available. Breakfast and lunch is served in The Artisan Rooms, a less formal and elaborate dining experience.

Zoe and Neil also run Penmaenchuf Hall (page 194) as part of the Seren collection.

WALES

CENTRAL ENGLAND AND WALES

Old Radnor, Radnorshire

Old Radnor, Presteigne LD8 2RH

Tel 01544 350655
email mail@harpinnradnor.co.uk
website www.harpinnradnor.co.uk

Nearby Offa Dyke Path, Radnor Valley, Hay Festival
Location in Old Radnor, near Walton. Close to Welsh border
Food breakfast, lunch, dinner
Price ££-£££
Rooms 3; 2 double with bathroom and 1 suite with bathroom
Facilities dining room, sitting room, terrace,
Credit cards MC, V
Children welcome (extra charge)
Accessibility not suitable
Pets dogs welcome (extra charge)
Closed Mondays and Tuesdays
Proprietors The Bridges

The Harp Inn
Village inn

A hardcore new entry to the guide. There are just five bedrooms done in restrained good taste with up-to-date fitting and it's family owned and managed by the Bridges.

The food, pub classics plus imaginative modern dishes, gets warm responses. The views are wonderful, overlooking the Radnor Valley about a mile into Wales from the border It's a useful starting point for long or short walks on the waymarked Offa's Dyke Path and Mortimer Trail. Cycling, mountain biking and golf are nearby.

The building is an authentic, mellow old longhouse inn (see below) with slate floors, oak beams and antique settles. It's dog friendly, but care is taken to exclude dogs from some of the eating areas. 'A beautiful, peaceful, friendly place' says a recent guest.

Longhouses probably originated in Devon and were commonly built in the 14th to 18thCs with thatched roofs. Their length allowed animals to be sheltered in one part and humans the other, a practical solution for farmers who then adopted them in other parts of the country.

WALES

CENTRAL ENGLAND AND WALES

Penally, Pembrokeshire

Penally, near Tenby, South Pembrokeshire SA70 7PY

Tel 01834 843033
email info@penally-abbey.com
website www.penally-abbey.com

Nearby Tenby; Colby Woodland Garden; Upton Castle, Pembroke Castle
Location in Penally village 1 mile from Tenby; with ample car parking
Food breakfast, dinner, afternoon tea **Price** £££
Rooms 12 (8 rooms in the Main House and 4 in the Coach House), all double and double-twin. All rooms have hairdryer, Nespresso machine, bathrobes, Bramley toiletries **Facilities** Drawing Room, Sun Room, dining room, bar, private courtyard events space with bar and garden **Credit cards** MC, V
Children accepted **Accessibility** no special facilities
Pets dogs welcome (1 dog policy)
Closed never **Proprietors** Lucas and Melanie Boissevain

Penally Abbey
Country house hotel

Ever since the Middle Ages, this has been recognized as one of the spots from which to appreciate the broad sweep of the Pembrokeshire coast and National Park from Tenby to Giltar Point. The links golf course wasn't there, but the ruins of the medieval chapel which gave this Gothic country house its name are still in the secluded and well-tended gardens. Many of the windows and doors all have the characteristic double curve ogee arches. There is a comfortable and well furnished drawing room with an open fire, a welcoming bar far from the world's woes and weather, and a tall, candle-lit dining room. The restaurant serves up a menu inspired by local Pembrokeshire ingredients. An atmospheric courtyard can be used for small weddings and celebrations.

Bedrooms are comfortable, and well equipped with fresh linen: some you could play cricket in and are furnished traditionally, some in quite a grand style. St Deiniol's Lodge now houses a further five rooms, decorated in more contemporary style.

The Boissevains took over Penally in 2014. Melanie, an interior designer, has set about putting her unique mark on the decoration, while Lucas aims to put Penally on the culinary map.

WALES

CENTRAL ENGLAND AND WALES

Penmaenpool, Gwynedd

Penmaenpool, Dolgellau, Gwynedd
LL40 1YB

Tel 01341 212121
email reservations@penmaenuchaf.co.uk
website www.penmaenuchaf.co.uk

Nearby Mawddach Estuary; Snowdonia; Cader Idris, Portmeirion.
Location off A493 Dolgellau-Tywyn road; with ample car parking
Food breakfast, lunch, dinner
Price £££
Rooms 14 double and twin with bath; all rooms have phone, TV, iPod dock, hairdryer, minibar, wi-fi
Facilities sitting rooms, library, 2 dining rooms, bar; garden, helipad, trout and salmon fishing
Credit cards DC, MC, V
Children well-behaved children welcome
Accessibility restaurant only **Pets** accepted in 1 room by arrangement
Closed 8 days in Dec, 10 days in Jan
Proprietors Neil and Zoe Kedward

Penmaenuchaf Hall
Country house hotel

Not far from the market town of Dolgellau, Penmaenuchaf Hall's drive winds steeply up a wooded hillside from the south bank of the Mawddach Estuary to this sturdy grey stone Victorian manor house. Set on terraces in 21 acres of grounds, the views across Snowdonia must have been top of the list of reasons that brought the original builder – a Lancashire mill owner – to this peaceful spot at the foot of Cader Idris. A rose garden and a water garden add a charm of their own to the beautiful setting.

Retiring Mark Watson and Lorraine Fielding sold Penmaenuchaf to Neil and Ze Kedward who run the Seren collection of Pembrokeshire hotels (so it's a sister to Narbeth Grove page 191). They preserved the softened Victorian character of the house so that, from the imposing main hall you are drawn to the warmth and light of the ivory morning room, the sitting rooms and the library.

The same sympathetic treatment carries through to the bedrooms – fine fabrics are married with fine furniture and only the beds are baronial. If you are not tempted by the excellent walking in the surrounding hills, you can doze in the sunny conservatory, or eat in the oak-panelled garden room restaurant, Llygad yr Haul.

WALES

CENTRAL ENGLAND AND WALES

Skenfrith, Monmouthshire

Skenfrith, Monmouthshire, NP7 8UH

Tel 01600 750235
email reception@thebellatskenfrith.co.uk
website www.thebellatskenfrith.co.uk

Nearby Brecon Beacons National Park; Ross-on-Wye; Hereford; Hay-on-Wye; Abergavenny; Monmouth.
Location beside river, off minor road on edge of village in own grounds; ample car parking
Food breakfast, lunch, dinner, afternoon tea
Price £££ **Rooms** 11 doubles
Facilities bar, dining room, function room; terrace, garden, bakery.
Credit cards MC, V
Children welcome, but not for evening meals unless over 8
Accessiblity wheelchair access to restaurant and ground floor only
Pets accepted if not left unattended (£20 per dog) **Closed** Sunday evenings, Mondays and Tuesdays
Proprietors Sarah Hudson and Richard Ireton

The Bell at Skenfrith
Country hotel

Though contemporary and cosy rarely coincide, this is one place that convincingly combines the two. Tucked into the fold of a hill in the Welsh Marches, it has all the ingredients for a winter break that metropolitans could wish for: a huge inglenook radiating heat, surrounded by sofa, settle and rocking chair; a candle-lit, flagstone dining room serving locally sourced modern British dishes by Chef Joseph Colman – planned around seasonal vegetables and fruits, some grown in The Bell's kitchen garden – along with a well-organised wine list; and 11 delightful, simple-sophisticated bedrooms. There is also an on-site bakery.

Formerly a 17thC coaching inn, The Bell stands on the Monnow River close to Skenfrith Castle in an unchanged village. When the river flooded the village in 2020 it prompted a renovation and a smart update of the downstairs spaces.

There are wonderful walks in the area; six circular routes leaving from the door have been created by the hotel, with picnics provided. When you get back, you can enjoy a Welsh cream tea while easing your sore feet.

WALES

CENTRAL ENGLAND AND WALES

Tal-y-llyn, Gwynedd

Tal-y-llyn, Tywyn, Gwynedd LL36 9AJ

Tel 01654 761247
email info@dolffanogfawr.co.uk
website www.dolffanogfawr.co.uk

Nearby Cadair Idris, Snowdonia National Park, sandy beaches at Aberdyfi, Tywyn and Barmouth, Coed y Brenin Forest, Tal-y-llyn railway, Ynys Hir RSPB reserve, Dyfi Osprey Project **Location** Tal-y-llyn Valley at the foot of Cadair Idris mountain and overlooking Tal-y-llyn lake. **Food** breakfast, dinner **Price £ Rooms** 4; 3 double/twin, 1 double; all with shower and/or bath, Sky TV, wi-fi, hairdryer, L'Occataine toiletries **Facilities** guest sitting room with log fire, dining room, garden, private off-road parking, spa, secure storage for mountain bikes or fishing tackle, fishing on over 13 miles of local rivers and a mountain lake. **Credit cards** MC, V **Children** accepted over 7 **Accessibility** not suitable **Pets** by prior arrangement **Closed** Nov-mid Mar **Proprietors** Alex Yorke and Lorraine Hinkins

Dolffanog Fawr
Country guesthouse

Recommended by a trusted reporter, this unpretentious Welsh farmhouse, has four bedrooms done up in contemporary-traditional style, with restrained good taste. All the basics are spot on: Egyptian cotton sheets, best quality beds. Three of the rooms have window seats for pondering the views across the Tal-y-Llyn valley, with the superb Cadair Idris almost on the doorstep. A top-end, modern B&B, run by friendly Alex and Lorraine, and their son Morgan, who live in a separate wing. Guests can feel private in their own sitting room and dining room. A set-menu dinner is prepared four days a week by Lorraine, who spent years working alongside top chefs. Ingredients are largely taken from Welsh larder, including its renowed black beef and wild Dysynni sea trout – and served 'dinner party style' around a large oak table (with the option to eat separately.)

Think about coming here to enjoy the coast as well as the mountains – it's only half an hour from the sea. The scenery around here, north of the Dovey estuary, is exceptionally wild and beautiful, and less overrun than Snowdonia. While the main route up Cadair Idris starts from nearby Minfford, a non-standard route to the top begins within half an hour's walk of Dolffanog Fawr.

WALES

CENTRAL ENGLAND AND WALES

Three Cocks, Powys

Three Cocks, near Brecon, Powys
LD3 0SL

Tel 01497 847215
email bookings@threecockshotel.co.uk
website www.threecockshotel.co.uk

Nearby Brecon Beacons; Hay-on-Wye; Hereford Cathedral; Black Mountains.
Location in village, 11 miles (18 km) NE of Brecon on A438; ample car parking
Food breakfast, lunch, dinner
Price £-££
Rooms 7 double and twin, 6 with bath/shower, 1 with shower
Facilities sitting room, reception room with TV, dining room, breakfast room; large garden
Credit cards MC, V
Children welcome over age of 12
Accessibility difficult
Pets not accepted
Closed Jan
Proprietors Jess and Jack

Three Cocks
Country B&B

The building is a charming ivy-covered 15thC coaching inn in the Welsh hills, constructed around a tree (still in evidence in the kitchen) and with its cobbled forecourt on the most direct route from Hereford to Brecon. Inside, carved wood and stone walls continue the natural look of the exterior, with beams and eccentrically angled doorways serving as proof positive of antiquity. Under the new ownership of Jess and Jack charmingly friendly and enthusiastic atmosphereto draw people great distances to the warm welcome and roomy restaurant with its lace-covered tables. There are plenty of places where you can sit in peace, and residents have a drawing room of their own, in keeping with its public oak-panelled counterpart but with more light, stone and fabric in evidence. There is now also a coffee shop and bar, leading on to the extensive gardens, serving refreshments and light lunches.

Bedrooms are modest but comfortable and well equipped, with dark oak furniture and pale fabrics. The food is honest, hearty British fayre, making full use of the wealth of local sources, including the Black Mountain Salmon Smokery, as well as local cheeses and meats. Roy uses local merchant Tanners as his wine cellar, importing an eclectic range of wines from around the world.

WALES
CENTRAL ENGLAND AND WALES

Abergavenny, Monmouthshire

The Angel Hotel/The Walnut Tree Inn/restaurant

The Angel Hotel and The Walnut Tree restaurant are closely associated – the Griffith family, owners of The Angel, also have an interest in The Walnut Tree, which is run by Shaun Hill. The two places mark out Abergavenny as a useful gourmet base for exploring the Black Mountains.

Inside The Angel there's plenty of stylish architecture and various cosy bars and sitting rooms that are contemporary but still welcoming. The bedrooms are calming, with cream walls, wooden furniture and smart bathrooms; for more privacy there are seven self-catering cottages nearby.

It's a ten-minute taxi ride from The Angel to The Walnut Tree restaurant (which has two cottages), where Shaun presents a menu of uncomplicated yet sublime dishes.

15 Cross Street, Abergavenny, Monmouthshire NP7 9AA

Tel 01873 857121
email reservations@angelabergavenny.com
website www.angelabergavenny.com
Food breakfast, brunch, lunch, dinner, afternoon tea and on-site bakery
Price ££ **Closed** Christmas Day
Proprietor Caradog Hotels Ltd

Llyswen, Powys

Llangoed Hall
Country house hotel

With 23 bedrooms this (on the face of it) large and conventional country house hotel is a little outside the guide's territory, but our series editor Fiona Duncan rates it very highly. The house is imposing and beautifully restored by the late Sir Bernard Ashley, and wife Laura, of wallpaper and fabric fame. It houses his notable collection of 20thC British paintings.

Despite its formality, it's the type of place where guests are encouraged to be themselves – to curl up on the sofa, even play the piano. The rooms are charmingly done with antiques and pictures, fine linen, new bathrooms – guests will want to linger.

The food by Sam Brodie is imaginative. Those after a traditional Sunday lunch could find it helpful to know that it appears in the guise of a taster menu: crisps, purées and emulsions.

Llyswen, Brecon, Powys, Wales LD3 0YP

Tel 01874 754525
email enquiries@llangoedhall.com
website www.llangoedhall.co.uk
Food breakfast, lunch, dinner, afternoon tea
Price £££-££££ **Closed** never
Manager Calum Milne

MIDLANDS

CENTRAL ENGLAND AND WALES

Ashbourne, Derbyshire

Mappleton, Ashbourne, Derbyshire
DE6 2AA

Tel 01335 300900
email info@callowhall.co.uk
website www.callowhall.co.uk

Nearby Chatsworth House; Haddon Hall; Hardwick Hall.
Location 0.75 mile (1 km) N of Ashbourne off A515; with ample car parking
Food breakfast, lunch, afternoon tea, dinner **Price** £££
Rooms 15 in main house. Plus 2 self-catering treehouses and 11 smaller 'hives' sleeping 2-5.
Facilities sitting room, private dining room, inormal 'garden room' bar; garden, fishing **Credit cards** AE, DC, MC, V **Children** welcome
Accessibility suitable rooms in main house **Pets** dogs friendly rooms
Closed never
Proprietors Ed Burrows and Charles Randall

Callow Hall
Country hotel with treehouses

Since our last edition this place has probably had the most drastic update thanks to nature-inspired new owners 'Wildhive'. Set in extensive grounds at the entrance to the Peak District National Park, the hotel overlooks the stunning landscape of the Dove valley. The legacy of old owners the Spencers (master bakers in Ashbourne) is somewhat preserved in the main building, a fine Victorian country house hotel with flagstone floors, crackling fires and an excellent dining spaces. However, staying in the building is no-longer the only option. Now, spread through the grounds, woodlands and wild meadows are large treehouses and smaller 'hives' elevated above the ground. Set away from the house and with wrap-around decks the focus here is isolation in nature.

In their relaxed restaurant, 'The Garden Room, they serve many of their home-grown ingredients which can by enjoyed in front of floor-to-ceiling windows. Outdoors is always centre stage.

Carved antiques and family heirlooms mingle with period repro furniture. Ask for a decent-sized room when you book: one or two are on the small side for the price. Staff are helpful yet unobtrusive.

Reports welcome.

MIDLANDS
CENTRAL ENGLAND AND WALES

Ashford-in-the-Water, Derbyshire

Fennel Street, Ashford-in-the-Water, Bakewell, Derbyshire, DE4 1QF

Tel 01629 814275
email riversidehousehotel@btconnect.com
website www.riversidehousehotel.co.uk

Nearby Chatsworth; Haddon Hall; Bakewell.
Location 2 miles (3 km) NW of Bakewell off A6, at top of village, next to Sheepwash Bridge; with ample car parking
Food breakfast, lunch, dinner
Price £££
Rooms 14; 1 executive suite, 13 double/twin, all with bath/shower; all rooms have phone, TV, hairdryer
Facilities 1 sitting room, conservatory, bar, 4 dining rooms; garden
Credit cards AE, DC, MC, V
Children welcome over 16
Accessibilty possible to 4 rooms
Pets not accepted **Closed** never
Chef Patron Tom Lawson

Riverside House
Restaurant-with-rooms

Nestling in one of the Peak District's prettiest villages, this stone-built, ivy-clad house, has an idyllic setting in its own secluded grounds, bordered by the river Wye. The village is aptly named – on our inspector's visit during a spate of heavy rain, the river was threatening to encroach, but the hotel's manager was coping admirably, sandbags at the ready, with the possibility of a flood alert.

Chef-patron Tom Lawson has maintained a refreshingly plain style, entirely in keeping with the house's Georgian origins. A large plant-filled conservatory leads into a cosy snug with a recessed carved-oak mantelpiece and open fire. There is an elegant, comfortable sitting room and a variety of well-equipped bedrooms of different sizes. Rooms in the newer Garden wing overlook the river.

Crucial to Riverside is its reputation for fine food served in the Rafters restaurant which offers imaginative dishes such as *mille-feuille* of marinated salmon with beetroot *confit*, and celery and wild mushroom *strüdel*; there's an intriguing selection of cheeses, too – Lincolnshire Poacher, Belineigh Blue and Gubbeen.

MIDLANDS

CENTRAL ENGLAND AND WALES

Barford

Lower St, Barford St Michael,
Banbury OX15 0RH

Tel 01869 338160
email info@thegeorgebarford.co.uk
website www.thegeorgebarford.co.uk

Nearby Banbury, The Cotswolds, Bleinheim Palace
Location close to M40, convenient for Banbury and Oxford
Food breakfast, lunch, dinner
Price ££-£££
Rooms 3; 2 double with bathroom and 1 suite with bathroom
Facilities dining room, sitting room, terrace, conservatory
Credit cards MC, V
Children welcome
Accessibility limited only
Pets dogs welcome in some rooms
Closed never
Proprietors Michael Regan

The George Inn
Village inn

Copper-bottomed, all-round quality, plus an individual vibe. The 16thC thatched building's location, in a low-key village, is upstaged by its neighbours a few miles west in the Cotswolds, but being in a real village rather than tourist spot can be part of the charm. Our reporter stayed in Room 1: spacious for its reasonable price tag. Just as good were the eclectic furnishings: an antique mahogany hanging cupboard; bedside lamps, both different; a super-wide, very comfortable bed; beamy ceiling.

The ground floor has been opened up in the usual dining pub manner, enabling all comers to co-exist seamlessly: locals at the bar; a chatty hen party around the fireside space; then two further dining areas the far side of the bar. The Conservatory at the rear can seat up to 40 at one long table, but the layout is usually for smaller parties. The food is reasonably priced and outstanding: freshly cooked restaurant dishes such as local venison and red wine casserole or vegetable and lentil stew alongside gastropub staples. Our reporter's chicken schnitzel was knock-out. On the drinks list Constantia dessert wine is evidence of the sophistication and know-how of new, hands-on owners. They are getting the basics right and providing imaginative touches such as the 60s album covers decorating a whole wall and the neon George Inn installation in the Conservatory.

Barnsley, Gloucestershire

Barnsley, Cirencester,
Gloucestershire GL7 5EF

Tel 01285 740421
email info@thevillagepub.co.uk
website www.thevillagepub.co.uk

Nearby Cotswold Water Park, riding, Cirencester, Daylesford Organics
Location Barnsley village with free parking
Food breakfast, lunch, dinner
Price £££
Rooms 6, all have bath/shower
Facilities restaurant, bar as well as access to spa and cinema at Barnsley House (across the road)
Credit cards AE, DC, MC, V
Children welcome
Accessibility no special facilities
Pets welcome
Closed never
Proprietors Timothy Oulton

The Boot
Country pub

Don't come here for authenticity or the laid-back village pub atmosphere. This place, formerly The Village Pub was recently brought by designer Timothy Oulton. After one month serious reonvations the rebranded Boot is now a great spot if you are after something of chic, contemporary sister Barnsley House's luxury and style at half the price. Still, it's a classic Cotswold haven: warm and inviting, with low wooden ceiling beams, intresting artworks and well chosen antique furniture. Highlights of the quirky artefacts displayed around the building include a fossilised dinosaur tooth.

The bedrooms are not large, but have creamy, sophisticated good looks and top bathrooms. They are colourful but not garish.

It would be worth coming for the food alone. The menu, devisde by Chef John Jewell, consists of imaginative variations on classic English dishes, beautifully presented. For drinking, as this is first and foremost a local pub, there is an extensive wine, cocktail and beer list. Local ales are best enjoyed sipped from custom pewter tankards.

In a prime location for exploring the Cotswolds, the hotel also provides free bicycle hire.

MIDLANDS

CENTRAL ENGLAND AND WALES

Birmingham

St Paul's Square, Birmingham
B3 1QU

Tel 0121 272 0999
email info@siantpaulshouse.com
website www.saintpaulshouse.com

Nearby Birmingham Hippodrome, Birmingham Museum and Gallery, Gas Street Basin, Ikon Gallery, The Bullring
Location Birmingham business district, near Snow Hill and New Street ttrain stations
Food breakfast, lunch, dinner
Price ££-£££
Rooms 34; doubles, singles and king doubles all with bathrooms
Facilities restaurant, bar, terrace
Credit cards all major
Children welcome
Accessibility some suitability
Pets no
Closed never
Proprietors Adrian and Sharon Harvey

Saint Paul's House
City hotel

After more than 30 years, here is the first hotel in Birmingham we feel right for the guide. Its charm is down to the location and its large, welcoming ground floor bar-dining-relaxation area. Leafy St Paul's Square is the city's last surviving Georgian square, its centrepiece the handsome church of St Paul's. Compared with other districts of the city, it's gracious, unhurried and the building style is relatively harmonious. A curious logo hangs above the main entrance: a pair of pliers and a geometry compass set one quarter open. This is the Jewellery Quarter.

Mellow, exposed brickwork is the main feature of the bar-dining area. It's urban-contemporary without being try-hard. Some tables are conventional height, some chest height, convenient for quick eats or a drink. The large walk-around bar offers 30 different gins while the gastro-cafe food is reasonably priced. Over to one side, near a door leading to a staircase and lift, is the hotel reception desk. The hotel part of the operation feels as if it might be an afterthought, but once you've reached your room you should be more than happy. Prices for these comfortable rooms are keen for a city centre. Bath-shower rooms are sparkling and mainly white tiled. Mattresses and linen are irreproachable quality. You can park in the hotel's large car park for a reasonable charge.

MIDLANDS

CENTRAL ENGLAND AND WALES

Bishop's Castle, Shropshire

The Square, Bishop's Castle,
Shropshire SY9 5BN

Tel 01588 638403
email
stay@thecastlehotelbishopscastle.co.uk
website
www.thecastlehotelbishopscastle.co.uk

Nearby Ludlow, Shrewsbury, Clun, Welshpool, Welsh borders, Offa's Dyke, South Shropshire Hills, Bishop's Castle centre, arts and crafts shops
Location overlooking Bishop's Castle, around 30 mins away from Ludlow and Shrewsbury
Food breakfast, lunch, dinner
Price £
Rooms 13; double, single and twin (Master, Standard, Smaller) all with en-suite bath or shower **Facilities** 3 bars, restaurant, garden, terrace
Credit cards MC, V **Children** welcome **Accessibility** not easily accessible
Pets welcome **Closed** never
Proprietors Henry & Rebecca Hunter

The Castle Hotel
Town hotel

Built in 1719 by Lord Carnarvon, on the site of an old motte and bailey, the Castle Hotel stands overlooking the town of Bishop's Castle surrounded by Shropshire countryside. They do things traditionally here: wooden panelling, roaring open fires, chalk board menus, bar billiards and a fine selection of real ales.

The 12 rooms are spacious, pretty and unpretentious, with wooden furniture, original features and views right over the gardens, town and countryside. Some have high, gabled ceilings.

With Ludlow only down the road, the kitchen has a fine range of suppliers from which to choose, and makes good use of them. The menu has the same traditional feel as the hotel, but with a modern twist. Meals are hearty, healthy and fresh. Guests can dine in one of the three bustling bars or more serenely in the oak-panelled restaurant, The Oak Room. In the summer, many eat outside on the vine-covered terrace, overlooking the fishponds. At least five real ales are usually on tap, and a comprehensive wine list is also on hand.

Ludlow, Shrewsbury and mid-Wales are all within easy reach, and the South Shropshire hills offer some excellent walking. Bishop's Castle is a pretty little town with plenty of antique shops and tea rooms.

MIDLANDS

CENTRAL ENGLAND AND WALES

Bledington, Oxfordshire

The Grn, Chipping Norton OX7 6XQ

Tel 01608 658365
email info@kingsheadinn.net
website www.thekingsheadinn.net

Nearby Chipping Norton, Oxford, Blenheim Palace
Location 6 miles from Chipping Norton and 4 miles from Stow on the Wold.
Food breakfast, lunch, dinner
Price ££-£££
Rooms 12; some in main building others in courtyard
Facilities dining room, pub, courtyard
Credit cards MC, V
Children welcome
Accessiblity suitable
Pets dogs welcome
Closed never
Proprietors Nicola and Archie Orr-Ewing

The Kings Head
Village inn

We revisited for this edition and were struck afresh with how naturally the building dovetails into its classic Cotswold village location. At the edge of a large unspoiled green, intersected by streams, with swings for the children and bench-tables close by, a set designer couldn't have done better. Inside, its rustic character has been faithfully preserved, a warren of cosy eating and drinking areas encircling the central bar. Maybe it would be even better if there was a space for flopping on sofas and armchairs.

The menu, with nine starters and 13 mains has more choice than many a gastropub. The devilled lamb's kidneys are a major draw, but don't overlook the somewhat unusual offerings such as ribollita soup; baked Vacherin with roast garlic; split pea, lentil and coconut dal; shin of beef with swede mash. The drinks menu takes care of drivers: among ten choices is Zingi bear, a low-alcohol ginger ale which thirsty farmers used to slurp at work, then afterwards spike with spirits.

Six bedrooms in the pub and six around a courtyard are unpretentious, comfortable enough and fairly priced. As we went to press owners Nicola and Archie had maintained standards here for 25 years, offering a friendly welcome and overseeing contented, motivated staff. A well-designed leaflet describes three circular walks from the pub.

MIDLANDS
CENTRAL ENGLAND AND WALES

Bourton-on-the-Hill, Gloucestershire

Bourton-on-the-Hill, Moreton in Marsh, Gloucestershire GL56 9AQ

Tel 01386 700413
email enquiries@horseandgroom.info
website www.horseandgroom.info

Nearby Chipping Campden, Daylesford, Stratford-upon-Avon.
Location follow A44 from Moreton-in-Marsh and Horse & Groom is at top of hill on left-hand side
Food breakfast (included in price of room), lunch, dinner
Price ££-£££
Rooms 5 double; all with TV, Bramley produces, tea/coffee, wi-fi
Facilities TV, hairdryer, wi-fi, garden, restaurant
Credit cards MC, V
Children welcome
Accessibility no access
Pets welcome in main bar area, and most bedrooms (enquire when booking)
Closed never
Proprietors Epicurean Inns

Horse and Groom
Pub-with-rooms

While long-term regulars might pine after the affable welcome from previous owners Will and Tom Greenstock, they won't find much else changed. Now run by Epicurean Inns, the pub-with-rooms is now a more low-key and countrified affair (it's dog-friendly, with a more neutral colour scheme) but it's still full of character.

The fun starts in the kitchen and its seasonal, daily changing menu, with offerings often changing in the course of service as one successfully finished dish becomes replaced with a fresh alternative. Atmosphere in the dining room is laid-back and service energetic and friendly.

Each of the five bedrooms is light and spacious and abounds with finesse and modern finery. While some may find the shapes and colours in the rooms a little too eclectic for their taste, many will think it's rather invigorating to offer chequered chairs in one room or vibrant metallics in another. A pristine view of the Cotswolds helps to compensate for some noise from the road and the downstairs pub that affects one or two rooms.

A hearty breakfast is served and, like dinner, offers fresh ingredients and local produce. Prices are very reasonable, and visitors come away saying the Horse & Groom is an 'imaginative' but 'unpretentious' place which won't stand still.

MIDLANDS

CENTRAL ENGLAND AND WALES

Bourton-on-the-Water, Gloucestershire

High Street, Bourton-on-the-Water,
Gloucestershire, GL54 2AN

Tel 01451 822 244
email info@dialhousehotel.com
website www.dialhousehotel.com

Nearby Burford, Blenheim, Upper and Lower Slaughter
Location in the heart of the village with large hotel car park
Food breakfast, lunch, tea, dinner
Price £££-££££
Rooms 13 rooms
Facilities bar, sitting-room, garden
Credit cards all major
Children over 12
Accessibile a garden room is accessible by wheelchair
Pets well-behaved dogs allowed in bar area, but not in rooms
Closed one week in Jan
Proprietor Haley Davies

Dial House
Country hotel

The Dial House attracts a certain type of client and that type of client will like it very much. It's a place to forget boardroom worries, and enjoy being pampered. In the summer, Bourton-on-the-Water can be crowded, so the neat garden behind the hotel gives guests a place to escape the hordes.

The place is spotless. Rooms are furnished comfortably, and a number of them have been recently refurbished. Bathrooms have roll-top free-standing baths, Elemis toiletries and piles of thick white towels.

A small bar downstairs caters for all tastes, including a selection from a local brewery. A sitting-room for residents has a log fire in winter and brightly coloured modern chairs, for the owners are careful not to let this honey-coloured 17th century house become too old-fashioned. The two recently refurbished dining rooms are cosy and relaxed, serving breakfast, afternoon teas, and dishes combining both English and Mediterranean influences, with classical and modern techniques. Try the spicy meatballs with *linguine*.

MIDLANDS

CENTRAL ENGLAND AND WALES

Burford, Oxfordshire

99 High Street, Burford,
Oxfordshire OX18 4QA

Tel 01993 823151
email stay@burford-house.co.uk
website www.burford-house.co.uk

Nearby Cotswold Wildlife Park;
Blenheim Palace; Broadway.
Location middle of Burford High
Street; parking in street or free car
park nearby
Food breakfast, lunch, dinner
Price ££
Rooms 6 doubles with bath and
shower; all rooms have TV, wi-fi,
hairdryer
Facilities Bar area, dining room,
courtyard garden
Credit cards AE, MC, V **Children**
welcome
Accessibility no ground floor rooms
Pets not accepted in rooms, but welcomed in bar and garden
Closed Christmas
Proprietors Steven and Karen
Nolan
Manager Scott Hoare

Burford House
Town house hotel

Without disturbing its historical integrity, you'll find 21stC comforts in the 15thC Cotswold stone and black-and-white timbered house in the heart of Burford. The whole place positively gleams with personal care and attention, with fresh flowers, books and magazines in the smartly decorated, dark-beamed bedrooms, and their own belongings dotted amongst the public furniture. The Italian-inspired restaurant and bar area are a real hit with the locals and tourists, bringing a relaxed and informal atmosphere for the downstairs bit. There is also a garden room looking out on to the lovely courtyard garden.

Upstairs there are six bedrooms, three with four-posters and a few of these also have huge free-standing baths. Each thoughtfully organized room is full of character, and each has an immaculate bathroom. Breakfast (included in the price of the room) is well above average, served in the dining room looking out on to the High Street.

MIDLANDS

Burford, Oxfordshire

Sheep Street, Burford, Oxfordshire
OX18 4LR

Tel 01993 823155
email info@lambinn-burford.co.uk
website www.cotswold-inns-hotels.co.uk/lamb-inn/

Nearby Minster Lovell Hall;
Cotswold villages; Blenheim Palace.
Location in village; with car parking
Food breakfast, lunch, dinner
Price £££
Rooms 17 double and twin with bath or shower; all have phone, TV, hairdryer, wi-fi
Facilities 3 sitting rooms, dining room, bar; garden
Credit cards AE, MC, V
Children welcome
Accessibility 1 ground-floor bedrooms **Pets** dogs in room by prior arrangement
Closed never
Proprietors Cotswold Inns and Hotels
Manager Bill Ramsay

The Lamb
Town inn

If you want some respite from Burford's summer throng, you won't do better than The Lamb, only a few yards behind the High Street, but a haven of tranquillity — particularly in the pretty walled garden, a view endorsed by a recent inspection.

Inside the creeper-clad stone cottages, you won't be surprised to find traditional pub trappings (after all, The Lamb has been an inn since the 15th century), but you may be surprised to discover 17 spacious beamed bedrooms decorated with plush fabrics and antiques. All are different Shepherd, for example, has a vast antique four-poster bed and a little attic-like bathroom, Malt (in what was once the neighbouring brewery) has a lavish canopy over the bed and large stone mullion windows.

Head chef Piotr Galski produces the daily-changing menus served in the dining room, looking on to the geranium-filled patio. Coffee is served there, or in one of the sitting rooms, both of which have comfortable chairs and sofas grouped around open fires.

The Lamb Inn has been part of the Cotswold Inns and Hotels collection since 2005. Reports welcome.

MIDLANDS

CENTRAL ENGLAND AND WALES

Clearwell, Gloucestershire

Clearwell, Royal Forest of Dean, Gloucestershire, GL16 8JS

Tel 01594 833046
email info@tudorfarmhouse-hotel.co.uk
website www.tudorfarmhousehotel.co.uk

Nearby Clearwell Caves & Puzzlewood within 2km, Monmouth 11km, Chepstow 18km, Bristol 50km, Cardiff 700km
Location Clearwell village, in the Forest of Dean and Wye Valley
Food breakfast, lunch, afternoon tea, grazing menu, dinner
Price ££-££££
Rooms 20 double (4 can be twin); all have TV, wi-fi, hairdryer, coffee/tea facilities inc. a Nespresso machine, bathrobes **Facilities** gardens (and 14 acres SSSI land) - walks, sitting room with log burner
Credit cards MC, V, AM
Children welcome
Accessibility ground floor rooms available **Pets** accepted in 3 rooms, £10 per night **Closed** never
Proprietors Colin and Hari Fell

Tudor Farmhouse
Country hotel

Clearwell is a small west Gloucestershire village near the Welsh border surrounded by fields, so this place feels countrified and peaceful even though you enter from the village high street. Until recently it was a farm and although transformation has been achieved in several stages, it all hangs together. The 20-plus rooms, cottages and suites are placed around various buildings, but the feel is small and intimate. Old stonework and timber has been preserved in the public areas, there are log burning stoves, country antiques and freshly cut rustic flowers.

The bedrooms are stylish yet homely – contemporary but not wannabee-trendy. Hari and Colin Fell have paid attention to the basics – pocket sprung mattresses, good linen, thick towels, duck down pillows – and achieved an imaginative, unstuffy but stylish overall decorative effect.

Chef Rob Cox uses locally sourced ingredients where possible in his traditional dishes with a modern twist: a popular dish is seared sea bream with braised leeks. The menu has a sensible range of offerings from light lunchtime bites to full celebration dinners. It's becoming a local food destination. There's plenty to do around here: golf, fishing, canoing. They'll even tell you the best spots for a wild swim.

Clipsham, Rutland

Main Street, Clipsham, Rutland
LE15 7SH

Tel 01780 410355
email info@theolivebranchpub.com
website
www.theolivebranchpub.com

Nearby Burghley, Belvoir Castle, Rutland Owl and Falconry Centre
Location in the centre of Clipsham
Food breakfast, lunch, dinner
Price ££-££££
Rooms 6 en-suite; all rooms have TV, radio, tea and coffee making facilities; wifi
Facilities Patio, garden, pub
Credit cards MC, V
Children welcome
Accessibility fully wheelchair-accessible room
Pets well-behaved dogs accepted in some rooms (£10 charge) **Closed** Christmas night, Boxing day, New Year's day **Proprietors** Sean Hope and Ben Jones

Beech House
Country Inn

The Beech House is where you sleep, but the Olive Branch began it all and the two, though divided by the road, are really indivisible. So good was the food in the pub (named to mark the end of a quarrel with a farmer; this is not an ordinary place) that rooms were needed to house those who had travelled to enjoy it. What looks like a pretty doll's-house was bought and six en-suite rooms were made, decorated with fashionable modern colours and furnished with a mix of rather striking antique and modern pieces.

The thoughtful management has provided a fully wheelchair-accessible bathroom in the ground floor room. There are four types of tea in the bedrooms and fresh coffee for the cafetière; a Roberts radio, and a choice of duvets or sheets and blankets.

MIDLANDS — CENTRAL ENGLAND AND WALES

Fairford, Gloucestershire

The Market Place, Fairford, Gloucestershire, GL7 4AA

Tel 01285 712535
email info@thebullhotelfairford.co.uk
website thebullhotelfairford.co.uk

Nearby Tewkesbury Abbey; Malvern Hills.
Location on River Coln, 6m east of Cirencester, 4m west of Lechlade
Food breakfast, lunch, afternoon tea, dinner
Price ££££
Rooms 21; 3 standard double, 3 superior double, 6 luxury double, 6 twin, 2 family **Facilities** 24hr reception, wi-fi, on and off-site parking, restaurant, bar, sitting room, baggage store
Credit cards AE, DC, MC, V
Children welcome
Accessibility bar is wheelchair accessible but rooms are not
Pets not allowed **Closed** never
Proprietor Sebastian and Lana Snow

The Bull
Country hotel

A welcome addition to Sebastian and Lana Snow's family of Cotswold pubs, The Bull is a bigger, more bustling affair, situated in Fairford's pretty Market Square in a building dating back to the 15thC. Inside, they've executed their signature shabby-chic style with extra flair. There are the usual Alpine touches, such as cow-skin rugs and mounted antlers. There's also a muraled sitting room, and an elegant mustard morning room. Guests can eat in the intimate restaurant, or the sultry burnt-orange Stables (horse rails intact). Or, if they're feeling fancy, the magisterial Bull Room, with its own bar, chandeliers, and a long table seating 40 – ideal for raucous dinners. Like any good pub, it's cosy, with several roaring hearths and rich fir-green walls, with flashes of original stone.

Upstairs, the 21 rooms, decorated by Joe Titchener and Lana Snow, are proper Costwold affairs, complete with Wold Garden toiletries and Costwold Woollen Weavers throws – painted in soothing greys with judicious splashes of colour.

With stiff competition from trendy pubs in the area, their strength is, undoubtedly, the food. Chef Sebastian oversees a menu of exceptional pub fare, full of robust flavours: try his twice-baked Double Gloucester cheese soufflé.

MIDLANDS
CENTRAL ENGLAND AND WALES

Faringdon, Oxfordshire

Faringdon, Oxfordshire SN7 8RF

Tel 01367 870382
email info@troutinn.co.uk
website www.troutinn.co.uk

Nearby Vale of the White Horse; Kelmscott Manor; Chimney Nature Reserve; Blenheim Palace; Bampton; 20 mins from Oxford town centre
Location on the River Thames in the Cotswolds
Food breakfast, lunch, dinner
Price ££
Rooms 6; all with TV, radio
Facilities bar, dining room, garden
Credit cards DC, MC, V
Children welcome
Accessibility 4 accessible rooms
Pets welcome **Closed** Christmas and Boxing Day
Landlord Simon Young

The Trout at Tadpole Bridge Bed-and-breakfast

In this little-known, idyllic spot in Oxfordshire, the river flowing under Tadpole Bridge's diminutive span is, in fact, the Thames. Many customers arrive by boat, for a pint of ale or a night ashore. The Trout's garden runs down to the water, where there are moorings for patrons using the pub.

The old brick inn has the hallmarks of a modernised pub-with-rooms, but in landlord Simon Young's hands they add up to an unpretentious, family-friendly place to stay. There are lovely bedrooms that make you stop in surprise, a clutch of faithful regulars propping up the bar. Staff are local and cheerful.

The Trout, where the infant Thames is at its most peaceful, trickling under Tadpole Bridge, provides the most delightful base for a weekend away: downstream are the wildflower meadows and wading birds of the Chimney Nature Reserve; across the fields is Bampton, one of the oldest villages in the county; Blenheim Palace is within easy reach.

Great Rissington, Gloucestershire

Great Rissington, Gloucestershire
GL54 2LP

Tel 01451 820388
email enquiry@thelambinn.com
website www.thelambinn.com

Nearby The Slaughters; Stow-on-the-Wold; Burford; Sudeley Castle.
Location 4 miles (6 km) SE of Bourton-on-the-Water, 3 miles (5 km) N of A40; with ample car parking
Food breakfast, lunch, dinner
Price ££
Rooms 14; 4 suites in The Lamb Inn, 2 garden suites, 5 pub rooms, 2 stable rooms, all with bath or shower; all rooms have TV, wi-fi
Facilities sitting room, bar; garden
Credit cards AE, MC, V
Children welcome
Accesiblity not suitable
Pets accepted in bedrooms by arrangement
Closed never
Proprietors Paul and Jacqueline Gabriel

The Lamb Inn
Country inn

If you follow the River Windrush as it rises westwards from Burford, and then roughly follow its curve from the north (where it has given Bourton-on-the-Water its name), you will arrive in Great Rissington, deep in the Cotswolds. Overlooking gently rolling farmland and built from the local stone, the original elements of this inn are 300 years old. Taken over in the year 2000 by Paul and Jackie Gabriel, The Lamb is still very much a pub, indeed it is enough of a pub to merit a recommendation in a national guide to good beer. But it also now has two elements that many other inns lack – good board and lodging. Board comes in the shape of a surprisingly large – and comfortingly busy – restaurant. It does a roaring trade in traditional dishes freshly prepared from the best of local produce, often with a modern twist. Prices are reasonable: on our latest visit just before going to press we enjoyed the lamb shoulder (£26) and the pie of the day (£19).

The bedrooms are bright, fresh and individually designed, and more than half have space for sitting as well as sleeping. All bathrooms have recently been renovated, and updating the rooms of this 400 year-old property is an ongoing project.

MIDLANDS

CENTRAL ENGLAND AND WALES

Hambleden, Oxfordshire

Hambleden, Henley-on-Thames, Oxfordshire RG9 6RP

Tel 01491 571227
email enquiries@thestagandhuntsman.co.uk
website www.thestagandhuntsman.co.uk

Nearby Hell-fire caves, Clivedon, Henley-on-Thames, The Hughenden Manor
Location Hambleden village, just off Skirmett Road
Food breakfast, lunch, dinner
Price ££
Rooms 8 doubles with private bathrooms **Facilities** bar, restaurant, beer garden **Credit cards** all major
Children welcome
Accessibility not suitable
Pets welcome in some rooms and all public areas apart from the restaurant
Closed never
Proprietor David Holliday

The Stag & Huntsman
Village inn

The Stag and Huntsman is a Chilterns institution and a welcoming hub for the community. Taken over from Urs Schwarzenbach in 2023 by hotelier-publican David Holliday of Sika Inns, this building is leased from Urs and the Culden Faw Estate - 3,500 acres of explorable woodlands, chalk valleys, farmland and the river Thames.

The place thrives, even with a more sober appearance than other similar places. The handsome dark green livery may stray from contemporary colour palettes, but it's authentic and a refreshing change. It's said that architect Ptolemy Dean, who restored The Stag and Huntsman on behalf of the Culden Faw Estate, cried out "That's the colour!" as an innocent man strolled past in a dark green Barbour.

The whole place has echoes of elderly relatives – in a pleasing way – right down to the tessellated tile floors and the narrow staircase. But it has attitude – we were pleased to find a retro Roberts radio in our room.

The food is superior pub fare and as we went to press Chef Dom Robinson was about to take over the kitchen. We anticpate good things and would welcome reports on how he gets on.

MIDLANDS
CENTRAL ENGLAND AND WALES

Hambleton, Rutland

Hambleton, Oakham, Rutland
LE15 8TH

Tel 01572 756991
email hotel@hambletonhall.com
website www.hambletonhall.com

Nearby Burghley House; Rockingham Castle; Stamford, Belvoir Castle.
Location 2 miles E of Oakham on peninsula jutting into Rutland Water; with ample car parking
Food breakfast, lunch, dinner
Price ££££
Rooms 15 double and twin with bath; all rooms have phone, TV, hairdryer
Facilities sitting rooms, 3 dining rooms, bar; garden, swimming pool, tennis, helipad; fishing, golf, sailing, riding all nearby **Credit cards** AE, DC, MC, V **Children** accepted
Accessibility some rooms accessible via lift **Pets** by arrangement **Closed** never **Proprietors** Tim and Stefa Hart

Hambleton Hall
Country house hotel

If you're planning a second honeymoon, a break from work or a weekend away from the kids, this Victorian former shooting lodge in the grand hotel tradition is a sybaritic paradise, from which only your wallet and your waistline will suffer. The location is unrivalled, standing in stately grandeur on a wooded hillock, surrounded by manicured lawns, surveying the expanse of Rutland Water. The interior is sumptuous. In her design of the rooms, Stefa Hart uses rich, heavy fabrics in some of the bedrooms, and shows a preference for delicate colours. The rooms still have their original mouldings and are furnished with fine antiques and paintings. Bedrooms with a view over the water are the most sought-after and expensive.

Many people are drawn here by the wizardry of Michelin-starred chef, Aaron Patterson. He works his magic on only the freshest of ingredients, whether Hambleton beef, sea bass or veal sweetbreads. One of the joys of staying here is that you can blow the cobwebs away with an exhilarating walk from the front door of the hotel as far as you want around Rutland Water, birdwatching as you go.

Some time ago the Harts opened a home bakery – Hambleton Bakery – that makes a variety of breads and cakes. We particularly like their Hambleton Sourdough loaf.

MIDLANDS
CENTRAL ENGLAND AND WALES

Hampton-in-Arden, Solihill

Shadowbrook Lane, Hampton-In-Arden, B92 0DQ

Tel 01675 446080
email info@hamptonmanor.com
website www.hamptonmanor.com

Nearby Birmingham airport; Birmingham train station; Solihull; Stratford upon Avon; Royal Leamington Spa; Warwick; Birmingham City Centre
Location in 45 acres of woodland
Food breakfast, lunch, dinner, snacks, room service, afternoon tea
Price ££-££££
Rooms 15 doubles; of which 8 can be twinned. All come with fresh coffee to grind, bluetooth audio system, home-baked cookies, toiletries from 100 Acres **Facilities** bar; lounge; restaurant; 2 beauty treatment rooms; 45 acres of woodland
Credit cards AE, DC, MC, V
Accessbilty one room specially adapted **Pets** not accepted **Closed** Dec 23rd - Dec 28th
Proprietor Joshua Oakes, House Manager

Hampton Manor
Manor house hotel

Original and refreshing. Owner, James Hill employs a young team, and the result is rejuvenating. The feel of this grand, old 15-bedroom manor house is unexpectedly relaxed, but every bit as professional as you'd expect. Hampton Manor could well be leading the way for the next generation of independent hoteliers.

Each of the 15 rooms has been thoughtfully decorated and furnished with contemporary designer John Reeves' Louis Collection. Bathrooms are stunning and come with tasteful mosaics and monsoon showers. The bedrooms are opulent, with deep-wine hues, velour furnishings and oversized headboards.

Enjoy a drink before dinner in the cosy residents' bar (Fred's Bar). Two restaurants can be found at either end of the walled garden - Smoke and Grace & Savour. There is also a bakery. Service is personal and friendly, making Hampton Manor seem more like a restaurant-with-rooms than a hotel in a manor house.

The grounds are almost as grand as the house itself: 45 acres of majestic woodland. You'll often see James' father working on his tractor. The nearby village of Hampton-in-Arden is picturesque, and well worth the short walk.

MIDLANDS

CENTRAL ENGLAND AND WALES

Hereford, Herefordshire

Castle Street, Hereford
HR1 2NW

Tel 01432 356321
email info@castlehse.co.uk
website www.castlehse.co.uk

Nearby Hereford Cathedral, chained library, Mappa Mundi, cider museum, Offa's Dyke
Location In Hereford city centre on Castle Street; valet parking
Food breakfast, lunch, dinner
Price £££
Rooms 24; 17 suites, 3 doubles, 4 singles, all with bath, TV, phone, video player, mini hi-fi, fridge, safe
Facilities lounge, dining room, bar, gardens, terrace
Credit cards AE, DC, MC, V
Children welcome
Accessibility one adapted room
Pets not accepted
Closed never
Proprietor George Watkins

Castle House
Town house hotel

Life goes at a slower pace in this rural part of England and Hereford is the ideal county town: tight-knit, accessible and tranquil, yet with world-class attractions in its fine cathedral and Chained Library. Castle House is an elegant Grade II listed town mansion whose charming gardens overlook the old Castle moat. The cathedral and shops are nearby, yet there is absolute quiet: no traffic noise, just birdsong and the quack of ducks. We can think of few lovelier, or better sited, city hotels in Britain.

Past the pillared entrance, you find an impressive hall, with wooden central staircase and reception tucked neatly out of sight. To one side: a private room for guests and to the other, a spacious restaurant and sitting room. French doors open on to the pretty garden where the hotel's new, waterside restaurant and bar overlook the Hereford Castle moat.

Upstairs are 15 luxury guest rooms of various shapes and sizes, all with ensuite bathrooms. The hotel has been revamped over the last few years, including 8 new rooms in Number 25, a townhouse just a minute away from the main house.

The management is excellent and the food imaginative, served by head chef Gabor Katona.

MIDLANDS

CENTRAL ENGLAND AND WALES

Hough-on-the-Hill, Lincolnshire

Hough-on-the-Hill, Grantham Road, Lincolnshire NG32 2AZ

Tel 01400 250234
email armsinn@yahoo.co.uk
website www.thebrownlowarms.com

Nearby Belton House, Lincoln Cathedral, Lincoln Castle, Belvoir Castle, Tattershall Castle
Location 5-10 minutes from A1, village of Hough on the Hill
Food breakfast, dinner (Tues-Sat), Sunday lunch
Price £-££
Rooms 5; 1 in the barn conversion, 4 in the pub, all with en suite, TV, hairdryers, wi-fi, phone **Facilities** bar, restaurant, terrace **Credit cards** MC, V
Children accepted over 8
Accessibility 1 room on ground floor in barn conversion, but some steps into the pub
Pets not accepted
Closed Christmas Day and Boxing Day, 1-14th Jan
Proprietors Paul and Lorraine Willoughby

The Brownlow Arms
Restaurant-with-rooms

Lorraine Willoughby has worked at The Brownlow Arms since she was 17; she and Paul now own and run it together.

The rooms are stylishly decorated under the acute eye of Paul. We entered our room through a wide lobby, beyond which our room opened out. The dramatic focal point of the room was a white bed framed by a huge antique oak mantelpiece on the wall behind, padded in the middle to create a headboard, with a capacious red sofa at the end of the bed. The other rooms in the inn and house next door are decorated in fresh checks and stripes, and displayed an equally impressive attention to detail (not to mention well-equipped with television, radio, and ironing board).

The restaurant makes a refreshing change from modern, wood-floored pub dining rooms – you get warm panelling, stone fireplace and high-backed, medieval-style striped pattern chairs. The dining room has recently been refurbished, as has the patio terrace, where you can eat and drink in the summer. We couldn't fault the food: all the dishes (such as bresaola with gazpacho jelly and parmesan crisp) were gracefully and swiftly presented.

This place gives value for money – the bedrooms could easily be in a luxury town house hotel at double the price.

MIDLANDS
CENTRAL ENGLAND AND WALES

Kelmscott, Oxfordshire

Kelmscott, Lechlade,
Gloucestershire, GL7 3HG

Tel 01367 253543
email info@theploughinnkelmscott.com
website www.theploughinnkelmscott.com

Nearby cycling, horse riding, sailing, indoor climbing, tennis, Kelmscott House, festivals
Location Oxford, Cheltenham & Cirencester are approx. 25 min drive; based near stretch of Thames Path
Food lunch & dinner Tue-Sun, closed for food on Mon
Price £-££
Rooms 8; 7 double, 1 single, all with wi-fi, TV, shower
Facilities bar, restaurant, free parking, childrens menu, highchairs
Credit cards all major
Children welcome
Accessibility no special facilities
Pets not allowed
Closed never
Proprietor Sebastian and Lana Snow

The Plough
Country inn

The most low-key of Sebastian and Lana Snow's three Costwold pubs (a stone's-throw from the more party-centric Five Alls in Filkins and The Bull at Fairford, page 212), The Plough is a quintessentailly cosy country inn, aptly situated in the idyllic village of Filkins. The decoration of its diminutive interior is wisely understated, letting the 17thC features speak for themselves: low beamed ceilings, flagstone floors, and antique wooden benches set before the toasty wood-burning stove. A few small but effective flourishes give it the shabby-chic stamp of the Snow pubs, such as a pair of oversized pheasant-feather lamp shades mounted on old wheels, casting a warm dappled glow on the dining area.

If the interior is understated, the food packs a punch. Sebastian, who's worked as a chef for 30 years, has devised a menu that's both earthy and sophisticated. We enjoyed chicken liver pâté with spiced plum chutney and toasted brioche, followed by succulent partridge, savoy cabbage and red wine jus: boisterous, rich and gamey.

Upstairs, eight cosy bedrooms have been decorated by Sebastian's interior designer sister Miranda. They're proper country affairs, with plaid throws and views over Cotswold-stone houses. They're also well equipped, and, in this out of the way location, you couldn't hope for a more peaceful sleep. An ideal base for exploring nearby Kelmscott House.

MIDLANDS

CENTRAL ENGLAND AND WALES

Kingham, Oxfordshire

Church Street, Kingham OX7 6YA

Tel 01608658389
email theteam@thewildrabbit.co.uk
website www.thewildrabbit.co.uk

Nearby Churchill and Sarsden Heritage Centre, The Slaughters; Stow-on-the-Wold; Burford
Location Kingham
Food breakfast, lunch, dinner (no food served Monday night)
Price ££-£££
Rooms
Facilities Bar, Restaurant, outdoor dining
Credit cards MC, V, AE
Children no
Accessibilty difficult, enquire
Pets some dog friendly rooms
Closed never
Proprietors Lady Bamford

The Wild Rabbit
Country hotel

Two endearing flop-eared topiary bunnies flank the entrance to this place - another successful outpost of Lady Bamford's Cotswolds Empire - fashioned from bushes at a former inn close to her Daylesford farm shop, café and Bamford Haybarn Spa.

Our room, The Boar, was chilly, but it did have aromatic Bamford toiletries, attractive beams and scrubbed stone walls, a desk and a big bed. The rooms have reasonable space - the self-contained Beehive is especially large, popular with families of four.

Downstairs there's a big buzzing dining space and, adjacent, a generous bar area with comfy seating for those who simply want a drink at the bar. Carol Bamford was determined to make this a casual meeting place for locals, and she has succeeded. Since the kitchen has been taken over by Chef Sam Bowser the menu has become more focussed on organic and locally foraged ingredients. Once or twice a week he goes to the Daylesford market garden to talk to the growers which then gives rise to menu changes. Expect unusual cuts of meat, a refined take on bar snacks and hearty desserts.

Langar, Nottinghamshire

Langar, Nottinghamshire
NG13 9HG

Tel 01949 860559
email info@langarhall.co.uk
website www.langarhall.com

Nearby Belton House; Chatsworth; Sherwood Forest; Lincoln Cathedral, Belvoir Castle, Nottingham.
Location in village behind church; with ample car parking
Food breakfast, lunch, dinner
Price £££
Rooms 12 doubles; 1 room has shower, all others have baths; all rooms have phone, TV, hairdryer
Facilities sitting rooms, dining rooms, bar; garden, croquet, fishing, helipad
Credit cards MC, V **Children** welcome
Accessibility 1 ground-floor bedroom
Pets accepted by arrangement
Closed never
Proprietor Lila Aurora

Langar Hall
Country house hotel

Since Imogen Skirving (who, on her father's death, turned their family home into a hotel to prevent its loss) died in 2016, Langar Hall has been taken on by her granddaughter Lila, who has managed to preserve the unique experience created by Imogen. People who stay here feel more like guests in a beautiful Georgian stuccoed country house than customers in a hotel. The library appears to be totally unchanged, with hundreds of books available to leaf through with a drink or two before dinner. The food is superb and the wine list well judged.

The best bedrooms are airy, with furniture appropriate to the house that Imogen wanted to save, and enjoy glorious views of the Vale of Belvoir. For exercise, you can play croquet or stroll round the village church. Best of all is the friendliness of the hostess and her staff. Imogen wanders around the dining room, alighting at tables of single, bored businessmen and exchanging any sort of gossip, while nothing is too much trouble for the chef or staff. When a reporter realised, at 12.45 am, after a very good dinner, that he had forgotten his wash bag, an assortment of toothbrushes, toothpaste and razors was provided. We revisited recently and enjoyed the Langar Hall show as much as ever.

MIDLANDS — **CENTRAL ENGLAND AND WALES**

Malpas, Cheshire

Wrenbury Rd, Malpas SY14 8HN

Tel 01829 720300
email info@cholmondeleyarms.co.uk
website www.cholmondeleyarms.co.uk

Nearby Chester, Macdonald Hill Valley Spa and golf club, Cholmondeley Castle Gardens, BeWILDerwood adventure park, Alderford Lake, Beeston Castle
Location at the intersection of Wrenbury Rd and
Food breakfast (included), lunch and dinner
Price ££
Rooms 6 doubles with bathrooms all with showers. Mr Chip and Professor Dumbledore have baths
Facilities restaurant/bar
Credit cards MC, V
Children welcome
Accessibility difficult, 3 ground floor only
Pets dogs welcome in ground floor rooms (£10 per night)
Closed never
Proprietors Tim Bird and Mary Mclaughlin

Cholmondeley Arms
Pub with rooms

A stylish, playful option for a country break. Dog-forward and gin-obsessed, the repurposed schoolhouse has a particularly stylish, comfortable dining area.

The old headmaster's lodge was renovated in 2022 and contains stylish bedrooms. The room names are painted on each door, simulating chalk on a blackboard, and feature famous fictional headteachers. Decoration is a balance of reclaimed materials and contemporary furniture. Inky landscapes by a local artist adorn the walls; everything is balanced and friendly. The downstairs rooms are dog-friendly, so those with allergies should book an upstairs room.

Over in the schoolhouse, the theme is a Victorian classroom. Blackboards, desks, pews and other period furniture dominate. Order your food at the Central Oak bar - cheerful British classics that won't remind you of school dinners. There's a selection of large and small plates, not forgetting jam roly poly. The gin list upstages the wine list by offering 375 different items, plus gin workshops and tastings.

MIDLANDS

CENTRAL ENGLAND AND WALES

Malvern Wells, Worcestershire

Holywell Road, Malvern Wells,
Worcestershire WR14 4LG

Tel 01684 588860
email
reception@cottageinthewood.co.uk
website
www.cottageinthewood.co.uk

Nearby Malvern Hills; Eastnor Castle; Worcester Cathedral.
Location 2 miles (3 km) S of Great Malvern off A449; with ample car parking
Food breakfast, lunch, dinner
Price £££
Rooms 30 double and twin with bath or shower; all rooms have phone, TV, hairdryer
Facilities sitting room, dining room, bar; garden
Credit cards AE, MC, V
Children welcome
Accessibility ground-floor rooms in annexe **Pets** accepted in ground-floor rooms, £10 per night
Closed never
Proprietors Nick and Julia Davies
Manager Michael Pearson

The Cottage in the Wood Boutique country hotel

Three buildings form this glossy little hotel perched, very privately, in seven wooded acres, high above the Severn valley and with a superb vista across to the Cotswolds thirty-something miles away (binoculars provided). There are bedrooms in all three buildings, taking the hotel over our usual size for this guide; but the smartly furnished Georgian dower house at its heart is so intimate, calm and comfortable that we decided to relent.

A short stroll away is the rebuilt Coach House, where rooms are smaller but have the best views, and Beech Cottage with four cottage-style bedrooms. Apart from its food, the restaurant (modern English cuisine) has two other substantial qualities: windows that let you see the view and a wine list that lets you roam the world. Walkers can get straight out on to a good stretch of the Malvern Hills and for tourers the hotel provides leaflets giving concise notes on everything that's worth visiting for 50 miles (80 km) around. For the rest of us, there's a very well stocked bar and a free video library.

This place is no longer family run. We'd be interested to hear how the hotel is faring under new ownership. Bedrooms have recently been refurbished – reports welcome.

MIDLANDS
CENTRAL ENGLAND AND WALES

Neenton, Shropshire

Neenton, Bridgnorth, Shropshire
WV16 6RJ

Tel 01746787955
email info@pheasantatneenton.co.uk
website
www.pheasantatneenton.co.uk

Nearby Ludlow, Shropshire Hills AONB, Brown Clee Hill, Severn Valley Railway, Ironbridge, Attingham Park
Location on the B4264
Food breakfast, lunch, dinner
Price ££
Rooms 3; 2 double with bathroom and 1 twin with bathroom
Facilities lounge, pub, restaurant, garden, climbing frame
Credit cards MC, V
Children welcome
Accessibility ground floor only
Pets dogs welcome
Closed Mondays
Proprietors Neenton Community
Director John Pickup

The Pheasant
Village inn

This lovingly revived inn sits proudly in the inconspicuous but welcoming village of Neenton. It was derelict until 2013, when the community invested time and money into reinstating the pub to its rightful place at the heart of their village. Staff and locals collaborate to give guests a warm welcome. Nooks, comfortable sofas and fireplaces ooze traditional country-pub style but with in a refreshed contemporary twist.

The dining room, an airy, oak-framed extension, leads into a well-cared-for garden and orchard with a small climbing frame for children. The menu explores locally sourced, seasonal ingredients. Head chef Mark Harris works closely with Slow Food Ludlow, non-profit venture that encourages and celebrates eating well, eating locally and eating thoughtfully.

Each of the three smart rooms is uncluttered and bright with large beds and fresh flowers. One of them has expansive views over the rolling hills of Shropshire. The bathrooms are good-looking and calmly decorated, but none offer bathtubs, only showers.

This is more than just a stopover: the countryside, the locals' energy, and their passion for the place are the stuff of good memories.

MIDLANDS

CENTRAL ENGLAND AND WALES

Norton, Shropshire

Bridgnorth Road, Norton, Near Shifnal TF11 9EE

Tel 01952 580240
email
reservations@hundredhouse.co.uk
website www.hundredhouse.co.uk

Nearby Telford, Ironbridge Gorge Museum, Severn Valley steam way, The Long Mynd (walk).
Location just off the M54 from junction 4, on the A442 between Telford and Bridgnorth, with car-parking **Food** breakfast, lunch, dinner **Price** £–£££ (min 2 night stay)
Rooms 9; 8 doubles, 1 single, all with bath; all have TV, phone, tea and coffee making facilities, hairdryer **Facilities** dining room, bar, brasserie; herb garden, beer garden, conference rooms **Credit cards** AE, MC, V **Children** welcome
Accessibility difficult
Pets well behaved dogs (£10 charge)
Closed Christmas day/ night, Boxing Day night, New Years day/night
Proprietors Phillips family

Hundred House Hotel
Village inn

'Quite extraordinary, a pleasant surprise around every corner' says a recent guest. The historic building, originally a 1550s courthouse, is a delightful escape. Push open the stained glass doors, and you're immediately greeted by soft, dim lighting, warm wooden floors, intricately panelled walls, inviting fireplaces, and bundles of dried herbs and flowers hanging from the ceilings. Salvaged from a nearby stately home, the oversized fireplaces add to the enchantment. The eccentric decoration of the bedrooms, with their hand-painted walls (and radiators), four-poster beds, hand-sewn curtains and swings, may not appeal to conventional tastes, but each room has a cosy, whimsical ambience. The house and garden blend seamlessly into a delightfully chaotic experience. You feel like going on a treasure hunt to discover the wacky details. We especially enjoyed the stone teddy bears having picnics beside a Frankenstein's monster carousel horse welded on to a tractor seat. The country pub fare menu is curated by co-manager and executive chef Stuart and is big on herbs from the garden. A useful base for exploring the Shropshire hills or the local Industrial Revolution towns, such as Ironbridge. People leave this place feeling cheerful - perhaps even as if they're been in fairyland.

MIDLANDS

CENTRAL ENGLAND AND WALES

Oxford

92-94 High Street, Oxford
OX1 4BN

Tel 01865 799599
email info@oldbank-hotel.co.uk
website www.oldbank-hotel.co.uk

Nearby Oxford colleges; Botanical Gardens; Sheldonian Theatre.
Location in city centre, with ample car parking
Food breakfast, lunch, dinner; room service
Price £££-££££
Rooms 42; 40 double and twin, 1 suite, 1 Junior Suite; all rooms have phone, TV, complimentary wi-fi, Bluetooth DAB radio, fresh flowers, tea and coffee making facilities, treat filled mini-bar, air-con and safe
Facilities restaurant, bar, courtyard
Credit cards AE, DC, MC, V
Children accepted
Accessibility 1 specially adapted room, most other rooms have lift/elevator access
Pets not accepted
Closed never
Proprietor Jeremy Mogford

Old Bank Hotel
City hotel

Hardly a quintessential charming small hotel because of its size, but we still think Old Bank Hotel is a good central Oxford address. What was, until the 1990s, a venerable bank with a fine Georgian façade, is now a cool, sophisticated hotel with a buzzing restaurant. It has kept up its high standards since we last visited.

The building has much to recommend it. The best bedrooms are graced with floor-length windows or, in the Tudor part, beams and deep window seats under lattice windows – the Junior Suite (room 45), in this style (see above), is particularly charming. All the bedrooms feature handmade beds and marble bathrooms – with striking artwork from the owners' private collection decorating rooms, corridors and restaurant.

As well as a hotel, the Old Bank has become the 'in' place to eat in Oxford. The Quod Restaurant & Bar stretches across the former banking hall. Most guests will enjoy the buzz and bonhomie that emanates from this always packed meeting place (service can be slow), with a wide-ranging menu. Staff are welcoming, helpful and knowledgeable.

MIDLANDS

CENTRAL ENGLAND AND WALES

Oxford

1 Banbury Road, Oxford OX2 6NN

Tel 01865 310210
email info@oldparsonage-hotel.co.uk
website www.oldparsonage-hotel.co.uk

Nearby Oxford colleges; Botanical Gardens; Sheldonian Theatre.
Location 5 minutes' walk from city centre, at N end of St Giles, close to junction of Woodstock and Banbury Roads; limited car parking
Food breakfast, lunch, dinner; room service and afternoon tea
Price £££ **Rooms** 35; 30 double and twin, 1 single, 4 suites, all with bath; all rooms have phone, TV, hairdryer, wi-fi **Facilities** sitting room, dining room, bar, garden library; terrace, roof garden **Credit cards** AE, DC, MC, V **Children** welcome **Accessibility** some accessible rooms **Pets** not accepted **Closed** never **Proprietor** Jeremy Mogford

Old Parsonage Hotel
City hotel

Talk about contrast. The two best hotels in Oxford, Old Bank House (see opposite), and this one are in the same ownership – Jeremy Mogford. The Old Parsonage is much more typical of our guide, occupying a characterful, wistaria-clad house that has been owned by University College since 1320. Compared to its sleek, hip younger sibling, it seems at first quaint and old-fashioned, yet there is no themed olde worlde charm here, despite the great age of the building.

A decade ago, there were major renovations to the hotel. In addition to five new bedrooms, a garden library has been added for guests. The development of these new areas is in line with the rest of the hotel – wool, linen and velvet have been used in the rooms, and a colour scheme that centres on plum, deep red and grey. There is a brand new Old York stone floor downstairs.

Since then the restaurant has been rebranded as The Parsonage Grill, but reports tell us it's retained the intimate and Bohemian atmosphere that marked it out before, even with new furniture and decoration. We would welcome reports on the new look.

MIDLANDS — CENTRAL ENGLAND AND WALES

Ramsden, Oxfordshire

The Royal Oak, High Street,
Ramsden OX7 3AU

Tel 01993 868213
website www.royaloakramsden.com

Nearby Blenheim Palace, North Leigh Roman Villa, Cotswold Wildlife Park, Oxford
Location in village
Food Breakfast for guests, lunch, dinner, Sunday lunch, bar snacks
Price ££-££££
Rooms 5; 4 doubles plus The Stable which sleeps up to 6
Facilities On-site bar and restaurant, outdoor dining area, parking
Credit cards AE, MC, V
Children accepted
Pets welcome in pub, in rooms by arrangement
Accessibility public rooms only
Closed restaurant only, Sun eve, Mon eve
Proprietor Tim Bevan

The Royal Oak
Village pub-with-rooms

In an unspoiled village, sitting opposite the church and war memorial, the location feels peaceful. A London couple who have a house here give the place glowing reports, describing it as a welcoming home from home. There are just five bedrooms - nothing wrong with that - but it suggests that the focus is on the food and for sure the menu here is impressive not for its range of dishes but for unusual, sophisticated add-ons. For instance, the wild boar burger comes with autumn fruit aoli; the butternut squash and pumpkin tarka dhal is served with coconut yogurt; and the rump steak gets gorgonzola and bone marrow butter. Some of the offerings are nicely unusual in their own right, for example among the small plates are toasted chilli cheese cornbread and roasted chestnuts with rosemary and sage sea salt. We detected a welcome effort to keep the prices friendly: four out of the seven mains cost £19 as went to press.. The wine list, with 25 reds and 20 whites, also shows experimental flair, going off piste with wines made in Uruguay, Georgia and Japan. However, the jewel in the crown is the characterful, light dining area at the rear (The Barn) with pale wooden floor boards.

The smallest bedroom, Wilcot, is reasonably priced for the space provided. A very happy Cotswold pub.

MIDLANDS

CENTRAL ENGLAND AND WALES

Repton, Derbyshire

12 Boot Hill, Repton, Derby
DE65 6FT

Tel 01283 346047
email info@thebootatrepton.co.uk
website www.thebootatrepton.co.uk

Nearby Peak District National Park, Calke Abbey, Hardwick Hall, Shipley Country Park, Repton school
Location Repton
Food breakfast, lunch, dinner, roast dinners
Price ££-£££
Rooms doubles, twins and 1 suite
Facilities bar, restaurant, outdoor seating
Credit cards all major
Children accepted
Pets welcome
Accessibility not suitable
Closed never
Proprietor Pat Hammond

The Boot
Country inn

Is Repton a village or is it a school? School buildings and pupils (in term time) are everywhere. This inn, down a side street leading from the central cross roads faces an old school wall concealing a cricket pitch. So the location is pleasant enough and the red brick building, whose ground floor may have been a cobbler's workshop, has some character. But the essence of the charm here is delicious food at the most competitive prices we've seen in a long time. The chef, Matt Allsop, has worked his way up the kitchen since 2014 and we suspect he's a real craftsman. No pretentious cheffy egotism, just dedication to getting "the maximum out of whatever ingredients you're using." He likes "lots of stuff going off' - ie intense, varied flavours. Try his fried chicken with oriental glaze, or the pork belly - all will be clear. The menu also offers everyday pub staples such as burgers and fish and chips.

Rooms were fairly priced when we visited. Maintaining this quality at such prices requires artful management and the small team which runs the mini group, Bespoke Inns, to which The Boot belongs, is almost a family enterprise - owner Pat Hammond's daughter Emily plays a key role. As we went to press the other local properties were The Dragon at Willington, with a charming canal-side location, and Harpur's in Melbourne.

MIDLANDS

CENTRAL ENGLAND AND WALES

Rhydycroesau, Shropshire

Rhydycroesau, Near Oswestry,
Shropshire, SY10 7JD

Tel 01691 653700
email stay@peny.co.uk
website www.peny.co.uk

Nearby Erdigg; Llanrhaedar waterfall; Powys Castle; Pistyll Rhaedar waterfall
Location 3 miles (4.5 km) West of Oswestry on the B4580. Hotel is 3 miles (4.5 km)down on that road on the left
Food breakfast, dinner, afternoon tea of clotted cream, jam and scones; light lunch on request.
Price ££
Rooms 12 double; all with bath and shower; all rooms have TV, hairdryer, modem point, tea and coffee making facilities, phone
Facilities dining room, sitting room, bar, reading room; garden
Credit cards AE, MC, V
Children welcome
Accessibility 1 ground-floor room
Closed 21st of Dec for 4 weeks
Pets by arrangement
Proprietors Mr and Mrs Hunter

Pen-y-Dyffryn
Country hotel

Driving through the windy lanes cutting through the Shropshire hills from Oswestry, you can easily miss this attractive Georgian House tucked away off the main road. It nestles serenely among trees and green fields and you will be taken aback by the views that stretch (on a clear day) to the Welsh mountains. The dining room and sitting areas are decorated in warm colours; open log fires for the chilly winter evenings are perfect. If you prefer to drink or dine outside, there's a delightful little patio stretching round the side of the hotel. Look closely and you'll see modern touches about the place, such as abstract art.

The bedrooms are large, spacious and comfortable, with large fluffy towels provided in all the en suite bathrooms (some with spa baths and Jacuzzis) and fresh flowers on arrival. Four of the bedrooms are in the coach house, which is ideal for guests with animals. They each have spectacular views and their own private little patio. Chef Dave Morris has been here for 15 years and his cooking is perfect for the place – we enjoyed goats' cheese and maple syrup mousse and rose veal with Madeira cream sauce. The small bar by the entrance is staffed by helpful staff who can advise you on sightseeing, walking, or shopping in Wales or Shropshire.

MIDLANDS

CENTRAL ENGLAND AND WALES

Rowsley, Derbyshire

Rowsley, Derbyshire DE4 2EB

Tel 01629 733518
email reception@thepeacockatrowsley.com **website** www.thepeacockatrowsley.com

Nearby Haddon Hall, Chatsworth, rivers Wye and Derwent
Location beside A6, between Matlock and Bakewell
Food breakfast, lunch, dinner; room service
Price ££-£££
Rooms 15; 14 doubles and 1 suite, 2 with four-poster, all en suite; all rooms have phone, TV, tea and coffee making facilities, hairdryer
Facilities bar, conference rooms, private dining and restaurant, fishing, golf nearby **Credit cards** AE, DC, MC, V **Children** accepted, but not on Friday or Saturday
Accessibility not suitable **Pets** dogs £10 per night, not in public rooms
Closed 9th-26th Jan **Proprietor** Lord Edward Manners
Managers Laura Ball

The Peacock at Rowsley
Country hotel

Just inside the door of the Peacock is a bowl of water and a basket for your dog. This is a sportsman's hotel, though an aesthete would be just as happy here; the pictures are outstandingly good. The River Wye – the only water in the country where wild rainbow trout breed naturally – is what the sportsmen come for. It is said to be the finest dry fly trout fishing in the land and the Head River Keeper from Haddon Hall is on hand to help you enjoy it. The Hall (Thornfield in BBC TV's *Jane Eyre*) is a nearby outing for days when the fish won't bite.

The Peacock, built in the 17th century, was once Haddon's dower house. Now it has all the comforts and convenience that modern visitors expect. Furnished with a mixture of old pieces and comfortable modern upholstery, there is an aura of antique furniture wax and wood smoke. In the bedrooms, fresh flowers, mahogany dressing tables and top-notch beds will make you feel at home. Uniformed staff are attentive and friendly – occasionally a little too much so for old-fashioned tastes. A great ledger in the hall records the fishermen's daily successes and disappointments. Whatever their luck on the river bank, they will not be disappointed in this handsome, well-run hotel.

Sheffield

92 Brocco Bank, Sheffield, S11 8RS

Tel 0114 2661233
email hello@brocco.co.uk
website www.brocco.co.uk

Nearby close by are the city centre, Weston Park Museum, Millennium Gallery and the Winter Gardens; a short drive away are Chatsworth House, Bakewell and the Peak District; 45km Robin Hood Airport
Location just off Ecclesall Road, opposite Endcliffe Park
Food breakfast, lunch, dinner, snacks, afternoon tea (pre-booking and at weekends only)
Price £-££££
Rooms 8; 6 double and 2 twin. All with wi-fi, Nespresso machine, kettle, organic cosmetics, hairdryer.
Facilities wi-fi, restaurant, heated terrace, guest lounge, free parking.
Credit cards AE, MC, V
Children accepted
Accessibility one specially adapted room **Pets** on terrace only; not allowed in hotel or restaurant area
Closed never
Managers Pam and Nicola

Brocco on the Park
City hotel

Picasso and Sheffield: you wouldn't link the two, but the artist had a direct influence on the interior design at Brocco. Picasso is thought to have stayed here in 1950 while attending the Peace Congress in Sheffield. Its emblem was Picasso's dove, and there are a series of avian touches on each of the eight bedrooms. Doves adorn bedroom walls, some baths are egg-shaped and room keys fit into miniature birdhouses near the door: touches which create a warm and personal atmosphere. There's another reason for the avian design: the 'park' in 'Brocco on the Park' is Endcliffe Park, which lies directly opposite the hotel, and is a city-centre haven for birds. Many of the bedrooms overlook the 'living roof' and beyond to the grassy park. The 'living roof' is exactly that: a flat roof imaginatively carpeted with grass and other plants.

When previous owner Tiina Carr purchased Brocco it was in a state of near disrepair. She has worked tirelessly, overseeing a stylish transformation. Brocco now accommodates a near-perfect fusion of solid British character and Scandinavian charm and Tiina's legacy is now in the hands of an abitious all-female management team

The food at the all-day restaurant is popular and the atmosphere relaxed, friendly and contemporary without trying too hard. We think prices are fair for a city-centre establishment of this standard.

MIDLANDS — CENTRAL ENGLAND AND WALES

South Leigh, Oxfordshire

Station Road, South Leigh, OX29 6XN

Tel 01993 656220
email oxford@artistresidence.co.uk
website
www.artistresidenceoxford.co.uk

Nearby Oxford: 15 min drive away, The Cotswolds: 15 min drive, 1.5 hrs from London
Location the peaceful village of South Leigh
Food breakfast, lunch, dinner, Sunday lunch
Price ££-££££
Rooms 15: 3 farmhouse loft suites, 1 farmhouse suite, 10 doubles and 1 private shepherd's hut. Farmhouse loft rooms can accommodate children with cot. Wi-fi, flat screen TV, organic Bramley toiletries, Roberts radio, mini fridge, Nespresso coffee machine
Credit Cards all major **Children** welcome **Accessibility** pub only
Pets allowed in some rooms
Closed never **Proprietor** Charlotte and Justin Salisbury

Artist Residence Oxford **Village inn**

Young artists don't actually decorate this place, but their work hangs on the walls, and the creativity and originality of founders Justin and Charlotte are still intact here at their fourth hotel. A thatched gingerbread house, with five bedrooms tucked away in its eaves, it's a 16thC inn bursting with authenticity and original features: flagstone floors, open hearths, a wooden bar and settles, complemented by William Morris wallpapers (breaking the Farrow & Ball mould, good to see). As with the other four Artist Residences (pages 39, 68, 99 and 119), there are lively hints of contemporary quirk, from Connor Brothers artworks to neon prints by Andy Doig.

The Connor Brothers were also responsible for designing the restaurant, The Mason Arms, which serves dishes that are both satisfyingly rustic and sophisticated.

The bedrooms are decked out with reclaimed furniture, Volga furnishings and hung with eclectic paintings. Our series editor, Fiona Duncan, stayed in The Farmhouse Suite – a rustic bolt-hole built into the rafters, with exposed beams, slanted walls and a freestanding copper bath. So lovely, she thought she'd never want to leave.

MIDLANDS

CENTRAL ENGLAND AND WALES

Stratford-Upon-Avon

Church Lane, Shottery, Stratford-Upon-Avon, Warwickshire CV37 9HQ

Tel 01789 532320
email info@burnsidestratford.co.uk
website www.burnsidestratford.co.uk

Nearby Stratford-Upon-Avon, Anne Hathaway's cottage, Warwick Castle, Upton House
Location on Church Lane SW of Stratford-upon-Avon
Food breakfast, lunch, dinner, sunday lunch
Price ££-£££
Rooms 24; Deluxe Double, Executive King, Grand Super King or Luxury Family Suite. 1 self-catering cottage **Facilities** restaurant, bar, parking, airport meet and greet, tour assistance
Credit cards MC, V
Children welcome
Accessibility lift, wheelchair ramp, ground floor rooms
Pets no
Closed Never
General Manager Lee Chatwin

Burnside
Village hotel

Walking from the heart of Stratford-upon-Avon to the once-village, now-absorbed suburb of Shottery could well have been the same journey a young, courting Shakespeare regularly undertook to visit Anne Hathaway. The location of this place is its best feature, with plenty of historical and cultural appeal and, a short drive from the Cotswolds. Bought from the Shakespeare Heritage Trust in 2017, having been unoccupied and 'haunted' for over 100 years, this hotel is a friendly and affordable option when visiting the area.

The 25 rooms in the main building are perhaps a little too corporate, but are comfortable and clean. The bathrooms are bright, no baths. Their self-catering Brookside Cottage (bottom left) has a more traditional, quirky character: exposed beams, wonky walls, thatched roof, real wooden floorboards. The restaurant is nicely lit, has fresh flowers on the tables and is gently decorated with contemporary wooden panels. Locals come for popular Thursday curry nights and Sunday dinners. The Saddle Bar is in a private nook where guests are encouraged to perch upon, yes, horse saddles (less adventurous guests can find regular chairs).

With its relaxed atmosphere and approachable staff this place is an affordable and comfortable option in a quiet corner of a famous town.

MIDLANDS

CENTRAL ENGLAND AND WALES

Tetbury, Gloucestershire

Near Tetbury, Gloucestershire
GL8 8YJ

Tel 01666 890391
email reception@calcotmanor.co.uk
website www.calcotmanor.co.uk

Nearby Chavenage; Owlpen Manor; Westonbirt Arboretum.
Location 3 miles (5 km) W of Tetbury on A4135; with ample car parking
Food breakfast, lunch, dinner
Price ££££
Rooms 35; 22 double and twin, 7 family suites, 6 family rooms, all with bath or shower; all rooms have phone, TV, hairdryer
Facilities 2 sitting rooms, dining room; garden, swimming pool, croquet, 2 all weather tennis courts; playroom, crèche, Spa, gym.
Credit cards AE, DC, MC, V
Children welcome (crèche)
Accessibility 4 ground-floor bedrooms
Pets by arrangement
Closed never
Proprietor Richard Ball

Calcot Manor
Country house hotel

This 15thC Cotswold farmhouse has been functioning as a hotel since 1984. Richard Ball took over Calcot Manor from his parents when they retired, and with a team of dedicated staff continues to provide the highest standards of comfort and service while preserving a calm and relaxed atmosphere. The lovely old house itself was a sound choice – its rooms are spacious and elegant without being grand – and the setting amid lawns and old barns, surrounded by rolling countryside, is all you could ask for.

Furnishings and decorations are carefully harmonious, with rich fabrics and pastel colours throughout. A converted cottage provides seven family suites, designed specifically for parents travelling with young children. There's an Ofsted registered crèche and babsitting service to take the children off your hands.

Richard Davies is head chef of both the Conservatory Restaurant and the adjoining Gumstool Inn, which is more informal and moderately priced. In the restaurant, you might dine on champagne poached halibut with sea vegetables and a mussel saffron nage, or Calcot organic beef with a *béarnaise* sauce, French beans and artichokes.

MIDLANDS

CENTRAL ENGLAND AND WALES

Worfield, Shropshire

Worfield, near Bridgnorth,
Shropshire WV15 5JZ

Tel 01746 716497
email admin@oldvicarageworfield.com
website www.oldvicarageworfield.com

Nearby Ludlow; Severn Valley Railway; Ironbridge Gorge Museum.
Location in village, 8 miles (12 km) W of Wolverhampton, 1 mile off A454, 8 miles (12 km) S of junction 4 of M54; in own grounds with ample car parking
Food breakfast, lunch, dinner
Price ££
Rooms 14 double, 1 family, all with bath and/or shower (some have jacuzzi baths and private patio access); all rooms have phone, TV, minibar, hairdryer
Facilities 2 sitting rooms, 3 dining rooms, 1 with bar **Credit cards** AE, DC, MC, V **Children** welcome
Accessibility 1 specially adapted bedroom **Pets** accepted in bedrooms
Closed never **Proprietors** David and Sarah Blakstad

Old Vicarage
Restaurant-with-rooms

When this substantial red-brick vicarage was converted into a small hotel in 1981, every effort was made to retain the Edwardian character of the place – restoring original wood block floors, discreetly adding bathrooms to bedrooms, furnishing the rooms with handsome Victorian and Edwardian pieces, carefully converting the coach house to four 'luxury' bedrooms (one of which, 'Leighton', has been specially designed for disabled guests). Readers have praised the large, comfortable bedrooms, named after Shropshire villages and decorated in subtle colours, with matching bathrobes and soaps.

Attention to detail extends to the sitting rooms (one is the conservatory, with glorious views of the Worfe valley) and the three dining rooms. The award-winning Orangery restaurant has a daily-changing menu and an impressive cheeseboard. It's top-class English cuisine, ambitious and not cheap. It's served at polished tables by cheerful staff, with views over the rolling Shropshire hills (it makes a lovely wedding venue). There is a reasonably extensive wine cellar.

MIDLANDS

CENTRAL ENGLAND AND WALES

Baslow, Derbyshire

Baslow, Derbyshire, DE45 1SP

Tel 01246 582311
email info@cavendish-hotel.net
website www.cavendish-hotel.net
Food breakfast, lunch, dinner
Price £££
Closed never
Manager Philip Joseph
Proprietor Chatsworth Estate

The Cavendish
Country house hotel

The name doesn't suggest a personally-run small hotel, but 'Cavendish' is appropriate because the hotel is on the glorious Chatsworth Estate of the Dukes of Devonshire, surname Cavendish. In 2018 this became part of the Devonshire Hotels Group but is still managed by Philip Joseph who has worked here for over 30 years. Until this edition it was a whole-page entry but following a disappointing experience there we now include it as a half page. No mistake, it's a good place, with charm, even grace and good taste, but with getting on for 30 bedrooms and more planned it is becoming a little large for the guide, bearing in mind its country location. The restaurant serves ambitious, highly priced food.

Biggin-by-Hartington, Derbyshire

Biggin-by-Hartington, Buxton, Derbyshire SK17 0DH

Tel 01298 84451
email enquiries@bigginhall.co.uk
website www.bigginhall.co.uk
Food breakfast, lunch, dinner
Price ££-£££
Closed first three weeks in Jan
Proprietor James Moffett

Biggin Hall
Country house hotel

A gaggle of geese may follow you up the path to this friendly 17thC house. Popular with walkers, it's ideal to come back here after a day's trek: sink into a well-worn chair by a crackling fire and enjoy a drink in a relaxed, cosy atmosphere. Rooms are attractively decorated, with personal touches and stone mullioned, leaded windows. The roofs slope steeply. Breakfast is generous. Dinner (set menu with vegetarian options, changing daily) is excellent for the price – like home dining, but at the house of a very good cook.

MIDLANDS — CENTRAL ENGLAND AND WALES

Chipping Campden, Gloucestershire

The Square, Chipping Campden, Gloucestershire GL55 6AN

Tel 01386 840330
email reservations@cotswoldhouse.com
website www.cotswoldhouse.com
Food breakfast, lunch, dinner; afternoon tea **Price** ££££
Closed never **Proprietors** Bespoke Hotels **Manager** Craig Webb

Cotswold House Hotel & Spa Town hotel

Described by one reader as 'the place to stay' in Chipping Campden, Cotswold House can claim to be a very popular hotel and Spa. Set in a fine street, the building, dating from 1650, was renovated in 1999, with new rooms and the new coach house, where clean modern lines, gas log fireplaces and broad exposed beams definitely add to the place. In the main hotel, an impressive spiral staircase leads to well-appointed rooms, which are a similar standard to those in the coach house.

You have the choice of two restaurants: the relaxed Bistro on the Square and the formal Fig Restaurant. Alongside the coach house, a Mediterranean-style garden, attractively lit in the evening, is perfect for an after-dinner stroll.

hipping Campden, Gloucestershire

High Street, Chipping Campden, GL55 6AT

Tel 01386 840317
email reception@noelarmshotel.com
website www.noelarmshotel.com
Food breakfast, lunch, dinner
Price £££-££££
Closed never
Proprietors Bespoke Hotels

Noel Arms

Town hotel

This place scores effortlessly for location. It's in one of the Cotswold's most charming towns at the foot of the Cotswold Way, with great opportunities for walks. It oozes charm and historic atmosphere – the honey-stone building dates back to the 14thC. One bedroom has a four-poster in which the future Charles II allegedly slept when on the run during the Civil War.

The Noel Arms also has a reputation for excellent brasserie food. Talented chef Indunil Sanchi cooks high-quality pub fare alongside dishes inspired by his Sri Lankan heritage: the curries have won numerous plaudits. For £10 you can use the spa at Costwold House (above) down the road.

MIDLANDS

CENTRAL ENGLAND AND WALES

Ilmington, Warwickshire

The Howard Arms
Village inn

Equidistant between Stratford-upon-Avon and Moreton-in-Marsh, this is useful for Stratford and the Cotswolds.

It's laid back: locals drink at the bar and the place has an easy-going charm. But there's professionalism too: our bags were carried upstairs and when the television didn't work in our room, it was dealt with at once.

The food is exactly what one wants in a 400-year-old stone-built inn, with pretty arched windows, a mix of old furniture and giant polished flagstones. Expect comforting dishes such as steamed suet pudding and sticky toffee pudding – all at sensible prices.

There are three rooms above the pub and five in a low-key garden wing. They are excellent, if somewhat formulaic.

Lower Green, Ilmington,
Warwickshire CV36 4LT

Tel 01608 682226
email info@howardarms.com
website www.howardarms.com
Food breakfast, lunch, dinner
Price ££-£££
Closed never
Manager Pawel Sobisek

Ironbridge, Shropshire

Library House
Bed and breakfast

Reliable B&B (rooms from £75) with high standards in the heart of the Ironbridge World Heritage Site, opposite the Ironbridge itself and centrally located for the shops, pubs and restaurants. Smart decoration and authentically Georgian features and furniture throughout. The three bedrooms are more homely, and well equipped. The hosts Tim and Sarah Davis welcome guests personally, with afternoon tea and homemade cake served on arrival, and are strong on advice on where to eat and what to see – ask for their Ironbridge walks. Free passes to the local car parks are a genuine bonus.

A church bell rings nearby, day and night, but it's a light sound which doesn't disturb.

Severn Bank, Ironbridge, Near
Telford, Shropshire TF8 7AN

Tel 01952 432299
email info@libraryhouse.com
website www.libraryhouse.com
Food breakfast, lunch, dinner
Price £-££
Closed never
Proprietors Sarah and Tim Davis

CENTRAL ENGLAND AND WALES

MIDLANDS

Leintwardine, Herefordshire

Leintwardine, Craven Arms, SY7 0JU
Tel 01547 540806
email upperbuckton@gmail.com
website www.upperbuckton.co.uk
Food breakfast
Price £
Closed occasionally
Proprietors Mary and Johnathon

Upper Buckton Farm
Bed and breakfast

A B&B and working farm set in 400 acres of unspoiled Teme Valley, this is a quintessentially charming small place to stay. Run by friendly owners Mary and Johnathon, you'll receive a personal welcome and the benefit of their local knowledge. The farmhouse itself is packed with homely comforts. The bedrooms are quaint and understated, and decorated with antique furniture, while neutral shades and thick fabrics dominate. The dining room has an open fireplace – used in winter – and decorated with Georgian period furnishing and 19thC oil paintings.

Breakfast can be enjoyed outside in warmer months with expansive views across the lawn and to the unspoilt Herefordshire landscape.

Nether Westcote, Oxfordshire

Nether Westcote, Oxfordshire OX7 6SD

Tel 01993 833030 **email** info@thefeatherednestinn.co.uk **website** www.thefeatherednestinn.co.uk
Food lunch, dinner, afternoon tea
Price £££-££££ **Closed** Mondays, Christmas Day **Proprietors** Tony and Amanda Timmer

The Feathered Nest Country Inn **Country inn**

Another converted Cotswold inn, less formal but just as comfortable as some country house hotels.

Tony and Amanda Timmer's four bedrooms may be coyly named (eg. Cuckoo's Nest, Cockerel's Roost), but they are a blend of the practical, the luxurious and the countrified.

The food in the homely but elegant dining room is as impressive as the bedrooms. The pub fare served in the bar (where the stools are fashioned from riding saddles) is also above average. The wine list features unsung 'boutique' growers from around the world.

The Feathered Nest wouldn't work everywhere, but in the Cotswolds it does.

MIDLANDS — CENTRAL ENGLAND AND WALES

Northleach, Gloucestershire

West End, Northleach, Gloucestershire GL54 3EZ

Tel 01451539889
email bookings.wheatsheafinn@youngs.co.uk **website** www.cotswoldwheatsheaf.com **Food** breakfast, lunch, dinner **Price** £££-££££
Closed never **Proprietors** Young's

The Wheatsheaf Inn
Country inn

Blanketed in ivy and brimming with city dwellers escaping to the country for the races, this 17thC coaching inn has been taken over by Young's since the last edition. We're still won over by the interiors: an attractive dining area, gleaming with polished wood; the relaxed Game Bar; the treatment room. The location is not special, but the bedrooms are great: imaginative wallpapers and fabrics, zinc bath, comfortable beds. The food from chef Peter McCallister doesn't miss a beat, featuring dressed-up pub food and country classics. Breakfast isn't cheap, but we enjoyed the pancakes with bacon and maple syrup.

Northleach, Gloucestershire

High St, Lower Oddington GL54 0UR

Tel 01608692872
email guest.services@daylesfordstays.com **website** www.thefoxatoddington.com **Food** breakfast, lunch, dinner, bar snacks **Price** £££-££££
Closed never **Proprietors** Lady Bamford

The Fox at Oddington
Country inn

A good place, successful and often buzzing, but this guide gives it a half page because its charm is rather contrived. A deep pocket has allowed the old pub to be comprehensively made over in order to dish up countryside chic to a generally upmarket Cotswold crowd. A bright, expansive interior with multiple seating areas has been imposed, rather than adapted organically to retain as much as possible of the old charm. Expect knee-length tweed shooting trousers, well groomed pets and high-definition modern artwork of foxes. On our last visit we perched in a cosy nook beside the fire and picked at some expensive but tasty bar snacks. Good gastropub food, immaculate bedrooms and bathrooms. Sister establishment of The Wild Rabbit, page 221.

MIDLANDS

CENTRAL ENGLAND AND WALES

Shipton-under-Wychwood, Oxfordshire

High Street, Shipton-under-Wychwood, Oxfordshire OX7 6BA

Tel 01993 830500
email hello@thecrownshipton.com
website www.theshavencrown.co.uk
Food breakfast, lunch, dinner
Price ££
Closed Christmas day - 4th/5th Jan
Manager Abilio Oliveira

The Shaven Crown
Country house hotel

The Shaven Crown Hotel, as its name suggests, has monastic origins; it was built in 1384 as a hospice to nearby Bruern Abbey, and many of the original features remain intact – most impressively the medieval hall, with its beautiful double-collar braced roof and stone walls decorated with tapestries and wrought ironwork. The hall forms one side of the courtyard garden, which is decked with flowers and parasols, and on a sunny day is a lovely place in which to enjoy wholesome pub lunches. Some of the bedrooms overlook the courtyard, others are at the front of the house and suffer from road noise – though this is unlikely to be a problem at night. An extensive refurbishment to the ground floor and bedrooms in 2022 complements the historic setting well.

Stamford, Lincolnshire

St Martins, Stamford, Lincolnshire PE9 2LJ,

Tel 01780 766 412
email enquiries@thebullandswan.co.uk **website** www.hillbrookehotels.co.uk/the-bull-and-swan **Food** breakfast, lunch, dinner
Price ££-£££ **Closed** never
Proprietors Hillbrooke
Manager Peter Brighouse

The Bull and Swan
Town inn

Quaint is an over-used description for inns in old buildings, but here it really does fit. This historic inn on the High Street of Stamford's St Martins district is mainly 17thC and has been sympathetically made over in the usual quirky-luxurious style of the Hillbrooke mini chain.
Well-chosen antiques rub shoulders with top-quality beds and pristine white linen in the nine bedrooms. Most of the rooms are a fair size. There is a pleasasnt kitchen garden where they host film and pizza nights during the summer.
Food is better-than-average country inn fare using local ingredients. A drinking club for a 17thC Earl of Exeter and friends was based here, and members' nicknames eg The Badger are used for the rooms. Burghley House can be reached on foot.

MIDLANDS

Stamford, Lincolnshire

St Martins, Stamford, Lincolnshire
PE9 2LJ

Tel 01780 750070
email enquiries@thewilliamcecil.co.uk
website www.thewilliamcecil.co.uk
Food breakfast, lunch, dinner
Price ££-£££ **Closed** never
Proprietors Hillbrooke
Manager Peter Brighouse

The William Cecil
Town hotel

With 27 rooms this is somewhat outside our usual size, but the unstuffy staff make it feel like a smaller place. The atmosphere is relaxed but gracious, as you would expect from a house on this scale.

They've got the basics right here, including the quality beds, the Egyptian cotton linen and the intelligent use of space. Design and furnishings are nicely in keeping with the building, and the overall effect is perhaps more harmonious than other Hillbrooke hotels.

It's just along the road from The Bull & Swan (see opposite), and part of the same group. This guide doesn't normally favour chains, but the Hillbrooke philosophy shares much with ours: no managers in suits, no staff uniforms, no name badges.

Bildeston, Suffolk

High Street, Bildeston, Suffolk IP7 7EB

Tel 01449 740510
email reception@thebildestoncrown.co.uk
website www.thebildestoncrown.com

Nearby Lavenham, Long Melford, Constable Country, Wool Town Walks **Location** 10 mins on A1141/B115 from Hadleigh
Food breakfast, lunch, afternoon tea, dinner, snacks **Price** ££
Rooms 11 double, 1 twin; all have bath/shower
Facilities bar, lounge, 2 dining rooms, courtyard, 2 function rooms; fishing, riding, shooting, tennis
Credit cards AE, MC, V
Children welcome
Accessibility lift, Room 2 has access, 'drop off' point with step-free access to hotel **Pets** dogs accepted, £10 per night **Closed** Christmas Eve, Christmas Day and New Year's Day evenings
Proprietors The Buckle Family

The Bildeston Crown
Village inn

This handsome, custard-coloured Inn has been a steady landmark of sleepy Bildeston since the 14th century. Recently bought back under the management of Nedging Hall Estate and the Buckle family, this place continues to deliver a warm-hearted welcome.

Entering via the courtyard terrace it is a slight surprise to step into a well-lit, smart and contemporary space. The downstairs rooms are unstuffy and spacious with the entire ground floor given over to tables and smart dining chairs in a series of rooms with attractive, boldly painted walls. All winter long a log burner crackles from a large brick fireplace.

From the food to the fresh flowers there is a conscious drive to source as much as possible from the estate. Executive Chef Freddie Fallon has devised a broad menu of quality seasonal produce.

The rooms are lovely, with pretty fabrics and charming touches. Some bathrooms are due an update but ours had a great bathroom, with a rolltop bath and large shower.

Their weekend rates, in particular, are steep, but the Sunday-night dinner, bed and breakfast package (from £140-185 for two, depending on the room) is a good deal.

Brancaster, Norfolk

Brancaster, Staithe, Norfolk
PE31 8BY

Tel 01485 210 262
email
reception@whitehorsebrancaster.co.uk
website
www.whitehorsebrancaster.co.uk

Nearby Holkham Hall, Brancaster beach, Norfolk lavender, Burnham Market, Sandringham Estate Peddars Way
Location on A149 coast road with ample car parking
Food breakfast, lunch, dinner
Price ££-££££
Rooms 15; 5 family rooms, 10 doubles (4 can be twin), all with bath and shower; all rooms have phone, TV, hairdryer, wi-fi
Facilities dining area, sitting room, conservatory, restaurant, bar, garden, terrace, courtyard **Credit cards** MC, V **Children** accepted
Accessibility 1 room with low-rise bath and ground floor access
Pets dogs in some rooms
Closed never
Proprietor Nye family

The White Horse
Village inn

This is certainly not the most attractive building in the guide but once inside you should get the point. First you walk into a bar area for non residents, with a local community atmosphere; this melts seamlessly into a more 'residential' area with reception desk and seating; and this gives way to the big, airy conservatory dining room with its scrubbed pine tables and extraordinary view out over a network of creeks and marsh across Brancaster Staithe to Scolt Head Island – one of England's most distinctive coastal panoramas. You could easily while away most of a morning or afternoon here, followed by lunch or dinner, and still not be tired of the view.

Your room, either upstairs or in the green-roofed Garden Rooms, will be comfortable and cleanly decorated and furnished in a modern style with seaside colours and Lloyd Loom chairs.

The kitchen, captained by Chef Fran Hartshorne serves good food – no more or less than you'd expect for the price. Try the seafood platter which featues salmon from the on-site artisanal Staithe smokehouse.

The White Horse is a lesson in how to transform what was a horrible old pub in a fabulous situation into thriving 21st century operation.

EAST ANGLIA AND REGION

Cambridge

2 Gonville Place, Cmabridge CB1 1LY

Tel 01223 366611
email office@gonvillehotel.co.uk
website www.gonvillehotel.co.uk

Nearby Cambridge University, Fitzwilliam Museum, Kettle's Yard
Location Cambridge city centre
Food breakfast, lunch, afternoon tea, dinner
Price £££-££££
Rooms 8; doubles with en-suites
Facilities dining room, garden, terrace, bar, atrium, spa, Ev charging, laundry service, discounts at local gym, free bike hire
Credit cards MC, V, AE
Children welcome
Accessibility suitable, including spa
Pets some dog friendly rooms
Closed never
Manager Malcolm Wyse

Gresham House at the Gonville City hotel

A charming small hotel in Cambridge? Of course, it's long been needed as an alternative to the conventional hotels such as the University Arms. The Gonville, radically refurbished and updated in 2019, with 90-plus bedrooms, looks like just another hotel but it conceals, at the back, a handsome little 19thC building, Gresham House. Here there are just eight smart rooms, all different, with the use of a large sheltered garden, and a feeling of being removed from the bustle. You can dip in and out of the main hotel building for food, drink and socializing, or by-pass it.

The location, on the south side of Parker's Piece, SE of the city centre, is central enough to do the main Cambridge sights on foot.

A medium sized bedroom in Gresham House cost £290 as we went to press - what you would expect given the location. The hotel organizes tours of the city sights in the vintage Bentleys swankily parked outside the front door. There's a car park for residents, first come first served. Call the hotel's main number and you're answered by a theatrical voice listing the various options - room reservations, restaurant, and so on. Its super-plummy old-school tones belie what is a buzzy, contemporary place to stay.

Cley-next-the-Sea, Norfolk

Cley-next-the-Sea, Holt, Norfolk
NR25 7RP

Tel 01263 740209
email info@cleywindmill.co.uk
website www.cleywindmill.co.uk

Nearby Sheringham Hall; Cromer Lighthouse; Holkham Hall.
Location 7 miles (11 km) W of Sheringham on A149, on N edge of village; with ample car parking
Food breakfast, dinner on request
Price ££
Rooms 9 double, all with bath/shower. Self-catering options.
Facilities sitting room, dining room, garden
Credit cards MC, V
Children welcome
Accessibility difficult
Pets accepted in some rooms
Closed bed-and-breakfast closed for Christmas and New Year; self-catering let available during this time
Proprietor Natalie and Varian Bush

Cley Windmill
Converted windmill B&B

Imagine staying in a 'real' windmill. That is the sense of adventure that this place can induce even in the most world-weary. Memories of Swallows and Amazons or the Famous Five crowd in as you climb higher and higher in the mill, finally mounting the ladder to the look-out room on the fourth floor. Superb views over the Cley Marshes, a Mecca for bird-watchers.

The sitting room on the ground floor of the Mill is exceptionally welcoming – it feels well used and lived-in, with plenty of books and magazines, comfortable sofas, and an open fire. Bedrooms in the Mill feel rather like log cabins – much wood in the furniture and fittings. They are pretty rooms, with bathrooms ingeniously fitted in to the nooks and crannies.

Since our last edition, Cley Mill has changed hands. The new owners are Natalie and Varian Bush alongside their young children. There has been maintenance and restoration, but the basic formula remains unchanged. A new bedroom has been added right at the very top of the windmill – reached by a steep ladder, it is only for the adventurous and fit, but the view makes it worthwhile. Try to book well in advance. The Bushes also own a deli which supplies the B&B with fresh, local produce. With a cafe attached, it is worth the short walk into the village.

Dedham, Essex

High Street, Dedham, CO7 6DF

Tel 01206 323351
email office@thesuninndedham.com
website www.thesuninndedham.com

Nearby Dedham Vale Area of Outstanding Natural Beauty (nearby), Flatford Mill (1m), Constable's Haywain (1m), Beth Chatto Garden (5m), Manningtree and Mistley (7m) **Location** in village centre, opposite St Mary's Church **Food** breakfast, lunch, dinner, cream tea **Price** ££ **Rooms** 7; 6 doubles and 1 double/twin. All have TV, radio, tea and coffee making facilities, wi-fi, hairdryer
Facilities bar, lounge, restaurant, terrace, garden, bikes
Credit cards AE, MC, V
Children welcome
Accessibilty not suitable **Pets** dogs allowed in bar and oak room, and in rooms by arrangement - enquire before **Closed** 24-27th Dec
Proprietors Charlotte Green and Dominique St Rose

The Sun Inn
Village inn

On the Essex/Suffolk border, in Constable country, a buttercup yellow coaching inn stands at the centre of the village of Dedham. Piers Baker took over the scruffy old building twenty years ago and filled it with antiques, upmarket furniture and paintings. The result is homely and authentic. The reception is at the front elm bar, where patrons sip local ales. There is a split-level sitting room with a cosy open fire, and a beamed dining area with parquet floors and fresh flowers.

Most of the seven bedrooms face Dedham High Street and the huge windows of St Mary's church opposite, with the periodic chiming of bells reminding you of the quaintness of this rural village. One room faces the back of the inn, offering more peace to light sleepers. There are painted, wardrobes, Robert radios, and paintings that carefully match the colour schemes. The four-poster and half tester beds are the most remarkable, but all rooms are comfortable and well equipped.

In good weather, The Sun Inn does justice to its name: at breakfast, tables are draped in white linen, brightening the dining room. At lunch and dinner the menu includes local fish and game, and many items have a Mediterranean twist (you might find pappardelle with lamb ragu, but also poached salt cod among the choices).

Dedham, Essex

Stratford Road, Dedham,
Colchester, Essex CO7 6HN

Tel 01206 322367
email maison@milsomhotels.com
website
www.milsomhotels.com/maisontalbooth

Nearby Sir Alfred Munnings Museum at Castle House, Colchester, Ipswich, Constable Country, Suffolk Heritage Coast **Location** bypass Colchester A12 northbound, take left signposted Dedham, follow signs for Maison Talbooth **Food** breakfast, lunch at hotel **Price** ££££ **Rooms** 12; all double, 7 can be twin, all have bath/shower, one has additional bunk beds; terrace; all have free soft-drinks, mini bar, hairdryer, wi-fi, Sky HD TV **Facilities** sitting rooms, garden room, day spa, pool, tennis court **Credit cards** all major **Children** welcome **Accessibility** 5 downstairs rooms **Pets** dogs welcome **Closed** never **Proprietors** Milsom family

Talbooth House & Spa
Country house hotel

A welcome addition to our Essex section – under an hour and a half drive from London – this smart, rather plain-looking Victorian house is hard to beat for lavish comfort.

With new suites, a spa, pool, and tennis court this place is ever expanding under the consistent leadership of the Milsom family who, since our last edition have rebranded this place from Maison Talbooth to Talbooth House and Spa.

The 12 poet-themed suites have a decadent Sixties feel: quilted fabrics and luxury drapes; charcoal greys and muted greens; and patterned wallpaper that contradicts the all-new modern bathrooms.

Down the road, Le Talbooth, also under the Milsom ownership, is the gastronomic hotspot of the area. It remains a popular place to eat even after 50 years, and still exudes the feel of its Sixties heyday. There's an exceptional wine list and a blend of old-and-new style cooking. If you don't feel like going out, light snacks can be served in your room. The hotel's Range Rover takes you to and from the restaurant, or anywhere else nearby.

EAST ANGLIA AND REGION | CENTRAL ENGLAND AND WALES

Great Waldingfield, Suffolk

Great Waldingfield, Sudbury, Suffolk CO10 0TL

Tel 01787 372428
email bookings@theoldrectorycountryhouse.co.uk
website www.theoldrectorycountryhouse.co.uk

Nearby Lavenham, Long Melford, Bury St Edmunds, Sudbury
Food breakfast, dinner only by arrangement when booking the whole house
Price ££-££££
Rooms 7; all double, two ground floor, all have bath/shower; 3 in the main house, 4 in The Old Stables annex
Facilities drawing room, honesty bar, swimming pool, tennis court, free wi-fi
Credit cards MC, V
Children welcome
Accessibilty difficult
Pets clean dogs accepted
Closed rarely
Proprietor Frank Lawrenson

Rectory Manor House
Country house hotel

Much of the charm of this tucked-away rectory lies in the way owner Frank Lawrenson has thoroughly restored its original character – it's in superb condition, but uncompromised by trendy, contemporary add-ons. All the rooms have bathrooms and are individually decorated: subtle pastel shades reign, with delicately floral cushions and curtains. There is a sense of space everywhere, but especially in the drawing room, and to complete the gracious but relaxed atmosphere guests get a high level of unobtrusive but personal attention from Frank and his team, including a butler. The books, the honesty bar and copious, well presented information on what to see and do in the area make you feel at home. One concession to contemporary design is the swimming pool's curved roof, open on one side, making it an indoor-outdoor pool – used mainly in the summer-time. When exploring the grounds don't miss the mulberry tree, it' claims to be one of the oldest in Suffolk.

We sense that this place is always on the move. It's making a foray into environmentally friendly technology, including a Biomass boiler and a conservation programme in partnership with local artisans. Staying here means you have the satisfaction of making a contribution to their cause.

EAST ANGLIA AND REGION **CENTRAL ENGLAND AND WALES**

Great Wilbraham, Cambridge

10 High St, Great Wilbraham, Cambridge CB21 5JD

Tel 01223 827444
email info@carpentersarmswilbraham.co.uk
website www.carpentersarmswilbraham.co.uk

Nearby 14 km from Cambridge City Centre
Location Great Wilbrahim
Food breakfast, lunch, dinner
Price ££-£££
Rooms 3; 2 double with bathroom and 1 suite with bathroom
Facilities garden, terrace, bar, restaurant, coffee machines in rooms
Credit cards MC, V
Children welcome, cots available
Accessibilty not suitable
Pets dogs welcome
Closed never
Proprietors Chestnut Group

Carpenters Arms
Village Inn

A contemporary inn carved out of an old pub with four bedrooms, as little as 20 minutes from the centre of Cambridge, so it could be a base for exploring the university city. Great Wilbraham is a pleasant but ordinary East Anglian village surrounded by relentlessly flat countryside, so the Carpenters imaginative recent conversion into an up-to-date inn by the Chestnut group is a pleasant contrast.

The key features of the design's impact are floor-to-ceiling glass, plus a kitchen open on two sides to the eating area. The entrance lobby is a glass atrium and the whole of one side of the large dining area is glass. You look into a large garden, a relaxed outdoor eating area. Sliding doors complete the indoor-outdoor experience, which hits the spot in warm weather. Most country inns are brown and dark, but this is colourful and bright, even modestly eye-popping - see the vivid orange banquettes and an expanse of boldly colourful wallpaper. Two of the bedrooms have minimal space, but to reflect that are fairly priced - at times they cost less than £100. Try staying in central Cambridge for that.

The chef describes his fare as modern pub food done well, but this could be modest. Among the six mains we noticed a gluten-free chicken schnitzel, a courgette risotto, and veal - ie pub food with quite a sophisticated twist.

Harwich, Essex

The Quay, Harwich, Essex
CO12 3HH

Tel 01255 241212
email pier@milsomhotels.com
website
www.milsomhotels.com/thepier

Nearby Harwich sights including Electric Palace Cinema, Ha'penny Pier, Redoubt fort, golf **Location** on quayside in old town; own off-road car parking for 25 cars
Price ££ **Food** breakfast, lunch, dinner **Rooms** 14; all doubles with own shower or bath, phone, TV, wi-fi, minibar **Facilities** 2 restaurants, bar, terrace, sitting room, private dining facilities, house party service, sailing arranged on yacht or traditional Essex craft **Credit cards** AE, DC, MC, V **Children** accepted
Accessibility suitable
Pets dogs allowed (in bedrooms and in the NAVYARD bar and terrace)
Closed never
Proprietor Milsom family

The Pier
Seaside town hotel

Here's a good place for a weekend – if you like the sea, ships, and industrial seascapes. Picture-book pretty it isn't; atmospheric, absorbing and 'real' it most certainly is. The Pier, with its distinctive blue and white façade, designed to resemble a Venetian *palazzo*, was built in 1864 to accommodate overnight passengers from Harwich to the European mainland. It was from here, too, in 1620, that the Mayflower set sail for the New World.

The Pier restaurant on the first floor is relaxed and informal, specializing in locally caught seafood – with the option to dine on the balcony with views over the harbour. There's also the continental-styled NAVYÄRD bar, with 115 gins (and counting) to choose from (open from 9am). Check-in is at the bar, and bags are promptly taken to your room. All the rooms are several cuts above what you would expect for the price (deep, white-sheeted beds, natural sea colours on tongue-and-groove panelling), but with only £10 each between a 'standard', a 'superior' and a 'deluxe' it pays to go for the largest – and get the view.

The Pier has been owned for nearly 40 years by the Milsom family. Like their other establishments, Talbooth House and Spa and Kesgrave Hall (pages 250 and 255), it's a close-knit operation, with long-serving locals on the happy team.

Horndon-on-the-Hill

High Rd, Horndon on the Hill, Stanford-le-Hope SS17 8LD

Tel 01375 642463
email info@bell-inn.co.uk
website www.bell-inn.co.uk

Nearby Leigh on sea, Southend On Sea, Mersea Island, Tilbury Fort, Hadleigh Casle
Location Hordon-on-the-Hill village
Food breakfast (at the Ostlers), lunch, dinner
Price ££-££££
Rooms 26; doubles, suites and snug rooms All have power-shower, bath, TV, Noble Isle toiletries, wi-fi
Facilities dining room, courtyard, pub, garden
Credit cards all major
Children welcome
Accessibility not suitable
Pets no
Closed never
Proprietors The Vereker family

The Bell
Country pub

Horndon on the Hill, with its clapboard houses and spilling window boxes, feels like a secret. The village was once the hub of the local wool trade, sheep grazed the land down to the Thames and this inn has been at its heart since the 15thC. Today it's still a proper pub, with locals drinking ale and a buzzy community atmosphere, but other things have changed.

The Vereker family have owned and run The Bell for 80 years and, over three generations they have expanded the accommodation and developed a successful restaurant. The bar menu (no booking) is delicious and beautifully presented while the restaurant has a seasonal, changing menu, with vegetables and herbs from the garden and meat from the butcher next door. The service is efficient and friendly and makes the place feel genuinely family run. The 26 bedrooms vary considerably across three adjacent buildings. All are full of character and individuality: in High House there are suites to accommodate families (large airy rooms, high ceilings). In the old inn winding, creaky staircases lead up to rooms with historic connections (Henry VIII and Anne Boleyn are said to have stayed, perhaps Lord Nelson too). Top floor rooms are snug. All the rooms have a crisp, clean, comfortable feel.

EAST ANGLIA AND REGION

CENTRAL ENGLAND AND WALES

Kesgrave, Suffolk

Hall Road, Kesgrave, Ipswich IP5 2PU

Tel 01473333741
email reception@kesgravehall.com
website www.milsomhotels.com/kesgrave-hall/

Nearby Kesgrave, Suffolk Coast
Location just north of Ipswich
Food brasserie open all day, cream tea, pop-up restaurants on Fridays
Price ££-££££
Rooms 23; all en-suite with King sized beds
Facilities four spa packages, meeting rooms, restaurant
Credit cards MC, V
Children welcome
Accessibility some access
Pets allowed
Closed never
Proprietors Geraldine and Paul Milsom, Misolm Hotels

Milsom's Kesgrave Hall

A converted country mansion with a long history, having been a boarding school and a wartime RAF base, Kesgrave Hall's impressive white exterior stands in 38 acres of grounds on the outskirts of Ipswich, and looks out on to a vast lawn.

Its 23 rooms, split between the main house and outbuildings, are clean and contemporary, with top bathrooms (the best rooms come with free-standing bathtubs) and pleasant views across the grounds.

The restaurant is open all day and leads on locally sourced meat and seafood. It's a relaxed place, with a no-bookings policy, an open kitchen and an unusual method of ordering: guests write down their choices on a notepad and pass it to a waiter. This won't be to everyone's taste, but it's a novel idea that makes you feel under less pressure to order quickly.

This place is also ideal for private functions, having three event rooms for birthdays, meetings and corporate away days, as well as The Hangar, a separate building for weddings and large parties.

Kesgrave Hall's luxurious new spa opened in spring 2020. Built to blend in with the woodland, it is an ideal retreat from a busy life and the beautifully designed interiors create a peaceful environment.

EAST ANGLIA AND REGION

CENTRAL ENGLAND AND WALES

King's Lynn, Norfolk

King's Staithe Square, King's Lynn, Norfolk PE30 1RD

Tel 01553 660492
email info@thebankhouse.co.uk
website www.thebankhouse.co.uk

Nearby the Custom House, King's Lynn Minster, The Corn Exchange **Location** on the quayside, accessible via the A10, A17 and A47; ample parking.
Price ££-£££
Food breakfast, all day food, afternoon teas, Sat and Sun brunch
Rooms 12; singles, doubles, large doubles all with TV, radio, telephones, wi-fi, tea and coffee making facilities and guidebooks **Facilities** bar, brasserie, terrace, sitting area, parking **Credit cards** MC, V
Children welcome; under 5s free, £10 per night for cot, £20 per night for children under 12
Accessibility some, ramps both inside and out and WC
Pets allowed on request
Closed never **Proprietor** Anthony and Jeanette Goodrich

Bank House Hotel
Town house hotel

This is the sister hotel of The Rose & Crown in Snettisham (page 262). It's just as quirky and historic as its sibling. The Grade II listed Georgian townhouse started life as the home of a rich King's Lynn merchant, but in the 1780s was set up as the first branch of what is now Barclays Bank. A dent in the wooden floor is still visible, maybe left behind by the nervous shuffling of 18thC account holders. Careful design brings out the history of the building, but this place is far from old fashioned. Traffic-light bright chairs decorate the waterside terrace outside, whilst inside the armchairs are bright green and magenta. Rooms are airy, but could do with an update and some are a little small. Most have river views; a few look out on to King's Staithe Square.

The brasserie and bar are relaxed and welcoming, made up of a number of different areas from which you can choose according to how formal you're feeling. We think that the most sympathetic area is the former counting house – all dark, polished wood and original flooring. Dishes vary from the standard (burgers, fish and chips) to the exotic, and are prepared using local ingredients whenever possible. Bank House is brilliantly situated for exploring this historic town. The Corn Exchange theatre is nearby and pre- and post-theatre dining can be arranged.

King's Lynn, Norfolk

Lynn Road, Grimston, King's Lynn, Norfolk PE32 1AH

Tel 01485 600250
email info@conghamhallhotel.co.uk
website www.conghamhallhotel.co.uk

Nearby Sandringham; Ely; Norwich.
Location 6 miles (10 km) NE of King's Lynn near A148; with parking for 50 cars **Food** breakfast, lunch, dinner **Price** ££££
Rooms 26; 15 in the main house, 11 garden rooms, 11 double, 2 suites, all with bath, 1 single with shower; all rooms have phone, TV, room larders with small fridges, Nespresso machines **Facilities** 2 sitting rooms, bar, dining room; garden, spa, indoor swimming pool, tennis, croquet, putting
Credit cards DC, MC, V
Children welcome (over 7 in restaurant) **Accessibility** restaurant only
Pets dogs allowed in some rooms
Closed never
Proprietor Nicholas Dickinson

Congham Hall Hotel & Spa Country house hotel

'Quintessentially English' is how some guests describe their stay here. Practically everything about this white 18thC Georgian house, set in 40 acres of lawns, orchards and parkland, is impressive. The spacious bedrooms and public areas are luxuriously furnished and our reporter found the service to be solicitous and efficient and the staff helpful and welcoming. Cooking (in the modern British style) is adventurous and excellent, making much use of home-grown herbs. The restaurant is a spacious, airy delight, built to look like an orangerie, with full-length windows overlooking the wide lawns of the parkland, where the herb gardens are an attraction in their own right. Visitors stop to admire the array of 600 herb varieties and to buy samples, from angelica to sorrel. The restaurant doors open on to the terraces for pre-dinner drinks and herb garden strolls.

Personal attention is thoughtful. The hotel keeps a book of special walks, devised by the previous owners, the Forecasts, and can arrange clay pigeon shooting on site, subject to availability. Reports welcome.

Long Melford, Suffolk

The Green, Long Melford, Suffolk
CO10 9DN

Tel 01787 312356
email info@theblacklionhotel.com
website www.blacklionhotel.com

Nearby Long Melford church; Melford Hall; Kentwell Hall.
Location in village 3 miles (5 km) N of Sudbury, overlooking village green; with car parking
Food breakfast, lunch, afternoon tea, dinner
Price £££
Rooms 10; 8 double, 1 suite, 1 family room; all have bath/shower, TV, tea and coffee making facilities, superfast wi-fi, Noble Isle bath products
Facilities sitting room, 2 dining rooms, bar
Credit cards AE, MC, V
Children welcome
Accessibiltiy no special facilities
Pets dog-friendly
Closed never
Proprietor Philip Turner

The Black Lion
Country hotel

Long Melford is a famously attractive Suffolk village, and The Black Lion is at the heart of it, overlooking the green. Since becoming the latest member of the Chestnut Group the hotel – set in an elegant 19thC building – has undergone an extensive renovation.

The new interiors are smart yet warm, retaining The Black Lion's signature antique style with a more elegant feel: roaring fires, oil paintings and mounted antlers create a pleasant, countrified atmosphere. The set-up features a new conservatory, which can be used as a space for private parties, and leads on to their new terrace where guests can dine *al fresco*.

Bedrooms, either 'snug' or 'luxury' are soothing, in pastel olives and creams, with pleated headboards and wool throws.

Their already delicious food has gone up a notch under chef, Justin Newton. The focus is on pub classics, full of flavour whilst being refined. Dinner might include twice baked soufflé with braised celery, salt baked beetroot and walnut granola, and is served in their restaurant, conservatory, bar or lounge.

We'd be interested to hear reports on how the new management are getting on.

Mistley, Essex

High Street, Mistley, Essex CO11 1HE

Tel 01206 392821
email info@mistleythorn.co.uk
website www.mistleythorn.co.uk

Nearby Colchester 7 miles, Ipswich 8 miles, Stour Estuary
Location Mistley High Street, car park for 5 cards and street parking
Food breakfast, lunch, dinner, afternoon tea
Price ££-£££
Rooms 12; all have television, iPod dock, tea/coffee facilities, wi-fi; 3 rooms have small kitchen facilities
Facilities restaurant, bar, separate dining area that can be used for private functions (up to 30 people)
Credit cards AE, MC, V
Children welcome
Accessiblity suitable
Pets well-behaved dogs in some rooms
Closed Christmas day
Proprietor Sherri Singleton and David McKay

The Mistley Thorn
Village inn

In the 1700s, a wealthy, local landowner had plans to turn Mistley into a fashionable saltwater spa, but his scheme never came off. Be prepared for a place that's semi-industrial and rough at the edges.

Two 18thC towers rise from a churchyard on the edge of the town, and the High Street has prettily painted Georgian terraces. The Mistley Thorn is a former Victorian public house, outside of which you get the smell of Horlicks emanating from the Edme Maltings factory along the road. Opposite is the Stour Estuary, upstream from Harwich. We liked The Mistley Thorn as much for its setting as for the food and accommodation.

It's run with panache by Californian Sherri Singleton. Her menu majors on local seafood, including Mersea oysters and Colchester natives when in season. There's Suffolk Red Poll beef and Sutton Hoo chicken.

Our top-floor room, with a view of the Stour, was somewhat cramped, but it was freshly decorated and had a well-equipped, airy bathroom. Other rooms are larger, and all of them have views across Stour Estuary, as well as homely touches such as home-made cookies and dressing gowns. We heard some traffic noise in the morning.

EAST ANGLIA AND REGION

Morston, Norfolk

Morston, Holt, Norfolk
NR25 7AA

Tel 01263 741041
email reception@morstonhall.com
website www.morstonhall.com

Nearby Sandringham; Felbrigg Hall; Holkham Hall; Brickling.
Location 2 miles (3 km) W of Blakeney on A149 coastal road opposite entrance to quay and seal trips; ample car parking
Food breakfast, Sun lunch, dinner
Price ££££
Rooms 13; 7 double and twin in main hotel, plus 6 pavilion suites; all rooms have phone, TV, hairdryer
Facilities sitting room, sun lounge, conservatory, dining room, orangery; garden, croquet **Credit cards** AE, DC, MC, V
Children welcome
Accessibility 1 ground-floor bedroom
Pets accepted in bedrooms
Closed B&B only on Mondays
Proprietors Galton and Tracy Blackiston

Morston Hall
Country hotel

Don't be put off by the rather severe-looking flint exterior of this solid Jacobean house on the North Norfolk coast. Inside, the rooms are bright and airy, painted in summery colours and overlooking a sweet garden, where a fountain plays in a lily pond and roses flourish. The *raison d'être* of Morston Hall is its dining room, the responsibility of Galton Blackiston, who shot to fame as a finalist in ITV's 'Chef of the Year'. He has since won huge acclaim for his outstanding modern European cuisine and, the icing on the cake, a Michelin star in 1999. His set four-course menu changes daily and might feature: confit of leg of duck on sautéed Lyonnaise potatoes with thyme-infused jus or grilled fillet of sea bass served on fennel duxelle with sauce vierge. The carefully-stocked wine cellar offers a comprehensive selection of (not overpriced) wines from all over the world. Galton and his wife, Tracy, also organize wine-tasting dinners and cookery lessons. He gives a number of half-day cookery demonstrations and runs two three-day residential courses each year. Most of the large bedrooms are decked out in chintz fabrics, with armchairs and all the little extras, such as bottled water, bathrobes and large, warm, fluffy towels.

EAST ANGLIA AND REGION

Sculthorpe, Norfolk

Lynn Road, Fakenham NR21 9QG

Tel 01328 633001
email hello@sculthorpemill.uk
website www.sculthorpemill.uk

Nearby Walsingham Abbey, Sandringham, Holkham Hall, Fakenham
Location off the A148
Food breakfast (included), lunch, dinner, bar snacks
Price ££-£££
Rooms 7; doubles all have bath/shower, wi-fi, smart TV's, hairdryer, tea and coffee
Facilities dining room, pub, garden, river views
Credit cards MC, V
Children welcome
Accessibilitiy no special access
Pets welcome
Closed some winter closures
Proprietor Siobhan Peyton and Caitriona Peyton

Sculthorpe Mill
Country inn

The charm is definitely in the location, a remote spot on the River Wensum, here narrow and fast flowing. But it's also in the old mill building's exterior, which is mellow and pleasing and in the spacious ground floor with separate drinking areas where several groups can hang out without treading on toes. Out the back is an exceptionally pretty and natural garden with natural water channels and an enticing covered dining area plus tables under sunshades. On the first floor is a characterful, beamy dining room serving very good food. Its reputation has grown steadily since opening a few years ago: hands-on owner-managers Siobhan and Catriona are sometimes run off their feet - from time to staff are short - understandable in remote north Norfolk.

The bedrooms are reasonably comfortable and spacious and fairly priced, some with views over the adjacent nature reserve. Sculthorpe is one of the best new places in north Norfolk to open since our previous edition, within easy reach of the coast, whether for a drink, good food or just to relax in the garden with its background river music.

EAST ANGLIA AND REGION

Snettisham, Norfolk

Old Church Road, Snettisham, Norfolk PE31 7LX

Tel 01485 541382
email info@roseandcrownsnettisham.co.uk
website www.roseandcrownsnettisham.co.uk

Nearby Peddars Way, Houghton Hall, RSPB Snettisham, North Coast beaches, Holkham Hall, Sandringham, Norfolk Lavender, Burnham Market
Location off B1440, in centre of Snettisham village with ample car-parking
Food breakfast, lunch, dinner
Price ££ **Rooms** 16; 1 twin, 15 doubles (4 can be split for twins); all rooms have phone, TV, wi-fi, air-conditioning, hairdryers, irons
Facilities 3 dining rooms, walled garden, bar, sitting room **Credit cards** V **Children** welcome **Pets** accepted **Accessibility** 2 ground floor rooms **Closed** never
Proprietors Anthony and Jeanette Goodrich

Rose and Crown
Village inn

We like the way this inn keeps both locals and visitors happy. There are plenty of activities nearby, it is situated near an area of outstanding natural beauty, and it is far better value for money than its grander neighbours in nearby villages. The oldest part of the inn is the bar, originally built for workers who erected the local church, and where locals and visitors enjoy the beer and a wide selection of sandwiches whilst sitting by the open fire, then totter off to their rooms, minding the wonky old flagstones on the way.

On the way to your room, admire owner Anthony Goodrich's sporting prowess: his old school photos adorn the walls. The bedrooms are smallish, but done out in a fresh, sea-sidey way, with all the creature comforts you would expect. If you need a substantial lunch or dinner, head downstairs to one of the three dining rooms that provide fresh, locally sourced food, including beef from the salt marshes at Holkham, seafood from Brancaster and game from the gentlemen in wellies in the back bar.

Parents can rest assured that their children will be safe in the walled garden, with its impressive climbing frame and play area. They can be watched from the terrace or the attached dining room/sitting room.

EAST ANGLIA AND REGION

Stoke by Nayland, Suffolk

Stoke by Nayland, Suffolk,
CO6 4SA

Tel 01206 263245
email info@angelinnsuffolk.co.uk
website www.angelinnsuffolk.co.uk

Nearby Guildhall; Dedham Vale; Flatford Mill; East Bergholt.
Location in village centre, on B1068 between Sudbury and Ipswich; small car park for 20 cars
Food breakfast, lunch, dinner
Price ££
Rooms 6 double, 2 twin, 4 with bath; all with TV, hairdryer, wi-fi
Facilities sitting room, 2 dining rooms, bar; garden, herb garden, beer garden
Credit cards MC, V
Children travel cots available
Accessibility not suitable
Pets accepted in pub only
Closed never
Proprietors Suffolk Country Inns

Angel Inn
Village inn

In the heart of Dedham Vale, this inn has long been known as a place to stay with good food, but in 2023 it reopened after a major refurbishment. The result is chic and bang up to date, yet retaining the charm of its ancient timber framed buildings and flagstone floors. Original works of art from the owners' own collection – Old Masters to Modern British – add depth.

The courtyard garden has been redesigned with attractive plantings, seating, and a pergola which connects the inn with the annex and car park.

Head chef Ruben produces contemporary, imaginative dishes using local seasonal ingredients and to call it fine dining isn't enough. It's both classic and innovative and offers the added interest of a flavour of his native Spain. Pastry chef Gabi makes superb sourdough bread and delicious, artistic desserts and *petit fours*.

The tasting menu is a draw – apparently most guests choose it – and there is a vegetarian version.

There are pleasant local walks and much to explore nearby in Constable Country. Dedham, Flatford Mill and the Munnings Museum are a short drive; newly renovated Gainsborough's House in Sudbury is further.

EAST ANGLIA AND REGION | **CENTRAL ENGLAND AND WALES**

Swaffham, Norfolk

Ash Close, Swaffham, Norfolk
PE37 7NH

Tel 01760 723845
email enquiries@strattonshotel.com
website www.strattonshotel.com

Nearby Norwich; North Norfolk coast.
Location down narrow lane between shops on main street; with car parking
Food breakfast, lunch, dinner
Price £££
Rooms 14; 7 doubles, 7 suites, all with bath or shower; all rooms have phone, TV, hairdryer, minibar, iron
Facilities 2 sitting rooms, dining room, bar, cafe/deli
Credit cards MC, V
Children welcome
Accessibility difficult
Pets welcome in specific rooms
Closed Christmas
Proprietors Vanessa and Les Scott

Strattons Hotel
Town hotel

Strattons has long summed up everything we are looking for in this guide. When Les and Vanessa Scott bought this elegant listed villa in 1990 they had a very clear vision of what they wanted to create, decorating it with their unique artistic flair (they met as art students). Bedrooms are positively luxurious. Plump cushions and pillows jostle for space on antique beds, books and magazines fill the shelves. Their style extends to the smart bathrooms – one resembling a bedouin's tent. The two beautifully furnished sitting rooms, *trompe l'oeil* hallway and murals painted by a local artist are equally impressive. A reader writes: '20 out of 20 for staff attitude, value for money, quality of accommodation… An absolute delight.'

Les and Vanessa's daughter Hannah has now been running the hotel with her husband for nearly twenty years – keeping it very much a family affair. They've expanded the hotel to include extra bedrooms, and an on-site cafe – with a lifestyle/interiors shop is in the pipeline. The food is special too. They now have a resident head chef, although Vanessa (an acclaimed cookery writer) continues to oversee its operations. The seasonal menu plucks produce from their nearby orchard and allotment, and is cheerfully served by the small team of staff in the cosy basement restaurant.

EAST ANGLIA AND REGION

Thorington, Suffolk

Walnut Tree Farm, Thorington,
Halesworth IP17 3QP

Tel 07733 262797
email info@huskthorington.co.uk
website www.huskthorington.co.uk

Nearby Thorington Hall, Thorington Theatre, Suffolk Coast, Walberswick
Location just off the A12
Food breakfast, lunch, dinner
Price ££-£££
Rooms 6; 4 double barn rooms with bathrooms and 2 converted grain silos
Facilities dining room, sitting room, natural swimming pool, cooking courses
Credit cards MC, V
Children not suitable
Accessibility some
Pets dogs welcome
Closed weeknights
Proprietors Katy Taylor and Joey O'Hare

Husk
Farm supper-club-with-rooms

In Italy this would be accurately described as an *agriturismo* (similar to Glebe House Coombeshead pages 77 and 56). It's the centrepiece of a working farm run by Katy Taylor and Joey O'Hare with serious dedication to their environment and to cooking. Joey is a professional chef who has appeared on MasterChef: the Professionals and both have wine qualifications. At their popular weekend supper parties they host around a dozen, both locals and overnight guests, house party style at a long, carved oak table. Monday to Thursday they are at work on the farm, producing sustainably grown fruit, vegetables and other crops. Their food is very good: inventive, fresh home cooking of the highest quality. Our reporter's main course was a cabbage leaf stuffed with pheasant, all the ingredients home grown. The rooms are comfortable, individual and thoughtfully equipped. Ours, £260 including breakfast, amounted to a suite, with a separate living area. No TV.

The location is in unspoiled, but not outstanding countryside, close to several east Suffolk places to visit including Aldeburgh and Minsmere bird reserve. It's just what we look for: a cross-over between private home, guesthouse and B & B. Husk is the collective noun for a group of hares - the countryside here is full of them - and Joey's surname is O'Hare.

EAST ANGLIA AND REGION

Thorpe Market, Norfolk

Cromer Road, Thorpe Market,
Norwich, Norfolk NR11 8TZ

Tel 01263 832010
email office@theguntonarms.co.uk
website www.theguntonarms.co.uk

Nearby Cromer, Holt, Holkham Hall, Houghton Hall, The Sainsbury Centre of Art
Location just off the A149 on Elderton Lane
Food breakfast, lunch, dinner
Price ££-££££
Rooms 8 double in the main building, all have bath/shower; 4 Coach House rooms (next door) and 4 Barn house suites **Facilities** restaurant, sitting area, bar, The Stamp Rooms
Credit cards AE, MC, V
Children welcome, £15 per night for additional bed
Accessibility one fully adapted room in the coach house on the ground floor.
Pets 5 dog friendly rooms £10 per night
Closed Christmas Day
Proprietor Ivor Braka

The Gunton Arms
Country pub-with-rooms

One of the most impressive refurbished inns in East Anglia, possibly in the country. It's a substantial, flint-walled building in flat, spreading Norfolk parkland. Money did not deter the owner, art dealer Ivor Braka, from achieving the result he wanted. Although cash does not guarantee success, here it has come together to great effect with Braka's vision and high standards, and designer Robert Kime's flair.

Downstairs is a series of rooms which manage to feel traditional, cosy and stylish – and are full of surprises. Cropping up everywhere is outstanding contemporary art, much of it amusingly sexual. Tracy Emin's plates above the bar shocked one straightlaced couple so much that they got their solicitor to write a complaining letter. Country folk and Londoners seem to mix easily in the bar-dining area. The food is straightforward, including steaks cooked, memorably, on an open wood fire. The bedrooms are enchanting. If you find yourself in Ellis, look twice at the prints by the dressing table, but not if you were offended by Tracy Emin's plates.

EAST ANGLIA AND REGION

Walberswick, Suffolk

Main Street, Walberswick, Suffolk
IP18 6UA

Tel 01502 722112
email
info@anchoratwalberswick.com
website
www.anchoratwalberswick.com

Nearby local beach and river are both a 2 minute walk, Minsmere RSPB centre, golf courses at Aldeburgh, Thorpeness and Southwold, Dunwich forest **Location** just off the B1387, 15 minute drive from Southwold **Food** breakfast, lunch, dinner **Price** ££ **Rooms** 10; 6 garden rooms (3 are dog-friendly), 4 rooms in the main building; all en-suite with a bath and/or shower, all rooms have wi-fi, TV **Facilities** 2 sitting rooms, dining room, bar **Credit cards** AE, MC, V **Children** welcome **Accessibility** suitable **Pets** accepted in 3 Garden Rooms, 2 seating areas of pub and outdoor terraces **Closed** Christmas day **Proprietors** Mark and Sophie Dorber

The Anchor
Village inn

A place that stands out because of the hosts, says our series editor, Fiona Duncan. Almost twenty years ago the Dorbers acquired this formerly run-down pub in the village where Sophie Dorber grew up. (She and Mark had run the popular White Horse pub in Parson's Green, Fulham. Sophie did the food, he was the landlord, with a special interest in wine and beers from the world over.)

The Anchor is far from boring now: it's a comfortable place, popular with the locals. The staff are attentive (unless overrun at peak times), and sometimes funny (watch out for Luke's unexpected quips). Sophie's food is full of flavour and Mark has done something unique with the wine list: matched dishes with not just wines but beers too. He'll even tell you what beer to drink with you breakfast porridge.

Don't be misled by the building's nothing-special exterior. The ten bedrooms (four in the main building, six more spacious chalets in the garden) aren't as inviting as the colourful bar and restaurant – in fact they're simple, but they are priced for what they are. Bathrooms have underfloor heating.

It's a terrific weekend getaway, with much of interest nearby – the town of Southwold, and the famous Walberswick reedbeds – a birder's paradise.

Wells-next-the-Sea, Norfolk

The Buttlands, Wells-next-the-Sea
NR23 1EU

Tel 01328 710206
email info@theglobeatwells.co.uk
website www.theglobeatwells.co.uk

Nearby Norfolk Coast Path
Location just off the A39 in the village of Allerford
Food breakfast, lunch, dinner, picnic baskets on request
Price ££-£££
Rooms 29; 19 double/twins with bathroom in main house and 10 in The Arch House
Facilities dining room, cosy bar, courtyard, terrace
Credit cards MC, V
Children welcome
Accessibility suitable
Pets dogs welcome
Closed never
Proprietors Philip Turner

The Globe Inn
Coastal Inn

Tucked away in a small square with a green in the popular Norfolk coast town of Wells, this has a relatively secluded location. Inside, the atmosphere is traditional inn with many a cosy niche seating area and with enough contemporary, often colourful statements to remind you that it was recently refurbished and redesigned by the Chestnut Group, still a smallish collection (16 as we went to press) with a reputation for sensitively yet imaginatively converted East Anglian places to stay.

In summer expect the bustle of families with kids and dogs (it's very dog friendly) and in winter a calmer vibe with locals chilling in front of the fires.

Past the bar areas you find your way to the restaurant at the back where the food is pub classics combined with dishes focussing on local produce, not least North Sea crab and fish.

The 19 bedrooms in the main house all have individual designs but are in harmony with the early 19thC building and plenty of colourful touches. Another ten rooms are in The Arch House on the edge of town. Both are a few minutes' walk from the coastal marshland and creeks separating the town from the sea, and here you get the classic Norfolk Coast experience. A sister hotel, The Carpenter's Arms at Great Wilbraham, is on page 252.

EAST ANGLIA AND REGION | CENTRAL ENGLAND AND WALES

Cheltenham

131 The Promenade, Cheltenham
GL50 1NW

Tel 01242822939
email reservations@no131.com
website www.no131.com
Food breakfast, lunch, dinner, bar snacks
Price £££-££££
Closed very rarely
Proprietors Country Creatures

131 The Promenade
Townhouse hotel

Behind this classic Georgian townhouse exterior is a contemporary and lively food-forward place to stay. Renovated by Georgia and Sam Pearman, founders of the Lucky Onion group and now the Country Creatures hotel group, they want every aspect of your stay from the furniture to the meals to be something you may not have seen in any home or hotel every before. Mismatched chairs, red bath tubs, and antiques are theatrically arranged under the high ceilings.

Downstairs there is 'Yoku', an upmarket Sushi bar and the 'Terrace' restaurant serves small pates of exciting flavours; Beetroot relish with Coconut yoghurt, Gin-cured fish, and grilled pears with duck.

Coltishall, Norfolk

Church Loke, Coltishall, Norfolk,
NR12 7DN

Tel 01603 737 531
email info@norfolkmead.co.uk
website www.norfolkmead.co.uk
Food breakfast, lunch, dinner, afternoon tea, picnic hampers
Price ££-££££
Closed rarely Proprietors James Holliday and Ann Duttson

Norfolk Mead
Village hotel

The Norfolk Broads aren't known for their hotels, which is why we were gratified to come across this charming riverside address. The hotel comes with its own boat to ferry guests up the river Bure, spotting herons and otters whilst chugging past stretches of idyllic countryside. Back in the handsome Georgian house they can spoil themselves with an 'Aromassage' from Catherine's healing hands.

James Holliday and Anna Duttson, who bought and refurbished the hotel in 2013, make a kindly and hands-on team. The interiors are very smart, albeit a little bland for the taste of our series editor, Fiona Duncan, but the tranquility of location and spot-on hospitality more than compensate.

EAST ANGLIA AND REGION | **CENTRAL ENGLAND AND WALES**

Lavenham, Suffolk

The Swan Hotel & Spa
Village hotel

The Swan's exterior competes head-on with the quaintest, but the recently refurbished interior is the reason to stay.

The down-at-heel, pokey old coaching inn has been made to look fresh without losing its essential character. The brasserie, overlooking the garden, works especially well. The beamy bedrooms are not as interesting as the ground floor spaces, but you may enjoy the test of finding your way back to your room through the labyrinth of passages and quirky floor levels. The Gallery Restaurant's food, in a reconstruction of a medieval timbered hall, is enjoyable, the wine list expertly chosen.

High Street, Lavenham, Suffolk
CO10 9QA

Tel (01787) 247477
email info@theswanatlavenham.co.uk
website www.theswanatlavenham.co.uk
Food breakfast, lunch, afternoon tea, dinner **Price** ££-££££ **Closed** never
Proprietor TA Collection

Norwich, Norfolk

38 St Giles
Town bed-and-breakfast

This sophisticated and recently downsized bed-and-breakfast in the heart of Norwich can claim to be one of the best in the city. The breakfasts here are particularly acclaimed – imaginative jams, fresh pancakes and homemade granola. The Norfolk breakfast is a particular favourite with guests – one recent visitor describing it as 'the best British breakfast' around.

Bedrooms are an interesting marriage of traditional and contemporary design. Period features such as large fireplaces and generous bay windows give a lovely old-fashioned feel, while contemporary chaise longues, colourful silk curtains and modern wooden furniture make each room feel chic and cool. Welcome treats, such as homemade brownies, are left for guests.

38 St Giles Street, Norwich, Norfolk NR2 1LL

Tel 01603 662944
email bookings@38stgiles.co.uk
website www.38stgiles.co.uk
Food breakfast
Price ££-££££
Closed never
Proprietor Dennis and Holly Bacon

EAST ANGLIA AND REGION

Orford, Suffolk

Orford, Woodbridge, Suffolk, IP12 2LJ

Tel 01394 450205
email info@crownandcastle.co.uk
website crownandcastle.co.uk
Food breakfast, lunch, dinner
Price ££££
Closed never
Proprietor The Hotel Folk

CENTRAL ENGLAND AND WALES

The Crown and Castle
Restaurant-with-rooms

There's been a hostelry here for eight centuries, but today's inn is a quirky, late-19thC building that has an immediately welcoming feel. The Trinity restaurant makes a beguiling place for an informal lunch or smarter dinner (an excellent breakfast, too). When Fiona Duncan visited she felt that there were some jarring notes, such as funky wall and ceiling lights. Her bedroom (in the outbuilding) was smart, with a pretty headboard, but lacked personality. Stock furniture, plain grey walls, and a 'no smoking' notice made it less of a welcoming sanctuary than rooms she has stayed in for the same price. Since then they've refurbished a number of rooms as well as the restaurant. We'd be interested to hear reports, as it's a useful address in an interesting area.

Southwold, Suffolk

Market Place, Southwold, Suffolk IP18 6EG

Tel 01502 722186
email swan.hotel@adnams.co.uk
website www.adnams.co.uk/hotels/the-swan
Food breakfast, lunch, dinner
Price ££-££££
Closed never
Proprietors Adnams

The Swan Hotel
Town hotel

Some years back, The Swan, a Southwold institution like its sister hotel The Crown, had a bold and judicious refurbishment. Bedrooms have taken on a contemporary coastal look, with bright-coloured furnishings, bespoke modern lighting and furniture. They're also spacious, with sumptuous sitting areas, striking Tall Boy beds and decent bathrooms.

The hotel is largish, and quite conventional for this guide, but the staff and on-hand butlers are helpful, giving individual attention, including a gin and tonic on arrival. There are also two restaurants, with short menus of interesting dishes. The Still Room has a special ambience.

THE NORTH-WEST / NORTHERN ENGLAND

Area introduction

The far north of England divides neatly into two areas: the north-west and the north-east. The north-west includes Cumbria, some of North Yorkshire, Lancashire and Merseyside. The north-east is a large band of territory stretching from the Humber Estuary up to the Scottish border, taking in most of the rest of North Yorkshire, the Yorkshire Dales and the large, wild county of Northumberland, together with County Durham and some heavily industrialized counties such as Teeside. Cumbria and the Yorkshire Dales have the richest crop of charming small hotels for the obvious reasons: their wonderful mountain and moorland scenery, terrific walking and many numinous ancient monuments and historic houses. For visitor numbers, Cumbria is up there with Devon and Cornwall, and getting there by train from London is much quicker.

Below are some useful back-up places to try if our main selections are fully booked:

Seatoller House
Country guesthouse, Seatoller
Tel 017687 77218
www.seatollerhouse.co.uk
Sociable guest-house.

Kelleth Old Hall
Self-catering, Kelleth
Tel 015396 23344
www.kelletholdhall.co.uk
Delightful, idiosyncratic, one-room country retreat

Hotel du Vin
Townhouse hotel, Harrogate
Tel 01243608121
www.hotelduvin.com
Richly furnished chain hotel overlooking The Stray.

Goldsborough Hall
Country house hotel, Goldsborough
Tel 01423 867321
www.goldsboroughhall.c
Historic, luxurious hotel

Haley's Hotel
Town house hotel, Leeds
Tel 0113 2784446
www.haleys.co.uk
Useful address for Leeds, with friendly, local staff.

The Wensleydale Heifer Village hotel, West Witton Tel 01969 622322
www.wesleydaleheifer.co.
Characterful, themed bedrooms in Yorkshire Dales

Mount Pleasant Farm
Self-catering, Whashton
Tel 01748 822784
www.mountpleasantfarmhouse.co.uk Top-end B&B in 1850s farmhouse.

Northcote
Country House Hotel, Lan
Tel 01254 240555
www.northcote.com
A few minutes drive from Forest of Bowland.

The White Horse and Griffin Hotel and restaurant, Whitby
Tel 01947604857
www.whitehorseandgriffin.com
17thC building in town centre.

Ambleside, Cumbria

Borrans Rd, Ambleside LA22 0EH

Tel 015394 33605
email hotel@rothaymanor.co.uk
website www.rothaymanor.co.uk

Nearby Ambleside (10 minute walk), Lake Windermere, Borrowdale (50 minutes), Blackwell, Wordsworth museum, Townend
Location Ambleside
Food breakfast, lunch, afternoon tea, dinner
Price ££-£££
Rooms 23; doubles and suites with bathroom spread across annexe and main house
Facilities dining rooms, lounges, terrace, grounds, hotel-organiszd lake swims, laundry service
Credit cards MC, V
Children welcome
Accessibility some, 1 wheelchair adapted room
Pets dog friendly rooms and one dog friendly dining space
Closed Jan
Proprietors Jenna and Jamie Shail

Rothay Manor
Boutique country hotel

This strays a little but not far from our usual territory. It is a straightforward, smart country house hotel with 23 bedrooms but the location on the edge of Ambleside has a unique appeal and charm: you're in an oasis of large grounds surrounded by fencing, removed from Lake District tourist razzmatazz, in your own calm world. The N tip of Lake Windermere is close, but out of sight.

The main building, which contains 15 rooms - has the feel of a smaller place - parts of it could almost be a local inn. Old panelling has been retained, but painted with contemporary colours. Prints of local mountain and fell scenes some by distinguished artists such as Francis Towne adorn the walls. The wallpapers are bold, maybe too bold for some. The furniture is traditional and rustic. You can choose between fine dining in the dining room or bistro food in an informal eating area. The bedrooms are luxurious and individually designed and decorated but manage not to spill over in to fussiness.

This is a launch pad for any number of Lakes expeditions. It's about 50 minutes by car from the far end of Borrowdale, where starting at Seathwaite there's the classic hike up to Styhead Tarn. For a unique and stimulating description of this expedition, see *Walks for Mind and Spirit*, published by Duncan Petersen.

Askham, Cumbria

Askham, near Penrith, Cumbria
CA10 2PF

Tel 01931 712350
email enquiries@askhamhall.co.uk
website www.askhamhall.co.uk

Nearby Askham village, River Lowther, Penrith, Ullswater 20 mins by car, walks from the door and fishing **Location** in own grounds, 10-minute drive from Penrith and the M6; ample car-parking
Food breakfast, lunch (café only), dinner
Price £££-££££
Rooms 16; all with own bath or shower **Facilities** restaurant, private gardens, heated outdoor swimming pool, spa, hot tub, cafe, converted barn, medieval hall and garden pavilion for weddings **Credit cards** all major **Children** welcome, catering arrangements to be discussed **Accessibility** no special facilities **Pets** dogs accepted by prior arrangement **Closed** Jan and first 2 weeks of Feb **Proprietors** Charles Lowther

Askham Hall
Country house hotel

One of the most exciting developments in Lake District accommodation for a long time. The young owner, Charles Lowther (half brother of the present Earl of Lonsdale) and his family have created a 'hometel' – a home from home hotel out of Askham Hall, on the edge of the Lake District. After driving through Lowther Park and reaching the pretty village of Askham, the hall's gates are a little way down the hill from the houses. The main building dates back to the 13thC and is accompanied by a charming listed 17thC garden and medieval pele tower.

Charlie has given serious thought to making this place super-relaxed, more like staying in a private house than a hotel. Its one-off location in a family home gives it an added twist of originality.

Their eclectic, occasionally quirky country house style decoration and furniture is all different. A professional kitchen, devotedly led by Head Chef Richard Swale, produces sophisticated food from a small menu with an impressive wine list, served in their recently upgraded Conservatory dining room and restaurant, Allium.

The Lowthers' other place to stay nearby is The George and Dragon near Penrith (page 283).

THE NORTH-WEST | NORTHERN ENGLAND

Austwick, North Yorkshire

Austwick, Settle, North Yorkshire
Dales LA2 8BY

Tel 01524 251224
email info@thetraddock.co.uk
website www.thetraddock.co.uk

Nearby the Yorkshire Dales National Park, Settle Carlisle Railway and 3 Peaks of Ingleborough, Whernside and Pen-Y-Ghent **Location** 1 mile off the A65 between Skipton and Kendal; with ample car-parking
Food breakfast, lunch, dinner, bar snacks, afternoon & cream tea
Price ££-£££
Rooms 14; 3 shower only, 3 bath and shower; 5 luxury doubles & 3 suites, all with Plasma TV, phone, hairdryer, tea/coffee facilities, fruit and water
Facilities 2 dining rooms, 3 sitting rooms, 1 bar; garden and patio
Credit cards MC, V
Children welcome **Accessibility** limited **Pets** £10 per dog **Closed** never **Proprietors** Jane, Bruce, Paul and Jenny Reynolds

The Traddock
Country hotel

'Traddock'? It means a trading paddock, and this hotel stands in a field that was forever used for just this purpose. It's a grey stone house on the edge of a mostly pretty village, part of the scenery and ideally located for the big walks in the south-western Yorkshire Dales. A feeling of being in its skin charcterizes the whole place. Renovated and fully refurbished by the Reynoldses in 2002, original features and country antiques sit comfortably alongside new furniture and fabrics in confident country house taste. The three sitting-rooms, one spacious and well proportioned, are quirkily linked by the bar, the standing area in front of it doubling as a passage.

Our reporter's room was again in good country house taste – pine chest, pine wardrobe, rusty-red wall paper nicely offsetting cream-yellow paintwork. With the lounge featuring a log fireplace and canine-companions allowed all year round, the hotel provides a cosy base from which to explore the beauty of the area.

THE NORTH-WEST | NORTHERN ENGLAND

Bashall Eaves, Lancashire

Clitheroe Rd, Bashall Eaves,
Clitheroe BB7 3DA

Tel 01254 826227
email enquiries@theredpumpinn.co.uk
website www.theredpumpinn.co.uk

Nearby Forest of Bowland
Location Bashall Eaves village, short drive from Clitheroe **Food** breakfast and supper
Price ££-£££
Rooms 8 doubles in main building, 4 glamping yurts with double beds, and 4 shepherd huts, one with wood-fired hot tub
Facilities dining room, sitting room, terrace,
Credit cards all major
Accessibility two ground floor rooms
Pets dogs welcome in some rooms areas (sur-charge)
Closed Never
Proprietors Fran and Jonathan

Red Pump Inn
Pub and B&B

Couples who go into hospitality from jobs they don't like almost always get our vote. Fran wanted out of her office job, Jonathan was up for a new venture and they had always dreamed of running a rural B&B. But in 2014 this old pub came on to the market.. Jonathan had run a restaurant in his 20s and understood what it takes. As business took off they added glamping yurts and shepherds' huts, more than doubling the room count. These are beautifully fitted out and rightly popular. Being outdoors in the large garden brings guests a step closer to the grand views to the Forest of Bowland.

The occasional downside of yurts and shepherds' huts is that although they are perfectly waterproof, rain on the roof can keep light sleepers awake, so bear this in mind if you book.

Fran and Jonathan are hands-on owner-managers with the energy and dedication to give guests personal attention. The food gets enthusiastic responses but please note the steak restaurant has closed - instead Fran offers a variety of supper dishes on weekend evenings.

The Red Pump? Jonathan says the name is a mystery and that extensive research has led to nothing. There's a red pump in the car park, but no one knows its history.

THE NORTH-WEST
NORTHERN ENGLAND

Borrowdale, Cumbria

Borrowdale, Keswick, Cumbria
CA12 5UY

Tel 017687 77247
email reservations@leatheshead.co.uk
website www.leatheshead.co.uk

Nearby Derwent Water; Buttermere; Castlerigg Stone Circle.
Location 3.5 miles (5.5 km) S of Keswick, off B5289 to Borrowdale, in 3 acres of grounds; car-parking
Food breakfast, afternoon tea, lunch, dinner
Price ££ **Rooms** 11 double and twin, all with shower, some with bath; all rooms have phone, TV, hairdryer, wi-fi
Facilities 2 sitting rooms, dining room, bar; garden
Credit cards MC, V **Children** not accepted **Accessibility** 1 ground-floor room **Pets** not accepted
Closed 3 weeks in Jan
Proprietor Jane

The Leathes Head
Country hotel

In the beautiful Borrowdale valley near Derwent Water, perched in its own wooded grounds, this Lakeland stone Edwardian house was originally built for a Liverpool ship-owner. Many of its period features, the plasterwork and wood-panelled ceiling in the hall, are still there but are now accompanied by more contemporary Cumbrian products and natural materials. The bar has been dressed with Kirkstone Brathay slate, Cumbrian oak, and a basket light weaved with willow harvested near Cockermouth. The hotel interiors have been crafted stylishly by local artisans.

Sustainability is an increasingly important part of the operation. Produce from the garden (worth exploring) shows up frequently in the menus.

It is informal enough to attract the walkers and climbers who return year after year for the glorious fells ringing the valley. All the bedrooms are comfortable and individually furnished. Bathrooms are modern and light. The three-acre grounds include lawns big enough and level enough to play boules or croquet – and flat areas are few and far between in this region. The real challenges are the fells beyond the gate, and the hotel can help here too, with its extensive collection of walking guides. There are also lake cruises, water sports and mountain biking in the area.

THE NORTH-WEST

NORTHERN ENGLAND

Bowland Bridge, Cumbria

Bowland Bridge, Grange-over-Sands, Cumbria, LA11 6NN

Tel 015395 55549
email
hello@hareandhoundslakes.com
website
www.hareandhoundslakes.com

Nearby Cartmell Fell, Windermere, Bowness, Kendal, World of Beatrix Potter
Location just off the A5074
Food breakfast, lunch, dinner
Price ££-£££
Rooms 4; doubles with ensuites
Facilities pub, dining room, garden, private parking, snug
Credit cards MC, V
Children welcome
Accessibility pub only
Pets dogs welcome
Closed never
Proprietors Andrew Black and Simon Rayner-Langmead

Hare and Hounds
Village inn

Arriving in Bowland Bridge you could feel you're in a sleepy, lost village. But step into this pub and you'll get a lively buzz. Guests, locals and walkers seem to have a common cause: the wonder of the fells around Lake Windermere (and retreating when the weather turns). The lively atmosphere arises partly from the enthusiasm of American co-owner Andrew Black, whose friendliness and curiosity encourage a sense of community among the guests. Restoring this quintessential country pub is the joint venture of long-time friends and day-dreamers, Andrew and Simon Rayner-Langmead.

With quirky artworks, including a Tracy Emin, the Hare and Hounds has energized this old Cumbrian village, and its reputation is growing. Each of the four bedrooms (delightfully named in the vernacular of Cumbrian Shepherds: Yan (one), Tyan (two), Tethera (three), Methera (four) is a testament to classic country cottages, with a palette of warm and inviting hues of earthy tones and soft, muted greens. The daily menu offers a selection of classic Cumbrian dishes and traditional fare. The pub often hosts residencies for talented chefs, so the menu will change. Breakfast is ordered the night before using a checklist. Fresh milk is put outside your room every morning.

THE NORTH-WEST

NORTHERN ENGLAND

Bowland Bridge, Cumbria

Bowland Bridge, Grange-over-Sands
LA11 6NW

Tel 015395 68486
email info@masonsarmsstrawberrybank.co.uk
website www.masonsarmsstrawberrybank.co.uk

Nearby Holker Hall, Hawkshead Brewery, Blackwell Arts & Crafts House, Cartmell Fell
Location overlooking the Winster Valley; access from A5074
Food breakfast, lunch, dinner
Price £-££
Rooms 2 cottages with kitchen and sitting rooms, sleeping 4/6; 5 2-level suites, with sitting areas; all have welcome basket, hairdryer, towels, iron & board
Facilities bar, garden, restaurant
Credit cards MC, V
Children welcome
Accessibility pub accessible but no adapted rooms
Pets welcome (by pre-arrangement)
Closed never
Proprietor Individual Inns

The Masons Arms
Country inn

Despite its peaceful setting on the edge of two country lanes overlooking Windermere, the Masons Arms is far from quiet. Following a generous investment by new owners Individual Inns (Robinsons Brewery) in 2019, this local institution has retained its spirited atmosphere - the pub downstairs gets fairly cramped. It's traditional and rustic with a roaring fire, and, more important, food that can't be faulted. The extensive menu of their award-winning kitchen specializes in hearty pub fare, enhanced by strong flavours and local ingredients: for example, lamb Cartmel – slow roasted shoulder of lamb cooked on the bone, served with garden peas, rosemary and garlic mash and shallots. You can eat in the lovely, heated outdoor seating area, with views across Windermere (which you'll find busy even in colder months).

The quality and spaciousness of the bedrooms mark it out as more than a pub with rooms. The Strawberry Bank Suite is elegantly designed with a four-poster bed, exposed ceiling beams and a freestanding roll-top bath set in a marble niche. Several of the rooms have their own private terraces. You can order breakfast hampers in advance. There's a separate cottage with its own kitchen and sitting area, and two bedrooms on two levels with their own seating areas.

THE NORTH-WEST / NORTHERN ENGLAND

Bowness-on-Windermere, Cumbria

Bowness-on-Windermere, Cumbria
LA23 3JP

Tel 015394 43286
email
reception@lindethfell.co.uk
website www.lindethfell.co.uk

Nearby Windermere Steamboat Museum; Lake Windermere (currently closed).
Location 1 mile (1.5km) S of Bowness on A5074; with ample car-parking
Food breakfast, lunch, dinner and afternoon tea
Price ££
Rooms 14; 12 double and twin, 2 single, 9 with bath, 5 with shower; all rooms have phone, TV, hairdryer
Facilities 2 sitting rooms, dining room, bar; garden, lake, croquet, bowling green
Credit cards MC, V
Children accepted
Accessibility access possible to ground-floor bedroom
Pets not accepted
Closed 3 weeks in Jan
Proprietors Hindle family

Lindeth Fell
Country house bed-and-breakfast

Staying at Lindeth Fell is like visiting a well-heeled old friend who enjoys making his visitors as comfortable as possible, and is justifiably proud of the view from his house. The Hindle family (who also run nearby Storrs Hall Hotel) bought this place from the Kennedy family in 2023. Keen to expand on its exisiting reputation they now serve lunch, dinner and afternoon teas.

Approached through trees, and set in large mature gardens glowing with azaleas and rhododendrons in spring, Lindeth Fell's wood-panelled hall leads to a pair of comfortable and attractive sitting rooms and a restaurant where large windows let in the tremendous view. Weather permitting, drinks and tea can be taken on the terrace, and the same warm weather might even allow for a game of croquet. Upstairs, the rooms vary in size and outlook, and both qualities are reflected in their price. All the rooms are comfortably furnished and pleasingly decorated.

As we went to press the hotel was about to close temporarily for redecorating the public spaces. Reopening was scheduled for spring 2024. Reports welcome.

THE NORTH-WEST

NORTHERN ENGLAND

Bowness-on-Windermere, Cumbria

Crook Road, Bowness-on-Windermere, Cumbria LA23 3JA

Tel 015394 88600
email reception@linthwaitehouse.com
website www.leeucollection.com

Nearby Windermere Steamboat Museum; Lake Windermere; Beatrix Potter's Hilltop
Location 1 mile (1.5km) S of Bowness off the A5074; with ample car parking
Food breakfast, lunch, dinner
Price ££-£££
Rooms 36 double and twin with bath; all rooms have phone, TV, hairdryer; wi-fi
Facilities sitting rooms, conservatory, dining rooms, bar; terrace, garden, veranda, plunge pool
Credit cards AE, MC, V
Children accepted
Accessibility one specially adapted room **Pets** accepted
Closed never
Proprietor Leeu Collection

Linthwaite House
Country house hotel

This Edwardian country house is a very professionally-run place with a unique style. The reception rooms are filled with palms, wicker furniture and old curios as well as antiques. Painted decoys, well-travelled cabin trunks and oriental vases help to evoke days of leisure and service in the far reaches of the Empire.

Service here manages to be crisp and amiable at the same time: you are made to feel that you are on holiday and not on parade. Whether you eat in the richly coloured dining room or the Mirror Room, the food has come from Chris O'Callaghan's kitchen – well-thought-out menus, beautifully presented. Bad luck, though, if you're under seven: it's an early tea for you, without the option.

Of the bedrooms, the best look directly towards Windermere, some are in a modern annexe, and there is quite a variation in size. They all have style though, with thoughtful use of fabrics and furnishings, and bathrooms that are attractive rather than utilitarian. Beyond the terraces outside are 14 acres of lawn, shrubs, woods and a small lake.

THE NORTH-WEST
NORTHERN ENGLAND

Brampton, Cumbria

Brampton, Cumbria CA8 2NG

Tel 016977 46234
email farlam@farlamhall.co.uk
website www.farlamhall.co.uk

Nearby Hadrian's Wall; Lanercost Priory; North Pennines (Area of Outstanding Natural Beauty)
Location 3 miles (5 km) SE of Brampton on A689, NE of (not in) Farlam village; with ample car parking
Food breakfast, dinner; afternoon tea (pre-booking essential)
Price ££££
Rooms 12 double with bath; all rooms have phone, TV, hairdryer
Facilities 2 sitting rooms, dining room, wi-fi; garden, croquet
Credit cards MC, V
Children accepted over 5
Accessibility 2 ground-floor bedrooms **Pets** welcome
Closed 2 weeks in Jan
Proprietors Joe and Kathy

Farlam Hall
Country house hotel

'Charming family, quiet surroundings, excellent food,' are the phrases that encapsulate Farlam Hall. Since 1975 the Quinion family has assiduously improved their solid but elegant Border country house. It has its roots in Elizabethan times, but what you see today is essentially a large, Victorian family home, extended for a big family and frequent entertaining. No coincidence that it makes such a good hotel.

The dining room and public rooms are discreet and the atmosphere is one of traditional English service and comfort. The bedrooms vary widely, with some decidedly large and swish. Nevertheless, all are luxurious and charmingly done out, and some have beautiful views of the grounds flocked with sheep.

In 2019 Americans Joe and Kathy became the new owners of Farlam Hall. Once regular guests, now proprietors, the couple did a total refurb of the interior and bought in Hrishikesh Desai as chef-patron. With half an acre of the ground dedicated to growing produce the Cedar Tree restaurant serves a fresh and varied tasting menu described as 'French, with spice'. Farlam Hall is well placed to explore Hadrian's Wall and the Northumberland Coast.

Clifton, Cumbria

Clifton, Near Penrith, Cumbria
CA10 2ER

Tel 01768 865 381
email enquries@georgeanddrag-onclifton.co.uk
website www.georgeanddrag-onclifton.co.uk

Nearby Ullswater; Lowther Castle
Location come off the M6 at junction 39 towards Shap, continue for 10 minutes and you will come to Clifton; has its own car park
Food breakfast, lunch, dinner
Price ££-£££
Rooms 6; superiors, single and family rooms
Facilities restaurant, bar, private dining room, garden, courtyard
Credit cards all major
Children welcome
Accessibility public areas only
Pets welcome in rooms and bar but not restaurant, small charge for dogs
Closed Christmas
Proprietor Charles Lowther

George and Dragon
Country inn

Recently reopened and sensitively restored after a being gutted by a fire in 2022, this place – a charming village tavern – is back at the heart of its community. The owner Charles Lowther and his mother, Caroline, Countess of Lonsdale, took over in 2008 and their warm welcome is still infectious.

The works have kept the bar as its focal point and allow for an uninterrupted view all the way to the far side of the colourful wooden-panelled restaurant. The open bar and grill is still at its heart and the menu has also had a revamp thanks to chef, Gareth Webster. The focus is on tasty, locally sourced, enhanced pub fare. Venison and beef features large and most of the produce comes directly from the Lowther Estate where Charles breeds Shorthorn cattle.

Bedrooms are homely, some a little awkwardly shaped, but redeemed by stylish furshishing, luxury bath products and comfortable beds. It's a great, affordable base from which to explore the Lake District, or stopover when travelling on the M6.

Guests can be taken stalking by the Estate's head stalker and there are one or two good fishing spots nearby. The George and Dragon is the little sister of Askham Hall, page 274, where Charles Lowther spent his childhood. Come for lunch, dinner or to while away the time amongst regulars with a pint of ale.

THE NORTH-WEST / NORTHERN ENGLAND

Crosthwaite, Cumbria

Crosthwaite, Lyth Valley
LA8 8HR

Tel 015395 68237
email info@the-punchbowl.co.uk
website www.the-punchbowl.co.uk

Nearby Lake District National Park, Grizedale Forst Park, Windermere, Kendal
Location just N of the A5074 between Bowness and Levens
Food breakfast, luch, tea, dinner
Price ££
Rooms 9 doubles; all with bath and shower
Facilities restaurant, bar, sitting rooms
Credit cards AE, MC, V
Children welcome
Accessibility not suitable
Pets not accepted
Closed never
Proprietors Richard Rose and Amanda Robinson
General Manager Claudiu Onofrei

The Punch Bowl
Country inn

Richard and Amanda have been running the Punch Bowl for almost 30 years. They have done it up in contemporary style, using mushroomy off-white shades from heritage paint makers. Tiny high-intensity downlighters make the free-standing roll-top bath and expensive taps glitter. Little bottles of as-it-were home-made shampoo and body lotion have hand-written labels. The power shower is excellent. The bath towels are enormous. The tongued and grooved wainscoting is painted Cooking Apple Green. More original is the old-style Roberts radio beside the bed tuned to Classic FM and playing when you first come in: perhaps a bit self-conscious, but not disagreeable.

The kitchen team, headed by Arthur Bridgeman-Quin, draws people from far and wide to eat quite luxurious and very imaginative dishes, made with great flair. William Nicholson's woodcuts of Twelve Sports, a polished refectory table with a bowl of fashionable green foliage and a dish of used corks give the room the air of a smart London restaurant, though the waitresses at the Punch Bowl are much nicer than their big city counterparts. The same dishes are obtainable in the bar for those who want to eat more informally. The surrounding countryside is lovely, the welcome genuine. A truly charming small hotel.

THE NORTH-WEST — NORTHERN ENGLAND

Grasmere, Cumbria

Keswick Road, Grasmere, Cumbria, LA22 9RN

Tel 015394 35250
email info@theforestside.com
website www.theforestside.com

Nearby Dove Cottage and the Wordsworth Museum, Sarah Nelson's Grasmere Gingerbread Shop, Heaton Cooper Studio
Location on at foot of Butter Crag; at end of a private drive approx. 300m off A591 Ambleside to Keswick Road. In 43 acres
Food breakfast, lunch, dinner
Price £££-££££
Rooms 20; 12 double, 5 of which can accomodate extra guests; 8 twin. All have wi-fi, TV, tea and coffee tray, hairdryer, toiletries
Facilities bar, restaurant, sitting room. private dining room, 43 acres of grounds **Credit cards** all major
Children over 12s welcome in restaurant **Accessibility** 1 adapted rooom, with roll-in wet room **Pets** 6 dog-friendly rooms, 2 dogs max (£20 per day) **Closed** 7-12th Jan
General Manager Gareth Newton

Forest Side
Restaurant-with-rooms

Our series editor Fiona Duncan had misgivings when she entered Forest Side's slick interior, which seemed a little out of step with the hotel's handsome slate-built exterior and Lakeland setting. These fears were quickly allayed by a warm Northern welcome, and the hotel soon stole her heart. Owner Andrew Wildsmith has lavished £4 million as well as his attention to detail, which made Hipping Hall – his other hotel – such a success.

The interiors are beautifully done: expect genuine Lincrusta walls, shimmery velvet sofas and bird of paradise wallpapers. At first they may seem a little too carefully composed and 'designer', but this belies what is in fact a well-thought out symbiosis between the hotel with its natural setting and local traditions: wool from sheep in the surrounding fields is used for carpets and beds, waiters are dressed in Pendle Tweed hacking jackets, and local pottery is used for dining.

The hotel's *raison d'être* is its food: a stand out culinary experience commandeered by chef Paul Leonard whose passion for foraging and processes like pickling, distilling and curing, makes for a menu that is both satisfyingly earthy yet light and modern. You will be pleasantly surprised by some unusual ingredients, including salsify root and seaweed custard.

THE NORTH-WEST
NORTHERN ENGLAND

Great Eccleston, Lancashire

Cartford Lane, Little Eccleston, Lancashire, PR3 0YP

Tel 01995670166
email office@thecartfordinn.co.uk
website www.thecartfordinn.com

Nearby Fylde Coast, Forest of Bowland, River Wyre, Lancaster Castle, Blackpool Tower
Location Great Eccleston
Food breakfast, lunch, dinner, afternoon tea at onsite deli
Price £££-££££
Rooms 8; 2 treehouse cabins, 2 river view suites, 1 penthouse suite, 2 river rooms, 1 ground floor room
Facilities dining room, sitting room, delicastessen, art and furnitre shop, Bowland and Bay Artisan foodie tours
Credit cards MC, V, AmEx
Children no
Accessibilty difficult, enquire
Pets no
Closed Jan
Proprietors Julie and Patrick Beame

The Cartford Inn
Riverside hotel

In a little-visited corner of the North West, on a peaceful bend of the river Wyre, this place's real heart, soul and energy is that of owners Patrick and Julie Beame. This husband-wife duo's passion for their community seeps into every nook of this old 17thC Inn. The hotel and its adjoining bar, restaurant, onsite deli, and gallery are also an vibrant showcase for local artisans and creatives.

Since 2007, the hotel has evolved from a dilapidated old coach house into a trendy boutique. We stayed in their newly constructed, chic, treehouse-esque rooms, which perch on stilts overlooking the orchard and river. These converted shipping containers are calmly decorated with stylish furniture, quirky artwork and soft natural materials.

The menu is adventurous and, with locally sourced ingredients, embraces the flavours of different cuisines: tangy ceviche, pakora with zhoug, merguez sausages, French gateaux and banana blossom. Patrick has worked closely with a vineyard and a local distiller to develop a unique line of wine and a gin that echo the flavours often found in his kitchen. Breakfast is equally impressive and in the daylight the same space is transformed, with its floor-to-ceiling windows offering dramatic views towards the Bowland Fells. For foodies, creatives, and curious explorers, this hotel is a destination in itself.

THE NORTH-WEST — NORTHERN ENGLAND

Hawkshead, Cumbria

Near Sawrey, Hawkshead, Ambleside, Cumbria LA22 0JZ

Tel 015394 36393
email mail@eeswyke.co.uk
website www.eeswyke.co.uk

Nearby Hill Top; Lake Windermere; Grasmere.
Location in hamlet on B5285, 2 miles (3 km) SE of Hawkshead; with car parking
Food breakfast, dinner
Price ££
Rooms 8 double and twin, 2 with bath, 6 with shower; all rooms have TV, hairdryer, hospitality tray
Facilities 2 sitting rooms, dining room; garden
Credit cards MC, V **Children** accepted over 12
Accessibility not suitable
Pets not accepted
Closed never
Proprietors Richard Lee

Ees Wyke
Country house

Esthwaite Water, to the east of Windermere, has been kept safely in private hands, so has escaped the development that has ravaged some of the other Lakes. Ees Wyke, a gem of a white-painted Georgian mansion, is perched above park-like meadows that roll gently down to the reed banks on the shore, punctuated here and there by sheep and mature trees. As well as unmarred views, Richard has happily discovered the secret of making people feel instantly at home.

This is a well-kept house, with everything just so, even down to a plentiful supply of games and books for those inclement days. In the dining room are beautiful large windows to show off the view (these are new since Beatrix Potter stayed here for her holidays), with crisp white tablecloths. The dinners run to three generous and unhurried courses and the price/quality ratio of the wine list is definitely tipped in your favour. The bedrooms are attractive and generously proportioned, most with small but well-equipped bathrooms, and comfortable enough to allow you to build up the strength you need to tackle the truly heroic Lakeland breakfast.

THE NORTH-WEST — NORTHERN ENGLAND

Kirkby Lonsdale, Cumbria

6 Market Street, Kirkby Lonsdale

Tel 01524271965
email email@sun-inn.info
website www.sun-inn.info

Nearby Ingleton Waterfalls, Sizergh Castle, Levens Hall, Yorkshire Three Peaks, Casterton Golf Course
Location Along the A65
Food breakfast, lunch, dinner
Price ££-£££
Rooms 11
Facilities dining room, bar
Credit cards MC, V
Children welcome
Accessibility ground floor bar and restaurant only
Pets dogs welcome
Closed never
Proprietors Jenny and Iain Black

The Sun Inn
Pub with rooms

Characterful, un-complicated and classically Olde English, this place sits in the heart of charming market-town Kirkby Lonsdale. Our reporter marvelled at how he had never stumbled across the location before, with its attractive northern charm and its proximity to North Yorkshire, Lancashire and, of course, the Lake District.

Inside this white-washed 17thC Inn the downstairs is open plan and cosy with wood-burners, exposed-brick beams, dark red walls, wood panelling and antique chairs. Smart and friendly, the space is popular with families, foodies and walkers.

The wine and beer selection is notably extensive and good value and is accompanied by a brasserie-bordering-on-gastropub style menu devised by keen forager, Chef Joe Robinson. Our reporter Jonathan enjoyed his meal of 'typical English fayre' although was distracted by an unharmoniously loud background music. However, owners Jenny and Iain, reassure us that this was unusual and that calm has been restored.

The bedrooms are as spacious as a building of this age allows - some more awkward than others. Tastefully done and attractive, all 11 rooms have a calm and contemporary countryside feel. Affordable and snug, this place is an excellent pit stop for long journeys along the M6.

THE NORTH-WEST — NORTHERN ENGLAND

Loweswater, Cumbria

Loweswater, Cockermouth CA13 0RU

Tel 01900 85219
email info@kirkstile.com
website www.kirkstile.com

Nearby Buttermere, Honister Pass, Whinlatter Forest, Cockermouth
Location towards Loweswater
Food breakfast, lunch, dinner, picnic baskets on request
Price ££-£££
Rooms 9; one twin, doubles, king-size doubles including 1 family suite and one family annexe room
Facilities dining room, sitting room, brewery
Credit cards MC, V
Children welcome
Accessibilty 3 ground floor rooms
Pets dogs welcome,
Closed never
Proprietors Roger and Helen Humphries

Kirkstile Inn
Country Inn

Outside, it's a familiar two-storey whitewashed Lake District stone building with black window frames. Inside, the bedrooms are smart, contemporary and in restrained good taste - you could be in the Home Counties - but with pleasant antique pieces to offset the new fabrics: here a four poster, there a large free-standing clothes cupboard or a handsome marble-top chest of drawers. All is harmonious and comfortable. A recent guest considered her room 'clean and immaculately comfortable' and the service 'exemplary'.

Few places in the Lake District do the combination of characterful, beamy inn, comfort and fabulous surroundings as well as this. Kirkstile is on the western side of the Lakes near Crummock Water, a little removed from the central and eastern visitor honeypots, which can be a plus in itself. 'The surrounding scenery is out of this world' says the same guest. Owners Roger and Helen Humphreys take an active interest but friendly, competent general manager Anna is in charge day to day.

THE NORTH-WEST | NORTHERN ENGLAND

Penrith, Cumbria

Another Place, The Lake, Ullswater, Watermillock CA11 0LP

Tel 01768486442
email life@another.place
website www.another.place

Nearby Lake District National Park
Location 10 minutes from the M6, 15 minutes from Penrith
Food breakfast, lunch, dinner
Price £££-££££
Rooms 40 rooms in main building plus 6 shepherd huts
Facilities dining areas, bar, lounge, swimming pool, treehouse, terrace, spa treatments
Credit cards MC, V, AE
Children allowed
Accessibilty access to most spaces
Pets dogs welcome
Closed never
Proprietors Watergate Bay

Another Place Lakeside
Country hotel

Inspired by its sister hotel, Watergate Bay in Cornwall, this place brings something new to the Lake District. By including it, we go a little off piste, but what's provided here is unique. The location between lake and hills is both calming and inspiring.

Rooms vary in size, and some are large. Twenty rooms in the main building have recently been upgraded and repainted in fresh new colours. However, the traditional lakeside style has been retained, with dark brown furniture and cosy seating areas. The other 20 rooms have a contemporary style.

The tucked-away shepherd huts have more of a country feel: the cushions in muted earth colours match the wooden wall panels, and the snug living spaces are complete with log burners.

After an active day of lake swimming, kayaking, paddle boarding, pilates, massages and more, retreat to one of three dining areas. The formal Rampsbeck Restaurant offers a three-course menu based on seasonal and local produce. The Glasshouse is new and close to the shore with panelling which harks back to the Victorian era, and a modern wood-fired pizza-oven. Service is relaxed but prompt. The casual dress code might leave guests confused about who is staff and who isn't.

Prices are in line with Lake District rates, but the big choice of activities gives added value.

THE NORTH-WEST

NORTHERN ENGLAND

Sawrey, Cumbria

Near Sawrey, Ambleside, Cumbria, LA22 0LF

Tel 015394 36334
email info@towerbankarms.co.uk
website www.towerbankarms.co.uk

Nearby Hilltop (NT), between Esthwaite Water and Windermere.
Location beside B5285 near Sawrey; some car parking
Food breakfast (residents only), lunch, dinner
Price ££
Rooms 4; 2 doubles, 1 twin, 1 superior double, all with shower; all rooms have TV, tea and coffee making facilities
Facilities bar, restaurant
Credit cards AE, MC, V
Children welcome on premises until 9pm
Accessibility not suitable
Pets accepted in bar and overnight in rooms
Closed Winter hours from November to early February
Proprietor Anthony Hutton

Tower Bank Arms
Country inn

Beatrix Potter pilgrims need look no further. This simple inn, a short walk from Hilltop (NT), where many of Miss Potter's books were written, is surely where Mr MacGregor allowed himself an occasional dram and it is to be seen – distantly – in The Tale of Jemima Puddleduck.

It looks more like a cottage than a pub, only the ticking clock over the porch suggesting otherwise. The inn caters for many people staying in B&Bs in the village and the owner wants the exterior to look unpretentious, feeling that walkers with muddy boots or those on budgets might otherwise be put off. Dinner is extremely popular so don't forget to book. For £9.75 at lunchtime enjoy dishes such as Cumbrian beef & ale Stew (with herby dumplings and mashed potato), in surroundings grander than one would expect at that price, with Wedgwood china and linen napkins. It is not a posh place or a large one – three doubles and one twin room – but it is clean and tidy and the flagstoned bar offers the comfort of a wood-fired range and a number of good beers. Don't come here expecting tea on the lawn or room service. But if your imagination is fired by a view of the street where Mrs Tabitha Twitchet or the Sandy-Whiskered Gentleman strolled, this could be for you.

NORTHERN ENGLAND — THE NORTH-WEST

Shibden Mill, West Yorkshire

Shibden Mill Fold, Halifax, HX3 7UL

Tel 01422 365840
email enquiries@shibdenmillinn.com
website www.shibdenmillinn.com

Nearby Halifax, Shibden Hall, Calderdale Industrial Museum, Square Chapel Arts Centre
Location beside B5285 near Sawrey; some car parking
Food breakfast, lunch, afternoon tea, dinner
Price ££-£££
Rooms 11; 6 standard, 3 superior, 1 small double and 1 suite with private terrrace.
Facilities bar, restaurant
Credit cards All major
Children welcome
Accessibility downstairs only
Pets no
Closed never
Proprietor Max and Caitlin Heaton

Shibden Mill
Pub-with-rooms

At the shady bottom of what is almost a gorge but in fact a very steep-sided valley, your greeting is the soothing sound of flowing water from the river running through. The inn, with its long history, is a popular local destination, fronted by a large car park (a filled in millpond) which only slightly detracts from the charm. Once inside you should be taken by the authentic period interior with its mellow 18th and 19thC furniture.

We've overlooked it in previous editions but since the pandemic the modern British food, several notches up from gastropub fare, has been getting better and better. The sophisticated tasting menu, at £70 per person as we went to press, offered nine courses. How about cod, bacon dashi, mussels and girolles? Five matched wines by the glass cost £35.

The bedrooms and bathrooms, some recently refurbished, are comfortable but will appeal to the 40-60 year olds rather than the 20s and 30s.

Outside is a dining and drinking area, busy on summer weekends, which manages to coexist with the posh food indoors. An attractive oasis in a generally industrial area with few outstanding places.

THE NORTH-WEST

Ullswater, Cumbria

Ullswater, Cumbria, CA11 0PH.

Tel 01768 482874
email stay@glenriddinghouse.com
website www.glenriddinghouse.com

Nearby at centre of Lake District National Park, Helvellyn (3 m)
Location on shores of Ullswater. Free parking.
Food breakfast, packed lunch (pre-arranged), afternoon tea, dinner (pre-booked)
Price ££££
Rooms 4; 1 suite-ensuite, 3 double-superior-ensuite; all Regency style with bathrobes, shower/wetroom or bathroom, toiletries, seating area, TV, wi-fi, refreshment tray, views
Facilities breakfast room, dining room, landscaped gardens, ample parking
Credit cards AE, MC, V
Children not allowed
Accessibility some, enquire before
Pets not allowed
Closed enquire before
Proprietors Inn Collection Group

Glenridding House
Boutique bed-and-breakfast

Darwin declared this place to be 'magnificently beautiful' when he holidayed here in 1881 – and that rings true today. The Grade II-listed villa, built in 1815, is bursting with classic Regency elegance. The current owners spent seven years carefully restoring it to former glory, starting with its striking wrap-around latticed balcony, complete with outdoor furniture and direct access to all the bedrooms. Their real *raison d'être*, however, is the location on the shores of Ullswater, with a path down to the lake for easy-access swimming. It's surrounded by the dramatic fells and crags of the Lake District, with opportunities for great walks.

The bedrooms continue the Regency theme, with oak floors, window shutters and brass Victorian bedsteads (many have four-posters). Egyptian cotton bedding and bathrobes are matched with exquisite showers, wetrooms or bathrooms.

Breakfast, served in the lovely Darwin Lakeview Room, includes a full English as well as choices such as Manx kipper fillets, and a simple but excellent dinner can be pre-arranged. This might include wild baked salmon with new potatoes, followed by sticky toffee pudding. Hospitality extends to afternoon tea, with an array of scones and jams set up before the French windows in the sitting room, with views across the lake.

Wasdale Head, Cumbria

Wasdale Head, Seascale, Cumbria
CA20 1EX

Tel 019467 26229
email reception@wasdale.com
website www.wasdale.com

Nearby Hardknott Castle Roman Fort; Ravenglass and Eskdale Railway; Wastwater; Scafell Pike.
Location 9 miles (14.5 km) NE of Gosforth at head of Wasdale; with ample car parking
Food breakfast, bar and packed lunches, dinner
Price ££
Rooms 18; 9 doubles, 3 suites, all have telephone and TV; also 6 self-catering apartments
Facilities sitting room, dining room, 2 bars; garden **Credit cards** MC, V
Children accepted
Accessibility 2 ground floor rooms
Pets accepted in 9 rooms, 5 self-catered apartments and all public areas except the restaurant
Closed never **Proprietors** Nigel and Lesley Burton

Wasdale Head Inn
Mountain inn

The Wasdale Head is in a site unrivalled even in the consistently spectacular Lake District. It stands on the flat valley bottom between three major peaks – Pillar, Great Gable and Scafell Pike (England's highest) – and only a little way above Wastwater, England's deepest and perhaps most dramatic lake.

Over the last decade and a half, the old inn has been carefully and thoughtfully modernized, adding facilities but retaining the characteristics of a traditional mountain inn. The main sitting room of the hotel is comfortable and welcoming, with plenty of personal touches. The bedrooms are not notably spacious but they are adequate, with fixtures and fittings all in good condition. There are also six self-catering apartments in a converted barn, and three suites.

The dining room is heavily panelled, and decorated with willow pattern china and a pewter jug collection. There is also now a children's menu. Food is considerably better than you would expect of a mountaineering inn, served by young, friendly staff. There are two bars. The one for residents has some magnificent wooden furniture, while tasty bar food is served in the congenial surroundings of the public bar, much frequented by walkers and climbers.

Whitewell, Lancashire

The Inn at Whitewell, Forest of Bowland, near Clitheroe, Lancashire BB7 3AT

Tel 01200 448222
email reception@innatwhitewell.com
website www.innatwhitewell.com

Nearby Browsholme Hall; Clitheroe Castle; Blackpool.
Location 6 miles (9.5 km) NW of Clitheroe; with ample car parking
Food breakfast, picnic lunch on request, dinner, bar meals
Price ££
Rooms 25 double and twin, 1 suite, all with bath and/or shower; all rooms have phone, TV and bluetooth speakers
Facilities dining rooms, bar; garden, fishing, cycling route, golf nearby, wine tasting
Credit cards DC, MC, V
Children welcome
Accessibility 2 ground-floor rooms
Pets welcome **Closed** never
Proprietor Charles Bowman

The Inn at Whitewell
Country inn

Past and present come together with great effect at this welcoming inn with a glorious situation, on a riverbank plumb in the middle of the Forest of Bowland. In the 14th century it was a small manor house where the Keeper of the Forest lived. Today, some of the original architecture survives and rooms are furnished with antiques, but modern comfort is the order of the day, with, for example, bluetooth speakers in all the bedrooms. Most of these are spacious and attractive, with warm lighting and prints clustered on the walls; many contain an extra sofa bed; a couple have four-posters. To keep romance alive, you can book one of the rooms with a fireplace and snuggle up to a cosy peat fire or wallow in the deep vintage baths.

Food is an important consideration here. English dishes feature predominately on the menu – seasonal roast game or grilled fish, followed by wicked homemade puddings and a selection of farmhouse cheeses. Alternatively, bar meals are on offer at lunchtime and in the evening. Just past the bar is a small shop that sells a great selection of wines, books, and other bits and bobs. Be sure to check the terms and conditions of the inn before making a booking.

THE NORTH-WEST
NORTHERN ENGLAND

Windermere, Cumbria

Ambleside Road, Windermere,
LA23 1AX

Tel 015394 448222
email stay@cedarmanor.co.uk
website www.cedarmanor.co.uk

Nearby Windermere Lake,
Holehird Gardens, Blackwell House,
Hill Top (Beatrix Potter), Dove
Cottage (Wordsworth)
Location on A591 next to St Mary's
Church
Food breakfast, afternoon tea,
lounge and room service **Price** ££ -
££££ **Rooms** 10; 8 double (2 can be
twin), 2 double suites with separate
dining/sitting room; all have tea/coffee facilities, TV, wi-fi
Facilities 2 sitting rooms, bar, dining room, garden and patio, giftshop
Credit cards MC, V, debit cards
Children welcome, 2 rooms have
sofa beds, only 10+ in dining room
Accessibility no special facilities
Pets not allowed **Closed** 1 week for
Christmas, 3 weeks in Jan
Proprietor Jonathan Kaye

Cedar Manor
Boutique hotel

A short walk north of Windermere, hidden behind trees and greenery, stands Cedar Manor with its grey brick façade and mullioned windows – built in the 19thC by the same architect who designed nearby St Mary's Church.

Its owners, Caroline and Jonathan Kaye are a friendly, hands-on couple with an eye for detail. There are two comfortable sitting rooms decorated with imaginative wallpaper and harmonious colours. One leads to a wooden carved bar, while the other displays a collection of arts, crafts and jewellery – all for sale, and made by local artists. Bedrooms and bathrooms are gracefully decorated, with canopied beds and furniture made to fit by local craftsmen. The award-winning detached Coach House Suite features a dining area and a twin spa bath. In the evening, relax with a drink in the patio by the great cedar tree.

Their candlelit restaurant offers a short but excellent menu, focussing on modern English cuisine – save room for dessert.

Jonathan, who used to manage the exclusive Raffles nightclub in Chelsea, hosts weekly backgammon nights, as well as the yearly Lake District backgammon championship. There is friendly banter, relaxed organisation and informal mingling – Cedar Manor in a nutshell.

Windermere, Cumbria

Crook Road, near Windermere,
Cumbria LA23 3NE

Tel 015394 88818
email hotel@thegilpin.co.uk
website www.thegilpin.co.uk

Nearby Windermere Steamboat Museum; Holker Hall; Sizergh Castle; Kendal; Grasmere.
Location on B5284 Kendal to Bowness road, 2 miles (1 km) SE of Windermere; with ample car parking
Food breakfast, lunch, dinner
Price £££ **Rooms** (Gilpin Hotel) 14 double and twin with bath; 6 Garden Suites with hot tubs; (Gilpin Lake House) 6 suites with bath, 2 double and twin with shower; all rooms have phone, TV, minibar, hairdryer.
Facilities (2 sitting rooms, 4 dining rooms; garden, swimming pool, sauna, hot tubs, jetty spa, boat house, private lake **Credit cards** AE, DC, MC, V **Children** accepted over 7 **Accessibility** limited, call to discuss **Pets** not accepted **Closed** never **Proprietors** Cunliffe family

Gilpin Hotel & Lake House **Country house hotel**

Just occasionally, whether by luck or judgement, you can arrive somewhere that tells you to congratulate yourself on your choice of hotel before you even step through the door: Gilpin Hotel & Lake House is one of these happy places. Barney Cunliffe's great grandmother lived in this Edwardian house for 40 years, and when his parents came 25 years later, it had become a rather ordinary B&B. Now, with manicured grounds and gleaming paint, quite substantially and wholly sympathetically enlarged and set on a peaceful hillside with moor beyond the boundary, you are to some extent prepared for the warm welcome and deep-pile comfort waiting for you inside. This is a highly professional and well-staffed operation, yet still driven by the enthusiasm of owners whose unmistakeable priority is the happiness of their guests.

If your tastes run to good pictures, fine furniture and immaculate service you will be happy; if they include excellent and imaginatively presented food with more than the occasional touch of outright luxury, you will be happier still; and if you want a large, thoughtfully decorated room, probably with its own sitting area, and a bathroom to talk about when you get home, then you're in luck.

The hotel also has five detached spa lodges.

THE NORTH-WEST   NORTHERN ENGLAND

Windermere, Cumbria

Holbeck Lane, Windermere,
Cumbria LA23 1LU

Tel 015394 32375
email stay@holbeckghyll.com
website www.holbeckghyll.com

Nearby Lake Windermere.
Location 3 miles (5 km) N of
Windermere, E of A591; with ample
car parking
Food breakfast, light lunch, dinner
Price ££££
Rooms 23 double, all with bath; 4
suites; all have phone, TV, hairdryer
Facilities 2 sitting rooms, 2 dining
rooms; garden, health spa, tennis,
croquet, Jacuzzi
Credit cards AE, DC, MC, V
Children welcome
Accessibility 3 lodge rooms
Pets accepted in the Lodge rooms
Closed 2 weeks Jan
Director Ross Marshall

Holbeck Ghyll
Country house hotel

An award-winning hotel in a classic Victorian lakeland house, ivy-clad with steep slate roofs and mullioned windows – plus oak panelling and art noveau stained glass. Our latest reporter had a 'friendly welcome' and was impressed by its superb position, providing both privacy from the bustle of Windermere and grand lake views from the immaculate gardens; also indeed by the two comfortable sitting rooms, both homelike and beautifully furnished.

The buildings have been refurbished to very high standards in a traditional, slightly formal style – though proprietors and staff alike are friendly and relaxed. Bedrooms and bathrooms are beautifully and individually decorated, very spacious, some with their own sitting room. At the top of the house is a 'very special' four-poster room. In the Lodge nearby are six further rooms (four are self-catering), with breathtaking views.

The food remains a clear attraction: pre-dinner canapés are served while you select from the inventive daily-changing menus. Tasting menus, an exclusive Chef's table experience and a more casual Lounge menu are on offer as ex-head chef turned director Ross attempts to develop the hotel into more of a restaurant-with-rooms.

There is a jogging trail from which you can spot deer and red squirrels.

THE NORTH-WEST — NORTHERN ENGLAND

Wiswell, Lancashire

8 Vicarage Fold, Wiswell, Clitheroe
BB7 9DF

Tel 01254 822218
email enquiries@freemasonswiswell.co.uk
website www.freemasonswiswell.com

Nearby Clitheroe Market, Pendle Hill, Whalley Bridge,, Forest of Bowland
Location just north of Blackburn
Food breakfast, lunch, dinner
Price ££-£££
Rooms 4; 2 doubles with bathroom and 2 suites with bathroom
Facilities pub, TV's, nespresso machines, bathtubs, private dining rooms
Credit cards MC, V
Children welcome
Accessibility to ground floor rooms and pub
Pets dogs welcome in ground floor rooms
Closed never
Chef-owner Steven Smith

Freemasons
Pub-with-rooms

Popular with city dwellers escaping Manchester and Liverpool this Ribble Valley pub-with-rooms is a foodie Mecca. The menu, devised by Steven Smith, gives a new meaning to gastro-pub food. The cosy first floor is neatly decorated with hunting lodge memorabilia and has low ceilings, exposed beams and flagstone floors. A smart private dining space upstairs is also available. We had the sampling menu - unforgettable, but pricey.

The accommodation is a new addition to the pub and makes a calm retreat from the busy restaurant. Named after country animals, the four rooms have trendy wooden cladding and contemporary furnishings. All have bathtubs, and in the two mezzanine rooms, Mr. Fox and Mr. Hare, the baths are on their own levels.

This makes a useful base for exploring the local countryside and historical towns, such as Clitheroe with its castle and market square, as well as walking trails and cycling routes. Parking near the hotel is awkward: try to find a space on one of the roads road running either side of the pub.

THE NORTH-WEST

Arkengarthdale, North Yorkshire

Arkengarthdale, nr Richmond,
North Yorkshire DL11 6EN

Tel (01748) 884567
email info@cbinn.co.uk
website www.cbinn.co.uk
Food breakfast, lunch, dinner
Price ££
Closed Christmas Day
Proprietors Charles Cody

Charles Bathurst Inn
Country inn

Charles Cody turned this once derelict inn in Arkengarthdale into something special. It is very popular with Dales people, to whom it is important socially, and this may have made it a bit clannish, even self-satisfied. The bedrooms have glorious views. They are light and modern, with homely touches and some period furniture. Downstairs, the ambience is darker and more masculine. A large and tempting menu of locally-sourced dishes is painted on the vast mirror at one end of the room. The inn is halfway along the Coast to Coast walk and those setting out from here can expect a hearty breakfast and good advice, well-made sandwiches for lunch and a Thermos of something warm.

Reports welcome.

Aysgarth, North Yorkshire

Aysgarth, Leyburn DL8 3SR

Tel 01969 663775
email info@aysgarthfallshotel.com
website www.aysgarthfallshotel.com
Food breakfast, lunch, afternoon tea, dinner
Price £-££
Closed never
Proprietors The Brook Group

Aysgarth Falls
Country hotel

Following the retirement of previous owners this place has had a contemporary restoration making it more than just a useful address. Downstairs it's essentially a big bar, eating and dining area, congenially decorated, with a pleasant atmosphere and well above-average food – try the Korean chicken or other pub classics.

Bedrooms are neat, newly refurbished in pleasant neutral colours and have new bathrooms. It's well placed, of course, for the famous Aysgarth Falls but also for the many Wensleydale walks and sights.

Barngate, Cumbria

Drunken Duck Inn
Country inn

So named after a Victorian landlady who found her ducks lying on the nearby crossroads. Presuming them dead, she started to pluck them; but soon realized that they were actually blind drunk, and not dead in the slightest. This inn has real character and charm. The bar/pub is delightful and exactly as you would hope an old country inn should look and feel. The menu in the bar and dining room is extensive, yet not overambitious.

Ambling round the side of the inn you will come across the 'deluxe' and 'superior' rooms. Each is individually decorated with contemporary yet comfortable furniture and fabrics, and has the added perk of private garden sitting areas. The standard bedrooms in the main house are also tastefully done out, if a little cramped.

Barngate, Ambleside, Cumbria, LA22 0NG

Tel 015394 36347
email info@drunkenduckinn.co.uk
website www.drunkenduckinn.co.uk
Food breakfast, lunch, dinner
Price ££–£££
Closed Christmas Day
Proprietors Stephanie Barton

Bowness-on-Windermere, Cumbria

The White House
Country hotel

Almost awkwardly located in the heart of Bowness-On-Windermere this place follows a trendy room-service-only model. Check in is by text, there are no keys just access codes and without communal areas there is no chance of bumping into other guests. This is unusual, but has a certain appeal for travellers wanting to remain contactless.

We liked the colourful and contemporary option this place offers to an area saturated with samey country-style hotels. It's bold walls and tiles against the original stone walls offers a unique metropolitan feel to what is one of the oldest buildings in this busy tourist town.

A short walk from Windermere and its many pubs and restaurants, this place is something different. Reports please.

Robinson Place, Bowness-on-Windermere LA23 3DQ

Tel 015394 88408
email nick@whitehousewindermere.com
website www.whitehousewindermere.com
Food no
Price ££ **Closed** never
Proprietor Grant Smith

Crosthwaite, Cumbria

Great Langdale, Ambleside
LA22 9AQ

Tel (015394) 37272
email olddungeonghyll1@btconnect.com website www.odg.co.uk
Food breakfast, packed lunch, dinner, bar meals Price ££ Closed 20 to 26 Dec Proprietors Neil and Jane Walmsley

The Old Dungeon Ghyll
Country hotel

Neil and Jane Walmsley have been the proprietors here since 1983 and have continued to improve and develop this popular family hotel retaining as many old features as possible. Once, many a climber chose to stay here. They were a pretty uncritical bunch (any kind of a roof was a luxury), but now all bedrooms have bathrooms. There is a comfortable residents' sitting room with an open fire, a busy hikers' bar (open to the public) as well as the warm guests' bar and a snug dining room offering wholesome, uncomplicated food. Neil and Jane hold occasional charity folk festivals, and there are music nights in the bar every Wednesday.

Langho, Lancashire

Langho, Blackburn, Lancashire BB6 8BE

Tel 01254240555
email reception@northcote.com
website www.northcote.com
Food breakfast, lunch, dinner Price £££-££££ Closed never
Proprietors Nigel Haworth

Northcote
Country house hotel

Half close your eyes and this solid 1800's Victorian mansion could be a restaurant-with-rooms, though in fact it offers all the comforts of a top country hotel. Food is the focus here, Nigel Haworth having won many local and national awards. His cooking is firmly rooted in local ingredients, but its edge is the fresh, clean flavours and imaginative rather than trendy presentation. A cheese flavoured icecream partnering the summer pudding arrived in a cone on a wooden rack. The service is charming , the atmosphere friendly and food-and-wine oriented, much influenced by Nigel's long standing collaborator, Craig Bancroft.

This place has a formidable local reputation. It's 26 bedrooms are spacious.

THE NORTH-WEST | NORTHERN ENGLAND

Liverpool

The Hargreaves Building, 5 Chapel Street, Liverpool L3 9AG

Tel 0151 236 6676 **email** info@racquetclub.org.uk **website** www.ainscoughs.co.uk **Food** breakfast, lunch, dinner; no lunch Sat, closed Sun **Price** ££ **Closed** 24th-26th Dec; weddings only until early Jan **Proprietors** Martin and Helen Ainscough

The Racquet Club
Town hotel

A good-value place that defies the chain-hotel atmosphere of central Liverpool. Book in advance as weddings are prioritised at weekends – about 120 per year. The design (devised by Martin Ainscough) is thoroughly quirky. For instance, stag heads line the stairs, leading up to an enormous moose head on the first floor. Throughout the corridors, there are prints of Georgian aristocracy as well as modern art – some local, some bizarre. Bedrooms are cosy and comfortable. Rooms two and three have hand-carved detail on the beds' headboards and polished antique furniture. The Ainscoughs who bought the place nearly 30 years ago have been carefully expanding their hospitality empire to include a pub in Bispham Green, and a famous old Windermere hotel, the Miller Howe.

Liverpool

Stanley Dock, Regent Rd, Liverpool L3 0AN

Tel 0151 559 1444 **email** info@titanichotelliverpool.com **website** www.titanichotelliverpool.com **Food** breakfast, brunch, afternoon tea, dinner, grill **Price** ££-£££ **Closed** never **Proprietors** Titanic Hotels

Titanic Hotel
City hotel

A little off-piste for us due to the number of rooms, but this place is a truly special addition to Liverpool's hotels. Former ship building warehouse, the Titanic Hotel sits proudly in the regenerated Stanley Docks. A popular outdoor terrace, where drinks and meals can be served, overlooks the water and the many reminders of the area's industrial past.

The transformation from warehouse to hotel has been well thought out and thoughtful. The rooms retain the large windows, steel beams and brick walls but are all furnished with comfortable, well designed furniture and chic fixtures and fittings. Tucked away in the cavenous basement, under a vaulted ceiling, is a swimming pool and spa.

THE NORTH-WEST — NORTHERN ENGLAND

Settle, North Yorkshire

The Golden Lion Settle

Near the centre of Settle where many a Dales walk or trek starts or finishes, this gets praise for delicious and imaginatively presented food.

The log burner with firewood stacked either side is the public area's welcoming hub: it will draw you in for a slow fireside drink. There's a choice of two dining spaces besides the bar area. Choose from pub classics and ambitious restaurant dishes.

We like the restrained, comfortable style of the bedrooms with intelligent use of pretty painted furniture.

Duke Street, Settle
BD24 9DU

Tel 015394 37272
email relax@goldenlionsettle.co.uk
website www.goldenlionsettle.co.uk
Food brunch, sandwiches, dinner
Price ££-£££ **Closed** never
Proprietors Daniel Thwaites

Ullswater, Cumbria

Howtown House
Country hotel

Howtown Hotel is the Real Thing. It is a house that has been in the same family for well over a century. Nothing is too much trouble for the Baldrys. The place is as clean as a museum. The scenery around is staggering. Since out last edition they have transitioned into almost entirely private rental.

The cosy little snug with stained glass in the windows might be where the Swallows & Amazons' uncle, Captain Flint, met his friends. Other public rooms are grander, lighter, more like drawing-rooms. The bedrooms are equally comfortable and impressive. Downstairs, Toby jugs, brass warming pans, the heads of foxes hunted in the 1930s, and oil paintings make the hall seem like an antiques shop.

Ullswater, Penrith, Cumbria CA10 2ND

Tel 017684 86514
email david@howtown-hotel.com
website www.howtoewn-hotel.co.uk
Food breakfast, lunch, afternoon tea, dinner, picnics
Price ££-£££ **Closed** never
Proprietors The Baldrys

THE NORTH-EAST

NORTHERN ENGLAND

Alnmouth, Northumberland

24-25 Northumberland St,
Alnmouth NE66 2RA

Tel 01665 463001
email info@thewhittlinghouse.co.uk
website
www.thewhittlinghouse.co.uk

Nearby Alnwick Castle,
Northumberland Coastline,
Lindisfarne, Alnmouth beach
Location Alnmouth, just off the
A7068, 1 hour from Newcastlle
Food breakfast, lunch, sunday
lunch, dinner
Price ££-£££
Rooms 3; 2 double with bathroom
and 1 suite with bathroom
Facilities dining room, bar
Credit cards MC, V
Children welcome
Accessibilty to ground floor only
Pets dogs welcome
Closed never
Proprietors Richard Sim and Tom
Leslie

The Whittling House
Seaside hotel and restaurant

On the Northumberland Coast where we've never previously found a true charming small hotel, this 2020 opening presents itself as a home from home. The ten rooms are up to date, cosy and comfortable. Some have views across the rooftops of Alnmouth to the sea - the building is on the town's one-way main street, which is not over-busy. The relaxed ambience continues in the bar and restaurant with flagstone floors, panelling and attractive fabrics.

Joint owner and chef Richard Sim often drops by to cook breakfast and has made a serious success (Michelin status) of The Potted Lobster in Bamburgh. His well presented and artfully cooked dishes range from classics (fish and chips) to potted lobster £48 and game tasting menus £45 on specified nights.

Richard and Tom Leslie co-own The Potted Lobster and another local restaurant as well as this place, so although a general manager runs it day to day it's virtually owner managed, capable of giving guests the sort of personal (but not intrusive) welcome we value.

Up the coast towards the border is Lindisfarne or Holy Island, reached by a causeway. A terrific walk around the 'island' is featured in *Walks for Mind and Spirit* the fascinating new walking guide by Duncan Petersen Publishing available at www.duncanpetersenpublishingltd.square.site

THE NORTH-EAST — NORTHERN ENGLAND

Aysgarth, Yorkshire

Aysgarth, Leyburn Yorkshire
DL8 3SR

Tel 01969663635
email info@stowhouse.co.uk
website www.stowhouse.co.uk

Nearby Leyburn and Hawes, Aysgarth Falls, Askrigg, Bolton Castle, Dales trekking
Location in the heart of Wensleydale
Food breakfast
Price £££
Rooms 7 double, all with bath/shower and Dales views
Facilities living room, honesty bar, snug, dining room - all with wood-burners, 2 acres of grounds
Credit cards all major
Children welcome
Accessibilty no special facilities
Pets dogs welcome in all rooms except Love is Blind and Badger
Manager Sarah and Phil Bucknall

Stow House
Bed-and-breakfast

A shot in the arm for Yorkshire Dales B&B: Sarah and Phil Bucknall have asked themselves what you don't get elsewhere in the national park and confidently provided it. First, a blend of old and new – often colourful, sometimes whacky fabrics and contemporary art co-exist with antiques in a 19thC vicarage. Second, chic modern bathrooms to a standard that travellers usually expect in city hotels. Third, their cocktails – which seem to aptly express Sarah and Phil's approach: friendly, hands-on, communicative hosts who make you feel better as you walk through the door. Their signature cocktail is the Corpse Reviver No.2.

Both worked in big London advertising businesses before launching Stow House in 2014, though their feel for what the customer wants is far from superficial. They've looked after the basics: the beds and linen are high quality; the rooms warm; breakfast well above average. As you'd expect of a vicarage, the seven rooms are spacious. Guests have the run of the house, with their own entrance, while Sarah and Phil live in an unobtrusive annexe. In other words, this is B&B-plus, with maximum privacy and independence for the guest, a choice of two downstairs sitting rooms and dinner provided for groups if ordered in advance. Prices above average, but fair.

THE NORTH-EAST — NORTHERN ENGLAND

Bolton Abbey, North Yorkshire

Bolton Abbey, Skipton, North Yorkshire BD23 6AJ

Tel 01756 718100
email res@devonshirehotels.co.uk
website
www.thedevonshirearms.co.uk

Nearby Castle Howard; Skipton Castle; Brontë Parsonage; Harewood House. **Location** on B6160 just N of junction with A59; in grounds with ample car parking **Food** breakfast, lunch, dinner, afternoon tea **Price** ££££ **Rooms** 40; 37 double and twin, 1 family, 2 suites, with a combination of bath/shower (requests for specific bathrooms must be made); all rooms have phone, TV, DVD, hairdryer **Facilities** 3 lounges, conservatory, restaurant, brasserie, 2 bars, gym, sauna, steam room, solarium, indoor swimming pool; garden, tennis, croquet, putting, helipad, fishing **Credit cards** all major **Children** not under 7 in restaurant **Accessibilty** rooms on the ground floor, and 1 specially adapted **Pets** accepted, £10 per dog **Closed** never **Manager** Adam Dyke

The Devonshire Arms Hotel & Spa **Country hotel**

As your helicopter whirls towards its helipad, you can see that the moorland of the Dales proper comes to within a mile or so of the 17thC Devonshire Arms. Follow the path down the bank of the Wharfe, which gives the valley its name, for the half mile from Bolton Abbey village to the stone bridge and you're there. Owned by the Duke and Duchess of Devonshire, the hotel is doubly graced since it contains antiques and paintings from Chatsworth, the family seat; the Duchess has masterminded their placement and the design of the interior. This is a hotel in two parts, old and new. The elegant old wears its years well and has happily grown out of exact right angles. The extension, which brought with it an indoor swimming pool, spa and gym, is settling in well.

The dining alternatives cover a similar spectrum. On the one hand is the quiet comfort of the classical Burlington Restaurant, and on the other a buzzy brasserie with dishes to suit most moods and a snappy wine list to go with them. The bedrooms also come in old and new varieties: the older win on character and the newer score better with their views. See also The Devonshire Fell (page 308).

Burnsall, North Yorkshire

Burnsall, Skipton, North Yorkshire
BD23 6BT

Tel 01756 729000
email res@devonshirehotels.co.uk
website www.devonshirefell.co.uk

Nearby Bolton Abbey Estate, Leeds, Harrogate
Location Burnsall village, just off the B6160
Food breakfast, lunch, dinner, afternoon tea
Price ££££-£££££
Rooms 16 doubles (some can be twin), all ensuite; 4 more planned
Facilities restaurant, bar, conservatory, wine cellar, Devonshire Spa located at The Devonshire Arms Hotel & Spa **Credit cards** all major
Children welcome
Accessibilty no lift to bedrooms, but wheelchair access points, trained staff **Pets** dog friendly rooms available, £10 charge per night
Closed no specific closure dates
Proprietors Duke and Duchess of Devonshire

The Devonshire Fell
Restaurant-with-rooms

Just outside picturesque Burnsall, the Devonshire Fell sits above the village, with great views across the River Wharfe. Located very close to the Bolton Abbey Estate, this is a less formal sister hotel to The Devonshire Arms (307).

The ground floor leads seamlessly from one room to the other with simple wooden floors, log fires and pretty shutters in the dining room. No chintz here: the stair carpets are pink-and-grey striped; the bedrooms have bedheads and Roman blinds in bright colours. Prints, black-and-white photographs and contemporary paintings decorate the walls.

Bedrooms are very comfortable, with good sheets. On a large tray you'll find quality coffee and tea, cakes, soft drinks and fresh milk. Our reporter appreciated the large flat-screen TV, and the unusual gels and shampoos.

Drinks are generally served in a cosy conservatory, often a contradiction in terms, but this one has a log fire at one end and was 'blissfully comfortable'. Dinner, from a small menu, was 'well thought out with local fish and meat. Presentation was elegant (don't expect huge Yorkshire platefuls). Fish and chips and homemade beefburgers were just right after a day walking the fells.' A superb place to stay for walkers, and dog friendly.

THE NORTH-EAST
NORTHERN ENGLAND

Byland, North Yorkshire

Byland, Coxwold, North Yorkshire
YO61 4BD

Tel 01347 868 204
email abbey.inn@english-heritage.org.uk
website www.english-heritage.org.uk/daysout/properties/byland-abbey/inn/

Nearby Byland Abbey
Location 2 miles from A170 between Thirsk and Helmsley
Food breakfast
Price ££-£££
Rooms 2 doubles, 1 twin, all ensuite, with TV
Facilities breakfast room, tea room in the summer
Credit cards MC, V
Children welcome
Accessibilty no special access
Pets not accepted
Closed never
Proprietor English Heritage

Byland Abbey Inn
Country bed-and-breakfast

The pairing of an isolated inn with starkly beautiful Cisterican abbey ruins is rare in Britain; sitting in the stone-walled Wass Room, one could almost be in France, in a *vieux logis* overlooking a *monument historique*. Hope to stay at full moon when they look particularly majestic. English Heritage, which maintains Byland Abbey ruins, bought the small 19thC inn some years ago and gave it a conscientious makeover, and it is now a Tearoom, attracting walkers, cyclists and tourists.

The three bedrooms are prettily decorated. The Mouseman, is notable for its specially commissioned Mouseman furniture made in nearby Kilburn. You can breakfast in the Coxwold room whilst gazing at the ruins, and then wander among them free of charge, probably alone. The Black Swan at Oldstead is Michelin-starred, and recommended for dinner, and the Stapylton Arms is within walking distance.

However, our most recent reporter found the prices too steep for what was on offer. The breakfast (no longer served in bed) was ample but basic, and the amenities in the rooms could have been improved. We'd be interested to hear reports on how English Heritage have addressed these issues – an inventive project which perhaps hasn't yet reached its full potential.

THE NORTH-EAST
NORTHERN ENGLAND

Cornhill-on-Tweed, Northumberland

Main Street, Cornhill-on-Tweed,
Northumberland TD12 4UH

Tel 01890 882424
email enquiries@collingwoodarms.com
website www.collingwoodarms.com

Nearby golfing, fishing, riding, cycling, sightseeing walks
Location near Berwick-Upon Tweed, Cheviot Hills, North Northumberland, Scottish Border
Food breakfast, lunch, dinner
Price £££
Rooms 15 all with digital televisions
Facilities brasserie, dining room, bar, library
Credit cards DC, MC, V
Children accepted
Accessibilty possible, ground-floor bedroom and bathroom
Pets not accepted, but kennels available
Closed never
Proprietor Ronald Watson
Manager Kristie Taylor

The Collingwood Arms
Town inn

'A more relaxing, solid, reassuring and unpretentious hotel would be hard to imagine,' comments our series editor, Fiona Duncan. A former coaching inn (the words 'Post Horses' still appear above the door), it sits on an old main road to Edinburgh, with the River Tweed below.

A stone building with a plain Georgian front, its name is from its original owners: a local merchant family with strong ties to the 19thC naval hero Vice-Admiral Collingwood. They left in 1955, but current owner Ronald Watson (who has two other establishments on Bamburgh) clearly respects the place's heritage: each bedroom is named after a ship in the Admiral's Trafalgar division. Colours and fabrics have been kept muted, and Persian rugs and antique furniture scattered throughout.

There are a few contemporary twists – a trendy, wood-floored pub-brasserie; simple, almost minimalist, headboards on beds – but these are thoughtful touches rather than needless trend-following. Attention to detail is evident, from the library-cum-sitting room to each of the 15 bedrooms.

Food is widely praised. You eat in a stylish, relaxing, parquet-floored restaurant or, if weather allows, out in the manicured gardens. Ingredients are fresh and locally sourced. When Fiona visited, she enjoyed her grilled black pudding and leek starter.

THE NORTH-EAST — NORTHERN ENGLAND

East Witton

Main Road, East Witton, Nr Leyburn, DL8 4SN

Tel 01969 624 273
email enquiries@thebluelion.co.uk
website www.thebluelion.co.uk

Nearby Yorkshire Dales, Ripon Cathedral, Jervaux Abbey, Brymor Dairy
Location on the A6108
Food breakfast (included), lunch, dinner
Price ££-££££
Rooms 15; doubles, suites and twins
Facilities dining room, pub, courtyard, outdoor seating
Credit cards MC, V
Children welcome
Accessibility limited, enquire
Pets some dog friendly rooms
Closed never
Proprietors Melanie and Sean

The Blue Lion
Pub-with-rooms

Atmospheric and authentic. It was left out of our previous edition because of uncertainty about future management, however this Wensleydale institution has forward-looking new owner managers, Melanie Jackson and Sean Rankin. Our chief editor Fiona Duncan stayed more than a decade back and loved it. Revisiting in 2023 we felt the same.

You'll instantly get the old Yorkshire feel: impressive original furnishings including an unusual curved settle in the bar; a range of drinking and eating areas from which to choose, spread over the ground floor; interesting historic prints and paintings. Menus chalked on blackboards focus you on the food, restaurant dishes rather than pub fare, for example pork tenderloin and Wagu black pudding Wellington with apple puree. Overall, the offering is traditional dishes with a imaginative twist, including grouse and partridge. Sunday lunch, two courses for £30.50 as we went to press seemed to be notable value.

Rooms, several in a courtyard outbuilding, are comfortable and handsomely decorated, with prices a little above average, but worth it for this historic place in a timeless Wensleydale village. The terrain here is gently domesticated: hilly, rising to grassy wooded tops, rather than grand moorland and craggy outcrops.

Grassington, North Yorkshire

Summers Fold, Grassington, near Skipton, North Yorkshire BD23 5AE

Tel 01756 752584
email reservations@ashfieldhouse.co.uk
website www.ashfieldhouse.co.uk

Nearby Skipton Castle, Gordale Scar, Janet's Foss, Ripon, Malham Cove, Bolton Abbey
Location in Grassington, just off the main square; with ample car parking
Food breakfast
Prices £-££
Rooms 8 double and twin with bath or shower; all rooms have TV, hairdryer, wi-fi
Facilities 2 sitting rooms, 1 with bar, dining room; garden
Credit cards MC, V
Children welcome over 10
Accessibility not suitable
Pets not accepted
Closed two weeks each year
Proprietors the Howard family

Ashfield House
Country bed-and-breakfast

Grassington, and Wharfedale in general, is a little-known Northern gem, especially for keen walkers. Tucked away off the main street is this small private stone and slate hotel, a peaceful sanctuary at the end of its own yard. What's more, and unlike anywhere else in Grassington, you can park your car there. Oak and pine furniture, bare beams and stone walls are combined with neat furnishings. The bedrooms are modestly sized with fresh, clean decoration and their own shower rooms.

The Howard family took over in 2016, with 30 years hotel experience already under their belt, and are incrementally putting their own stamp on the place. They've improved the car-parking facilities, decorated a couple of rooms and are in the process of improving the kitchen – so in the future, dinner might come into play again. In the meantime guests can enjoy a hearty breakfast laden with Yorkshire produce, and complimentary homemade cake on arrival.

Beyond the house, insulated from the bustle of the town, is a quiet walled garden with a table and chairs where you can simply sit and enjoy the sunshine if the prospect of a walk along the river seems too testing.

THE NORTH-EAST — NORTHERN ENGLAND

Harome, North Yorkshire

Harome, Nr Helmsley, North Yorkshire, YO62 5JE

Tel 01439 770397
website www.thestaratharome.co.uk

Nearby Helmsley market town, Castle Howard, Duncombe Park.
Location 2.5 miles SE of Helmsley off the A170, ample car parking
Food breakfast, lunch, dinner (restaurant in the Inn closed on Mon) **Price** £££
Rooms 9 doubles, 3 suites, all with bath or shower; all rooms have TV, radio, hairdryer, phone, tea and coffee making facilities
Facilities dining rooms, breakfast room, bar, sitting room; garden
Credit cards MC, V **Children** welcome **Accessibility** 4 ground-floor rooms **Pets** accepted in a couple of ground-floor rooms
Closed never
Proprietors Andrew Pern

The Star Inn
Country hotel

'One of the most comfortable, relaxing nights I have spent in a hotel' says a recent reporter. Wellies and umbrellas wait by the front door of Cross House (the Inn's guest house) in case you feel like having a stroll around the beautiful countryside.

Reopened in 2023 after fire damage prompted a rebuild and a refurbishment, this quirky thatched-cottage Inn has not lost its cheerfulness. The opulent sitting room is kept warm by the grand fire in the centre and once sat on the sofas with tea and seriously good cakes you can hardly make it to your room. When you do, you'll discover that they are immaculate, balancing the contemporary and the rustic perfectly with fantastic bathrooms (some with whirlpool baths).

Supper and lunch can be served in the Inn itself: just across the road. The pub and restaurant are bursting with charm and decorated in keeping with the 14thC thatched image, so expect old beams and secret little loft spaces in which to enjoy coffee; the rear terrace is a popular place to eat *al fresco* in the summer.

The restaurant, serving Andrew's 'modern Yorkshire' dishes, recently regained its Michelin star. Upstairs the fairytale private dining room has been decorated by local artists.

Hawes, North Yorkshire

Hawes, North Yorkshire DL8 3LY

Tel 01969 667255
email enquiries@simonstonehall.com
website www.simonstonehall.com

Nearby Pennine Way; Wharfedale; Ribblesdale.
Location 1.5 miles (2.5 km) N of Hawes on Muker road; with ample car parking
Food breakfast (residents only), bar lunch, Sun lunch, dinner
Price £££
Rooms 18 double and twin with bath and shower; all rooms have phone, TV, wi-fi
Facilities bar, lounge, brasserie, restaurant; garden, terrace
Credit cards AE, DC, MC, V
Children welcome
Accessibility ground floor only
Pets welcome in bar area and in certain bedrooms
Closed never
Owner Jake Dinsdale

Simonstone Hall
Country house hotel

Simonstone has undergone major refurbishment in the last few years, but still has the air of something special, helped by the friendliness of the staff. Outside, it is the same dignified, slightly forbidding, large Dales country house; but as you enter you will probably hear the lively chatter coming from the extensive bar area which is intended to re-create the hotel as a place that will attract local non-residents as well as overnight guests. To have this popular country pub within an essentially dignified old country hotel is nicely off-piste. The bar is smartly done out; the meals and range of wines by the glass are imaginative; waiters in black tie and apron, French bistro-style, bustle about. It gives the place an injection of life, but if you've come here for peace, or a romantic twosome, just walk down the corridor to the sitting room, hidden at the far end of the hall to provide guests with peace and quiet. You can enjoy dinner in both The Brasserie and The Four Fells restaurants.

All bedrooms now have bathrooms with showers. The luxury and superior bedrooms are in chic country house style with some bold statements contrasting painted panelling with bold wallpapers. Some have sleigh beds, others four-posters, many of them with absorbing views of the Dales.

THE NORTH-EAST
NORTHERN ENGLAND

Hawnby, North Yorkshire

Hill Top, Hawnby, near Helmsley,
North Yorkshire Y06 5QS

Tel 01439 330180
email info@theowlhawnby.co.uk
website www.theowlhawnby.co.uk

Nearby Rievaulx Abbey; Jervaulx Abbey; North York Moors.
Location at top of hill in village 7 miles (11 km) NE of Helmsley; with car parking
Food breakfast, lunch, dinner
Price ££
Rooms 9 double and twin with bath; all rooms have phone, TV, hairdryer
Facilities sitting room, bar, restaurant, garden
Credit cards MC, V
Children welcome
Accessibility difficult
Pets some dog friendly rooms
Closed Monday and Tuesday
Proprietors Peter and Sam Varley

The Owl
Country hotel

After a spectacular drive through rolling valleys and the unspoilt stone village of Hawnby, you come across this delightful country inn, formerly The Inn at Hawnby. The 'village pub' façade hides an exquisite country hotel that had been decorated with obvious flair, bold fabrics and warm tones throughout.

The hotel used to be part of the 13,000-acre Mexborough estate and has recently been taken over by restauranteurs Sam and Peter Varley. The kitchen produces a full *a la carte* menu, all from scratch and proudly incorporating produce from North Yorkshire's many farms and suppliers.

The Varleys have tidied up the outside of the Inn and the gardens, as well as giving the public rooms and bedrooms some attention, aiming to make them altogether cosier and more welcoming.

Reports continue to heap praise on The Owl: 'This charming country hotel ... is an ideal base for touring North Yorkshire; a gem with fabulous views, home cooking and friendly service'.

Hetton, North Yorkshire

Back Ln, Hetton, Skipton BD23 6LT

Tel 01756 730263
email reservations@angelhetton.co.uk
website www.angelhetton.co.uk

Nearby 10 minutes from Skipton train station, Linton Falls
Location A few minutes' drive from Grassington in the village of Hetton
Food breakfast, lunch, dinner
Price ££
Rooms 20 en-suite bedrooms, 7 suites, 5 studio rooms, 3 deluxe; overhead and walk-in showers
Credit cards MC, V
Children welcome, family-friendly suites available
Accessibility 2 accessible rooms, incl. wet room showers, widened doorways and grab rails
Pets 1 dog-friendly suite and 1 studio room, welcome in the bar area (main house), dog beds and bowls
Closed Monday and Tuesday
Proprietors Michael and Johanna Wignall with Jo and James Wellock

The Angel at Hetton
Country hotel

The Angel at Hetton has been reborn since the last edition as a superb new contemporary place to stay, worth a detour if only for the food. Chef Michael Wignall (once at Gidleigh Park, Devon) has returned to his northern roots to be awarded a Michelin star for sophisticated, inventive dishes such as squab with pak choi and spring onion.

The rooms, spread through the main building and two others nearby have a nicely clean modern style with neutral colour schemes in harmony with original features such as chunky beams. Some of the rooms have great fell views.

Hetton is a peaceful, tiny village – population 155 in 2011 – near Skipton. The main Angel building occupies one of its typical Yorkshire two-storey great stone houses. Family friendly.

Hunmanby, North Yorkshire

Stonegate, Hunmanby, North
Yorkshire YO14 0NS

Tel 01723 891333
email staciedevos@aol.com
website www.wranghamhouse.com

Nearby Scarborough Castle; North York Moors National Park.
Location behind church in village, 1 mile (1.5 km) SW of Filey; ample car parking
Food breakfast, lunch, dinner
Price ££
Rooms 12; Double, Twin, Super-King, Four-Poster and 2 Executive Suites available; 7 with bath, 5 with shower; all have phone, TV, hairdryer and welcome tray **Facilities** sitting room, dining room, bar; garden
Credit cards AE, MC, V
Children welcome
Accessibility 1 adapted room
Pets by arrangement
Closed Christmas and Boxing Day
Proprietors Peter and Stacie Devos

Wrangham House
Country house hotel

Wrangham House is a well-preserved and elegant Georgian former vicarage set in three acres of beautiful gardens. The main part of the house was built in 1700 and continues to be sympathetic to its period. The eponymous Francis Wrangham added a wing, now housing the restaurant, in 1810. Stacie and Peter Davos purchased Wrangham House in 2005, and set about restoring the house to its former glory – the pair are passionate about the house and its upkeep. Over the years this has involved refurbishing the kitchen, sitting room, dining room and most of the bedrooms, as well as giving the gardens some much-needed care and attention.

Peter, a talented cook, is in charge of the kitchen – and delights in using seasonal produce such as game and lobster – so there is always something new on the menu. Everything is freshly made and locally sourced. Peter and Stacie take pride in offering a personal and flexible service – guests on long stays have the opportunity to influence the menu by discussing their preferences with Peter, and early dinners will be arranged for families with young children. Reports welcome.

Lastingham, North Yorkshire

Lastingham, North Yorkshire
Y062 6TH

Tel 01751 417345/417402
email reservations@lastingham-grange.com **website** www.lastinghamgrange.com

Nearby North York Moors; Scarborough; Rievaulx Abbey.
Location at top of village, 7 miles (10 km) NW of Pickering; ample car parking **Food** breakfast, lunch, dinner **Price** £££
Rooms 12 and 1 self-catering cottage – The Old Reading Room; 10 double, 2 single, all with bath; all rooms have phone, TV, hairdryer, wi-fi **Facilities** sitting room, dining room; terrace, garden
Credit cards MC, V
Children welcome
Accessibility restaurant and garden
Pets accepted in bedrooms by arrangement, not in The Old Reading Room
Closed Dec to mid-Mar
Proprietors Jane, Bertie and Tom Wood

Lastingham Grange
Country house hotel

Lastingham Grange – a wistaria-clad former farmhouse – nestles peacefully in a delightful village on the edge of the North York Moors. Unlike many country house hotels, it manages to combine a certain sophistication – smartly decorated public rooms, friendly unobtrusive service, elegantly laid gardens – with a large dash of informality, which puts you immediately at ease. From the moment you enter, you feel as if you are staying with friends. Recently, we had this reaction from an inspector: 'Family feeling; very child friendly; charming rooms.–'

The main attraction is the garden. You can enjoy it from a distance – from the windows of the large L-shaped sitting room (complete with carefully grouped sofas, antiques and a grand piano) – or, like most guests, by exploring. There is a beautifully laid rose garden, enticing bordered lawns and an extensive adventure playground for children.

Bedrooms are perfectly comfortable, with well-equipped bathrooms, and have been totally redecorated since our last visit, when a reporter felt that they were somewhat downbeat in places. Paul Cattaneo and Sandra Thurlow produce traditional English meals for the daily-changing menu, prepared from fresh, local ingredients. Reports welcome.

THE NORTH-EAST

NORTHERN ENGLAND

Millgate, North Yorkshire

Millgate, Richmond, North Yorkshire DL10 4JN

Tel 07799880893
email millgate1@me.com
website www.millgatehouse.com

Nearby Cleveland hills; Swale valley; the Dales; Richmond.
Location in Richmond town centre
Food breakfast
Price ££-£££
Rooms 3; 2 superking doubles, 1 twin, all en suites
Facilities sitting room, dining room; garden for residents only
Credit cards not accepted
Children accepted over 10
Accessibility not suitable
Pets accepted (not in dining room)
Closed never
Proprietors Austin Lynch and Tim Culkin

Millgate House
Town B&B

Millgate House dates back to the early 1700s and, despite its relatively unassuming exterior, is full of surprises. Behind the street façade is a house of real charm and character, tastefully furnished with antiques and interesting pieces sourced from from all over the world. Below, and sloping away from the house, lies an award winning garden with excellent views across the river Swale towards the beautiful Cleveland Hills beyond.

What really sets Millgate House apart is its garden. Since scooping first prize in the National Royal Horticultural Society Garden Competition, the grounds have been featured in publications in the UK as well as internationally. The gardens are open all year round, and entry is free to house guests.

Breakfast is very good at Millgate House and dinners can be pre-arranged for parties of 16 and over. The accommodation on offer is of a high standard. All three bedrooms are warm and spacious with fine views, and each has its own large, airy bathroom with great period details. All of this, together with some outstanding care and service from owners Austin and Tim, make Millgate House a fine choice in this area.

Two nights minimum stay.

THE NORTH-EAST
NORTHERN ENGLAND

Nun Monkton, Yorkshire

The Green, Nun Monkton, York
YO26 8EW

Tel 01423330303
email enquiries@thealice-hawthorne.com
website www.thealicehawthorn.com

Nearby Beningbrough Hall, Yorkshire Heart Vineyard, All Saints Church
Location 14 minutes from A1 exit 47
Food breakfast (residents only) lunch and dinner Tues-Sat
Price ££
Rooms 12; selection of pub and garden rooms
Facilities restaurant, walk-in rainfall showers, room service, courtyard
Credit cards MC, V,
Children not under 16
Accessibility 1 wheelchair adapted room
Pets dogs welcome
Closed never
Proprietors Claire and John Topham, and Richard Harpin

The Alice Hawthorn
Village hotel

We like to make our reviews distanced, in contrast to the gushing approval of the pay guides who do compliments for cash, but here it's hard not to go overboard. The Alice Hawthorn is everything we want in a charming small hotel – for that is what it is, rather than a pub with rooms.

The location in Nun Monkton, a pretty, spread out village with a vast green, west of York. It's a rural village setting with the main building looking like a private farmhouse. The outbuildings at the back providing extra rooms are artful examples of timber interior construction at its best, also clad with timber outside and topped with silver corrugated iron roofs, a stylish yet appropriate echo of farm buildings, and necessary for planning permission.

The main house's public spaces and bedrooms are country house super-chic, stylishly original yet restful and harmonious. The food is well above average for the money, and the rooms are similarly well-priced.

Only a deep-pocketed investor working with talented hospitality experts could achieve this quality, and unsurprisingly the place is a partnership between John and Claire Topham, with their impressive record of Yorkshire inns (see also The Angel at Hetton) and Richard Harpin of the successful HomeServe plumbing and home maintenance business.

THE NORTH-EAST — NORTHERN ENGLAND

Pateley Bridge, North Yorkshire

Wath-in-Nidderdale, Pateley Bridge, near Harrogate, North Yorkshire HG3 5PP

Tel 01423 711306
email sportsmansarms@btconnect.com
website www.nidderdale.co.uk/sportsmansarms

Nearby Wharfedale, Wensleydale; Fountains Abbey, Bolton Abbey.
Location 2 miles (3 km) NW of Pateley Bridge, in hamlet; with ample car parking
Food breakfast, bar lunch, dinner
Price ££
Rooms 11; 9 double, 2 twin with bath or shower; all rooms have TV
Facilities 3 sitting rooms, bar, dining room; fishing
Credit cards MC, V **Children** accepted **Disabled** public rooms are ground floor **Pets** welcome by arrangement **Closed** Christmas Day, New Year's Day **Proprietors** Jane and Ray Carter

The Sportsman's Arms
Country hotel

Our latest inspection confirms that the Sportsman's Arms is going from strength to strength. The long, rather rambling building dates from the 17th century, and the setting is as enchanting as the village name sounds; the River Nidd flows across the field in front; Gouthwaite reservoir, a bird-watchers' haunt, is just behind; glorious dales country spreads all around.

Jane and Ray Carter have been running the Sportsman's Arms, with the help of a young enthusiastic team, for almost four decades now, and continue to make improvements. Bedrooms (two with four-posters) are light and fresh, with brand-new bathrooms. Six more rooms, four with views across open countryside, are located in the barn and stable block.

And then there is the food. The Sportsman's Arms is first and foremost a restaurant, and the large dining room is the inn's focal point, sparkling with silver cutlery and crystal table lights. The lively menu embraces sound, traditional local fare, as well as fresh fish and seafood brought in daily from Whitby. To back it up, there is a superb wine list – and an extremely reasonable bill.

THE NORTH-EAST   NORTHERN ENGLAND

Reeth, North Yorkshire

On the Green, Reeth, Richmond, North Yorkshire DL11 6SN

Tel 01748 884292
email enquiries@theburgoyne.co.uk
website www.theburgoyne.co.uk

Nearby Richmond Castle; Middleham Castle Aysgarth Falls, Wensleydale Railway.
Location 10 miles (16 km) W of Richmond on B6270; with car parking **Food** breakfast, packed lunch on request, Sunday lunch on first Sunday of month, dinner; room service **Price ££ Rooms** 10 double and twin with bath; all rooms have phone, flat screen TV, hairdryer, tea/coffee facilities
Facilities sitting room, dining room; garden, fishing, drying facilities, lock-up for bicycles
Credit cards MC, V
Children accepted
Accessibility ground-floor room
Pets dogs accepted by arrangement
Closed never **Proprietors** Sarah and Sean Usman

Burgoyne Hotel
Village hotel

The Burgoyne Hotel stretches its late-Georgian length along the top of the sloping green in Reeth. If you turn round and look the other way, you'll see why: the Swale valley is extremely pretty, and with only the green in front of it, the Burgoyne has an uninterrupted view. Inside, time, money and taste have conspired to produce something of a masterpiece to which has been added the magic ingredient of a warm welcome. There are two elegant and richly furnished sitting rooms on the ground floor with Medieval touches here and there: stone coats of arms on the fireplaces and 'Gothic' oak doors. The restaurant, where the snowy napkins, the crystal and the silver stand out against the cool blues of the decoration, is a kind of inner sanctum where head chef Sean Lord offers old-fashioned dishes with modern twists. The daily-changing menu uses Yorkshire produce, and is complemented by an impressive wine list.

The bedrooms, most of which face the valley, are beautifully appointed and deeply comfortable. Window seats offer pleasant perches for people who just want to sit and enjoy the view. Rather than hack space for bathrooms out of the well-proportioned rooms, one or two bathrooms are across the corridor – voluminous robes and slippers are provided for the short journey.

THE NORTH-EAST — NORTHERN ENGLAND

Richmond, North Yorkshire

Easby, Richmond, North Yorkshire, DL10 7EU

Tel 01748 826 066
email easby.hall@zen.co.uk
website easbyhall.com

Nearby The Yorkshire Dales, Easby Abbey, the market town Richmond with castle and Georgian Theatre Royal; waterfalls **Location** 4 miles from Scotch Corner (A1), 15 minutes from Darlington train station; overlooks the Swale river and ruins of Easby Abbey; ample private parking. **Food** breakfast, complimentary afternoon tea on arrival **Price** £££-££££ **Rooms** 3; super-king doubles (can become twin), 2 with bath/shower, 1 with shower, wi-fi, hairdryer, log burner/open fire, fridge, tea/coffee, radio/TV **Facilities** drawing room, 3 gardens with a summer house and winter hut with open fire. **Credit cards** none **Accessibility** 1 ground floor room but no special facilities **Pets** by arrangement **Closed** never **Proprietors** John and Karen Clarke

Easby Hall
Country house hotel

Easby Hall stands on a country lane outside Richmond. Our first impression: here's a well-proportioned and stylish home, recently renovated. The kitchen garden is impressive, with much companion planting and not a weed in sight.

Stroll into the elegant drawing room and you will stop dead in your tracks: beyond and below the 'infinity lawn' lie the tranquil, romantic ruins of Easby Abbey, surrounded by gently rolling woods and meadows. Couples marry in St Agatha church and walk up to Easby Hall for their reception.

The house is immaculately decorated using bold wallpapers and soft paint colours. The smallest bedroom, Abbey, has the views, but each is exceptional, with quite a tea tray: home-made biscuits, fresh mint for infusions and fresh flowers. Dinner is currently not provided, although a private chef can be brought in for groups by prior arrangement.

Breakfast was special, with an emphasis on organic produce largely sourced from their kitchen garden. Each table had pretty floral china and flowers from the garden. Coffee from a silver pot; seasonal home-made compote on offer (be it rhubarb with cardamom, blackcurrant or poached pear); poached eggs scattered with edible violas. Had the room overlooked the abbey ruins, it would have been even better.

THE NORTH-EAST — NORTHERN ENGLAND

Ripley, North Yorkshire

Ripley, Harrogate, North Yorkshire
HG3 3AY

Tel 01423 771888
email reservations@boarsheadripley.co.uk
website www.ripleycastle.co.uk

Nearby Ripley Catsle; York; Fountains Abbey and Studley Royal Water Gardens; Ripley Castle
Location in village centre, 3 miles (5 km) N of Harrogate on A61; with ample car parking
Food breakfast, lunch, dinner
Price ££
Rooms 23 double and twin; 5 rooms with shower only, 14 with shower over bath, 2 with bath only; hairdryer; minibar on request
Facilities sitting room, dining rooms, 2 bars; garden, tennis, fishing
Credit cards AE, MC, DC, V
Children accepted
Accessibility 1 specially adapted room, 8 ground-floor rooms
Pets accepted in some rooms only
Closed never
Proprietors Sir Thomas and Lady Ingilby

Boar's Head
Country house hotel

Anyone with a spare inn and enough paintings and antique furniture to furnish it could do worse than emulate Sir Thomas and Lady Ingilby's successful stewardship of the Boar's Head in Ripley. It is a thriving establishment with helpful, pleasant staff who do not leave your comfort to chance. A recent redecoration has refreshed the place, which is now has a more contemporary and uncomplicated feel.

There are bedrooms in the inn itself, lighter more contemporary ones in its cobbled courtyard, and across the road, in the peace and quiet of Birchwood House, are four of their six best rooms. All have fresh flowers, pristine modern bathrooms and thoughtful decoration.

The public rooms are warm and welcoming, filled with period furniture; seascapes and ancestors share the walls. There is a choice for dinner: you can either go to the relaxed bar/bistro (packed when we visited) or the richer candle-lit comfort of the restaurant to agonise over a choice that includes 'Yorkshire Cassoulet' – Yorkshire duck leg, Yorkshire sausage and Easingwold pork belly – or Ripley's Famous Mushroom Stroganoff. Fresh vegetables and game make seasonal appearances from the Ingilby estate, presided over by their castle.

THE NORTH-EAST — NORTHERN ENGLAND

Romaldkirk, County Durham

Romaldkirk, Barnard Castle, Co
Durham DL12 9EB

Tel 01833 650213
email hotel@rose-and-crown.co.uk
website www.rose-and-crown.co.uk

Nearby Barnard Castle; Egglestone Abbey; High Force.
Location in centre of village, on B6277, 6 miles (9.6 km) NW of Barnard Castle; with ample carparking **Food** breakfast, dinner, Sun lunch **Price** ££
Rooms 14; 13 double and twin, 2 rooms in Monk's Cottage, 1 family, 11 with bath, 3 with shower; all rooms have phone, TV, hairdryer, Bose sound systems
Facilities sitting room, dining room, bar, gun lockers, wi-fi
Credit cards AE, DC, MC, V
Children welcome
Accessibility in courtyard rooms
Pets accepted in 12 bedrooms
Closed Christmas Eve, Christmas Day, Boxing Day
Proprietors Thomas and Cheryl Robinson

The Rose and Crown
Country inn

The Rose and Crown was built in 1733 in this very pretty light stone village, which owes its original layout to the Saxons and its name to the patron saint of the church. Recently refurbished by owners Thomas and Cheryl Robinson, this place has gone from strength to strength. It is set in the centre of the three-green village. The bar is comfortingly traditional: real ales, natural stone walls, log fire, old photographs, copper and brass knick-knacks. Excellent pub food is at the heart of this inn, and can be enjoyed in either the relaxed bar area or the charming oak-panelled room. The menu often features seasonal ingredients and organic produce.

There are seven comfortable bedrooms, attractively decorated and furnished with antiques, in the main building. Five more have been added round the courtyard at the back, and open directly on to it. Since our last edition, the Monk's Cottage has been opened to provide two extra bedrooms. It overlooks the Saxon church next to the inn. This accommodation has an honesty bar and boot room – perfect for walkers.

THE NORTH-EAST | NORTHERN ENGLAND

Sheriff Hutton, North Yorkshire

High Sittenham, Sheriff Hutton,
York, North Yorkshire, YO60 7TW

Tel 01347 878386
email info@hallfarmhouseyork.co.uk
website
www.hallfarmhouseyork.co.uk

Nearby Bridlington, Robin Hood
Bay, Castle Howard, North
Yorkshire Moors, Scarborough and
Filey beaches, York, Whitby, Eden
Camp **Location** on a farm in the
Howardian Hills; ample parking
Food breakfast, evening meals on
request **Price** £-££
Rooms 3; 1 super-king/twin (also
has a sofa bed); 2 double. All have
bath/shower, TV, sofa, wi-fi,
hairdryer, coffee/tea facilities
Facilities on-site parking, lock up
facilities for bikes, garden
Credit cards cash or bank transfer
only **Children** welcome
Accessibility one ground floor room
Pets dogs not allowed in main
house, but can sleep in porch/boot
room (£10 sur-charge)
Closed Jan (makes exceptions)
Proprietors Sally Hemingway

Hall Farm House
Bed-and-breakfast

North Yorkshire has a chilly reputation: the North York Moors are bleak and windswept, the Yorkshire Wolds to the south a little less so, but still not exactly cosy when the wind blows in from the east. This Georgian farmhouse belies that reputation, sitting on a hill between the two in a relatively benign countryside, the Howardian Hills Area of Outstanding Natural Beauty. And once inside, the welcome is warm.

Owner Sally Hemingway goes out of her way to make her guests feel at home and have everything they need. Sally used to be a chef, so the food is unusually good. The full English breakfast is based on local produce; croissants and muffins are home-baked; jams and compotes are home-made from berries grown in the garden; afternoon tea, with freshly baked cakes, scones and biscuits is free. She will produce a three-course dinner if asked in advance.

The bedrooms are individually decorated in fresh but neutral colours, mainly creams and greys, with a few well judged splashes of colour or pattern. The garden bedroom, accessed from the garden, is more extrovert.

The Ebor Way and Centenary Way long distance trails go past the house, so this is a walker's stopover as well as being convenient base for York and Castle Howard.

THE NORTH-EAST | NORTHERN ENGLAND

South Dalton, East Yorkshire

West End, South Dalton, Beverley,
East Yorkshire, HU17 7PN

Tel 01430 810 246
email email@pipeandglass.co.uk
website www.pipeandglass.co.uk

Nearby Dalton Estate, St Mary's Church, Beverley Minster,
Location on the site of the original gatehouse to Dalton Park, on edge of the Yorkshire Wolds
Food breakfast (residents only), lunch, dinner, afternoon savouries, Sunday lunch, childrens menu
Price £££-££££
Rooms 9; all have super king-size bed, tea and coffee making facilities, air-con, wi-fi, TV, radio, bathrobes, Temple spa toiletries, hairdryer
Facilities restaurant, bar, garden, private dining room
Credit cards AE, DC, MC, V
Children welcome
Accessibility accessible restaurant, disabled toilet, one fully accessible room **Pets** not allowed
Closed Mondays
Proprietors James and Kate Mackenzie

The Pipe and Glass
Pub-with-rooms

The Pipe and Glass is based on a winning formula of rustic luxury: a cosy country pub serving up Michelin food. James Mackenzie and his wife Kate stress that it's first and foremost a pub – so expect hearty pub classics at their best, with an emphasis on local flavours. This includes barbecued rump of Yorkshire lamb, and Yorkshire rhubarb with pistachio Bakewell tart (they're particularly good at puddings). Nor are they a one-trick pony. Our hotel's editor, Fiona Duncan, was especially impressed by their five ground floor bedroom suites, individually decorated by local designer David Bird. Bold patterned wallpapers combine with sumptuous throws and walnut furniture make for a luxurious and comforting effect. All the rooms are well-equipped, and come with their own private garden patios. You can also have breakfast in bed.

The main pub and private dining areas have also been given the Bird treatment: cosy sitting areas, open fires and soft pools of lighting entice ramblers in from the Yorkshire Wolds to warm their feet with a pint. The pub's lack of pretension draws an eclectic crowd: local drinkers mix with smart diners who have driven some distance for the food, adding to the happy, relaxed atmosphere.

THE NORTH-EAST — NORTHERN ENGLAND

York

17 Blosson Street, York, YO24 1QA

Tel 01904 643238
email
reception@bar-convent.org.uk
website www.bar-convent.org.uk

Nearby York Minster, York Castle Museum, Yorkshire Museum, York city centre (1 km or less), York railway station (400 m) **Location** by the medieval gatehouse of Micklegate Bar, on the A1036 travelling E into York **Food** breakfast, light lunch, snacks, afternoon tea (book in advance) **Price** £-££ **Rooms** 20; 8 singles, 5 doubles, 5 twins, 2 triples; 16 have en-suite, 4 have shared bathroom; all have flat-screen TV, hairdryer, free wi-fi, tea/coffee making facilities **Facilities** sitting room, self-catering kitchen, garden, café, permanent exhibition, laundry **Credit cards** DC, MC, V **Children** welcome **Pets** guide dogs only **Accessibility** there's a lift but some corridors may be unsuitable for wheelchairs **Closed** end of Dec to start of Jan, Easter **Proprietor** The Bar Convent Trust

Bar Convent
City hotel

If you're looking for something different, the Bar Convent won't disappoint. It was founded in the 17thC by Frances Bedingfield as clandestine convent for the 'Ladies of the Bar', during a time of Tudor suppression. After a significant fundraising effort, it is now a 20-bedroom guesthouse, with a permanent exhibition celebrating its chequered past.

A Victorian winter garden sheltered by a glass roof is now the entrance hall, also accommodating the popular all-day café. A tangle of corridors and staircases lead up to the rooms, some with en-suites and some with shared bathrooms, offering great flexibility for single travellers and families alike. Two of the bedrooms, St Anna and St Joachim, are designed by Olga Polizzi, with tranquil blue and cream furnishings.

The white-and-gold Baroque chapel is a delight, and the garden is a real oasis. Certainly no other place in York can offer the experience of staying in a Grade I-listed building where a Catholic order was founded, wounded soldiers were cared for during the war and where families and children were sheltered from persecution. Our series editor Fiona Duncan says: As you might expect, it is memorable, tranquil and affordable; the sisters make Bar Convent a special place to stay

THE NORTH-EAST — NORTHERN ENGLAND

York

Grays Court, Chapter House Street,
York YO1 7JH

Tel 01904 612613
email office@graysscourtyork.com
website www.graysscourtyork.com

Nearby York Minster, St William's College, Railway Museum, Jorvik Viking Centre
Location Chapter House Street, off St. Maurice's Road, car parking at £15 per night
Food breakfast, lunch, dinner, afternoon tea
Price ££££
Rooms 11 doubles, 1 can be twin, all have bath/shower, with TV, safe, tea/coffee facilities, telephone, wi-fi
Facilities The Bow Room Restaurant, Long Gallery with bar, function rooms, library, garden
Credit cards all major
Children welcome
Accessibility no special facilities
Pets small dogs by prior arrangement
Closed Christmas
Proprietor Helen Heraty

Grays Court
Town house hotel

This iconic building in one of the England's most historically fascinating cities was built in 1091 to help establish the regime of William the Conqueror in the North of England. Two decades into its reincarnation as a hotel its strength is now its young and enthusiastic staff and its hands-on owner Helen. The location is good too, on a quiet street, with added peace and privacy from a small tree-lined courtyard for parking. With its recent update and atmospheric setting Grays Court is an upstanding local gem.

Michelin starred-chef Ian Doyle has devised a garden-inspired menu which is served in The Bow Room restuarant.

You enter by a long, comfortable sitting room, with original 11thC walls forming one side. Above is a long, imposing gallery with wonderful oak panelling (not much enhanced by the hung pictures). There's a small bar at one end, and a peaceful sitting-room/library on the same floor. The comfortable bedrooms were renovated in 2022, maintaining a classic style, with some show-stopper antiques in the mix, such as a William IV four poster bed (Willoughby room). The larger rooms have freestanding copper baths and all have windows with interesting views over the gardens, York Minster or out on to another interesting nook of the city.

SCOTLAND

Area introduction

From the fertile southern uplands bordering England to the dramatic mount ranges and sensational coasts of the Highlands and Islands, Scotland is varied a breathtakingly beautiful. Within a few hours' drive the scenery changes from gen rolling hills to craggy peaks. Visitors come to hike, climb, ski, play golf, fish, and explore Scotland's fascinating historical heritage and lively cultural life. Peo describe Scotland as being either 'Lowland' or 'Highland'. The lowlands, which are all low, lie south of a line drawn between Glasgow and Edinburgh. The Highlan though not all high, are north of this line. Our selection includes converted castl country manors, farmhouses and town houses. This edition has a number of int esting additions, thanks to reporter Jonathan Noble. Entries are indexed in alp order by place name, regardless of whether they are on the mainland or on an isla
Below are some useful back-up places to try if our main selections are fully booked:

Dornoch Station
Country hotel, Dornoch
Tel 01862 810351
www.bespokehotels.com
Overlooking Royal Dornoch Golf Course.

Crolinnhe
Bed-and-breakfast, Fort William Tel 01397 70379
www.crolinnhe.co.uk
Guesthouse with spectac views of Loch Linnhe.

Ednam House Hotel
Country house hotel, Kelso
Tel 01573 224168
www.ednamhouse.com
Traditional fishing hotel with great location on the Tweed.

Toravaig
Country House hotel Te
01471820200
www.skyehotel.co.uk
Country house overlook the sound of Sleat

SOUTHERN SCOTLAND

SCOTLAND

Closeburn, Dumfries and Galloway

Closeburn, Thornhill, Dumfries and Galloway DG3 5EZ

Tel 01848 331211
email info@trigonyhotel.co.uk
website www.trigonyhotel.co.uk

Nearby Drumlanrig Castle; Caerlaverock Castle; Caerlaverock Nature Reserve **Location** just north of Closeburn before the village of Thornhill; about 200 yards from the main road. **Food** breakfast, lunch Friday–Sunday, otherwise by reservation only **Price** ££-££££ **Rooms** 9; 4 doubles (2 can be twin), 4 superior (3 can be twin), one garden suite with heated conservatory and small private garden; all have bath/shower, TV and radio, hairdryer, tea and coffee making facilities. **Facilities** restaurant, gardens, bar, terrace; activities include: falconry, vintage car hire, land-rover safaris, salmon fishing, spa **Credit cards** MC, V **Children** welcome **Accessibilty** no special facilities **Pets** dogs welcome **Closed** never **Proprietors** Adam and Jan

Trigony House Hotel
Country bed-and-breakfast

Owners Adam and Jan bought Trigony House Hotel after deciding to quit the rat-race in York and move to the Scottish countryside. They've created a homely, family atmosphere founded on simple, honest comforts. Adam's food is a major draw. His unfussy classic dishes can be enjoyed in the informal bar or the slightly more formal restaurant, both with cosy wood-burning stoves. Inside and out, it's what you would expect of a former Edwardian shooting lodge: understated and handsome, ivy creeps up the exterior and a large trim front garden is perfect for dogs. The interiors don't try too hard and suit the building; muted colours are used throughout for understated ambience and the whole building is well maintained and a perfect size for the operation. The Garden Spa is a recent addition: kitted out with a Swedish hot tub and sauna cabin, it offers a selection of pampering holistic treatments.

Although tucked away in the countryside, there are lots of things to do. Adam and Jan have a wealth of suggestions for the area and often arrange things to do nearby and in the grounds. One of our favourite activities was driving around the winding Scottish country roads in a hired vintage Austin 14. Low-key walks and cycling routes are on hand, too.

SOUTHERN SCOTLAND

SCOTLAND

Cupar, Fife

Cupar, Fife KY15 5LH

Tel 01334 840206
email stay@thepeatinn.co.uk
website www.thepeatinn.co.uk

Nearby Edinburgh; Piscottie; St Andrews; golf courses; Dundee; Perthshire; East Neuk; Falkland Palace; The Secret Bunker **Location** from the B940 and 941 follow signs to the village of Peat Inn – in prominent position with parking **Food** breakfast, lunch and dinner Tuesday–Saturday inclusive **Price** £££-££££
Rooms 8; double and family suites **Facilities** private garden, restaurant, safe, parking **Credit cards** AE, MC, V **Children** welcome; under fives are free, over fives: supplement for sofa bed. Cots and high chairs available **Accessibility** to public areas and an adaptable ground-floor bedroom **Pets** not accepted
Closed Sun-Mon, Christmas and 10 days at the beginning of Jan **Proprietors** Geoffrey and Katherine Smeddle

The Peat Inn
Restaurant-with-rooms

This restaurant-with-rooms, a former 17thC coaching inn, has had a sterling reputation for more than 30 years. Originally owned by renowned chef David Wilson, it was taken over in 2006 by Geoffrey Smeddle and his wife Katherine, who are, according to one guest 'creating something quite special'.

A warm, professional welcome is ensured by Katherine and the front of house team, but the food is the big draw here. Geoffrey's dishes, which use only the best local and seasonal produce, are racking up awards. Typical dishes include poached longoustines with coriander and satay sauce, honey-glazed duck breast and hot strawberry soufflé. This award-winning restaurant isn't intimidating, though: it's split into three small areas, which, helped by the service, create a friendly, intimate atmosphere.

Upstairs, the eight suites are each individually designed, with the bedroom and living room set on two separate levels and bathrooms finished with Italian marble. Carpets are deep, fabrics are rich, and towels are thick and fluffy. Continental breakfast (home-made, of course) is served in your suite at a preferred time – a touch that might feel intrusive to some, decadent to others. It's almost impossible to find any fault with this place.

Glasgow

15 Woodside Place, Glasgow G3 7QL

Tel 0141 332 1263
email rooms@15Glasgow.com
website www.15glasgow.com

Nearby art galleries; all major attractions; shopping; bars; restaurants. **Location** city centre, in green area a 10 minute walk to city and West End attractions; free car-parking available on request
Food breakfast
Price ££
Rooms 5; 3 double (1 can be a twin), 2 suites, all have bath/shower, bath robes, TV, hairdryer, tea/coffee
Facilities guest sitting room, residents garden
Credit cards MC, V
Children welcome
Accessibility not suitable
Pets not accepted
Closed Christmas
Proprietor Lorraine Gibson

15 Glasgow
City bed-and-breakfast

Situated in a terrace of large, confident Victorian terrace houses near the city centre, 15 Glasgow was converted from offices into a B&B in 2009 by Shane and Laura McKenzie, and taken on by Lorraine Gibson in 2016. She's made a few changes (the rooms now have Scottish themed names, such as Tartan, Thistle and Heather) but the period features – original shutters, fireplaces, ceilings – are preserved, alongside a tasteful, design-led style. The rooms are spacious, with swish bathrooms and underfloor heating. The Charles Rennie Mackintosh Suite, the original first floor reception room of the house, is enormous, stunning whatever your taste, with feminine touches of pink, and three floor-length sash windows overlooking the private garden – and priced at a friendly £150 a night in peak season.

Breakfast is delicious, and served in the spacious ground floor sitting room or brought to your bedroom. There's a good amount of choice, with gems such as clementine-and-whisky marmalade, as well as the full Scottish, complete with haggis.

With its West End location and good value, Lorraine offers a great alternative to staying in a Glasgow hotel.

SOUTHERN SCOTLAND

SCOTLAND

Glasgow

1 Devonshire Gardens, Glasgow
G12 0UX

Tel 01413780385
email reception.glasgow@hotelduvin.com
website www.hotelduvin.com/locations/glasgow

Nearby Glasgow Museum and Art Gallery, Cathedral, Shopping centre
Location Central Glasgow
Food breakfast, lunch, dinner
Price ££-£££
Rooms 49; all rooms en suite, all have flatscreen TV, and showers or baths
Facilities drawing room, dining room, private function room
Credit cards AE, MC, V
Children welcome
Accessibility not suitable
Pets welcome
Closed never
Proprietor Hotel du Vin

One Devonshire Gardens City hotel

On an otherwise unassuming street of Glasgow's West End, Hotel du Vin's One Devonshire Gardens occupies no less than five Grade-II listed terraced town houses. Framed by stone columns and rows of trees pruned to perfect points, its high-end status is obvious at first glance. Inside, however, any intimidating grandeur is forgotten as you are immediately drawn into a cosy downstairs sitting room filled with plaid armchairs and crackling fireplaces where guests read and drink coffee. Impressive 19thC stained glass windows accompany you up the wide staircases that lead to the bedrooms. The bright and airy suites are a stark and slightly awkward contrast to the low-lit cosiness of downstairs, each individually decorated but all boasting the characteristically high ceilings and windows of Glasgow's Victorian town houses. Even the rooms, finished with dark, velvety wallpaper, are brightened with streams of natural light. The rooms are all different, and although the decoration follows a house style, it doesn't feel impersonal or bland. Some are perhaps a touch too bold in design, but most are thoughtfully and tastefully done. Despite its 49 rooms, One Devonshire Gardens achieves the feel of a smaller, more relaxed place without compromising on luxury. A quiet and intimate retreat from a busy city.

SOUTHERN SCOTLAND

SCOTLAND

Gullane, East Lothian

Main St, Gullane, EH31 2AB

Tel 01620 621111
email info@bonniebadger.com
website www.bonniebadger.com

Nearby Gullane Bents, Muirfield golf course, Direlton village and castle, Gullane Hill **Location** five miles west from North Berwick. A 10 minute detour form the A1
Food breakfast, lunch, dinner, picnic baskets on request
Price £££975
Rooms 12; 1 suite, 11 doubles.
Facilities dining room, sitting room 'The Garden Room', bar, garden
Credit cards MC, V, Amex
Children yes
Accessibilty access to ground floor only **Pets** some rooms dog friendly
Closed Jan
Proprietors Michaela and Tom Kitchin

Bonnie Badger
Restaurant with rooms

This is Edinburgh chef and restaurant entrepreneur Tom Kitchin's first venture into food with rooms, opened Decembers 2018 and a major addition to the area's lunching and dining possibilities. On the main street of Gullane (pronounced 'gullen'), it was built as an 18thC coaching inn, became a petrol station and then evolved back into a traditional inn – The Golf Inn. Its most recent incarnation as a stylish pub, restaurant and rooms cements this place is a destination in its own right.

First impressions are very good: smartly designed but not contrived, and friendly, competent staff. Don't miss the garden room which gives on to a stylish courtyard with an outdoor fire and barbecues.

The bedrooms, though stylish and comfortable, are a little – only a little – eclipsed by downstairs.

The star turn, however, is The Stables Restaurant with its high ceiling, unusual 'hoop' lighting and gastropub food – we enjoyed oysters with an intensely zingy vinegar and shallot sauce, thickly sliced smoked salmon with dill dressing and rye bread, a succulent Highland wagyu burger and an unusual take on ham and eggs. The free afternoon tea is exceptional and the bar stocks around 140 whiskies. Crispy pigs ears star in the pre-dinner nibbles.

Kilberry, Argyll

Kilberry, Argyll PA29 6YD

Tel 01880 770 223
email relax@kilberryinn.com
website www.kilberryinn.com

Nearby secluded beaches, distilleries, ferries to the surrounding islands
Location on the B8024 between Tarbert and Lochgilphead
Food breakfast, lunch, dinner
Price ££
Rooms 5 double with shower; all rooms have TV, hairdryer, tea and coffee, books
Facilities restaurant
Credit cards MC, V
Children over 12 welcome
Accessibility to restaurant and 1 bedroom
Pets dogs accepted by arrangement
Closed Dec-Mar and Mondays and Sundays
Proprietors Clare Johnson and David Wilson

The Kilberry Inn
Restaurant-with-rooms

This traditional whitewashed, red-roofed 'but'n'ben' cottage had long been run as an inn before David Wilson and chef Clare Johnson, who used to run the renowned Anchorage Seafood Restaurant in the nearby fishing village of Tarbert, took it on and set about transforming it into a modern restaurant with rooms. Gone is the former cluttered, rustic, 'twee' look. It has been replaced with minimal and contemporary decoration, with cosy log fires, beams and quarried stone-walls, hung with art from local painters. The inn has five comfortable, tastefully decorated double bedrooms with showers, in adjacent buildings.

The focus in the restaurant is on fresh, locally produced ingredients – crab, lobster, langoustine, scallops and fish are all caught within a few miles of the inn, and meat is all reared nearby. Dinner might be potted Kilberry crab, followed by Sound of Jura monkfish with pepperonata and piquillo pepper dressing, then Isle of Mull cheddar with biscuits and chutney to finish.

The inn is situated on a remote single track road on the Kintyre peninsula, with stunning views of the surrounding lochs and islands, and David thinks this remoteness makes arriving an adventure in itself. Reports welcome.

Kirkcolm, Dumfries and Galloway

Corsewall Point, Kirkcolm,
Stranraer, Dumfries and Galloway
DG9 0QG

Tel 01776 853220
email info@lighthousehotel.co.uk
website www.lighthousehotel.co.uk

Nearby Stranraer – ferry to Ireland, Loch Ryan, Iron Age fort, pony-trekking, golf.
Location remote; in own grounds with ample private car parking, air transfer arrangeable.
Food breakfast, lunch, dinner
Price ££
Rooms 11; 9 doubles, 2 suites, some can be twin-bedded; all rooms have phone, TV, hairdryer
Facilities 2 sitting rooms, restaurant, 20-acre grounds
Credit cards AE, MC, V
Children accepted
Accessibility 1 accessible room
Pets allowed in 2 of the suites
Closed never
Proprietor Helen Mason and John Harris

Corsewall Lighthouse
Lighthouse hotel

Remote – the last mile is down a track – on a windswept promontory north of Stranraer, this is a listed, 200-year old working lighthouse. The tower itself isn't part of the hotel, but the structure at its foot, the former lighthouse keeper's dwelling, houses the restaurant, public areas and some of the rooms. Other accommodation, including the suites, are in separate buildings, none more than three minutes from the hub.

Guests come here for a unique and romantic experience, the generally light rooms and dramatic seascapes, but not for style. It's mostly done out comfortably, but in a conventional, unpretentious way – you could hardly be anywhere else but a hotel. Some of the smaller rooms may not please perfectionists – but bear in mind it's an old building.

The food ('tremendous' says a reporter) wins general approval. Service is thoughtful and the welcome personal - new owners Helen and John live on site and you can often find them chatting to guests in the lounge and conservatory areas.

'Truly magical' says one reporter. 'Nothing beats going out after dinner to walk the shore and hear the waves exploding on the rocks' says another. Porpoise, seals and basking sharks can be seen off the coast. To climb the lighthouse tower you need permission in writing from the Northern Lighthouse Board.

SOUTHERN SCOTLAND

SCOTLAND

Melrose, Roxburghshire

Burts Hotel
Melrose, Scottish Borders TD6 9PL

Tel 01896 822285
email enquiries@burtshotel.co.uk
website www.burtshotel.co.uk

Food breakfast, lunch, dinner
Price £-££
Closed Never
Proprietors Henderson family

The Townhouse Hotel
Melrose, Scottish Borders TD6 9PQ

Tel 01896 822645
email enquiries@thetownhousemelrose.co.uk **website** www.thetownhousemelrose.co.uk

Food breakfast, lunch, dinner
Price £-££
Closed Never
Proprietors Henderson family

Burts and The Townhouse
Town hotels

Unusually for a Scottish border town, pleasant Melrose appeals to all sorts of visitor – it offers walking and fishing, as well as shopping, museums and Melrose Abbey. Similarly, the Hendersons' two places to stay, standing opposite each other in the town centre, accommodate a range of visitors' needs.

Burts (top photo) is secure in its reputation as a fishing hotel with great atmosphere. Jolly flowers tumbling out of every window at the front prepare you for an unstuffy atmosphere within. Upstairs, bedroom walls are decorated in an earthy range of colours, while a lively variety of fabrics and patterns in each room add bolder colours (four have been recently refurbished). Be sure to book dinner in advance, as the bistro is popular with locals – 'the hottest seats in town' we are told.

The Townhouse (bottom left photo) departs from the country sports ethos of its sister hotel. The rooms are similarly bold – intensely patterned walls, cushions and sofas, but more ambitious in colour scheme and size. Young city dwellers seeking a contemporary, uncluttered ambience will feel more comfortable here.

The menu offers local produce (as at Burt's), and is elegantly served, but we were underwhelmed by the drinking area in the lean-to conservatory at the back.

SOUTHERN SCOTLAND — SCOTLAND

Portpatrick, Dumfries and Galloway

Portpatrick, Dumfries & Galloway
DG9 9AD

Tel 01776 810471
email reservations@knockinaam-lodge.com
website www.knockinaamlodge.com

Nearby Logan; Ardwell and Glenwhan Gardens; Castle Kennedy.
Location 3 miles (5 km) SE of Portpatrick, off A77; in grounds; ample car parking
Food breakfast, lunch, dinner
Price ££££
Rooms 10; 3 double with bath, 7 double with bath and walk-in shower; all rooms have phones, TV's and hairdryer. One self-catering lodge also available
Facilities 2 sitting rooms, bar, dining room, outdoor dining space 'The Cove', garden, croquet, helipad
Credit cards AE, MC, V
Children welcome
Accessibility public rooms accessible (no ground-floor bedrooms)
Pets accepted in some spac
Closed never
Proprietor David Ibbotson

Knockinaam Lodge
Country hotel

Galloway is very much an area for escaping the hurly-burly, and Knockinaam Lodge complements it perfectly (as well as being the ideal staging post for anyone bound for the ferry at Stranraer to Northern Ireland). Succeeding proprietors of the Lodge have had a reputation for fine food and warm hospitality, and the tradition is still maintained with the help of an enthusiastic staff and owner, David Ibbotson.

The house, a low Victorian villa, was built as a hunting lodge in 1869 and extended at the turn of the century. It was used by Sir Winston Churchill as a secret location in which to meet General Eisenhower during the Second World War.

The rooms are cosy in scale and furnishings, the bedrooms varying from the stylishly simple to the quietly elegant. A key part of the appeal of the place is its complete seclusion – down a wooded glen, with lawned garden running down to a sandy beach. Children are welcome, and well catered for, with special high teas.

Since 2003 David has brightened up the place, completely redecorating and painting the exterior. Recently added is a stylish self-catering cabin, Shingle, whoses floor-to-ceiling windows offer extensive views across the Irish Sea.

The restaurant has a Michelin star, and the wine list has more than 450 bins.

SOUTHERN SCOTLAND

SCOTLAND

Sanquhar, Dumfries and Galloway

Sanquhar, Dumfries and Galloway, DG4 6JJ

Tel 01659 50270
email ian@blackaddiehotel.co.uk
website www.blackaddiehotel.co.uk

Nearby Drumlanrig Castle 8 miles; Dumfries House 18 miles; Dumfries 28 miles; Kilmarnock 30 miles; Ayr 32 miles **Location** on the banks of the River Nith, just outside the village of Sanquhar
Food lunch and afternoon tea (booking required), dinner (no booking required)
Price ££-££££
Rooms 7; all double, 3 can be twin, 2 are suites; all have wi-fi, tea and coffee facilities, homemade shortbread, HD TV
Facilities restaurant, garden
Credit cards AE, MC, V
Children welcome
Accessibility 1 suitable self-catering cottage with a ramp up to the front door and an extra large bathroom
Pets accepted, £10 surcharge
Closed never
Proprietors Paola and Anna

Blackaddie House
Country hotel

Husband and wife Ian and Jane McAndrew bought Blackaddie back in 2007. Since then, they have worked tirelessly to refurbish the property and now offer seven bedrooms – of which two are classed as suites – and two self-catering cottages. The Grouse Suite, which is the largest of all the rooms, has a jacuzzi and king-sized four-poster bed. The River Suite features a set of French windows that lead out on to the patio, where you can sit by the River Nith as it flows through the end of the garden.

Jane's detailed knowledge of the area includes suggestions for some great walking routes, not least Mennock Pass to Wenlockhead, which is only a short drive away. Ian, who is also the head chef, creates some fabulously presented dishes using locally sourced ingredients. The menu changes daily and includes a locally famed seven course tasting menu with matching wines. Ian was the youngest British chef to be awarded a Michelin star in 1980 and was crowned Scottish Chef of the Year in 2016: the food is that good.

If you're not too full after dinner, retire to the bar – where there's a choice of single malt whiskies – and relax by the log fire. Ian, a chatty and affable man who loves to meet his punters, can often be found mingling with guests in the bar when the kitchen closes.

SOUTHERN SCOTLAND

SCOTLAND

Allanton, Berwickshire

Allanton, TD11 3JZ

Tel 01890818260
email info@allantoninn.co.uk
website www.allantoninn.co.uk
Food breakfast, lunch, dinner
Price ££
Closed never
Proprietors William and Katrina Reynolds

Allanton Inn
Country Inn

We especially liked the pods for outdoor dining in the large garden with long views over Borders Countryside. In summer a pizza shack pops up here, attracting a jolly crowd.

Owner-managers William and Katrina have been at the Allanton since 2011, building up a respectable track record. Expect well above average, locally sourced food - Katrina is a local farmer's daughter and has top local contacts.

The bedrooms, one with mauve the dominant colour (to reflect the local moorland heather when in flower), have colour schemes echoing the landscape - silver greys of the rivers, green for fields, gold for the ripe corn.

Duns is a peaceful Berwickshire town and there's plenty of local history interest.

Edinburgh

Castlehill, The Royal Mile,
Edinburgh EH1 2NF

Tel 0131 225 5613
email mail@thewitchery.com
website www.thewitchery.com
Food breakfast, lunch, dinner
Price ££££
Closed never
Proprietor James Thomson

The Witchery by the Castle **Restaurant-with-rooms**

It takes its name from the hundreds of witches burned at the stake nearby, but The Witchery by the Castle is, thankfully, not macabre. However, it is Gothic and, above all, luxurious. It occupies a pair of 16thC buildings at the gates of Edinburgh Castle. Entering from a close off the Royal Mile, candle-light reveals painted ceilings and walls covered in tapestries and 17thC oak panelling rescued from a fire at St Giles Cathedral.

Suites, either above the restaurant or in an adjacent building, are plush and opulent, with antiques, historic paintings and dramatic colour schemes, and have views towards the Old Town or over the Royal Mile.

You can eat either in the award-winning restaurant of the same name; in the Secret Garden; or in The Tower.

SOUTHERN SCOTLAND
SCOTLAND

Gullane, East Lothian

Muirfield, Gullane, East Lothian
EH31 2EG

Tel 01620 842144
email enquiries@greywalls.co.uk
website www.greywalls.co.uk
Food breakfast, lunch, dinner,
afternoon tea **Price** ££££
Closed Jan to Feb
Proprietor ICMI Management

Greywalls
Country house hotel

Greywalls is a slick, expensive country house hotel, with – by our standards – quite a large number of bedrooms, but despite this we cannot resist including such a distinctive place. It is a classic turn-of-the-century house, and for golf enthusiasts – it overlooks the tenth green of the famous Muirfield championship course.

The feel of Greywalls is very much one of a gracious private house, although series editor Fiona Duncan felt it would have been cosier were it still family-run.

Dinner, served in a room overlooking the golf course, is superb – it's one of Albert Roux's Chez Roux outposts. Bedrooms are attractive and well-equipped, particularly those in the original house rather than the new wing.

Jedburgh, Roxburghshire

Jedburgh, Roxburghshire TD8 6PA

Tel 01835 863011
email sheila.whittaker@btinternet.com
website www.accommodation-scotland.org
Food breakfast **Price** £
Closed Nov-Mar
Proprietors Mr and Mrs Whittaker

Hundalee House
Bed-and-breakfast

Set back in the hills, this 18thC limestone manor house has been home to the Whittakers for a decade. They created the fine large garden, putting in flowering shrubs, adding peacocks and digging a pond for koi carp. Inside, the taste is even more exotic, reflecting their time in Egypt. Egyptian motifs hang on the walls and Egyptian hounds guard the fireplace in the sitting room, which has fine views of the Cheviot Hills to the south. Bedrooms may not be luxurious but one has a four-poster bed. Two others share a bathroom; these offer notable value and are useful for a family. Sheila Whittaker does not serve dinner, but her breakfasts are 'cooked and copious,' according to one teenage visitor.

SOUTHERN SCOTLAND

Kirkudbright

High St, Kirkcudbright DG6 4JG

Tel 01557 330402
email reception@selkirkarmshotel.co.uk
website www.selkirkarmshotel.co.uk
Food breakfast, lunch, dinner
Price ££
Closed never
Proprietors Sue and Chris Walker

Selkirk Arms
Seaside hotel

Plenty of thought has been given to making the bedrooms very different. However you respond to the design and decoration, which are sometimes pretty bold, the rooms are spacious and up to date. Kirkudbright is a pleasant fishing port at the head of a large estuary in under-visited Dumfries and Galloway. There's a local artist colony whose galleries and exhibitions give an extra dimension. It's possible that Robert Burns, national poet of Scotland, wrote *The Selkirk Grace* here. Familiar to genuine Scots, it is said as guests sit down to the traditional Burns night supper each January of haggis and bashed neaps (mashed root vegetables) and is humorously laconic:

> *Some hae meat and canna eat*
> *And some wad eat that want it…*

HIGHLANDS AND ISLANDS
SCOTLAND

Auldearn, Nairn

Auldearn, Nairn, IV12 5TE

Tel 01667 454896
email info@boath-house.com
website www.boath-house.com

Nearby Inverness, Nairn, Loch Ness, Balmoral Castle
Location off A96, near Nairn, ample parking
Food breakfast (residents only) lunch, dinner, Thursday to Sunday
Price ££££
Rooms 8 in main house, doubles to super-king. 2 private cabins with woodburners and outdoor fire pits. 1 4-bed self-catering Lodge with private garden
Facilities 2 sitting rooms, restaurant, walled garden with enclosed studio, sauna and cafe; golf, fishing, riding, clay shooting all available nearby
Credit Cards MC, V
Children welcome
Accessibility one ground floor cottage, restaurant is accessible
Pets accepted by arrangement
Closed never
Proprietors Jonny Gent

Boath House Hotel
Country House Hotel

This Grade A listed Georgian mansion was standing derelict until Don and Wendy Matheson found and fell in love with it in the early Nineties. Now revamped under unconventional hotelier, artist and founder of London's Sessions Arts Club restaurant Jonny Gent.

The main house has eight guest bedrooms, all tastefully decorated a calm, almost monastic simplicity. All have private bathrooms, and two have four poster beds. It stands in 20 acres of grounds, including a 2-acre lake and Victorian walled garden. Two 'studios'- stand-alone cabins - are also available.

The kitchen gardens provide many of the ingredients served in the award-winning restaurant, which ushers in guests and locals alike. The focus is on organic, locally–produced and seasonal food. Local seafood is delivered daily, and meat and cheese come from a nearby farm. Wild food items, such as wild mushrooms and herbs, are also on the menu when in season, and even honey comes from the hotel's own hives – organic food is a real passion here.

Jonny is keen to foster a friendly, informal atmosphere and wants the place to feel like home for the guests despite the grandeur of the house and sprawling grounds. Writers and artists are regularly invited for residencies.

HIGHLANDS AND ISLANDS
SCOTLAND

Badachro, Shieldaig Bay

Shieldaig Lodge, Badachro, Ross-Shire IV21 2AN

Tel 01445741333
email reservations@shieldaiglodge.com
website www.shieldaiglodge.com

Nearby Gairloch Beach, Loch Ewe, The Fairy Lochs, Badachro, Inverness Airport
Location just off the A832
Food breakfast, lunch, dinner, afternoon tea by prebrooking only
Price £££-££££
Rooms 12; 11 double, 1 single, 1 suite, 4 twin, 1 quadruple, 2 triple
Facilities whiskey and gin bar, 2 log fire lounges, library, games room with pool table, restaurant, fishing, private gardens, guided walks
Credit cards MC, V
Children welcome
Accessibility not suitable
Pets welcome in most rooms
Closed never
Proprietors Charlotte and Nick Dent

Shieldaig Lodge
Highland hotel

Functional, but human. Old Victorian houses, such as this, often have too much brown wood for modern taste, but Shieldaig Lodge manages not to be depressing.

The building itself is impressive – a substantial restored Victorian hunting lodge set in the beauty of the West Highlands and nestled next to Shieldaig Bay. It retains the charm of its 19thC origins. The muted colour palette, tartan pattern details and artfully positioned grandfather clocks underscore the old-fashioned home from home feel. Golden mirror frames and crystal chandeliers give a touch of elegance.

Each of the 12 bedrooms is quite sophisticated, complete with antique pieces and tartan details. We recommend, of course, a bedroom with a sea view. The Suite has a large bay window with an alluring view over the waters and hills – a cushy little niche for a morning coffee or immersing yourself in a book.

A serious selection of whiskies and gins is available at the Liberator bar, where you also have the opportunity to blend your own whisky under the guidance of the Lodge's whisky expert.

See also Widbrook Grange, Forss House and Broadford Hotel – sister hotels in the same collection.

HIGHLANDS AND ISLANDS

SCOTLAND

Balquidder, Perthshire

Balquhidder, Lochearnhead,
Perthshire FK19 8PQ

Tel 01877 384622
email monachyle@mhor.net
website monachylemhor.net

Nearby in the heart of Rob Roy country.
Location on private estate; turn off A84, 11 miles (17.5 km) N of Callander at Kingshouse Hotel, then follow single-track lane for 6 miles (9.5 km); well-signposted; ample car-parking
Food breakfast, lunch, dinner
Price ££-££££
Rooms 16 double, all with bath or shower; all rooms have phone, TV, hairdryer. Also The Cabin (sleeps 4) with own kitchen, and The Wagon (sleeps 4)
Facilities sitting room, bar, restaurant; terrace, garden, fishing, stalking **Credit cards** MC, V
Children well behaved children accepted over 12
Accessibility access easy
Pets accepted in 2 rooms
Closed Jan **Proprietors** Tom Lewis

Monachyle Mhor
Farmhouse hotel

A small, family-run farmhouse with a charm all its own. The setting is both serene and romantic: this was the home of Rob Roy MacGregor, approached along the Braes of Balquhidder and set beside Lochs Doine and Voil.

Rob and Jean Lewis came here in 1983 from Monmouth to farm the 2,000-acre estate, later opening it as a hotel. When they moved to the South of France, their enterprising son Tom took over and expanded the buisness. There's now a total of 16 rooms spread across the main house, Courtyard and Farmhouse, all very stylishly decorated with a medley of bold modernist strokes and well-chosen antiques. The Cabin and The Wagon – a 1950s Pilot Panther wagon restored by artist Sarah Kechington – are available for glamping. Tom's unstoppable empire now includes a fish shop, bakery, Mhor to Your Door (a mobile restaurant) and Mhor 84 – a roadside gastropub with seven rooms.

The award-winning restaurant takes 'locally sourced' to another level, shooting the lamb, pork, venison and game on-site, and foraging much of their vegetables and herbs. It's situated in a light and airy conservatory overlooking the two lochs.

For a relaxing, country break in magnificent scenery and with memorable food, Monachyle Mhor is hard to beat.

HIGHLANDS AND ISLANDS — SCOTLAND

Brachla, Inverness-shire

Brachla, Loch Ness-Side, IV3 8LA

Tel 01456 459469
email escape@loch-ness-lodge.com
website www.loch-ness-lodge.com

Nearby Loch Ness, Culloden, Isle of Skye, Glen Affric National Nature Reserve **Location** from Inverness follow signs for A82 Fort William/Loch Ness Road, Lodge is on the right after approximately 9 miles
Food breakfast, afternoon tea, pre-orderable packed lunches
Price £££-££££
Rooms 7 double with flat screen TV
Facilities drawing room, spa, garden, wi-fi throughout
Credit cards AE, MC, V
Children welcome (over 12)
Accessibility possible
Pets not accepted
Closed Jan
Proprietor Scott Sutherland
Manager Arran McMaster

Loch Ness Lodge
Highland bed-and-breakfast

Located just a stone's throw from the waters edge, this B&B offers unrivalled views across Loch Ness and the hills beyond. The lodge sits in its own cultivated gardens and acts as an ideal setting-off point to explore the surrounding highlands.

The emphasis at Loch Ness Lodge is on understated indulgence: it seems that nothing is too much for the staff (who will even provide you with satnav details for your excursions). Although dinner is no longer offered, the team are more than happy to recommend (and book) a restaurant nearby.

An onsite spa offers a range of restorative treatments and in the hotel itself there are plenty of calm spaces in which to curl up and unwind after a long day outdoors.

Breakfast is wide ranging and often centres on locally-sourced ingredients. The complimentary afternoon tea, with a variety of loose-leaf teas and home-made bakes, was a welcome addition and has proved popular with the regular guests.

Our room was particularly spacious, simply decorated in muted colours with dark wood furnishings, and came complete with sherry and our own view of the Loch – a luxury shared by all seven rooms.

HIGHLANDS AND ISLANDS

SCOTLAND

Broadford, Isle-of-Skye

Torrin Road, Broadford, Isle of Skye, IV49 9AB

Tel 01471822204
email reservations@broadfordhotel.co.uk
website www.broadfordhotel.co.uk

Nearby Cuillin Hills, Broadford Bay, Kinloch Forest, Castles.
Location 30 minute drive from Portree
Food breakfast, lunch, dinner
Price ££££
Rooms 11; 7 double, 2 superior double, 2 twin
Facilities restaurant, sitting room, terrace, bar
Credit cards MC, V
Children welcome
Accessibilty no access
Pets dogs welcome for an extra charge
Closed never
Manager Means Pert

The Broadford
Highland hotel

We have several hotels on Skye, but this is a welcome addition. We like it for its subtle style and stunning scenery and its location, comfortably nestled near the centre of the Broadford village just across the road from the sea.

Your first impression might be a curious combination of shabby and modern styles, but with a relaxed feel. It feels calm and warm, with splashes of vibrant colour here and there, velvet cushions on the beds and leather sofas, all creating a sense of homely comfort.

The 11 bedrooms are simple and comfortable. They are relatively small, but they are tastefully furnished with bright touches. A few of the rooms look out over Broadford Bay, where you might see fishing boats returning from the sea with their catch of the day. The Broadford Hotel claims to be the original home of the world-famous liqueur Drambuie, which was developed, patented and sold by John and James Ross, who owned the hotel towards the end of the 19thC. Legend or not, Drambuie is now the house speciality, which you can enjoy on the fine faux leather sofa looking out over the bay in the Spinnaker Bar.

See also Widbrook Grange, Forss House and Shieldaig Lodge - sister hotels in the same collection.

HIGHLANDS AND ISLANDS
SCOTLAND

Elgol, Isle of Skye

Elgol, Isle of Skye, IV49 9BL

Tel 01471 866330
email info@coruiskhouse.com
website www.coruiskhouse.com

Nearby Bonnie Prince Charlie's cave, boat trips take you to Loch Coruisk, islands of Rum and Canna, Cuillins, Neolithic settlements
Location Elgol village, 13 miles down a single track road from Broadford **Food** breakfast, dinner
Price ££-££££
Rooms 2 en-suites and 2 large suites (one suite, 2 adjoining doubles). All have king-size beds, bathrooms, hairdryer, tea/coffee facilities, fresh fruit, bathrobes, White Company toiletries.
Facilities parking, bar, sitting room with wood burning stove and TV
Credit Cards all major except AE
Children under 14s not allowed
Accessibility not suitable
Pets not allowed **Closed** Christmas, New Year, 20 Oct-28 Feb
Proprietors Clare Winskill and Iain Roden

Coruisk House
Restaurant-with-rooms

On the wilder side of the 'dinosaur isle' of Scotland (named for the fossils and footprints discovered here), Coruisk House can be found at the the end of a 13-mile single track, running through some of the most spectacular scenery in the Highlands. In Clare and Iain's cosy and informal restaurant, guests choose from a short but sublime menu that lets the local ingredients sing: shellfish such as langoustines, lobsters and hand-dived scallops are served with their perfectly appointed wine list, and an array of Highland malt whiskeys and gins (give advance notice for a delicious vegetarian option). Food writer Hattie Ellis called this 'the best food on Skye', but perhaps the greatest testament to this tiny restaurant on a far-flung isle is a booking list stretching months in advance.

The five bedrooms are perfectly hygge little havens, with sheepskin rugs and duck-down bedding, and views across the Sound of Sleat. Guests are welcomed into the couple's embracing hospitality with a glass of prosecco on arrival, and breakfasts that include peat-smoked salmon, Scottish pancakes and homemade compotes.

And Skye's the limit when it comes to activities: catch a boat from Elgol harbour (where Bonnie Prince Charlie fled in 1745) into the spectacular Loch Coruisk, to spot orcas, puffins and golden eagles.

HIGHLANDS AND ISLANDS
SCOTLAND

Fort William, Inverness-shire

Glenfinnan, Fort William,
Inverness-shire, PH37 4LT

Tel 01397 722235
email availability@glenfinnan-house.com
website www.glenfinnanhouse.com

Nearby Ben Nevis, Glenfinnan viaduct railway bridge, Shiel Cruises, Glenfinnan Monument, Fort William, Highland activities.
Location pass through Fort William and turn off the A82 to follow the A830 'Road to the Isles', west for 15 miles to Glenfinnan. Turn left just after the Glenfinnan Monument Visitor Centre
Food breakfast, dinner, bar food
Price ££-£££ **Rooms** 12 including some suites and family rooms
Facilities drawing room, playroom, garden, function/wedding facilities, bar, dining room **Credit Cards** AE, MC, V **Children** welcome
Accessibility not suitable **Pets** not accepted in restaurant **Closed** never
Proprietors Jane Macfarlane
Managers Manja & Duncan Gibson

Glenfinnan
Country house hotel

The owners of Glenfinnan House Hotel clearly value family time. That perhaps explains why children are so readily welcomed, why the hotel operates a no-TV policy, and why dogs are well and truly smothered when they stay. Rooms are comfortable rather than inventive, but the real charm lies elsewhere.

Chef/manager Duncan produces some outstanding things from the kitchen, using fine local produce such as salmon, mussels, beef or venison; some of his classic dishes, as well as various innovative options from the *a la carte* menu, can be enjoyed in both the dining room and the bar.

Most important, this is inspiring, mountainous country which adults and kids will love (the latter will enjoy the chance to visit famous scenes from the Harry Potter films). Loch Shiel cruises operate from nearby, with regular sightings of golden eagles, black-throated divers and red deer. In season, trips slightly further afield often bring you face-to-face with whales, dolphins, seals, puffins and otters.

HIGHLANDS AND ISLANDS — SCOTLAND

Fort William, Inverness-shire

Grange Road, Fort William, Inverness-shire PH33 6JF

Tel 01397 705516
email info@grangefortwilliam.com
website www.grangefortwilliam.com

Nearby Ben Nevis; 'Road to the Isles'; Loch Ness. **Location** on outskirts; from town centre take A82 direction Glasgow, then turn left into Ashburn Lane; hotel is at top on left; ample car parking
Food breakfast, tea and shortbread served on arrival
Price £££
Rooms 1 Superior Terrace Suite, with lounge, king-size bed, french doors leading to patio; 1 Garden Suite; all rooms have bath/shower, tea/coffee making facilities
Facilities breakfast room, sitting room; garden, sea loch close by
Credit cards by arrangement
Children not accepted
Accessibility not suitable
Pets not accepted **Closed** mid-Nov to Easter **Proprietors** Joan and John Campbell

The Grange
Bed-and-breakfast

This outstanding bed-and-breakfast is on the outskirts of Fort William, run with great flair by Joan and John Campbell. A ten-minute walk from the fairly charmless town centre brings you to this late Victorian house, set in pretty terraced grounds overlooking Loch Linnhe. There's the option of staying in the Terrace Suite in the main building, or in their cosy Garden Suite – both offering the visitor tranquil privacy with lovely views over the garden and Loch Linnhe.

A feminine touch is distinctly in evidence in the immaculate interior, which is decorated with admirable taste and a flair for matching fabrics with furnishings and fittings. First glimpsed, you might expect a stand-offish 'don't touch' approach from the owners, but nothing could be further from the truth at the Grange. Joan Campbell, responsible for the decoration, is naturally easy-going, with a great sense of hospitality.

Both suites are superbly, and individually, decorated and furnished, their bathrooms lavish and luxurious – it all comes as rather a surprise. A delightful place.

HIGHLANDS AND ISLANDS

SCOTLAND

Inverary, Argyll

1 Main Street East Inveraray Argyll
PA32 8TT

Tel 01499 302111
email info@thegeorgehotel.com
website www.thegeorgehotel.co.uk

Nearby Inveraray Castle, Loch Fyne, Highlands and Islands
Location Situated between the main street of Inveraray and the banks of Loch Fyne
Food Lunch served daily 12-5, dinner served daily 5-8
Price ££
Rooms 24; suites, master rooms, standard rooms, plus The Barn (a 4 bedroom house with a private courtyard)
Facilities Restaurant, pub, cocktail bar, garden bar
Credit cards All major
Children welcome
Accessibility restaurant but not rooms
Pets All rooms are dog friendly
Closed rarely
Proprietors The Clark Family

The George
Island bed-and-breakfast

In the small town of Inverary, tucked between the main street and the banks of Loch Fyne, The George Hotel has been in the Clark family since it first opened in 1860. Seven generations later, and now the longest running family owned hotel in Scotland, it has 24 rooms alongside a successful restaurant, pub and cocktail bar, but with the feel of a smaller place.

The historic pub is at the heart of the operation. Soft lighting, open fires and comfortable seating bring warmth to the centuries-old stone walls. Over 400 whiskies are an offer here, balanced precariously atop one another behind the bar.

Head chef Craig Thomson oversees the restaurant next door. The menu, all about fresh, local produce, offers venison from Inveraray and Loch Fyne oysters delivered daily. In summer, you can dine outside in the Garden Bar with its street food menu.

Upstairs are colourful bedrooms, filled with antiques, ornate wallpapers and open fires. Some are distinctly grand, particularly The Library Suite, with its full wall of Scottish literature. Velvet curtains and candle-lit bathtubs lean into the hotel's long history and traditional feel. The George is one of the older hotels on the site, but there is nothing tired about it. Its buzzy atmosphere brings the historic buildings alive for a satisfying blend of old and new that is hard to find.

HIGHLANDS AND ISLANDS

SCOTLAND

Isle of Eriska, Argyll

Isle of Eriska, Ledaig, Oban, Argyll
PA37 1SD

Tel 01631 720371
email office@eriska-hotel.co.uk
website www.eriska-hotel.co.uk

Nearby Oban; Isle of Mull; Inverary Castle; Glencoe.
Location on private island connected by road bridge; from Connel take A828 toward Fort William for 4 miles (6 km) to N of Benderloch village, then follow signs; ample car parking **Food** breakfast, lunch, dinner **Price** ££££ **Rooms** 16 in main house (deluxe and standard); 6 Hilltop Reserves; 2 self-catering cottages (each with 3 bedrooms) **Facilities** 3 drawing rooms, bar/library, dining room, indoor swimming pool, gym, sauna, garden; 6-hole golf course, driving range, tennis court, croquet, clay-pigeon shooting **Credit cards** AE, MC, V **Children** welcome **Accessibility** 2 adapted ground floor rooms **Pets** accepted **Closed** Jan **Proprietors** ICMI Management

Isle of Eriska Hotel
Island mansion

A splendid hotel that has the twin advantages of seclusion, since it is set on its own remote island, and accessibility: it is connected to the mainland by a short road bridge. And for those who like to keep themselves occupied during their stay, its leisure centre, which includes a magnificent 17-metre heated swimming pool, and its sporting opportunities, will appeal.

Built in 1884 in grey granite and warmer red sandstone, in Scottish Baronial style, the hotel is a reminder of a more expansive and confident era. If it reminds you in feel, if not in appearance, of Balmoral, you will not be surprised to learn that the original wallpaper on the first-floor landing is also found in the royal castle. In fact the experience of staying here is very much like being in an old-fashioned grand private house, comfortable rather than stylish, with a panelled great hall, and roaring log fires and chintz fabrics much in evidence. In the library-cum-bar you can browse through the books with a malt whisky in hand, while excellent six-course dinners are served in the stately dining room. The handsome bedrooms vary in size and outlook. In 2016 the hotel changed hands from the Buchanan-Smith family to ICMI Management.

HIGHLANDS AND ISLANDS

SCOTLAND

Isle of Mull, Argyll

Ise of Mull, Argyll and Bute, Scotland PA69 6ES

Tel 01681 705232
email info@tiroran.com
website www.tiroran.com

Nearby Iona, Staffa, castles, mountains, beaches and wildlife.
Location countryside, by a loch with a private beach, large gardens
Food breakfast, lunch, dinner, afternoon tea, room service
Price ££££
Rooms 10; 5 double/twin, 5 double, all have shower, all have TV, hairdryer, tea/coffee facilities **Facilities** 2 drawing rooms, conservatory and dining room, gardens, beach
Credit cards MC, V
Children welcome
Accessibility limited, 1 ground floor room with walk-in shower
Pets accepted, 4 rooms for pet owners
Closed rarely
Proprietors Laurence and Katie Mackay

Tiroran House
Country house hotel

An omission from earlier editions. This is about as good as a small country house hotel gets. It's secluded, but not remote, in large gardens beside a loch; you're face-to-face with terrific wildlife... but that is just a start.

One of our trusted reporters describes it as 'one of those gems' which the *Charming Small Hotel Guides* are all about, in fact it surpasses all our criteria.

He wrote of a recent visit: 'We were greeted on the doorstep by Laurence Mackay', who owns and runs the place with his wife Katie. 'The staff were a delight. The food was superb. The wine list is impressive and Laurence clearly knows a good deal about single malt whisky. The freedom from intrusive modern technology was a pleasure, although had I wanted to listen to some decent music for a quiet hour, there was discreet equipment to make it possible. The old world charm of the two very different sitting rooms, then a contrasting two-level dining room, as well as the seriously comfortable and tasteful bedrooms, makes this a seriously good hotel.'

There's also self-catering accommodation in separate buildings in the garden, with access to the hotel's facilities – perfect for families.

HIGHLANDS AND ISLANDS
SCOTLAND

Isle Ornsay, Isle of Skye

Isle Ornsay, Sleat, Isle of Skye
IV43 8QR

Tel 01471 833332
email hotel@eileaniarmain.co.uk
website www.eileaniarmain.co.uk

Nearby Clan Donald Centre; Aros Heritage Centre; Dunvegan Castle.
Location on water's edge, on estate between Broadford and Armadale in the S of the island, 20 mins drive from Skye Bridge or Mallaig ferry point; ample car parking
Food breakfast, lunch, dinner
Price £££
Rooms 16; 12 double, twin or triple, 4 suites
Facilities sitting room, 2 dining rooms, boutique shop, Gaelic Whisky, art gallery; anchorage for yachts, Fearann Eilean Gaelic Whisky and Gin
Credit cards MC, V
Children welcome
Accessibility limited
Pets dogs welcome by prior arrangement
Closed Januuary to mid March
Proprietor Lady Noble

Eilean Iarmain
Seafront hotel

Hearing the soft lilt of the voices of the staff is one of the pleasures of a stay at this traditional Skye hotel, and a sure sign that you are in the Hebrides. This is a bi-lingual establishment, and the friendly and welcoming staff are fluent in both Gaelic and English.

The hotel is part of an estate belonging to Lady Noble. Its three buildings are beautifully situated right on the water's edge, on the small rocky bay of Isle Ornsay, looking across the Sound of Sleat to the mainland Knoydart Hills beyond. If you are lucky, you may see otters on the shore.

The hotel's core is a white-painted Victorian inn, which comprises the reception area, two appealing dining rooms and six bedrooms. A further six bedrooms are in a building opposite, while the latest addition houses four split-level suites. All the rooms are traditional in character, hospitable and homely, with modern fittings and smart bathrooms. In each is a complimentary miniature bottle of whisky supplied from the distillery. The restaurant specializes in local fish, shellfish and game, and enjoys a local reputation.

HIGHLANDS AND ISLANDS
SCOTLAND

Killiecrankie, Perthshire

Killiecrankie, By Pitlochry,
Perthshire PH16 5LG

Tel 01796 473213
email hello@killiecrankiehouse.com
website www.killiecrankiehouse.com

Nearby Pitlochry; Pass of Killiecrankie; Blair Atholl; Glamis.
Location in 4 acres, 3 miles (4.5 km) N of Pitlochry, just off A9 on the B8079; ample car parking
Food breakfast, dinner Weds - Sat, Lunch on Fridays and Saturdays
Price ££
Rooms 5; super-king ensuites with showers and baths.
Facilities lounge, cook book library, 2 dining rooms, bar, conservatory, garden, whiskey tasting
Credit cards MC, V
Children over 12, but no children's menu
Accessibility restaurant only
Pets no
Owners Tom and Matilda Tsappis

Killiecrankie House
Restaurant with Rooms

Energetic, young chef-sommelier duo Tom and Matilda Tsappis took over the worn and weathered Killiecrankie House in 2020. At a crossroads in their lives and careers, juggling jobs in marketing and finance alongside running a popular supper club, they left London for this delightfully modest Scottish country hotel. Built as a private home for a local clergyman in 1840, it stands at the foot of the Pass of Killiecrankie, formed by the River Garry slicing through the surrounding granite hills. It has its own attractive grounds.

The stylish and moody bedrooms are elegantly uncluttered with country house fabrics and fine custom-made furniture and fittings. Bathrooms are spacious and all have free-standing bathtubs.

Downstairs, painted panelling in the bar helps make it a cosy, convivial place in which to gather for drinks, and an open kitchen adds to the interest. Tom's culinary vision is complex, influenced by Scotland and Japan, and the 12-course tasting menu showcases some spectacular local seafood. The food is beautifully presented, and wine pairings are available.

Old traditions have perhaps been supplanted for contemporary tastes but this remains a lovely place in which to relax and watch out for wildlife, including red squirrels and roe deer.

HIGHLANDS AND ISLANDS
SCOTLAND

Kingussie, Inverness-shire

Tweed Mill Brae, Kingussie, Inverness-shire PH21 1TC

Tel 01540 661166
email relax@thecross.co.uk
website www.thecross.co.uk

Nearby Highland Wildlife Park, Aviemore, Cairngorm Mountain Railway
Location in Kingussie just off the A9, 10 miles south of Aviemore. Large car park
Food breakfast, lunch, dinner, afternoon tea (prior booking advised)
Price ££££
Rooms 8 double and twin, all with bath; all rooms have phone, TV, hairdryer, tea/coffee **Facilities** 2 sitting rooms, restaurant; garden and garden terrace
Credit cards AE, DC, MC, V
Children welcome
Accessibility restaurant only
Pets accepted by arrangement
Closed Christmas, Jan (open for Hogmanay) **Proprietors** Joe and Sarah Jouhal

The Cross
Restaurant-with-rooms

Since the Jouhals took over in 2021 they have been focussing their efforts on becoming as sustainable as possible. The chef-manager duo continue to relish the ongoing challenge of upgrading this charming restaurant-with-rooms. They've rightly maintained standards in the kitchen, serving contemporary Scottish cuisine that wins awards. A huge amount of work and experience travelling and eating in great restaurants around the world informs the menu which still serves reasonably priced dishes. For example, the chicken liver parfait, which 'seemed to be created by a nerdy perfectionist. It was silky and musky, with a sprinkle of sea salt on the top, and a dark, sticky-sweet fig and apple jam, as well as two rough oatcakes, on the side. Joy.'

A trusted reporter recently confirmed that it's business as usual in this beguiling 19thC tweed mill, though we would welcome more reports on the nature of the welcome and the atmosphere. Besides good food, The Cross's charm is its secluded 4-acre setting, in a pretty valley above Kingussie with the River Gynack alongside, where you might see salmon swimming and herons fishing. The lofty sitting room is especially appealing.

HIGHLANDS AND ISLANDS
SCOTLAND

Kylesku, Sutherland

Kylesku, Sutherland IV27 4HW

Tel 01971 502 231
email info@kyleskuhotel.co.uk
website www.kyleskuhotel.co.uk

Nearby Loch Glencoul and Loch Glendhu, bird watching, wildlife spotting, fishing, walking, climbing, beaches
Location good parking. Access from A894, 35 miles N of Ullapool or 95 miles NW of Inverness.
Food breakfast, lunch, dinner
Price £-££
Rooms 8 double/twin rooms: 6 with bath/shower; 2 with private shower room. All rooms have tea/coffee, TV, hairdryer
Facilities wi-fi, residents' sitting room, bar, dining area and beer garden. **Credit cards** MC, V
Children welcome
Accessibility limited
Pets welcome
Closed Dec-Feb
Proprietors T Lister and S Virechauveix

Kylesku Hotel
Lochside hotel

'It's no beauty, but it is a charmer', writes a trusted reporter. A group of southerners, including Tanja Lister and Sonia Virechauveix, bought it in 2010 and set about renovation in stages. 'Above all else, it is warm and comfortable, which in north-west Scotland means it has plenty going for it.'

The public spaces of this 1680s coaching inn have responded well to renovation, with wonderful views from picture windows.

The food is not far behind other grander places nearby, such as The Albannach (see following page) – if not behind at all. The friendly enthusiasm with which it is prepared and presented adds to the charm. Bedrooms are fresh, plain and white-and-grey contemporary, with dots of understated colour here and there. The north end of the hotel is actually the village local and makes a cheery, cosy drinking place. 'An inexpensive, helpful small hotel that deserves to succeed'.

It's a handy stopping place on the road to Cape Wrath, the far north-western tip of mainland Britain, next to the old Kylesku ferry slip, and right by the Kylesku Bridge, in wonderful scenery. Fish for the dinner table are landed on the slip.

HIGHLANDS AND ISLANDS
SCOTLAND

Lochinver, Sutherland

Baddidarroch, Lochinver,
Sutherland IV27 4LP

Tel 01571 844407
email info@thealbannach.co.uk
website www.thealbannach.co.uk

Nearby Suilven and Canisp peaks, Achmelvich beach, boat trips to islands
Location Lochinver
Food breakfast, lunch, dinner
Price ££££
Rooms 5; 3 suites, 2 doubles
Facilities terraces, garden, slipway
Credit cards MC, V
Children over 12 accepted
Accessibility 2 specially-adapted rooms
Pets not accepted
Closed never
Proprietors Colin Craig and Lesley Crosfield

The Albannach
Country house hotel

'Up a small hill just outside the pretty port of Lochinver,' writes a trusted reporter, 'the building is not particularly attractive externally – but compared with the alternative places in Lochinver, where terms such as barracks and youth hostel come to mind – it is better than OK.'

Inside, the welcome is warm and the way they handle your booking during arrival is pleasantly personal. 'Our room was well heated, tastefully furnished and well equipped.' All the bedrooms are individually decorated and have views to the sea loch and mountains beyond.

The public parts have a Highland ambience, or as our reporter puts it, 'a slightly Gothic feel – my wife was a little anxious that on a dark staircase she might meet Norman Bates, or his mother.'

But the food is far from Gothic: as we went to press this was the most northerly Michelin-starred restaurant in Britain. Our reporter was given fat oysters as a pre-dinner appetiser, and the food thoroughly deserved its star.

Not inexpensive – without the Michelin star, it would be overpriced, but this is an interesting place in a terrific location, made better by the food. There's a self-proclaimed 'draconian' no smoking policy in the hotel, but the terrace is convenient for this purpose – umbrellas provided.

HIGHLANDS AND ISLANDS

SCOTLAND

Lochniver, Sutherland

Lochinver, Sutherland IV27 4LW

Tel 01571844122
email rachaelkellyhawkins@gmail.com
website www.glencanisp-lodge.co.uk

Nearby Arvreck Castle, Lochniver, North West Highland Geo Park, Bones Caves
Location 1.3 miles from Lochniver
Food breakfast, dinner, Sunday lunch
Price ££
Rooms 7; 4 double, 1 twin, 1 triple, 1 family suite
Facilities restaurant, lounge, garden
Credit cards MC, V
Children welcome
Accessibility access to restaurant and lounge
Pets accepted by arangement
Closed never
Proprietors Rachael and Sam Hawkins

Glencanisp Lodge
Highland hotel

Bought by the community of Assynt in 2005, Glencanisp Lodge has a quintessentially country house feel. With the path to Suilven (751m high with a distinctive shape) starting on their doorstep, it's a great base for exploring the Assynt wilderness.

The decoration of this 19thC hunting lodge maintains the Victorian charm that Sam and Rachael Hawkins, who run the hotel, have strived to preserve: wooden headboards in the bedrooms, tartan carpets and a stag's head in the dining room.

Almost everything served in the restaurant is Scottish and the menu changes daily, depending on what can be sourced locally. This could explain its limited choices, although we think that there is something to suit most people, including vegetarian options. Expect to see locally smoked salmon, local eggs, organic porridge, and homemade granola at breakfast. Glencanisp Lodge has seven spacious guest bedrooms, all with either private or en suite bathrooms, and four have king-sized beds. Most rooms have either a garden or mountain view, but the views from the public rooms make up for those that don't.

The lodge is an ideal base for walkers, with the white sandy beaches of the Loch Druim Suardalain coastline five miles away.

HIGHLANDS AND ISLANDS
SCOTLAND

Pitlochry, Perthshire

Higher Oakfield, Pitlochry,
Perthshire PH16 5HT

Tel 01796 473473
email bookings@knockendarroch.co.uk
website www.knockendarroch.co.uk

Nearby Blair Castle; Killiecrankie Pass; Loch Tummel, Edradour Distillery.
Location close to town centre, 26 miles (41 km) N of Perth on A9; ample car parking
Food breakfast, dinner
Price £-££
Rooms 12 double and twin, all with bath; all rooms have phone, TV, hairdryer, radio
Facilities 2 sitting rooms, dining room; garden
Credit cards AE, MC, V
Children accepted over 10
Accessibility limited
Pets not accepted
Closed mid-Nov to mid-Feb
Proprietor Struan and Louise Lothian

Knockendarroch
Town mansion

Pitlochry is a particularly agreeable Highland town, and Knockendarroch House is the place to stay. Built in 1880 for an Aberdeen advocate, it displays more château-esque elegance than Scottish Baronial pomp. It stands on a plateau above the town, surrounded by mature oaks (its Gaelic name means Hill of Oaks).

Furnished in careful good taste, the house feels gracious and welcoming. There are two interconnecting sitting rooms in which to relax, with log fire, white cornices and new carpets – all very soothing. The dining room is light and spacious, with many windows and some attractive furniture.

Most of the bedrooms have views; those from the second floor are spectacular. They are all well furnished and two have small balconies.

Guests attending the famous Pitlochry Festival Theatre (which began here at Knockendarroch) are served an early dinner, and a courtesy bus is laid on to take them to and from the town.

As we went to press we heard from some well-travelled 30-year-olds who stayed here recently and said the description above is spot on. They enjoyed the grandeur, the comfort and the good food.

HIGHLANDS AND ISLANDS

SCOTLAND

Port Appin, Argyll

Port Appin, Argyll PA38 4DF

Tel 01631 730236
email airds@airds-hotel.com **website** www.airds-hotel.com

Nearby Oban; Glencoe; 'Road to the Isles'; Ben Nevis.
Location between Ballachulish and Connel, 2 miles (3 km) off A828; ample car parking
Food breakfast, lunch, dinner; room service **Price** ££££ **Rooms** 8 double and twin, 3 suites, all with bath/shower; all rooms have Bulgari toiletries, bathrobes and slippers; phone, TV, hairdryer; 2 self-catering cottages. **Facilities** 2 sitting rooms, conservatory, dining room, whisky bar, garden and croquet lawn, shingle beach **Credit cards** DC, MC, V **Children** accepted; none under 8 in dining room after 7.30pm
Accessibility limited
Pets accepted, not in public areas
Closed last three weeks Jan
Proprietors Jenny and Shaun Mc Kivragan

Airds Hotel
Boutique luxury hotel

The owners of Airds have very sensibly taken every advantage of its superb location on the shores of Loch Linnhe: the dining room, the conservatory and many bedrooms face the loch. To capitalize further, they have also created, across the road, an attractive lawn and rose garden in which guests can sit and admire the view across the loch to the island of Lismore. The sunsets here are stunning.

Despite its fairly ordinary exterior, Airds Hotel is a smart and decorous establishment, impeccably run and maintained. The interior is elegant, with two sitting rooms prettily furnished with comfortable chairs, deep-pile carpets and open log fires. Each of the bedrooms are individually furnished and decorated with designer wallpapers and fabrics, and kitted out with fancy Bulgari toiletries. Fresh flowers, books and paintings are in abundance throughout the hotel.

The food at their recently modernized restaurant is highly praised and often features such local delicacies as Lismore oysters, smoked salmon or venison. Each day the dinner menu and wine list is left in your room, so that you can consult it at leisure, give your orders by late afternoon, and relax before dinner with an aperitif, confident that there will be no unecessary delays.

HIGHLANDS AND ISLANDS
SCOTLAND

Portree, Isle of Skye

Portree, Isle of Skye, IV51 9EU

Tel 01478 612217
email info@viewfieldhouse.com
website www.viewfieldhouse.com

Nearby Trotternish peninsula.
Location on outskirts of town, 10 minutes walk S of centre; from A87 towards Broadford, turn right just after national garage on left; with ample car parking
Food breakfast, packed lunch, dinner
Price ££
Rooms 11 double and twin, 10 with bath; all rooms have phone, radio, hairdryer **Facilities** sitting room, dining room, TV room, washer and tumble drier for guests
Credit cards MC, V
Children welcome
Accessibility one adapted room
Pets accepted, but not in public rooms
Closed mid-Oct to mid-Apr
Proprietors Iona Macdonald

Viewfield House
Country guesthouse

'It won't suit everyone,' writes our reporter, 'but for those seeking an age gone by, the experience would be memorable.'

This is an imposing Victorian country mansion, which, as the name suggests, has some fine views from its elevated position. The need for costly repairs to the roof prompted Evelyn Macdonald, Iona's great-grandmother, to open Viewfield House to guests. The distinctive character of the house was preserved; and though you will not lack for comfort or service, a stay here is likely to be a novel experience. The house is full of colonial memorabilia: stuffed animals, and birds; *objets d'art*; and a magnificent collection of oil paintings and prints.

The rooms are original, right down to the wallpaper in one instance (though all but one now have *en suite* bathrooms in the former dressing-rooms); there is a classic Victorian parlour and a grand dining room with a huge oak table, which seats up to 16 people. Dinner can be taken each evening at 7.30, by prior arrangement. Breakfast features a wide selection of cooked items including Mallaig kippers, smoked haddock and porridge.

Iona, and her partner Jasper run the day-to-day operations.

HIGHLANDS AND ISLANDS — SCOTLAND

Scarista, Isle of Harris

Scarista, Isle of Harris HS3 3HX

Tel 01859 550238
email timandpatricia@scarista-house.com
website www.scaristahouse.com

Nearby beaches; golf; boat trips.
Location 15 miles (24 km) SW of Tarbert on A859, overlooking sea; in 2-acre garden, with ample private car parking
Food breakfast, packed/snack lunch, dinner
Price ££££
Rooms 6; 2 double, 1 twin, 3 suites in Glebe House, all with bath; all rooms have phone, hairdryer
Facilities library, 2 sitting rooms, dining room
Credit cards MC, V
Children welcome
Accessibility limited
Pets by arrangement
Closed Dec-Feb
Proprietors Tim and Patricia Martin

Scarista House
Island guesthouse

Harris has little in the way of hotels, but Scarista would stand out even among the country houses of the Cotswolds.

The converted Georgian manse stands alone on a windswept slope overlooking a wide stretch of tidal sands on the island's western shore. The decoration is elegant and quite formal, with many antiques, but the atmosphere is relaxed and, by the open peat fires, conversation replaces television. The bedrooms, all with private bathrooms, have selected teas and fresh coffee, as well as home-made biscuits. Three of the bedrooms are in the main house, with three refurbished suites available in The Glebe building, just behind the house.

Tim and Patricia Martin continue to maintain a high standard. They aim to be welcoming and efficient, but never intrusive, and to preserve that precious private home atmosphere.

One of Scarista's greatest attractions, particularly rewarding after a long walk over the sands, is the meals. The imaginatively prepared fresh local and garden produce and an impressive wine list ensure a memorable dinner in the candle-lit dining room.

HIGHLANDS AND ISLANDS
SCOTLAND

Sleat, Isle of Skye

Sleat, Isle of Skye IV43 8QY

Tel 01471 833214
email reservations@kinloch-lodge.co.uk
website www.kinloch-lodge.co.uk

Nearby Clan Donald Centre.
Location in 60-acre grounds, 6 miles (9.5 km) S of Broadford, one mile (1.5 km) off A851; ample car parking
Food breakfast, lunch, dinner, afternoon tea
Price ££
Rooms 14 double, all with bath; all rooms have TV, radio, hairdryer
Facilities 3 sitting rooms, bar, dining room, spa, wi-fi; fishing
Credit cards AE, MC, V
Children accepted
Accessibility 1 ground-floor bedroom
Pets accepted by arrangement but not in public rooms
Closed Christmas
Proprietors Lord & Lady Macdonald

Kinloch Lodge
Country hotel

This white-painted stone house, in an isolated position with uninterrupted sea views, at the southern extremity of the Isle of Skye, now known as the North House, was built as a farmhouse around 1700 and later became a shooting lodge. But it escaped the baronial treatment handed out to many such houses – 'thank goodness,' says Lady Macdonald, whose style is modern interior-designer rather than dark panelling and tartan. It has that easy-going private-house air. The guests' sitting rooms are comfortably done out in stylishly muted colours; there are open fires, honesty bar and family oil paintings grace the walls. The dining room is more formal, with sparkling crystal and silver on the tables.

Bedrooms used to be rather small, but have recently been reconfigured to give more space, and all now have en-suites, some with roll-top baths. The South House has accommodation for the Macdonalds and five more double rooms for guests. This building is quite remarkable as it looks, both inside and out, as old as its 18th century neighbour, and includes a magnificent stone spiral staircase, as wells as a wealth of books, portraits and *objets d'art*.

The food, under Marcello Tully, at Kinloch Lodge is renowned – Lady Macdonald has written cookery books and gives cookery demonstrations.

HIGHLANDS AND ISLANDS

SCOTLAND

Spean Bridge, Inverness-shire

Loch Lochy, by Spean Bridge, Inverness-shire PH34 4EA

Tel 01397 712685
email info@corriegour-lodge-hotel.com **website** www.corriegour-lodge-hotel.com

Nearby Cawdor Castle; Urquhart Castle; Loch Ness; Glencoe.
Location on road to Skye, between Spean Bridge and Invergarry, in own grounds, 17 miles (27 km) N of Fort William on A82; ample car parking
Food breakfast, dinner
Price £££ **Rooms** 9; 7 double and twin, 2 single, all with bath/shower; all rooms have TV, hairdryer on request **Facilities** sitting room, bar, dining room; terrace, private beach, jetty, fishing, waterfall
Credit cards AE, DC, MC, V
Children welcome
Accessibility suitable
Pets not accepted
Closed end of Nov until the week before the Easter holiday
Proprietors Ian and Christian Drew

Corriegour Lodge
Lochside hotel & restaurant

A former Victorian hunting lodge commanding outstanding views over Loch Lochy and set in six acres of mature woodland and garden within the 'Great Glen'. With its own attractive private beach and jetty on the loch, as well as a fishing boat and the services of a private fishing school at its disposal, this is an obvious choice for keen anglers, as well walkers and climbers, pony trekkers and sailors.

When guests arrive they are always greeted by a member of the family, whether it be Christian, Ian or James; their friendliness and enthusiasm for the hotel they run is infectious. The decoration throughout the rest of the hotel is cosy and pleasant, with a log fire in the sitting room and magical views over the loch from the large picture windows in the restaurant. Many of the comfortable bedrooms have the same view.

Food is an important element here. The restaurant is Michelin Recommended, using local meat, fish and game. Expect bold flavours: for a main you could have Aberdeen Angus steak with anchovy butter and truffle *jus*, followed by an iced baileys parfait.

The staff are genuinely friendly and willing to help. Beacause of its location wi-fi is unavailable, but this are to be expected in old lodges and are more than made up for by the views and food.

HIGHLANDS AND ISLANDS
SCOTLAND

Strontian, Argyll PH36 4HY

Tel 01967 402257
email enquiries@kilcamblodge.com
website www.kilcamblodge.com

Nearby ferry to Isle of Mull and Skye; Castle Tioram; Glencoe.
Location Corran ferry to Ardgour from the A82 near Ballachulish, then follow A861 to Strontian; in 19 acres with ample car parking
Food breakfast, light lunch, dinner (formal dining in restaurant, informal dining in their Driftwood Brasserie)
Price £££
Rooms 11 double and suites, all with bath; all rooms have TV, hairdryer, phone **Facilities** 2 sitting rooms, bar, restaurant, brasserie, garden, private beach, fishing, mountain bikes
Credit cards MC, V
Children welcome
Accessibility no special facilities
Closed first two weeks of Dec & Jan
Pets dogs accepted by arrangement, £12 per night
Proprietors David and Sally Fox

Kilcamb Lodge
Lochside hotel

There is a sense of adventure in travelling to a hotel by ferry, particularly when it then involves a ten-mile journey, first alongside a loch and then over a pass through a steep-sided glen. Drop down through the glen, pass through the small village of Strontian, and there, in a romantic setting on the shores of Loch Sunart, is Kilcamb Lodge.

Originally built in the early 18thC, with Victorian additions, Kilcamb is a beautifully restored country house with ten bedrooms, some with a loch view. Set amidst lawns and woodland, filled in spring with the colours of rhododendrons, azaleas and many wild flowers, it is a romantic and calming bolthole, the perfect choice for nature lovers: sea otters, seals, pine martens, red and roe deer and golden eagles can all be seen.

The ground floor public rooms are pleasantly furnished with light and attractive pastel fabrics. There is a wonderful Victorian wrought-iron staircase and a large stained glass window. All the bedrooms are individually decorated and have triple-lined curtains (it stays light very late in summer). Chef Gary Phillips prepares fresh Scottish food using locally-sourced fish, shellfish and meat from the Ardnamurchan Peninsula.

HIGHLANDS AND ISLANDS
SCOTLAND

Colbost, Isle of Skye

Three Chimneys
Seaside restaurant-with-rooms

For 30 years chef Shirley Spear and her husband Eddie have run Three Chimneys as an award-winning seafood restaurant in an idyllic seaside location in the north-west corner of Skye. The six suites created in a new building called the House Over-By, are luxurious – if understated – rooms designed to blend with the seascape and the changing light. Each contemporary, spacious and high-ceilinged room has direct access to the beach; bathrooms are heavenly. Breakfast is served in a room overlooking the seashore and the islands in Loch Dunvegan.

As you would expect, the menu is a mainly fishy one, but Highland beef, lamb and game are also a feature, and the puddings are just as good. The kitchen is run by their new Head Chef, Scott Davies.

Colbost, Dunvegan, Isle of Skye
IV55 8ZT

Tel 01470 511258
email eatandstay@threechimneys.co.uk
website www.threechimneys.co.uk
Food breakfast, lunch, dinner
Closed 1st Dec – late Jan
Proprietors Shirley and Eddie Spear

Connel, Argyll

Ards House
Seaside hotel

This pretty Victorian villa has uninterrupted views westward over the Firth of Lorn to the Morvern Hills. Sunsets are truly spectacular.

The house itself tends to ramble, as additions have been made over the years to the original cottage. The most recent owners, Steve and Ilze Paterson, has retained the snug atmosphere, but no longer serves dinner. Breakfasts are especially generous. You could choose not only the usual fresh fruit salad, muesli and yoghurt but also kippers, smoked salmon and scrambled eggs, pancakes and bacon with maple syrup, haggis on toast (with whisky if you want).

Special terms are available for short breaks.

Connel, by Oban, Argyll PA37 1PT

Tel 01631 710255
email info@ardshouse.com
website www.ardshouse.com
Food breakfast
Price £
Closed Christmas and New Year
Proprietor Steve and Ilze Paterson

HIGHLANDS AND ISLANDS
SCOTLAND

Doune, Stirlingshire

Stirling Road, Doune, FK16 6AB

Tel 01786643399
email bookings@thewoodside-doune.co.uk
website thewoodsidedoune.co.uk
Food breakfast, lunch dinner
Price £
Closed never
Proprietors Stuart and Jo

The Woodside
Village pub with rooms

'Passionate and attentive' our reporter said of the staff at The Woodside. Recently opened, this is a cosy and modern option for a stay in Stirlingshire. A short drive from some of the country's most beautiful walks and also the hisorical city of Stirling the location of this charming pub with rooms.

A partidge-clad staircase leads tp the seven bedrooms, each thoughtfully decorated with contemporary tones and colourful furnishings. For an ex-coaching inn they are surprisingly spacious and all have ensuites, and comfortable beds.

The restaurant serves uncomplcated scottish ingredients and has plenty of options for different dietry requirements.

Muir of Ord, Ross-shire

Highfield, Muir of Ord, Ross-shire 1V6 7XN

Tel 01463 870090
email info@thedowerhouse.co.uk
website www.thedowerhouse.co.uk
Food breakfast
Price £££ **Closed** up to a month, off-season **Proprietors** Robyn and Mena Aitchison

The Dower House
Farmhouse bed-and-breakfast

This former Dower House of a baronial home, which burnt down in the 1950s, was converted from thatched farmhouse to charming Georgian cottage ornée style in about 1800. It became a hotel in 1988, and is still run by the same owners. Something of an oasis in the rugged landscape between the rivers Beauly and Conon, it is set in beautifully-maintained gardens and grounds. The elegant red dining room makes a stunning setting for evening meals, and Robyn's self-taught cooking does not disappoint. The sitting room has comfortable chairs, flowery fabrics and an open fire. The three bedrooms vary in size and furnishings and are fairly simple. The largest is the most luxurious, with an enormous bed and spacious bathroom. A two-bedroom self-catering flat is also available.

HIGHLANDS AND ISLANDS
SCOTLAND

Strachur, Argyll

Strachur, Argyll PA27 8BX

Tel 01369 860279
website www.creggans-inn.co.uk
Food breakfast, lunch, dinner
Price ££
Closed closed over Christmas and usually a couple weeks at the beginning of Jan
Proprietors The MacLellan family

Creggans Inn
Lochside hotel

Overlooking Loch Fyne, this former hunting lodge of the 3,000-acre Strachur Estate was first opened as an inn more than 40 years ago. The MacLellan family are still in charge, and have refurbished the place, starting with the sitting and dining rooms.

The food here is excellent: drawing heavily on local products such as scallops and langoustines from Loch Fyne, it is light, inventive and delicious. The wine list is unusually good.

A major natural advantage is the position of the inn. The views over Loch Fyne and across the Mull of Kintyre to the Western Isles are breathtaking. Many parts of the Strachur Estate, including the private flower garden, are open to guests.

Tarbert, Isle of Harris

Pier Road, Tarbert, Isle of Harris HS3 3DG

Tel 01859 502364
email stay@hotel-hebrides.com
website www.hotel-hebrides.com
Food breakfast, lunch, dinner
Price £-£££
Closed Christmas Day **Proprietors** Angus and Chirsty Macleod

Hotel Hebrides
Town hotel

A functional, modern hotel aimed at business travellers as well as tourists – and perhaps formulaic despite describing itself as a boutique hotel. Still, it's a useful address because it's 30 seconds from the ferry pier in Tarbert on the island of Harris where until now we've not found anywhere to recommend – in fact as we went to press there was nothing that reached this standard anywhere in the Outer Hebrides. Also, unusually, it has eight single rooms where you can stay for as little as £60 including breakfast. Some of the bedroom decorations are jarring, others plainer and more successful; the staff wear low-key uniforms, but it's owner-managed and its heart is in the right place.

HIGHLANDS AND ISLANDS

SCOTLAND

Thurso, Caithness

Forss, Near Thurso, Caithness
KW14 7XY

Tel 01847 861201
email anne@forsshousehotel.co.uk
website www.forsshousehotel.co.uk
Food breakfast, lunch, dinner
Price ££-£££ **Closed** 23rd Dec – 5th Jan **Proprietors** Ian and Sabine Richards

Forss House Hotel
Country house

Sabine and Ian Richards bought this mellow country house, built 1810, in 2004. They have redecorated in a way that makes it look unchanged, though itis in fact new and fresh.

You'll find tartan carpeting, a malt whisky bar, a sunny conservatory for breakfast and a shallow Georgian staircase leading up to the light and spacious first-floor bedrooms. The food is highly rated and we thought it lived up to its reputation.

There's excellent salmon fishing at hand along the Forss, which flows in an arc around the hotel. With open, easy casting, it's well suited to beginners and children as well as the more experienced. In spring and summer the banks – thick with wild

Urquhart, Morayshire

-Meft Road, Urquhart by Elgin IV30 8NH

Tel 01343 843063
mobile 0774 8867825
email info@oldchurch.eu
website www.oldchurch.eu
Food breakfast, dinner
Price £ **Closed** Nov-Apr
Proprietors Andreas Peter and Kyzysztof Plewicki

The Old Church of Urquhart **Village B&B**

A reader recommends this unusual, budget B&B – as we went to press two people can stay for as little as £66 including breakfast. Owners Andreas and Krzysztof have their own rooms in the converted church, and they are a presence, but you can feel private in the guest sitting room and dining room (dinner: £15 as we went to press). Bedroom decoration and furnishings are homespun and standardised. They also use the name 'B&B Parrandier'. Reports welcome.

HIGHLANDS AND ISLANDS
SCOTLAND

Walls, Shetland Islands

Walls, Shetland Islands, ZE2 9PD

Tel 01595 809307
email info@burrastowhouse.co.uk
website
www.burrastowhouse.co.uk
Food breakfast, light/packed lunch, dinner
Price ££
Closed Oct to Mar
Proprietor Pierre Dupont

Burrastow House
Seafront guesthouse

On the remote west side of Shetland, at the end of the single track road, on a rocky promontory overlooking Vaila Sound and the Island of Vaila, stands this calm, solid 18thC stone house. It has been run for the last thirteen years with enthusiasm by Pierre Dupont.

The four first-floor bedrooms in the main house are the ones to go for if you can. They are all large, one with a second bedroom which is perfect for children, and all have views. Some have splendid beds: a four-poster in one and a half-tester, draped in blue silk, in another. In the public rooms there are peat fires, books, an eclectic mix of furnishings and wonderful views from the windows. Pierre serves his natural, homely cooking in the cosy dining room.

IRISH REPUBLIC   IRELAND

Ireland area introduction

With a mild climate and a famously leisured way of life, Ireland (also described in tourist publications as the Emerald Isle) is a place of contrasts and changing light, of mountains, lakes and rivers, lush pastures, bog and wild moorland. There are 2,000 miles of coastline with small rocky coves, long sandy beaches and some of the highest cliffs in Europe. In the most remote parts of the country you can drive for miles without seeing anything but sheep. Among the most spectacular features are the golden beaches of Counties Wicklow and Wexford in the east, and the romantic lakes of County Sligo in the west. But if you want bright lights, music and good food, Ireland has any number of pubs that nightly celebrate the traditional Irish love of music and conversation.

Below are some useful back-up places to try if our main selections are fully booked:

Ballylickey Manor
Serviced self-catering,
Ballylickey Tel 353873347117
www.balllickyhouse.com
Elegant ex-shooting lodge

The Bushmills Inn
Coastal hotel, Bushmills Tel 02820733000
www.bushmillsinn.com
Former coaching inn near the Giant's Causeway.

Shores Country House
Bed-and-breakfast,
Castlegregory Tel 066 7139196 www.theshorescountryhouse.com
On Brandon Bay.

The Cliff Townhouse
Restaurant-with-rooms,
Dublin Tel 01 638 3939
www.clifftownhouse.ie
Airy, stylish restautant-with-rooms in central Dublin.

Rosturk Woods
Self-catering houses,
Mulranny Tel 087 6573840
www.rosturkwoods.ie
Secluded woodland houses near Clew Bay.

NORTHERN IRELAND   IRELAND

Magheralin, Co Armagh

58 Newforge Road, Magheralin,
Craigavon, Co Armagh BT 67 0QL

Tel 028 9261 1255
email enquiries@newforgehouse.com
website www.newforgehouse.com

Nearby Belfast (25 km); Mountains of Mourne (50 km).
Location clearly signposted, just off A3, through Magheralin, 1st left onto Newforge Road, with ample private car parking
Food breakfast, dinner
Price £££
Rooms 6 doubles with bath/shower; all rooms have phone, TV, DVD player, hairdryer, wi-fi
Facilities drawing room, dining room; large garden
Credit cards MC, V
Children under 1 and above 10
Accessibility dining room accessible
Pets not accepted
Closed 3 weeks over Christmas and New Year
Proprietors John and Louise Mathers

Newforge House
Country guesthouse

For Northern Ireland, this is about as sophisticated as a guesthouse gets, in fact it's almost a small hotel. Instead of sharing the owner's home, you have the run of it, not least the graceful drawing room. John and Louise Mathers, the young owners, live in one outbuilding, while John's father has another. Six generations of Mathers (a linen family) have lived here; the latest bowed to the fact that it was too big and converted it to a guesthouse, restoring it in the process. The Georgian interior has been respected, but the walls have that clean, smooth modern finish and there's an optimistic, airy atmosphere — windows are tall. The dining room has separate tables, so no communal dining. Another bonus: John is a trained chef, with a professionally fitted kitchen and the food is good: three courses (£44) with two choices at each course, ingredients fresh each day. There's a license, and a wine list. Give a day's notice for dinner.

Even the smallest of the six bedrooms, named after family members, is roomy, and all are individually decorated in the best of taste. In fact, they're as smart as many we've seen in chic city hotels, and the spacious bathrooms gleam.

You're guaranteed a peaceful night here since the house stands well back from a quiet road just outside Newforge.

NORTHERN IRELAND

IRELAND

Downpatrick, Co Down

Tyrella House. Downpatrick
Co Down

Tel 028 4485 1422
email tyrella.corbett@virgin.net
website www.hidden-ireland.com/tyrella **Food** breakfast; dinner on request, a day's notice needed. **Price** ££-£££
Closed never
Proprietor David Corbett

Tyrella House
Country house bed-and-breakfast

Staying at Tyrella as David Corbett's guest is to experience in a genuine way the vanishing lifestyle of the Northern Irish landed gentry. It's a fine country house, dating from the 18th century, down a longish drive, not another building in sight. The nicely proportioned rooms contain the accumulated brown antique furniture and possessions of four generations of Corbetts. Don't expect immaculate paintwork or a trim drive; do expect a relaxed welcome, a large bedroom, a comfortable bed and the feeling of being in a home. The food gets some pleasant compliments in the visitors' book. The house still stands in some 300 acres of its own, now used for equestrian events (David is a horseman) and has its own private beach, which guests can use.

IRISH REPUBLIC — IRELAND

Aghadoe, Co Kerry

Aghadoe, Lakes of Killarney,
Co Kerry

Tel 064 66 31711
email info@killeenhousehotel.com
website www.killeenhousehotel.com

Nearby Killarney, 4 miles (6 km); Muckross House; Gap of Dunloe.
Location in countryside, 4 miles (6 km) from Killarney; car parking
Food breakfast, dinner
Prices €€-€€€
Rooms 23; 8 championship, 15 standard; 8 with king-size double and single; 2 double, 5 twin, 2 single, 6 double and single; 22 with bath, 1 with shower; all rooms have phone, TV, radio, hairdryer
Facilities bar, sitting room; garden, terrace, tennis court, free wi-fi
Credit cards AE, DC, MC, V
Children welcome if well-behaved
Accessibility not suitable
Pets welcome
Closed 1 Nov to 1 Apr
Proprietors Michael and Geraldine Rosney

Killeen House Hotel & Rozzers Restaurant
Country house hotel

We had to visit a hotel with 'charming' as its e-mail address. And there it was: a charming small hotel, a rectory built in 1838 and given a bright new white front and architectural twiddly bits painted in red by Michael and Geraldine Rosney, who took it over in 1992. Michael is a jolly, amusing – and kind – person who used to manage the Great Southern Hotel in Killarney. He has created a warm, cosy, entertaining and lively little place, where he spoils his golfing clients and indulges their every whim. He sees them off in the morning and waits for their return in the evening, like an anxious parent. Then he is to be found in The Pub, 'possibly the only place in the universe that accepts golf balls as legal tender', where he dispenses Guinness and sympathy. Nothing is too much trouble for him: he puts phone messages in envelopes and distributes them himself. All this activity provides loads of fun for everyone, especially Michael, and you don't have to be a golfer to benefit from his generous spirit. Comfortable, spacious bedrooms are decorated in checks and plaids; there's a special one with a spa bath that he gives to regular guests as a 'thank you' for coming back again and again. Good showers; excellent food at Rozzers restaurant, one of the most popular in the Kerry area, with chef Paul O'Gorman at the helm.

Ardara, Co Donegal

Ardara, Co Donegal

Tel 353 086 17 65 431
website www.thegreengate.eu

Nearby Ardara (for tweed); Glenveagh National Park.
Location 1 mile (1.6 km) from Ardara, up a hill; with car parking
Food breakfast
Price €-€€
Rooms 3 adjoined thatched chalets, sleeping 7 altogether (extra beds possible), plus 1 honeymoon suite with sea and mountain views
Facilities garden, terrace
Credit cards not accepted
Children welcome, free for under 10s
Accessibility possible in 1 room
Pets dogs allowed
Closed Christmas
Proprietor Édouard Chatenoud
Manager Paula McMullen

The Green Gate
Cottage bed-and-breakfast

This little place, a tiny farmhouse with stone outbuildings, is bursting with charm. It was converted by a Frenchman who came to Donegal 15 years ago to write about "life, love and death". Paul Chatenoud left behind his musical bookshop and flat in Paris for a wilder existence on the top of a hill overlooking the Atlantic, and created what must be the most beautiful small B&B in Ireland. So much love and care has gone into this enterprise, mostly done with his own hands, from thatching the cottage roof to whitewashing the guest rooms.

Suce Paul died the B&B has been managed by Paula McMullen, who has stayed true to his vision, extending the same care and attention to her guests: hot water bottles, a map in each room, a bath in which you can rest your head back and gaze out of the window at the sky and sea. The garden is filled with primroses, fuscia and small birds, with hundreds, if not thousands, of orange montbretia up the lane.

Breakfast is an informal affair, to be taken at any time in front of the peat fire of her cosy kitchen. The guests chat with each other while Paula prepares a breakfast of coffee/tea, granola with yoghurt and fresh fruit, a full Irish or pancakes – her famous speciality. Fruit and veg are often plucked straight from the garden.

IRISH REPUBLIC — IRELAND

Ballymacarbry, Co Waterford

Glenanore, Ballymacarbry, Co Waterford

Tel 052 6136134
email hanorascottage@eircom.net
website www.hanorascottage.com

Nearby Dungarvan, 18 miles (29 km); Clonmel, 15 miles (24 km); Blackwater Valley.
Location in Nire Valley, 4 miles (6 km) out of Ballymacarbry; parking available
Food breakfast, packed lunch, dinner
Price
Rooms 10; all double/twin; all with Jacuzzi; all rooms with phone, TV, hairdryer; tea/coffee making facilities
Facilities garden, terrace, spa tub
Credit cards MC, V **Children** not accepted **Accessibility** none
Pets not accepted **Closed** Christmas week **Proprietors** Wall family

Hanora's Cottage
Riverside guesthouse

Changes have taken place since our last edition at award-winning Hanora's Cottage, built by a little bridge over the river in the beautiful Nire Valley for late owner Seamus Wall's great-grandmother. With the village school and church next door, the picturesque group of buildings and their setting made our inspector think of somewhere in the Pyrenees. The guest-house is a favourite with walkers, who come for the Comeragh Mountains and nearby forests and lakes. Mary Wall puts comfort high on her list and pampers her guests. She has added five new rooms, each with a spa tub, where guests may rest aching limbs and emerge refreshed for a candle-lit dinner in the new dining room. Food is prepared by the Walls' talented Ballymaloe-trained son, Eoin, and his wife Judith. In the new extension, brilliantly designed to fit with the rest of the building, Mary has put in a drying and boot room. Bedrooms are large, calm and peaceful, with thick carpets, and most have spa baths (superiors have double Jacuzzis). There are books by the beds, some Tiffany lamps, and quality bedlinen. The breakfast room looks out on to the little stone bridge and Seamus's renowned bread recipes are still being used. Plenty of fruit and freshly-squeezed juices, too. Ask for a front room if you want to fall asleep to the sound of the river.

Ballymote, Co Sligo

Ballymote, Co Sligo

Tel 087 9976045
email stay@templehouse.ie
website www.templehouse.ie

Nearby Sligo, 12 miles (19 km); Yeats Country; Lissadell House; Carrowkeel megalithic passage tombs.
Location on 1,000-acre estate, 4 miles (6 km) from Ballymote; parking available
Food breakfast, dinner
Price €
Rooms 10; all double/twin, all rooms have hairdryer and free wi-fi
Facilities garden, woodland, farm, lake fishing, boating, table tennis room, yoga
Credit cards MC, V
Children welcome, high tea in kitchen for under-12s
Accessibility difficult **Pets** dogs on leads (sheep); sleep in car **Closed** 15 Nov to 1 Apr
Proprietors Roderick and Helena Perceval

Temple House
Country house

Is this a dream? It begins as you enter the gates of a gentle, gracious world of its own. In parkland filled with fat sheep, this is a whopper of a Georgian mansion, the home of the Percevals since 1665. Much of what you see was refurbished in 1864 - and electricity was not put in until 1962. To be overcome by the grandeur would be easy were it not for the easygoing charm of Roderick and Helena Perceval together with their children and four dogs. Temple House is very much a home, and they want it to be enjoyed.

Bedrooms, with marble fireplaces and much of their original Victorian furniture, seem to be the size of football pitches – one is called the Half-Acre.

As shadows fall, you could take a walk across the farm land to the ruins of a 13thC Knights Templar castle and a Tudor house down by the lake. The family silver comes out for dinner – an experience in itself. Expect delicious dishes and freshly-baked bread. Guests dine together at a vast mahogany table and the atmosphere is that of a friendly house party. Big breakfasts.

Temple House is now also available for private rental. Groups of up to 20 can take the entire house for a fully catered gathering, with an additional cottage on the estate that can accommodate another eight people.

IRISH REPUBLIC — IRELAND

Ballyvaughan, Co Clare

Ballyvaughan, Co Clare, H91 CF60,

Tel 353 65 707 7005
email stay@gregans.ie
website www.gregans.ie

Nearby Aran Islands, Cliffs of Moher, Aillwee Cave; Doolin and Kilfenora village
Location 5 km south of Ballyvaughan village on the N67
Food breakfast, light lunch, afternoon tea, dinner
Price €€€-€€€€
Rooms 21 (Classic, Superior, Junior Suite or Premier Suite); all come with reading, bathrobes, radios, telephone, hairdryer, Bamford toiletries, shower/bath, tea/coffee, wi-fi
Facilities reflexology and massage, restaurant, sitting rooms, gardens
Credit cards all major
Children welcome
Accessibility fully accessible
Pets dogs allowed
Closed Dec, Jan and first half of Feb
Proprietors Simon Haden and Frederieke McMurry

Gregan's Castle
Country house hotel

This is not actually a castle. It's one of Ireland's Georgian houses, dating from 1750, and a relatively modest one at that, but exceptionally lovely all the same. The interior, both sweeping and intimate, has an elegant drawing room, charming corkscrew bar and a roaring fire. Simon, who was brought up here, trained in hospitality before returning, fortuitously with an interior designer wife. Frederieke has expertly wedded the house's traditional features and plentiful antiques with modern colours, lighting and artworks.

The real cherry on the cake, however, is its magical location in the heart of Burren, a limestone county scattered with ancient burial tombs, stone forts and ruins. It's no wonder J.R.R Tolkein was inspired to write *Lord of the Rings* when he stayed here in the 1950s.

The modern menu, locally sourced and whipped up by talented chef David Hurley, more than lives up to the hotel's high standards, as do the exceptional breakfasts.

English visitors currently only account 10 per cent of their guests. Our series editor Fiona Duncan implores English readers to visit: privately owned, family-run and staffed by passionate locals, this breed of hotel is a rarity in England, and well worth making a trip for – not least for the great rambling country around Middle Earth.

IRISH REPUBLIC   IRELAND

Cashel Bay, Co Galway

Cashel Bay, Co Galway

Tel 095 31111
email info@zetland.com
website www.zetland.com

Nearby Connemara, Roundstone, Clifden, Westport, Aran Islands, fishing (some deep sea), shooting, golf, scuba diving, horse-riding, climbing.
Location in gardens overlooking Cashel Bay, on N340 to Roundstone from Galway; car parking
Food breakfast, dinner
Price ?
Rooms 22 rooms, all with television, shaving points, hairdryers and tea and coffee making.
Facilities gardens, bar, restaurant, open fires, lounge, Wi-Fi
Credit cards AE, MC, V
Children welcome
Accessibility no special facilites (though there is 1 ground floor room)
Pets one room (with direct access to garden) is suitable for small dogs
Closed never **Proprietors** Prendergast family

Zetland House Hotel
Country house hotel

Guests remark that they feel as if they are stepping back in time as they drive up to the Zetland House. It's an imposing, 19thC sporting lodge, which broods over a landscape of bogs, mountains, beaches, lakes and little else.

Inside, it's all soft, golden lighting, polished wood, open fires and plaid armchairs. The bedrooms are furnished chintzily but luxuriously, with carved wooden furniture and floral fabrics. Most have mesmerising views. Standard rooms are uniformly comfortable, but the deluxe rooms are truly charming: one has a king-size, four-poster bed, and all have sea views.

Downstairs, the restaurant's main feature is its stunning views over Cashel Bay and the surrounding area. Guests shouldn't just expect to feast their eyes, though – the Zetland has recently won several awards for catering and hospitality. The chef uses only locally-produced, fresh products and seasonal herbs and vegetables, and the wine list is interesting. The bar is cosy and wood-panelled, and offers a selection of Irish whiskys, as well as the black stuff. 'Life moves at a different pace, here' says one guest. 'People have time to stop and chat to you.'

IRISH REPUBLIC — IRELAND

Castlelyons, Co Cork

Castlelyons, Nr Fermoy, Co. Cork

Tel 353 25 36349
email info@ballyvolanehouse.ie
website ballyvolanehouse.ie

Nearby Blarney Castle, Kinsale, St Ballycotton, Cashel Rock, lots of gardens, River Blackwater
Location set in 70 acres, 30 min from Cork; 45 min from airport
Food breakfast, picnic lunch (on request), dinner, afternoon tea
Price €€€-€€€€
Rooms 6; all with wi-fi, reading material, bath, tea/coffee, cookies; glamping on offer May-Sep
Facilities sitting room, dining room; trout lakes, walled and formal gardens, woodland, tennis courts
Credit cards V, MC
Children welcome
Accessibility not suitable
Pets 1 per room with no charge, enquire before **Closed** the week around Christmas (re-opens 4/5th Jan)
Proprietors Justin and Jenny Green

Ballyvolane
Country house hotel

Like many Irish hotels, Ballyvolane eludes classification. Somewhere between a hotel, guesthouse and B&B, it's also a historic country house that's been in the same family since 1953. Its interior is both grand and homely, with smart wooden floors, shelves of books, paintings and mirrors – and, loveliest of all, Italianate painted panels on their doors depicting flowers and birds. The mix of antique, retro and contemporary has a boho-chic feel, enhanced by quirky alternative offerings such as 'glamping' from May to September.

The six stately bedrooms in the main house are antique laden, but with all the modern comforts, paired with lovely old-fashioned bathrooms. A charming sense of informality pervades: although room keys are provided, most guests don't use them and dinner is served house party style on a large communal table (with the option to eat separately). Delicious suppers are prepared by chef Chris Jeffrey, using vegetables plucked from the magnificent walled garden. The team are also keen foragers: expect wild garlic, sorrel, pennywort and damsons, alongside a menu of game and salt-water fish.

Ballyvolane House is also home to Bertha's Revenge Gin, distilled onsite.

IRISH REPUBLIC — IRELAND

Clifden, Co Galway

Beach Road, Clifden, Co Galway

Tel 095 21369
email res@thequayhouse.com
website www.thequayhouse.com

Nearby Connemara National Park; Galway, 50 miles (80 km).
Location on quay, 3 minutes by car from Clifden town centre; car parking in road
Food breakfast
Price €€
Rooms 15; 5 superkings, 9 double (4 twin); all with bath or shower; all rooms with phone, TV, radio, hairdryer, balcony
Facilities sitting room; garden, terrace
Credit cards MC, V
Children welcome
Accessibility ground-floor rooms
Pets not accepted
Closed end Oct to end Mar
Proprietors Paddy and Julia Foyle

The Quay House
Town house hotel

Paddy Foyle is a celebrated mover and shaker in this rapidly-getting-very-hip little seaside town, where he was born in Room 12 of Foyle's Hotel. He is also the owner of the stylish Quay House, down on the harbour wall where the fishing boats tie up. A natural interior decorator, he has the boldness and panache of a set designer: the house, built in 1820 for the harbourmaster, is a stage for his fanciful ideas and outbursts of colour. You have the distinct sense you are in a production of some kind — is it an opera? a film? — as you pass through the wondrous rooms. A favourite theme is Scandinavian: washed-out, distressed paintwork; plenty of grey and Nordic blue; wooden panelling; striped fabrics. One room is a riot of blue *toile de jouy*; there's a Napolean Room at the top of the house; another has a frieze of scallop sea shells. It's pretty; it's fun. But Paddy is a restless pacer, always moving on, so expect changes. He's already stuck a bay on to the old flat-fronted house, bought the place next door and turned it into studios.

On a recent visit we were once again enchanted by the originality of the place, and found Paddy as full of charm as ever. A must if you are in this part of Ireland, and well worth a detour.

Dingle, Co Cork

Upper John Street, Dingle,
Co Kerry

Tel 066)9151518
email info@pax-house.com
website www.pax-house.com

Nearby Killarney, 42 miles (68 km); Mount Brandon; Tralee, 30 miles (48 km).
Location in countryside, half a mile (0.8 km) out of Dingle town; signposted on N86; car parking
Food breakfast
Price €€€
Rooms 13 all with choice of king bed or 2 single beds; 10 seaview bedrooms; all have walk-in shower, some also have separate bathtub
Facilities lounge, patio, terraces
Credit cards MC, V
Children accepted
Accessibility wheelchair access
Pets if well-behaved
Closed 1st Dec to 1st Mar
Proprietor John O'Farrell

Pax House
Guesthouse

There is an abundance of wild fuchsia in the hedgerows of the little lanes around Pax House, high on a green hill looking down over Dingle Bay. Before breakfast, you can take an early walk down to the shore, or, from the terrace, count the cows coming out of the milking parlour of the farm below this rather odd building that was once a retirement home. John O'Farrell took over from the Brosnan-Wrights in the summer of 2006, having worked in the hospitality business for more than 30 years, in such diverse places as Switzerland, Thailand, America and Spain. He has since repainted the house, all bedrooms have fresh flowers, and a collection of original paintings, prints and sculptures fill the house.

All rooms have walk-in showers, and some have seaparate bathtubs; cold taps produce water from the house's own spring well. John serves a notably varied breakfast, from a full Irish to pears in white wine, honey and clove syrup, and kippers in a lemon butter sauce. From the dining room you can see the field on Sleahead that starred in a film with Tom Cruise, and over to the Ring of Kerry. The silence on the green hill is blissful, but Dingle, a swinging little town, with its full share of traditional music, pubs and restaurants, much frequented by celebs, is only a short walk away.

Drinagh, Co Wexford

Drinagh, Wexford, Co Wexford

Tel 053 9158885
email info@killianecastle.com
website www.killianecastle.com

Nearby Wexford; Rosslare Harbour (Europort); Waterford Harbour; Kilmore Quay.
Location on a dairy farm, 3 miles (5km) from Wexford; 8 miles (13km) from Rosslare Harbour; car parking
Food breakfast
Price €
Rooms 8; 4 doubles, 2 triples, 1 twin, 1 single, tea and coffee available in all rooms
Facilities garden, terrace; tennis court; pitch & pitt course, golf driving range, farm walk
Credit cards all major cards
Children welcome
Accessibility not suitable
Pets not in house
Closed 18 Dec to 12 Feb
Proprietors Paul and Patrycja Mernagh

Killiane Castle
Farmhouse bed-and-breakfast

Those who already know Killiane Castle tend to have that special expression worn by people who have a secret they want to keep to themselves, for this is a remarkable place. The Mernaghs' early 17thC house was built inside the walls of a largely intact 15thC Norman castle, complete with tower (now listed). From the back rooms, you see the ruins of a small chapel in a field and the marshes running down to the sea. Down a leafy lane, miles from the main road, it seems centuries away from everywhere else. Twice a day, you can hear the hum of machines as the cows file in and out of the milking parlour.

In 2020, Jack and Kathleen Mernagh passed the business down to their son, Paul, who has worked in luxury hotels across the world. Paul and his wife Patrycja continue to provide warm hospitality to guests. Breakfast is especially impressive.

Some bedrooms overlook the weeping ash at the front of the house; some overlook the courtyard and castle walls to countryside beyond. All are spacious, well-equipped and comfortable.

IRISH REPUBLIC — IRELAND

Dublin

70 Adelaide Road, Dublin 2

Tel 01 475 5266
email info@kilronanhouse.com
website www.kilronanhouse.com

Nearby Grafton Street; National Gallery; Trinity College.
Location 5 minutes walk S of St Stephen's Green; free off-street parking
Food breakfast
Price €€-€€€
Rooms 23; 11 double (8 twin), 2 single, 2 family; all with shower; all with phone, TV, hairdryer; safe and free internet in reception
Facilities Lounge, Horse and Carriage Tours
Credit cards AE, DC, MC, V
Children over 10
Accessibility limited
Pets not accepted
Closed 23-25th Dec
Proprietors The Kinsella family

Kilronan House
Town B&B

This veteran, reasonably-priced Georgian guest-house in a quiet, leafy, residential street near St Stephen's Green has been in business for more than 40 years and is perfectly situated for walking to some of the city's most famous landmarks and shops.

Our reporter was impressed with the warm, yellow walls and parquet floor of the entrance hall and the welcoming reception area tucked under the stairs.

Bedrooms are on four 'creaking' floors, and it is a long climb to the top. Some are on the small side. Colours tend to be yellow again, with elegant fabrics and pretty, white-painted wrought-iron bedheads, some pine furniture, heavy off-white curtains and the odd print on the walls.

We were told of one room – below ground level – that was described as 'tiny', so it is clearly advisable to check in advance which rooms are available. The yellow sitting room has a big, gilt-edged mirror over the fireplace, antique furniture and a chandelier. The yellow extends to the breakfast room, with silver and white linens on the tables.

The overall feel of the place is old-fashioned and relaxed. In late 2013 the Kinsella family, who have been at the helm since 2008, refurbished the bedrooms and general areas – reports, please.

IRISH REPUBLIC — IRELAND

Dublin

31 Leeson Close, Dublin 2

Tel 01 676 5011
email stay@number31.ie
website www.number31.ie

Nearby St Stephen's Green; National Gallery; Grafton Street, Trinity College.
Location just off Lower Leeson Street; 5 minutes walk from St Stephen's Green; car parking
Food breakfast
Price €€€-€€€€
Rooms 20; 15 double (12 twin), 5 family; 17 with bath, 3 with shower; all with phone, TV, hairdryer, wi-fi; safe at reception **Facilities** sitting room, breakfast room, conservatory; garden
Credit cards all major
Children welcome
Accessibility not suitable
Pets not accepted
Closed 24, 25 and 26th Dec
Proprietor Richard Driehaus

Number 31
Town guesthouse

This is a very special and visually pleasing place: a mews house designed in the mid-1960s by controversial Dublin architect, Sam Stephenson, plus a Georgian house across the garden that was acquired in order to provide extra space. Only a plate on the wall with 31 on it indicates this is somewhere you may stay. The Stephenson building is modern and open-plan, with painted white brickwork and much glass, wood and stone; kilims hang on the wall. There's a little sunken sitting area, with a black leather sofa custom-built around the fire. French windows and wooden decking lead to the garden and the back of the Georgian house. Generous and delicious breakfasts (home-made breads, jams, potato cakes, granola) are cooked by Delia and served in a white upstairs room on long tables with fresh flowers, sparkling silver, and white linen napkins.

The mews house contains five stylish bedrooms and there are 15 more in the Georgian house. These have moulded ceilings and are painted in National Trust colours.

IRISH REPUBLIC — IRELAND

Goleen, Co Cork

Goleen, Co Cork

Tel 028 35225
email info@heronscove.com
website www.heronscove.com

Nearby Mizen Head; Cork, 75 miles (120 km); Bantry, 25 miles (40 km); Skibbereen, 24 miles (39 km).
Location on Goleen Harbour; car parking
Food breakfast, dinner (a la carte and set menu)
Price €
Rooms 4; 1 double, 2 twin, 2 double with a single bed; 1 with bath, rest with shower; all with TV, free wifi, hairdryer, electric blanket, tea/coffee tray
Facilities terrace
Credit cards AE, MC, V
Children by arrangement
Accessibility not suitable
Pets not accepted
Closed November to March
Proprietor Sue Hill

The Heron's Cove
Restaurant-with-rooms

Fish from trawlers on the West Cork coast are brought to the door of Sue Hill's white-painted, waterside restaurant, which offers 'fresh fish and wine on the harbour' and, most likely, a view of a heron. It is an idyllic spot, on this rugged stretch of the West Cork coastline. It is not surprising to hear from Sue that some of her guests do not want to do anything but simply sit and watch the tide come in and go out again. Three of the bedrooms in this modern house open on to balconies overlooking the little sheltered cove, and from the terrace of the restaurant on the ground floor – which is open from May to October – there are steps down to the shore. Guests are clearly those who relish the peace and quiet.

Along the upstairs landing runs a long shelf with a row of books. Bedrooms are well-equipped. There are posters of Aix-en-Provence on the walls and Sue has turned the staircase into a gallery for local artists. It's only a short walk to the village of Goleen and Sue sends all visitors off on the spectacular drive to Mizen Head, which is Ireland's most southwesterly point.

IRISH REPUBLIC — IRELAND

Gorey, Co Wexford

Gorey, Co. Wexford

Tel 053 942 1124
email reservations@marlfieldhouse.ie
website www.marlfieldhouse.ie

Nearby Waterford; Kilkenny; Wexford; Rosslare; beaches.
Location in 35-acre gardens and woodland, 1 mile (1.6 km) out of Gorey on R742 Gorey-Courtown road, or exit 23 off NII from Dublin/the south; with car-parking
Food breakfast, lunch, dinner
Price €€€€
Rooms 19 in main house; 17 double, 2 single, all with bath, phone, TV, hairdryer. Duck Lodge house; sleeps 4 **Facilities** sitting room, bar, dining room, sauna; garden, terraces, tennis, croquet, 2 restaurants: The Conservatory Fine Dining and The Duck Restaurant **Credit cards** AE, DC, MC, V **Children** welcome; high tea for those under 8
Accessibility suitable **Pets** dogs welcome by prior arrangement
Closed 2nd Jan – beginning Feb
Proprietors Bowe family

Marlfield House
Country house hotel

A sign in the drive of this stunning Regency house, once owned by the Earls of Courtown but since 1983 a Relais and Chateaux hotel (one of the best in Ireland), reads: 'Drive carefully, pheasants crossing'. Not only is this a preserve of good things for people, but it is pretty comfortable for animals, too. There's a little dog basket for a terrier beside the 18thC marble fireplace in the semi-circular architect-designed hall. Mary Bowe's peacocks, bantams, ducks and geese are cherished and indulged almost as much as her guests. This is a gorgeous place, a feast for the eyes because of the Bowe family's passion for interior decoration. Her taste is reflected in Waterford crystal chandeliers, little French chairs, gilded taps and a domed conservatory dining room. Garlanded with awards, the hotel has a tradition of warm hospitality and the Bowes' daughters, Margaret and Laura, are now in charge. Bedrooms are sumptuous and charming. Our favourites are the State Rooms, decorated with rich fabrics and fine antique furniture; the which French Room, with marble bathroom, overlooking the lake; and the Print Room, with views of the rose garden. Outstanding food.

IRISH REPUBLIC — IRELAND

Inis Meáin, Co Galway

Inis Meáin, The Aran Islands, Co. Galway

Tel 353 86 8266026
email post@inismeain.com
website www.inismeain.com

Nearby coastal and cliff walks, bird and wildlife watching, the island pub, ferry to other islands and mainland.
Location on Inis Meáin Island, reachable by ferry, plane, private boat or helicopter.
Food optional daily food delivery service
Price €€€€
Rooms 2 self-catering houses, can host up to 12 people each
Facilities kitchen, laundry, bicycles, fishing rod and binoculars provided
Credit cards MC, V
Children 12+
Accessibility not suitable
Pets not accepted
Closed Oct-Feb
Proprietor Ruairi and Marie-Therese de Blacam

Inis Meáin Island Stays
Self-catering accomodation

One and a half miles off the west coast of Ireland, Inis Meáin is a landscape of terraced limestone, higgledy-piggledy fields and hundreds of miles of dry-stone walls. Irish is the first language of the islanders, and traditional methods of farming, fishing, sport and music are a large part of their lives.

This place sits by the coast on a rocky outcrop. It's owned and run by Ruairi – a native – and his wife, Marie-Therese. Alongside winning a host of awards, they've stuck to their aim of showcasing the best of the island - huge windows offer amazing views.

After closing its restaurant in 2022, Inis Meáin now offers a daily food delivery service to its self-catering guests. Produce is home-grown and ingredients locally sourced where possible, continuing their commitment to simple but sophisticated cooking.

The bedrooms offer views of the coastline and island, and are uncluttered to let the landscape do the talking. Walls are painted in natural lime and furniture and flooring is simple polished wood. The de Blacams want the guests to 'appreciate the peace and quiet' so bicycles, books and fishing rods are provided in place of TVs. The couple get praise from guests for their warm welcome and attention to the small things.

IRISH REPUBLIC — IRELAND

Inistioge, Co Kilkenny

The Rower, Inistioge, Co Kilkenny

Tel 051 423614
email info@cullintrahouse.com
website www.cullintrahouse.com

Nearby Kilkenny, 19 miles (31 km); New Ross, 6 miles (10 km); Jerpoint Abbey; Waterford, ancient cairn nearby on farm.
Location in wooded countryside, 6 miles (10 km) from New Ross; car parking
Food breakfast, dinner (must be booked 48 hours in advance), self-catering options
Prices €-€€ (usually minimum stay 2 nights)
Rooms 6; 5 double/twin, 1 family; 2 with bath, 4 with shower; hairdryer; all rooms equipped with hot water bottle **Facilities** courtyard; gardens, bridge for viewing countryside
Credit cards most credit cards
Children welcome
Accessibility 1 ground-floor room, enquire before
Pets welcome by arrangement
Closed never
Proprietor Patricia Cantlon

Cullintra House
Country bed & breakfast

Patricia Cantlon is known for her long, leisurely, candle-lit dinner parties at the 250-year-old ivy-clad farmhouse where she was born. Guests have reported moveable eating times. When our reporter called, Patricia had several important jobs to do before getting under way in the kitchen: station herself outside the front door with palette and brushes to finish off a painting; race off to the vet with one of her cats. The day begins when a guest knocks on her door to alert her that people are up and about and waiting for breakfast (could be noon). Her informality and originality have won friends and admirers all over the world. They leave me sages in the visitors' book such as 'Great fun'; 'The house, the surroundings, the food, and most of all Patricia, were a magnificent find.' She has, in fact, created a bewitching retreat. The low-ceilinged house abounds in artistic extras such as the imaginatively-designed rooms in the green-roofed barn, and the conservatory, where Patricia lights banks of candles for pre-dinner drinks. There are log fires, long walks (there are countless acres of woodland to explore), conversations with cats and foxes, swimming with Patricia in the river. She's a natural hostess, with persuasive powers to make her guests feel they have entered a place that is not quite of this world. It

IRISH REPUBLIC / IRELAND

Leenane, Co Galway

Leenane, Co Galway

Tel 353-954-2222
email info@delphilodge.ie
website www.delphilodge.ie

Nearby Westport; Kylemore Abbey; Clifden; golf.
Location by the lake in wooded grounds on private estate; with car parking
Food breakfast, lunch, dinner
Price €€€
Rooms 12; 8 double, 4 twin, all with bath; all rooms have phone; hairdryer on request **Facilities** drawing room, billiard room, library, dining room; garden, lake
Credit cards AE, MC, V
Children welcome
Accessibility 2 ground-floor rooms
Pets not accepted
Closed mid-Dec to mid-Jan
General Manager Philip Counihan

Delphi Lodge
Fishing lodge

The 2nd Marquess of Sligo – who had been with Byron in Greece – thought this wild place as beautiful as Delphi, and built himself a fishing lodge here in the mid-1830s. When Peter Mantle, a former financial journalist, came across the house, it was semi-derelict. Falling under the same spell, he restored it with great care and vision, and Delphi is one of the finest and foremost sporting lodges in Ireland. Fishing is its main business, but everyone is made welcome here. He stepped back in 2011, and as we went to press the new manager was Philip Counihan.

On our visit, wood smoke was rising from the chimney, a new delivery of Crozes Hermitage was stacked up in the hall and Mozart was playing in the snug library overlooking the lake. Among the guests were a couple of bankers in their waterproofs, a novelist, and some Americans. Salmon are weighed and measured in the Rod Room, creating frissons of excitement and stories for the communal dinner table; the ghillies come in during breakfast to discuss prospects for the day. Bedrooms are unfussy but pretty, with pine furniture; larger ones have lake views. Book well ahead. Our most recent inspector was impressed: 'a unique and stunning location; the absolute country house experience.'

IRISH REPUBLIC — IRELAND

Lisdoonvarna, Co Clare

Lisdoonvarna, Co Clare

Tel 0657074025
email info@ballinalackencastle.com
website www.ballinalackencastle.com

Nearby The Burren; Ballyvaughan; Doolin Crafts Gallery.
Location in 100-acre grounds, 3 miles (5 km) S of Lisdoonvarna on R477; car parking
Food breakfast, dinner
Price €€
Rooms 12; 2 suites, 10 doubles; 10 with bath, all with shower; all with phone, TV, radio, hairdryer
Facilities lounge, pub, restaurant, wi-fi; garden
Credit cards MC, V
Children welcome
Accessibility not suitable
Pets well-behaved dogs in room; not in public areas
Closed end of Oct to end of Apr
Proprietors O'Callaghan family

Ballinalacken Castle Hotel **Country hotel**

This fascinating house, high on a green hillside with uninterrupted Atlantic views, was built as a 'villa' in the 1840s for John O'Brien, MP for Limerick. Not only does it have its own ruins of a 15thC O'Brien stronghold, but the entrance hall with cupola and green Connemara marble fireplace remains more or less unaltered. There is a newish, discreetish extension, but main house bedrooms have large, dark, old-fashioned pieces of antique furniture, huge wardrobes, and original shutters. From the bed in Room 4, you can see the Aran islands; and Room 7 has a view of the Cliffs of Moher. The lay-out is intriguing – mostly on one floor.

Chef Luca Mantoan has devised a seasonal and creative menu inspired by the locality: local shellfish features alongside baked St Tola's goat's cheese, Lisdoonvarna's smokehouse specialities and free-range lamb and beef.

The dining room has another cracker of a fireplace, turf fire, original wood floor, pink tablecloths. Nightcaps are served in the lounge bar, and you can steep yourself in the history of the place with locals and join in sing-alongs on weekend evenings, when live entertainment is laid on.

The O'Callaghans also offer self-catering accommodation in nearby Gentian Cottage.

IRISH REPUBLIC / IRELAND

Lisdoonvarna, Co Clare

Lisdoonvarna, Co Clare

Tel 065 7074026
email info@sheedys.com
website www.sheedys.com

Nearby The Burren; Ballyvaughan; Doolin Craft Gallery.
Location in centre of Lisdoonvarna, on edge of the Burren; car parking
Food breakfast, dinner (restaurant closed on Sundays, and intermittent in April)
Price €
Rooms 11; 5 double, 6 twin; 9 with bath, 2 with shower; all with phone, TV, hairdryer; ironing board
Facilities south-facing sun lounge, seafood bar, sitting room, restaurant
Credit cards AE, MC, V
Children welcome
Accessibility 1 ground floor room, enquire beforehand
Pets not accepted
Closed end Sep to Mar (opens in time for Easter)
Proprietors the Sheedy family

Sheedy's Restaurant & Hotel Restaurant-with-rooms

This small hotel was originally a farmhouse where the Sheedy family began looking after visitors to this little spa town (it has sulphurous springs) in 1855.

John Sheedy, ex-Ashford Castle head chef, has come home to cook; his delightful wife, Martina, looks after front of house and the wine list and adds her taste for contemporary design. Walls are painted in a moody grey colour called 'Muddy River'. Martina, who used to work at Mount Juliet, has also transformed the hotel, bringing in help from the nearby Doolin Craft Gallery, renowned for sharp, simple design in wool, crystal, linen and tweed. The lobby heralds the exciting shape of things to come, with shiny wood floor, little curved reception desk, a bit of exposed natural stone, paintwork in gentian blue and terracotta red.

John Sheedy's food is highly acclaimed and the restaurant has been given a completely new look to complement his celebrated 'Modern Irish' cooking. Seasonal ingredients, sourced form a expansive network of local suppliers, are served in generous portions.

For pre-dinner drinks and views over the rose and herb gardens, relax in the newly-added conservatory.

Bedrooms are being upgraded continuously. The aim is comfort, but with some modern design. Reports, please.

IRISH REPUBLIC — IRELAND

Mallow, Co Cork

Mallow, Co Cork, P51 KC8K

Tel 022 47156
email info@longuevillehouse.ie
website www.longuevillehouse.ie

Nearby Blarney Castle & Parklands.
Location on 400 acres of wooded estate, 3 miles (5km) W of Mallow on Killarney road; ample free car parking **Food** breakfast, daily lounge menu, afternoon tea, Sunday lunch, dinner - chef's seasonal menu plus tasting menu with optional wine pairings
Prices €€-€€€
Rooms 13; Super Kings, with en-suites
Facilities drawing room, bar, 2 dining rooms; on-site fly fishing, brandy distillery, falconry, badminton, Turner conservatory, bird watching, games room
Credit cards MC, V **Children** welcome **Accessibility** public rooms only **Pets** pet policy applies, please ask **Closed** midweek Jan – Mar; Mon and Tue all year
Proprietors William & Aisling O'Callaghan

Longueville House
Country house hotel

One of the finest country house hotels in Ireland: this elegant and imposing pink listed Georgian house on a 500-acre wooded estate has a three-storey block in the centre built in the 1720s, later wings, and a pretty Victorian conservatory. Inside, it is full of ornate Italian plasterwork, elaborately framed ancestral oils and graceful period furniture. The drawing room overlooks lawns and rows of oaks in the parkland; in the distance are the ruins of the family's Dromineen Castle, demolished under Cromwell, who dispossessed the family. But, after 300 years, they are back.

Longueville House has everything, including chef and patron William O'Callaghan, who, according to one leading food critic, cooks 'some of the finest food in Europe'. Almost all of his ingredients come from the estate farm and the walled kitchen garden. Find time for a tour of the orchards which provide apples for Longueville House's craft cider, visit the on-site 'crush house', and learn how apple brandy is distilled in the Calvados style.

Bedrooms are comfortable and filled with antiques. The ones at the front of the house have the best views. The Presidents' Restaurant is named after the portraits of Irish past presidents that hang on the walls. The wine list is superb, as is William's seven-course Surprise Tasting Menu.

IRISH REPUBLIC

IRELAND

Mountrath, Co Laois

Mountrath, Co Laois

Tel 0502 32120
email info@roundwoodhouse.com
website www.roundwoodhouse.com

Nearby walking, horse-riding, fishing; Slieve Bloom mountains.
Location in countryside, 3 miles (5 km) N of Mountrath on Kinnitty road; with gardens and ample car parking
Food full breakfast, five-course dinner
Price €€€
Rooms 10; 8 double (3 twin), 2 family rooms; all with bath; all rooms have central heating
Facilities drawing room, study, dining room, hall, library
Credit cards AE, DC, MC, V
Children very welcome
Accessibility not suitable
Pets accepted by arrangement
Closed 3 days at Christmas
Proprietors Hannah & Paddy Flynn

Roundwood House
Country house

A recent reporter reacted very well to the Flynns' operation. The house is 'not in perfect repair, but for the type of place they run, this didn't seem to matter': it's a 'wonderful place, and Hannah and Paddy really are charming and informal hosts'. The perfectly proportioned Palladian mansion is set in acres of lime, beech and chestnut woodland. The family have wholeheartedly continued the work of the Irish Georgian Society, who rescued the house from near-ruin in the 1970s. All the Georgian trappings remain – bold paintwork, shutters instead of curtains, rugs instead of fitted carpets, and emphatically no TV. Despite this, the house is decidedly lived in, certainly not a museum.

For Paddy's plentiful meals, non-residents sit at separate tables; residents usually sit together (though not obligatory) – fine if you like to chat to strangers, not ideal for romantic twosomes. After-dinner conversation is also encouraged over coffee and drinks by the open fire in the drawing-room. You may well find the hosts joining in.

Four pleasant extra bedrooms in a converted stable block we thought were cosier and of a better standard than those in the main house. It's very child-friendly (the Flynns have two girls), with a lovely big playroom at the top of the house, full of toys.

Rathnew, Co Wicklow

Newrath Bridge, Rathnew,
Co Wicklow, A67 TN30

Tel 0404 40106
email reception@hunters.ie
website www.hunters.ie

Nearby Mount Usher Gardens, Powerscourt Gardens; Russborough House; Glendalough; golf.
Location in gardens on River Vartry, in countryside half a mile from Rathnew; car parking
Food breakfast, lunch, dinner
Price €€€
Rooms 16; 15 double/twin, 1 single, 15 with bath, 1 with shower; all rooms with phone, TV, hairdryer; hot water bottle
Facilities gardens, terrace
Credit cards MC, V
Children welcome
Accessibility ground-floor room
Pets not accepted
Closed 24 to 26 Dec
Proprietors Gelletlie family

Hunter's Hotel
Coaching inn

The area around it is fast becoming part of Dublin commuterland, but not much changes here in this little island of constancy. In 1840, some Victorian travellers touring Ireland reported: 'We strongly recommend Mr Hunter's Inn at Newrath Bridge, which is, according to our experience, the most comfortable in the county.' The same applies today.

This is a delightful, proudly old-fashioned place, built as a coaching inn for several big houses in the vicinity. You would not be surprised if you were to hear the sound of horses' hooves and carriage wheels clattering into the enormous stable yard, or trunks being carried into the beamed front hall, which still has the tiled floor laid in 1720. Nothing clashes, nothing jars, to spoil the old world charm that brings people from far and wide. Present owners, Richard and Tom Gelletlie (great-great-grandsons of the original Mr Hunter) get complete strangers talking in the small bar, with bare, wide wooden floorboards, beams, and a print of the 1900 Grand National winner, Ambush 11, on the wall.

There is good, plain cooking; a lovely garden by the river; courtesy; glowing fires; charming bedrooms (ask for garden view); tea on the lawn; billowing wisteria.

IRISH REPUBLIC — IRELAND

Recess, Co Galway

Inagh Valley, Recess, Co Galway

Tel 095 34706
email inagh@iol.ie
website www.loughinaghlodgehotel.ie

Nearby Recess; Oughterard; Clifden; Galway.
Location in open country on shores of Lough Inagh; car parking
Food breakfast, lunch, dinner
Price €€€
Rooms 13; 1 triple, 4 twin, 8 double; all with bath and shower; all rooms have phone, TV, radio, hairdryer, trouser press; ironing board on request, room service
Facilities garden, lake, fishing, bicycles
Credit cards AE, DC, MC, V
Children welcome
Accessibility suitable ground-floor room **Pets** acccepted
Closed mid-Dec to mid-Mar
Proprietor Maire O'Connor

Lough Inagh Lodge Hotel Country hotel

This solid, well-proportioned Victorian shooting lodge, romantically placed on one of the most beautiful lakes in Connemara, was boarded up when Maire O'Connor and her late husband, John, came across it looking for somewhere suitable to run as a small hotel. Remarkably, some of the old sporting record books survive and may be read by guests. Little has been overlooked in the way of comfort. Each bedroom, named after an Irish writer, has a dressing room. Views are of water and The Twelve Bens mountains. Maire has kept to rich dark Victorian colours and polished wood; her careful attention to detail and service is reflected throughout the comfortable, cosy house. She arranges the fresh flowers, which are sent from Clifden. Rooms downstairs have inviting log fires and warm lighting. The green dining room with yellow curtains and gleaming, dark wood floor is delightful. Seafood and traditional wild game dishes are specialities of the kitchen. Loughs Inagh and Derryclare are on the doorstep; for walkers, there are miles of tracks through the wild and rugged landscape. The hotel also has a stable of bicycles.

Slane, Co Meath

Rossnaree, Slane, Co Meath

Tel 041 982 0975
email rossnaree@gmail.com
website www.rossnaree.ie

Nearby Dublin (40 mins); Newgrange, Knowth and Dowth (Bru na Boinne)
Location the Boyne Valley; in own grounds with ample car-parking
Food breakfast included; dinner (for 4 or more) to be booked in advance, afternoon tea, wood-fired pizza
Price €€
Rooms 4; 3 double, 1 twin; all with own bath or shower
Facilities guided tours; Rossnaree School of Art; fishing on the River Boyne; summer cooking courses
Credit cards DC, MC, V
Children welcome
Accessibility difficult
Pets acccepted on request
Closed Nov – Feb
Proprietor Aisling Law

Rossnaree House
Country hotel

This 200-acre wooded estate is a true taste of Ireland. The north side of Rossnaree looks towards the Hill of Slane, where St. Patrick lit his paschal fire in defiance of the pagan King of Tara; the neighbouring glen is where the Battle of the Boyne took place. The house was purchased by the Law family in the early days of the Irish Free State (1925). It is now managed by Aisling Law, great granddaughter of Irish revolutionary Maud Gonne.

Aisling is a talented artist. Each of the four bedrooms has a unique and carefully considered theme: the bird room with its subtle Oriental influences and murals with hand-painted birds and blossom trees; the tiger room with its four-poster bed, draped with Congolesewall hangings; the period style William Morris room, with original William Morris wallpaper; and the river room, with magnificent views across the River Boyne and the Megalithic sites of Bru na Boinne.   Breakfast happens in the dining room during winter, beside a crackling open fire, on a pretty mahogany dining table laid with antique china and silverware. In summer, you can take a picnic basket to the River Boyne. They have a small farm with geese, guinea fowl, hens and roosters.

Tours of Rossnaree are also available for visitors who book in advance.

IRISH REPUBLIC   IRELAND

Ardmore, Co Waterford

Ardmore, Co Waterford

Tel 024 87800
email info@cliffhousehotel.ie
website www.cliffhousehotel.ie
Food breakfast, lunch, dinner
Price €€€€
Closed 24th-26th Dec
Proprietors Barry and Gerri O'Callaghan

Cliff House Hotel
Restaurant-with-rooms

Outside our usual territory, this modern steel, glass and slate building drops down a cliff to the sea in a series of levels. They're connected by a lift and a spiral staircase; all the rooms face the water. The decoration is somewhat bland, except for the shell mirrors and lamps in reception, the jazzy bar and the lime-green spa. The charm is in the seaside setting, in the quality of the light that results, and in the charming local staff. Food (Michelin star), by Chef-Patron Tony Parkin is a fusion of Thai and French fine-dining, theatrically presented.

Ballingarry, Co Limerick

Ballingarry, Co Limerick

Tel 069 68508
email info@mustardseed.ie
website www.mustardseed.ie
Food breakfast, lunch, dinner
Price €€€
Closed Feb
Proprietors John Joyve

The Mustard Seed at Echo Lodge **Country house**

The Mustard Seed was opened over thirty years ago by the acclaimed chef Dan Mullane, who moved his kitchen to this former convent. Since his retirement in 2016 the hotel has continued to flourish under John Edward Joyce (who previously worked as its manager for nearly 25 years). The painted yellow house is ageing gracefully, while John has put his own stamp on the interior with opulent draperies and designer wallpapers. 'Foodies' continue to flock to the blue-walled dining room for smooth and professional service under chef Angel Pirev. Breakfast could be Kenmare smoked salmon with potato farle and crème fraiche, while dinner might include sophisticated dishes such as confit lobster and yuzu, vanilla purèe and lime gel.

IRISH REPUBLIC — IRELAND

Ballylickey, Co Cork

Ballylickey, Bantry, Co Cork

Tel 027 50073/50462
email info@seaviewhousehotel.com
website www.seaviewhousehotel.com
Food breakfast, lunch (Sun only), dinner **Prices** €€-€€€
Closed Nov-Easter
Proprietor Ronan and Suzanne O'Sullivan

Seaview House
Country hotel

Ronan O'Sullivan and his wife Suzanne are the third generation of O'Sullivans to take over Seaview House. The white Victorian house is a stone's throw from Ballylickey Bay.

Bedrooms are beautifully decorated in pastel colours and floral fabrics with stunning antique furniture – especially the bedheads and wardrobes. The rooms in the old part of the house are more individual.

There are two sitting-rooms – a cosy front room adjoining the bar and a large family room at the back. The menu changes daily, and the chefs are forever experimenting with new dishes, for example roast smoked pheasant on the day we visited.

The onsite Bathhouse (see sauna in picture) is a nice addition to the grounds.

Cashel, Co Tipperary

Main St, St. Dominick's Abbey, Cashel, E25 EF61

Tel 353 62 62002
email info@cashelpalacehotel.ie
website www.cashelpalacehotel.ie
Food breakfast, lunch, room service, dinner, afternoon tea, bar snacks
Prices €€€€
Closed never
Proprietors Magnier family

Cashel Palace Hotel
Country hotel

The historical setting of this place, in the shadow of the medieval Rock of Cashel, is quite special. Once occupied by Irish kings, saints and the first brewers of Guinness, the Rock can be viewed from some of Cashel Palace's 42 rooms.

Bought by the Magnier Family in 2016 the hotel underwent an impressive renovation. Consulting with architects, historians and locals has revived the tired building into a luxury option for exploring some of Ireland's best countryside.

Some might find it flashy, but there are friendly touches. After a romp up to the Rock of Cashel, or go by horse, unwind in the gym or spa.

IRISH REPUBLIC   IRELAND

Clifden, Co Galway

Ballyconneely Road, Clifden,
Connemara, Co Galway

Tel 095 21384
email info@ardaghhotel.com
website www.ardaghhotel.com
Food breakfast, bar lunch, dinner
Price €€ **Closed** Nov to Easter or
April 1 **Proprietors** Stéphane,
Monique and Serge Bauvet

The Ardagh Hotel
Coast hotel and restaurant

The view from the restaurant over Ardbear Bay is fabulous: light and colours constantly change; sunsets are memorable. Now run by a third generation of the family, this place maintains its combination of friendliness and reliable, discreet efficiency. The rooms are pristine and the hotel is decorated in a bright and contemporary style with an Alpine flavour that gives it charm.

Stéphane Bauvet can be found behind the front desk, or serving wine, and is always ready to help. The four large suites on the top floor have sea views, for the rest you should check when booking. Tucked under the eaves, a sunny sitting room for residents has piles of magazines and a profusion of greenery.

Cloyne, Co Cork

Cloyne, Middleton, Co Cork

Tel 021 4652534
email info@barnabrowhouse.ie
website www.barnabrowhouse.ie
Food breakfast, Sunday Lunch and
afternoon tea on weekends
Price €€
Closed Christmas week
Proprietor Geraldine Kidd

Barnabrow House
Country house

This could be called a cutting edge country house. No faded chintzes or family portraits here. Semi-minimalist interiors, with bold, bright colours and vast expanses of gleaming wood floors look as if they have come out of glossy magazines. Behind the rejuvenated main house is a coach house with floors painted white and elsewhere much orange, pink and yellow; a rustic cottage; and restaurant with an outdoor timber terrace. Hens provide fresh eggs; organic produce for the table comes from the kitchen garden.

Barnabrow House's main business is now weddings, but B&B is still available Sunday to Wednesday, and all week in the quieter months. Barnabrow, under chef Frank Topham, is now also open for lunch on Sundays.

IRISH REPUBLIC   IRELAND

Dublin

22 Adelaide Rd, Dublin, D02 ET61

Tel 353 1 9696598
email stay@thewilder.ie
website www.thewilder.ie
Food bar snacks, breakfast
Price €€€
Closed never
Proprietors Frankie and Josephine Whelehan

The Wilder
Townhouse hotel

This smart red-brick Gothic-style townhouse is only a short walk from the city's bustling centre. An excellent base for exploring Dublin but also a calm space in which to curl up with one of the many books (mainly Irish classics) which are perched throughout the hotel.

The interiors are contemporary and comfortable, with soft fabrics, bold patterns and smart modern fixutres and fittings. Historical features have been preserved. The Garden rooms, where breakfast is served, has high ceilings, big windows with a lovely iew of the leafy street outside. There is also a popular terrace. Some of the rooms are small but all have coffee machines, walk-in showers and black-out curtains.

Innishannon, Co Cork

Innishannon, Co Cork

Tel 021 4775121
email info@innishannonhotel.ie
website www.innishannonhousehotel.ie
Food lunch, dinner, BBQ
Price €€
Closed Feb
Proprietors Roche family

Innishannon House
Country hotel

This attractive, imposing 18thC house on the banks of the Bandon River is run by the Roche family. While maintaining the rustic country house style, each space feels clean and comtemporary. No. 16 is a cosy attic room with an antique bedspread, No. 11 a fascinating circular room with small round windows, a huge curtained bed and a newly built bathroom with a stand-alone bath.

Chef Cristain is in charge of the unpretentious but flavourful menu. Innishannon is not the last word in seclusion or intimacy: it runs conferences and wedding receptions with up to 200 guests. Reports welcome.

IRISH REPUBLIC / IRELAND

Kenmare, Co Kerry

Castletownbere Road, Kenmare, Co Kerry

Tel 064 41252
email muxnawlodge@eircom.net
website www.muxnawlodagekenmare.com
Food breakfast
Price €
Closed Christmas Eve and Day
Proprietor Hannah Boland

Muxnaw Lodge
Bed-and-breakfast

Charming, gabled Muxnaw Lodge was built in 1801, one of the oldest houses in Kenmare, set on a hillside overlooking the suspension bridge – and equipped with an all-weather tennis court.

Hannah Boland has created an attractive period style for her lovely old house, with painted magnolia and blue walls, brass beds and lovingly-polished antique furniture. In the bedrooms, she hides the modern electric kettles away in wooden boxes so they don't spoil the general look. In a bathroom at the back of the house, you may sit in the corner bath and look at the sea. For breakfast, fresh eggs from the butcher are cooked on Mrs Boland's big red AGA in the kitchen.

Kilgraney, Co Carlow

Kilgraney, Bagenalstown, Co Carlow

Tel 059 9775282
email bobbie@lorum.com
website www.lorum.com
Food breakfast, dinner
Price €€
Closed Dec-Feb
Proprietors Bobbie and Rebecca Smith

Lorum Old Rectory
Country B&B

There will come a moment in your stay at Lorum Old Rectory – perhaps during conversation at breakfast, or in the afternoon as you glimpse owner Bobbie Smith collecting herbs from the garden – when everything clicks. That is when you will realize just how refreshed you are after such a short time and just how pleasant a place Lorum is. Much of this is down to mother and daughter Bobbie and Rebecca, whose warm manner gets people talking, and whose quirky but clever grip of flavours in the kitchen oils the wheels.

The rich Irish heritage helps too, whether in the form of a fine view of Mount Leinster from your bedroom; the inviting furniture in the communal areas; or perhaps a trip into nearby Kilkenny, a historic town with medieval roots.

IRISH REPUBLIC — IRELAND

Kilkenny, Co Kilkenny

Butler House
Town house

This tall, grand Georgian house was once the dower house to Kilkenny Castle, family seat of the Earls of Ormonde. In the 1970s, the house was refurbished in contemporary style by Kilkenny Design, and the result is stunning.

The house has been refurbished again recently, with large spacious rooms, oak furniture and muted colours. The effect, with acres of white walls, is ordered, quiet and restful. Breakfast is now served in the Kilkenny Design Centre, a short stroll through the walled garden. Morning coffee, biscuits and cake are served on a pale oak table in the entrance hall. Superior bedrooms have bay windows and garden and castle views. Butler House is now run by the Kilkenny Civic Trust.

16 Patrick Street, Kilkenny, Co Kilkenny

Tel 0567722828
email res@butler.ie
Food breakfast
Closed 24 to 29 Dec
Proprietors Kilkenny Civic Trust
Manager Gabrielle Hickey

Newmarket-on-Fergus, Co Clare

Carrygerry House
Town house

Being so close to Shannon airport – a ten-minute drive away – this could have settled for being a commercial hotel. But the kindness and warm hospitality of Niall Ennis and his wife, Gillian, have made this old manor house a place to remember for those staying for either their first or last night in Ireland.

Carrygerry – built in the 18th century with a gable end and a remarkable courtyard entered through an archway – was a private house until as recently as the 1980s. Gillian is passionate about her house and she has filled it with antiques and pretty things. The house really seems to come alive in the evenings, when it positively glows in candle light. In the former coach house in the courtyard is a bar; some bedrooms are there, too.

Newmarket-on-Fergus, Co Clare

Tel 061 360500
email info@carrygerryhouse.com
website www.carrygerryhouse.com
Food breakfast, dinner
Price €€
Closed 24 to 27 Dec
Proprietors Niall and Gillian Ennis

IRISH REPUBLIC — IRELAND

Rathmullan, Co Donegal

Kilgraney, Bagenalstown, Co Carlow

Tel 353 7491 58188
email reception@rathmullanhouse.com
website www.rathmullanhouse.com
Food breakfast, lunch, afternoon snacks, pizzeria, formal dining **Price** €€€-€€€€ **Closed** Jan; from 9th Feb until Easter only open weekends **Proprietors** Mark and Mary Wheeler

Rathmullan House
Country hotel

Both outside and in, Rathmullan House is a feast. Built as a grand Georgian holiday home, its plentiful original features include a striking row of bay windows along the façade, as well as ornate ceilings, doorways and marble fireplaces once inside. The Indian colonial-styled sitting room is particularly lovely, and even the later addition of a Regency-style wing brings a welcome contemporary element.

Aside from the lovely surroundings, our series editor Fiona Duncan likens the experience of staying here to that of finding a hot water bottle in a chilly bed: tensions immediately evaporate under Mark and Mary's hospitality, not to mention the healing hands of their in-house masseuse. The food's outstanding too, served in their characteristically elegant restaurant.

Shanagarry, Co Cork

Shanagarry, Midleton, Co Cork

Tel 021 4652531
email res@ballymaloe.ie
website www.ballymaloe.ie
Food breakfast, lunch, dinner
Closed Christmas
Proprietors the Allen family

Ballymaloe House
Country house hotel

We can't resist this rambling, creeper-clad house set in rolling green countryside. Readers have been 'immensely impressed' and found the staff 'well-drilled, but jolly, with abundant charm'.

The Allens have been farming here for more than 70 years and started offering rooms long ago, adding more facilities over the years – rooms in extensions and converted out-buildings now outnumber those in the main house.

Despite quite sophisticated furnishings, the Allens have managed to preserve intact the warmth of a much-loved family home.

The menu, classic French and Irish dishes, is a wholesome collaboration between Chef Dervilla and local suppliers.

Woodstown, Co Waterford

Woodstown, Co. Waterford

Tel 051 382 549
Mobile 0248 6283
email gaultierlodge@yahoo.ie
website www.gaultierlodge.com
Food breakfast, afternoon tea on request
Price €
Closed beginning of Nov-beginning of Mar

Gaultier Lodge
Beach B&B

Well above average B&B in a handsome 18thC Georgian house with a five-star location beside the beach on Waterford Bay. Step straight out on to the broad sands. Busy, characterful hosts – Sheila (Irish) and her son Peter – who know their own minds. Smart, period-furnished bedrooms. Generous brunch. A guest reports confusion over bookings: get written confirmation, and pay any deposit required to be 100 per cent of the reservation.

Index – Hotel names

In this index, hotels are arranged in order of the first distinctive part of their name; other parts of the name are also given, except that very common prefixes such as 'The' and 'La' are omitted. More descriptive words such as 'Hotel', 'B&B', 'St', 'Maison' and 'Auberge' are included.

10 Castle Street, Cranbourne, 47
11 Cadogan Gardens, London, 169
131 The Promenade (New), Cheltenham, 269
15 Glasgow, Glasgow, 333
36 on The Quay, Emsworth, 111
38 St Giles St, Norwich, 270
41 Hotel (New), London, 117
42 The Calls, Leeds, 272

A

Airds Hotel, Port Appin, 362
Albannach, The, Lochinver, 359
Alexandra, The (New), Lyme Regis, 94
Alice Hawthorn, The (New), Nun Monkton, 320
Allanton Inn (New), Duns, 341
Alma, The, London, 118
Anchor Inn, The, Alton (Lower Froyle), 96
Anchor, The, Walberswick, 267
Angel at Hetton, The (New), Hetton, 316
Angel Hotel, The, Abergavenny, 198
Angel Inn, The, Stoke by Nayland, 263
Another Place Lakeside (New), Penrith, 290
Antonia's Pearls (New), Charlestown, 45
Aragon House (New), London, 169
Ardagh Hotel, The, Clifden, 402
Ards House, Connel, 368
Artist Residence Brighton, Brighton, 99
Artist Residence Bristol (New), Bristol, 39
Artist Residence London, London, 119
Artist Residence Oxford, South Leigh, 234
Artist Residence Penzance, Penzance, 68

Arundell Arms, The, Lifton, 58
Ashfield House, Grassington, 312
Askham Hall, Askham, 274
At the Chapel, Bruton, 42
Augill Castle, Kirkby Stephen, 272
Aysgarth Falls, Aysgarth, 300

B

Babington House, Frome, 93
Ballinalacken Castle Country House, Lisdoonvarna, 393
Ballylickey Manor House (New), Ballickey, 373
Ballymaloe House, Shanagarry, 406
Ballyvolane, Castlelyons, 382
Bank House Hotel, King's Lynn, 256
Bar Convent, York, 328
Bark House, The (New), Oakford Bridge, 65
Barlings Barn, Llanbrynmair, 186
Barnabrow House, Cloyne, 402
Barnsdale Lodge, Exton, 177
Bath Arms, Longleat, 59
Batty Langley's, London, 120
Bay Hotel, The, Coverack, 46
Beach, The, Bude, 43
Bear Hotel, The (New), Cowbridge, 180
Bear Hotel, The, Crickhowell, 177
Beaufort, The, London, 121
Beckford Arms, The, Fonthill Gifford, 50
Bedford, The (New), London, 122
Beech House, Clipsham, 211
Bell and Crown (New), Zeals, 86
Bell at Skenfrith, The, Skenfrith, 195
Bell, The (New), Horndon on the Hill, 254
Biggin Hall Hotel, Biggin-by-Hartington, 238
Bildeston Crown, The, Bildeston, 245

Index – Hotel names

Bingham Riverhouse, London, 123
Black Lion Hotel, Long Melford, 258
Blackaddie House, Sanquar, 340
Blue Lion, The (New), East Witton, 311
Boars Head (New), Ripley, 324
Boath House, Auldearn, 344
Bonnie Badger (New), Gullane, 335
Boot at Barnsley, The, Barnsley, 202
Boot, The (New), Repton, 230
Boscundle Manor Hotel, St Austell, 72
Boskerris, Carbis Bay, 44
Brama (New), London, 170
Braye Beach, Braye, 160
Broadstreet Townhouse, Bath, 90
Brocco on the Park, Sheffield, 233
Brook's Guesthouse Bath (New), Bath, 30
Brook's Guesthouse Bristol (New), Bristol, 40
Brownlow Arms, The, Hough-on-the-Hill, 219
Bull & Swan, The, Stamford, 243
Bull, The, Fairford, 212
Burford House, Burford, 208
Burgoyne Hotel, Ramsgill-in-Nidderdale, 322
Burnside, Stratford Upon Avon (New), Stratford-upon-Avon, 235
Burrastow House, Walls, 372
Burts Hotel, Melrose, 338
Bushmills Inn, The, Bushmills, 373
Butler House, Kilkenny, 405
Byland Abbey Inn, Byland, 309

C
Calcot Manor Hotel, Tetbury, 236
Callow Hall, Ashbourne, 199
Capital, The, London, 124
Carpenters Arms, The (New), Great Wilbraham, 252
Carrygerry House, Newmarket-on-Fergus, 405
Cartford Inn, The (New), Great Ecclestone, 286
Cary Arms, The, Babbacombe, 27
Cashel Palace Hotel (New), Cashel, 401
Casterbridge, The, Dorchester, 26
Castle Hotel, The, Bishop's Castle, 204
Castle House, Hereford, 218
Cat Inn, The, West Hoathly, 157
Cavendish, The, Baslow, 238
Cedar Manor, Windermere, 296
Chapel House, Penzance, 69
Charles Bathurst Inn, Arkengarthdale, 300
Chettle Lodge, Chettle, 92
Chiltern Firehouse, London, 26
Cholmondeley Arms, Malpas, 223
Church Street Hotel, London, 125
Cley Windmill, Cley-next-the-Sea, 248
Clifden Yurts, St Aubin, 163
Cliff House Hotel, Ardmore, 400
Cliff Townhouse, The, Dublin, 373
Coach and Horses, Kew Green (New), London, 126
Collingwood Arms, The, Cornhill-on-Tweed, 310
Colonnade, The, London, 127
Compasses, The (New), Littley Green, 26
Congham Hall Hotel & Spa, King's Lynn, 257
Coombeshead Farm (New), Lewanwick, 56
Corriegour Lodge, Spean Bridge, 366
Corsewall Lighthouse, Kirkcolm, 337
Coruisk House, Elgol, 349
Cotswold House Hotel & Spa, Chipping Camden, 239
Cottage in The Wood, The, Malvern Wells, 224
Covent Garden Hotel, London, 128

Index – Hotel names

Crab and Lobster, The, Sidlesham, 150
Creggans Inn, Strachur, 370
Cricket Inn (New), Beesands, 35
Crolinnhe, Fort William, 330
Cross, The, Kingussie, 357
Crown and Castle, The, Orford, 271
Cullintra House, Inistioge, 391
Culpeper, The (New), London, 170
Cynefin Retreat (New), Hay-on-Wye, 184

D

Delphi Lodge, Leenane, 392
Devonshire Arms, The, Bolton Abbey, 307
Devonshire Fell, The, Burnsall, 308
Dial House Hotel, Bourton-on-the-Water, 207
Dolffanor Fawr, Tal-y-llyn, 196
Dorian House, Bath, 31
Dornoch Hotel, Dornoch, 330
Dower House, The, Muir of Ord, 369
Driftwood Hotel, Rosevine, 71
Drunken Duck Inn, Barngate, 301
Dundas Arms, Kintbury, 168

E

Easby Hall, Richmond, 323
East End Arms, East End, 106
Edenwater House (New), Kelso, 343
Ednam House Hotel, Kelso, 330
Ees Wyke, Hawkshead, 287
Elephant at Pangbourne, The (New), Pangbourne, 172
Ennys, St Hilary, 73

F

Fairyhill, Reynoldston, 177
Falcondale, The (New), Lampeter, 185
Farlam Hall, Brampton, 282
Feathered Nest Country Inn, The, Nether Westcote, 241
Feathers, The (New), Woodstock, 177

Felin Fach Griffin, The, Felin Fach, 182
Fermain Valley, St Peter Port, 166
Fingals, Dittisham, 93
Fleur du Jardin, Castel, 161
Forest Side, Grasmere, 285
Forss House, Thurso, 371
Fort Road Hotel (New), Margate, 144
Fosse Farmhouse, Nettleton, 64
Fox and Grapes, London, 129
Fox, The, Oddington, 242
Franklin, The, London, 171
Freemasons at Wiswell (New), Wiswell, 299
Frog Street Farmhouse, Beercrocombe, 90

G

Gallivant Hotel, The, Camber, 102
Gallivant Littlestone Beach, The, Littlestone, 116
Gaultier Lodge, Woodstown, 407
George and Dragon, Clifton, 283
George at Egerton, The, Egerton, 110
George in Rye, The, Rye, 147
George Inn, The (New), Barford, 201
George, The (New), Inveraray, 352
George, The, Yarmouth, 159
Georgian House Hotel, The (New), London, 130
Georgian, The (New), Haslemere, 113
Gidleigh Park, Chagford, 26
Gilpin Hotel and Lake House, Windermere, 297
Glebe House (New), Southleigh, 77
Glencanisp Lodge (New), Lochinver, 360
Glenfinnan, Fort William, 350
Glenridding House, Ullswater, 293
Globe Inn, The (New), Wells-next-the-sea, 268

Index – Hotel names

Golden Lion (New), Settle, 304
Goldsborough Hall, Goldsborough, 272
Gore, The, London, 131
Grange, The, Fort WIlliam, 351
Gravetye Manor Hotel, East Grinstead, 107
Grays Court, York, 329
Green Gate B&B, The, Ardara, 377
Gregan's Castle, Ballyvaughan, 380
Gresham House at the Gonville (New), Cambridge, 247
Greyhound, The, Stockbridge, 154
Greywalls, Gullane, 342
Griffin Inn, The, Fletching, 112
Grosvenor at Hindon (New), Hindon, 54
Grosvenor, The (New), Stockbridge, 155
Grove of Narbeth, The, Narbeth, 191
Gunton Arms, The, Thorpe Market, 266
Gurnards Head, The, Zennor, 87

H

Haley's Hotel, Leeds, 272
Hall Farm B&B, Sheriff Hutton, 326
Hambleton Hall, Hambleton, 216
Hambrough, The, Ventnor, 174
Hampton Manor, Hampton-in-Arden, 217
Hanoras Cottage, Ballymacarby, 378
Harbour View, St Brelade, 164
Hare and Hounds Inn (New), Bowland Bridge, 278
Harp Inn, The (New), Old Radnor, 192
Hazlitts, London, 132
Headland Cottages, The, Newquay, 94
Heron's Cove, The, Goleen, 388
High Corner Inn (New), Linwood, 115
High Road House, London, 133
Highcliffe Contemporary Bed & Breakfast, Falmouth, 49
Holbeck Ghyll, Windermere, 298
Horn of Plenty, The, Gulworthy, 53
Horse & Groom, Bourton-on-the-Hill, 206
Hotel 55, London, 134
Hotel du Vin, Brighton, Brighton, 167
Hotel Du Vin, Bristol, Bristol, 91
Hotel du Vin, Harrogate, 272
Hotel du Vin, Tunbridge Wells, 26
Hotel du Vin, Winchester, Winchester, 158
Hotel Eilean Iarmain, Isle of Ornsay, 355
Hotel Endsleigh, Milton Abbot, 62
Hotel Hebrides, Tarbert, 370
Howard Arms, Illmington, 240
Howtown House, Ullswater, 304
Hundalee House, Jedburgh, 342
Hundred House, Norton, 226
Hunter's Hotel, Rathnew, 397
Husk (New), Thorington, 265

I

Idle Rocks, St Mawes, 74
Inis Meain Restaurant and Suites, Inis Meain, 390
Inn at Whitewell, The, Whitewell, 295
Innishannon House, Innishanon, 403
Isle Of Eriska Hotel, Isle of Eriska, 353

J

Jeake's House, Rye, 148
Jolly Sportsman (New), East Chilington, 104

K

Kelleth Old Hall, Kelleth, 272
Kilberry Inn, The, Kilberry, 336
KIlcamb Lodge, Strontian, 367
Killeen House Hotel & Rozzers Restaurant, Aghadoe, 376
Killiane Castle Country House, Drinagh, 385
Killiecrankie Hotel, Killiecrankie,

Index – Hotel names

356
Kilronan House, Dublin, 386
King John Inn, Tollard Royal, 95
Kings Head, Bledington, 205
Kinloch Lodge, Sleat, 365
Kirkstile Inn (New), Loweswater, 289
Knockendarroch House Hotel, Pitlochry, 361
Knockingham Lodge, Portpatrick, 339
Kylesku Hotel, Kylesku, 358

L

La Haule Manor, St Brelade, 165
Lamb Inn, Great Rissington, 214
Lamb, The, Burford, 209
Langar Hall, Langar, 222
Langford Fivehead, Lower Swell, 26
Laslett, The (New), London, 135
Lastingham Grange, Lastingham, 318
Leathes Head, The, Borrowdale, 277
Leonardslee House (New), Horsham, 114
Lewtrenchard Manor, Lewdown, 57
Library House, Ironbridge, 240
Lime Tree Hotel, London, 136
Linden House, Stanstead, 177
Lindeth Fell, Bowness-on-Windermere, 280
Linthwaite House, Bowness-on-Windermere, 281
Lion + Pheasant, Shrewsbury, 177
Llangoed Hall Hotel, Llyswen, 198
Llanthony Priory, Llanthony, 189
Loch and Tyne (New), Old Winsdor, 146
Loch Ness Lodge, Brachla, 347
Longuevile Manor, St Saviour, 26
Longueville House Hotel, Mallow, 395
Lord Poulett Arms, Hinton St George, 55
Lorum Old Rectory, Kilgraney, 404
Lough Inagh Lodge, Recess, 398

M

Marlfield House Hotel, Gorey, 389
Masons Arms, Branscombe, 38
Masons Arms, The, Bowland Bridge, 279
Master Builder's, The, Bucklers Hard, 101
Mayflower Hotel, London, 171
Mermaid Inn, The, Rye, 26
Milk House, The, Sissinghurst, 151
Millgate House, Millgate, 319
Milsom's Kesgrave Hall (New), Kesgrave, 255
Mistley Thorn, The, Mistley, 259
Monachyle Mhor, Balquidder, 346
Morston Hall, Morston, 260
Mount Pleasant Farm, Whashton, 272
Muxnaw Lodge, Kenmare, 404

N

Newforge House, Magheralin, 374
Noel Arms, Chipping Campden, 239
Norfolk Mead, Coltishall, 177
Norfolk Mead, Coltishall, 269
Northcote, Langho, 302
Number 31, Dublin, 387

O

Ockenden Manor, Cuckfield, 103
Old Bank Hotel, Oxford, 227
Old Church of Urquhart, The, Urquhart, 371
Old Coastguard, The, Mousehole, 63
Old Dungeon Ghyll, Great Langdale, 302
Old House Hotel, The, Wickham, 175
Old Parsonage, The, Oxford, 228
Old Quay House, Fowey, 51
Old Railway Station, The, Petworth, 173
Old Swan & Minster Mill, Minster, 177
Old Vicarage, The, Worfield, 237

Index – Hotel names

Old Whyly, East Hoathly, 108
Ollerod, The, Beaminster, 34
One Devonshire Gardens, Glasgow, 334
Orange, The, London, 137
Osborne House, Llandudno, 188
Owl, The, Hawnby, 315

P

Padstow Townhouse, Padstow, 66
Park House and Spa, Bepton, 98
Pax House, Dingle, 384
Peacock at Rowsley, The, Rowsley, 232
Pear Tree Inn, The, Whitley, 26
Peat Inn, The, Cupar, 332
Peat Spade Inn, Stockbridge, 156
Pembroke Arms, The (New), Wilton, 84
Pen Y Gwryd Hotel, Nant Gwynant, 190
Pen-y-Dyffryn, Rhydycroesau, 231
Penally Abbey, Penally, 193
Penmaenuchaf Hall, Penmaenpool, 194
Pheasant, The (New), Stannersburn, 272
Pier at Harwich, The, Harwich, 253
Pig at Combe, The, Gittisham, 52
Pig in wall, The, Southampton, 152
Pig near Bath, The, Bath, 32
Pig on the beach, The, Studland, 79
Pig, The, Brockenhurst, 100
Pipe and Glass, South Dalton, 327
Plas Dinas, Bontnewydd, 178
Plas Domelynilyn, Ganllwyd, 183
Plough, The, Kelmscott, 220
Plumber Manor, Sturminster Newton, 80
Prince Akatoki, The, London, 138
Princess Victoria, The (New), London, 139
Priory Hotel and Restaurant, The, Wareham, 83
Priory Steps, Bradford-on-Avon, 37
Punch Bowl Inn, Crosthwaite, 284
Pythouse Kitchen Garden, Tisbury, 82

Q

Quay House, The, Clifden, 383
Queens Head, The (New), Broadchalke, 41
Queensberry, The, Bath, 33

R

Racquet Club, The, Liverpool, 303
Rathmullan House, Rathmullan, 406
Reading Rooms, The, Margate, 145
Rectory Manor House, Great Waldingfield, 251
Rectory, The, Crudwell, 48
Red Lion Freehouse, East Chisenbury, 105
Red Lion, Somerset (New), Babcary, 28
Red Pump Inn, The (New), Bashall Easves, 276
Riverside House, Ashford-in-the-water, 200
Riverside Inn, The, Cound, 177
Rookery, The, London, 140
Rose and Crown, Snettishm, 262
Rose and Crown, The, Romaldkirk, 325
Rossnaree House, Riverstown, 399
Rosturk Woods, Mulranny, 373
Rothay Manor (New), Ambleside, 273
Roundwood House, Mountrath, 396
Royal Oak Ramsden, The (New), Ramsden, 229
Royal Oak, The, East Lavant, 109
Royal Oak, The, Swallowcliffe, 81
Royal Oak, The, Winsford, 85
Royal Oak, Yattendon, Yattendon, 176

S

Scarista House, Scarista, 364
Scarlet, The, Mawgan Porth, 26
Sculthorpe Mill, The (New),

Index – Hotel names

Sculthorpe, 261
Sea Garden Cottages, Tresco, 89
Seafood Restaurant & St Petroc's Hotel, The, Padstow, 67
Seatoller House, Seatoller, 272
Seaview Hotel, Seaview, 173
Seaview House, Ballylickey, 401
Selkirk Arms (New), Kirkudbright, 343
Shaven Crown Hotel, The, Shipton-under-Wychwood, 243
Sheedy's Restaurant & Hotel, Lisdoonvarna, 394
Shibden Mill Inn (New), Shibden, 292
Shieldaig Lodge, Badachro, 345
Shores Country House, Castlegregory, 373
Simonstone Hall, Hawes, 314
Sportsman's Arms, The, Pateley Bridge, 321
St Enodoc, Rock, 70
St Pauls House (New), Birmingham, 203
Stag & Huntsman, The, Hambleden, 215
Stanwell House Hotel, Lymington, 172
Stapleton Arms, The, Buckhorn Weston, 92
Star at Harome, The, Harome, 313
Star Castle Hotel, St Mary's, 88
Stow House, Aysgarth, 306
Strattons Hotel, Swaffham, 264
Strete Barton Guesthouse, Strete, 78
Sun Inn, The (New), Kirkby Lonsdale, 288
Sun Inn, The, Dedham, Dedham, 249
Swan Hotel, The, Lavenham, 270
Swan Hotel, The, Southwold, 271
Swan, The (New), Wedmore, 95
Sydney House Chelsea, London, 141

T
Talbooth House and Spa, Dedham, 250
Tawney, The, Stoke-on-trent, 177
Temple House, Ballymote, 379
The Broadford Hotel (New), Broadford, 348
The Henley, Bigbury-on-sea, 36
The Mustard Seed, Ballingarry, 400
The Pheasant (New), Neenton, 225
The Pheasant Inn, Shefford Woodlands, 149
The Talbot Inn, Mells, 61
Three Chimneys, Colbost, 368
Three Cocks, Three Cocks, 197
Three Horseshoes (New), Batcombe, 29
Tiroran House, Isle of Mull, 354
Titanic Hotel (New), Liverpool, 303
Tommyfield, The, London, 142
Toravaig House, Sleat, 330
Tower Bank Arms, Sawrey, 291
Town House Hotel, The, Melrose, 338
Traddock, The, Austwick, 275
Tresanton, St Mawes, 75
Trewornan Manor, St Minver, 76
Trigony House Hotel, Closeburn, 331
Trout at Tadpole Bridge, The, Faringdon, 213
Tudor Farmhouse, Clearwell, 210
Ty Mawr Country Hotel, Brechfa, 179
Tyddyn Llan, Llandrillo, 187
Tyrella House, Downpatrick, 375

U
Upper Buckton Farm, Leintwardine, 241

V
Viewfield House, Portree, 363

W
Wartling Place Country House Bed & Breakfast, Herstmonceux, 168
Wasdale Head Inn, Wasdale Head, 294

Index – Hotel names

Wasdale Head Inn, Wasdale Head, 294
Waterside Inn, The, Bray, 167
Wellington Arms, The, Baughurst, 97
Wheatsheaf Inn, The, Northleach, 242
White Horse and Griffin (New), Whitby, 272
White Horse, The, Brancaster, 246
White House, The (New), Bowness, 301
White House, The, Herm, 162
Whittling House, The (New), Alnmouth, 305
Widbrook Grange Hotel (New), Bradford-upon-Avon, 91
Wild Rabbit, The, Kingham, 221
Wilder, The (New), Dublin, 403
William Cecil, The, Stamford, 244
Winning Post, The, Winkfield, 176
Witchery by The Castle, The, Edinburgh, 341
Woodside, The (New), Doune, 369
Woolpack Inn, The, Totford, 174
Wrangham House, Hunmanby, 317
Wykeham Arms, Winchester, 175

Y
Yalbury Cottage, Lower Bockhampton, 60
Ynyshir, Eglwysfach, 181

Z
Zanzibar International Hotel, St Leonards-on-Sea, 153
Zetland House Hotel, Cashel Bay, 381
Zetter, The, London, 143

Index – Hotel locations

In this index, hotels are arranged in order of the names of the cities, towns or villages they are in or near. Hotels located in a very small village may be indexed under a larger place nearby. An index by hotel name precedes this one.

A

Abergavenny, Angel Hotel, The, 198
Aghadoe, Killeen House Hotel & Rozzers Restaurant, 376
Alnmouth, Whittling House, The (New), 305
Alton (Lower Froyle), Anchor Inn, The, 96
Ambleside, Rothay Manor (New), 273
Ardara, Green Gate B&B, The, 377
Ardmore, Cliff House Hotel, 400
Arkengarthdale, Charles Bathurst Inn, 300
Ashbourne, Callow Hall, 199
Ashford-in-the-water, Riverside House, 200
Askham, Askham Hall, 274
Auldearn, Boath House, 344
Austwick, Traddock, The, 275
Aysgarth, Aysgarth Falls, 300
Aysgarth, Stow House, 306

B

Babbacombe, Cary Arms, The, 27
Babcary, Red Lion, Somerset (New), 28
Badachro, Shieldaig Lodge, 345
Ballickey, Ballylickey Manor House (New), 373
Ballingarry, The Mustard Seed, 400
Ballylickey, Seaview House, 401
Ballymacarby, Hanoras Cottage, 378
Ballymote, Temple House, 379
Ballyvaughan, Gregan's Castle, 380
Balquidder, Monachyle Mhor, 346
Barford, George Inn, The (New), 201
Barngate, Drunken Duck Inn, 301

Barnsley, Boot at Barnsley, The, 202
Bashall Eaves, Red Pump Inn, The (New), 276
Baslow, Cavendish, The, 238
Batcombe, Three Horseshoes (New), 29
Bath, Broadstreet Townhouse, 90
Bath, Brook's Guesthouse Bath (New), 30
Bath, Dorian House, 31
Bath, Pig near Bath, The, 32
Bath, Queensberry, The, 33
Baughurst, Wellington Arms, The, 97
Beaminster, Ollerod, The, 34
Beercrocombe, Frog Street Farmhouse, 90
Beesands, Cricket Inn (New), 35
Bepton, Park House and Spa, 98
Bigbury-on-sea, The Henley, 36
Biggin-by-Hartington, Biggin Hall Hotel, 238
Bildeston, Bildeston Crown, The, 245
Birmingham, St Pauls House (New), 203
Bishop's Castle, Castle Hotel, The, 204
Bledington, Kings Head, 205
Bolton Abbey, Devonshire Arms, The, 307
Bontnewydd, Plas Dinas, 178
Borrowdale, Leathes Head, The, 277
Bourton-on-the-Hill, Horse & Groom, 206
Bourton-on-the-Water, Dial House Hotel, 207
Bowland Bridge, Hare and Hounds Inn (New), 278
Bowland Bridge, Masons Arms, The, 279
Bowness-on-Windermere, Lindeth Fell, 280
Bowness-on-Windermere, Linthwaite House, 281

Index – Hotel locations

Bowness, White House, The (New), 301
Brachla, Loch Ness Lodge, 347
Bradford-on-Avon, Priory Steps, 37
Bradford-upon-Avon, Widbrook Grange Hotel (New), 91
Brampton, Farlam Hall, 282
Brancaster, White Horse, The, 246
Branscombe, Masons Arms, 38
Bray, Waterside Inn, The, 167
Braye, Braye Beach, 160
Brechfa, Ty Mawr Country Hotel, 179
Brighton, Artist Residence Brighton, 99
Brighton, Hotel du Vin, Brighton, 167
Bristol, Artist Residence Bristol (New), 39
Bristol, Brook's Guesthouse Bristol (New), 40
Bristol, Hotel Du Vin, Bristol, 91
Broadchalke, Queens Head, The (New), 41
Broadford, The Broadford Hotel (New), 348
Brockenhurst, Pig, The, 100
Bruton, At the Chapel, 42
Buckhorn Weston, Stapleton Arms, The, 92
Bucklers Hard, Master Builder's, The, 101
Bude, Beach, The, 43
Burford, Burford House, 208
Burford, Lamb, The, 209
Burnsall, Devonshire Fell, The, 308
Bushmills, Bushmills Inn, The, 373
Byland, Byland Abbey Inn, 309

C

Camber, Gallivant Hotel, The, 102
Cambridge, Gresham House at the Gonville (New), 247
Carbis Bay, Boskerris, 44
Cashel Bay, Zetland House Hotel, 381
Cashel, Cashel Palace Hotel (New), 401
Castel, Fleur du Jardin, 161
Castlegregory, Shores Country House, 373
Castlelyons, Ballyvolane, 382
Chagford, Gidleigh Park, 26
Charlestown, Antonia's Pearls (New), 45
Cheltenham, 131 The Promenade (New), 269
Chettle, Chettle Lodge, 92
Chipping Camden, Cotswold House Hotel & Spa, 239
Chipping Campden, Noel Arms, 239
Clearwell, Tudor Farmhouse, 210
Cley-next-the-Sea, Cley Windmill, 248
Clifden, Ardagh Hotel, The, 402
Clifden, Quay House, The, 383
Clifton, George and Dragon, 283
Clipsham, Beech House, 211
Closeburn, Trigony House Hotel, 331
Cloyne, Barnabrow House, 402
Colbost, Three Chimneys, 368
Coltishall, Norfolk Mead, 177
Coltishall, Norfolk Mead, 269
Connel, Ards House, 368
Cornhill-on-Tweed, Collingwood Arms, The, 310
Cound, Riverside Inn, The, 177
Coverack, Bay Hotel, The, 46
Cowbridge, Bear Hotel, The (New), 180
Cranbourne, 10 Castle Street, 47
Crickhowell, Bear Hotel, The, 177
Crosthwaite, Punch Bowl Inn, 284
Crudwell, Rectory, The, 48
Cuckfield, Ockenden Manor, 103
Cupar, Peat Inn, The, 332

D

Dedham, Sun Inn, The, Dedham, 249
Dedham, Talbooth House and Spa, 250

Index – Hotel locations

Dingle, Pax House, 384
Dittisham, Fingals, 93
Dorchester, Casterbridge, The, 26
Dornoch, Dornoch Hotel, 330
Doune, Woodside, The (New), 369
Downpatrick, Tyrella House, 375
Drinagh, Killiane Castle Country House, 385
Dublin, Cliff Townhouse, The, 373
Dublin, Kilronan House, 386
Dublin, Number 31, 387
Dublin, Wilder, The (New), 403
Duns, Allanton Inn (New), 341

E
East Chilington, Jolly Sportsman (New), 104
East Chisenbury, Red Lion Freehouse, 105
East End, East End Arms, 106
East Grinstead, Gravetye Manor Hotel, 107
East Hoathly, Old Whyly, 108
East Lavant, Royal Oak, The, 109
East Witton, Blue Lion, The (New), 311
Edinburgh, Witchery by The Castle, The, 341
Egerton, George at Egerton, The, 110
Eglwysfach, Ynyshir, 181
Elgol, Coruisk House, 349
Emsworth, 36 on The Quay, 111
Exton, Barnsdale Lodge, 177

F
Fairford, Bull, The, 212
Falmouth, Highcliffe Contemporary Bed & Breakfast, 49
Faringdon, Trout at Tadpole Bridge, The, 213
Felin Fach, Felin Fach Griffin, The, 183
Fletching, Griffin Inn, The, 112
Fonthill Gifford, Beckford Arms, The, 50
Fort WIlliam, Crolinnhe, 330
Fort William, Glenfinnan, 350
Fort WIlliam, Grange, The, 351
Fowey, Old Quay House, 51
Frome, Babington House, 93

G
Ganllwyd, Plas Domelynilyn, 183
Gittisham, Pig at Combe, The, 52
Glasgow, 15 Glasgow, 333
Glasgow, One Devonshire Gardens, 334
Goldsborough, Goldsborough Hall, 272
Goleen, Heron's Cove, The, 388
Gorey, Marlfield House Hotel, 389
Grasmere, Forest Side, 285
Grassington, Ashfield House, 312
Great Ecclestone, Cartford Inn, The (New), 286
Great Langdale, Old Dungeon Ghyll, 302
Great Rissington, Lamb Inn, 214
Great Waldingfield, Rectory Manor House, 251
Great Wilbraham, Carpenters Arms, The (New), 252
Gullane, Bonnie Badger (New), 335
Gullane, Greywalls, 342
Gulworthy, Horn of Plenty, The, 53

H
Hambleden, Stag & Huntsman, The, 215
Hambleton, Hambleton Hall, 216
Hampton-in-Arden, Hampton Manor, 217
Harome, Star at Harome, The, 313
Harrogate, Hotel du Vin, 272
Harwich, Pier at Harwich, The, 253
Haslemere, Georgian, The (New), 113
Hawes, Simonstone Hall, 314
Hawkshead, Ees Wyke, 287
Hawnby, Owl, The, 315
Hay-on-Wye, Cynefin Retreat (New), 184

Index – Hotel locations

Hereford, Castle House, 218
Herm, White House, The, 162
Herstmonceux, Wartling Place Country House Bed & Breakfast, 168
Hetton, Angel at Hetton, The (New), 316
Hindon, Grosvenor at Hindon (New), 54
Hinton St George, Lord Poulett Arms, 55
Horndon on the Hill, Bell, The (New), 254
Horsham, Leonardslee House (New), 114
Hough-on-the-Hill, Brownlow Arms, The, 219
Hunmanby, Wrangham House, 317

I
Illmington, Howard Arms, 240
Inis Meain, Inis Meain Restaurant and Suites, 390
Inistioge, Cullintra House, 391
Innishanon, Innishannon House, 403
Inveraray, George, The (New), 352
Ironbridge, Library House, 240
Isle of Eriska, Isle Of Eriska Hotel, 353
Isle of Mull, Tiroran House, 354
Isle of Ornsay, Hotel Eilean Iarmain, 355

K
Jedburgh, Hundalee House, 342
Kelleth, Kelleth Old Hall, 272
Kelmscott, Plough, The, 220
Kelso, Edenwater House (New), 343
Kelso, Ednam House Hotel, 330
Kenmare, Muxnaw Lodge, 404
Kesgrave, Milsom's Kesgrave Hall (New), 255
Kilberry, Kilberry Inn, The, 336
Kilgraney, Lorum Old Rectory, 404
Kilkenny, Butler House, 405
Killiecrankie, Killiecrankie Hotel, 356

King's Lynn, Bank House Hotel, 256
King's Lynn, Congham Hall Hotel & Spa, 257
Kingham, Wild Rabbit, The, 221
Kingussie, Cross, The, 357
Kintbury, Dundas Arms, 168
Kirkby Lonsdale, Sun Inn, The (New), 288
Kirkby Stephen, Augill Castle, 272
Kirkcolm, Corsewall Lighthouse, 337
Kirkudbright, Selkirk Arms (New), 343
Kylesku, Kylesku Hotel, 358

L
Lampeter, Falcondale, The (New), 185
Langar, Langar Hall, 222
Langho, Northcote, 302
Lastingham, Lastingham Grange, 318
Lavenham, Swan Hotel, The, 270
Leeds, 42 The Calls, 272
Leeds, Haley's Hotel, 272
Leenane, Delphi Lodge, 392
Leintwardine, Upper Buckton Farm, 241
Lewannick, Coombeshead Farm (New), 56
Lewdown, Lewtrenchard Manor, 57
Lifton, Arundell Arms, The, 58
Linwood, High Corner Inn (New), 115
Lisdoonvarna, Ballinalacken Castle Country House, 393
Lisdoonvarna, Sheedy's Restaurant & Hotel, 394
Littlestone, Gallivant Littlestone Beach, The, 116
Littley Green, Compasses, The (New), 26
Liverpool, Racquet Club, The, 303
Liverpool, Titanic Hotel (New), 303
Llanbrynmair, Barlings Barn, 186
Llandrillo, Tyddyn Llan, 187
Llandudno, Osborne House, 188

Index – Hotel locations

Llanthony, Llanthony Priory, 189
Llyswen, Llangoed Hall Hotel, 198
Lochinver, Albannach, The, 359
Lochinver, Glencanisp Lodge (New), 360
London, 11 Cadogan Gardens, 169
London, 41 Hotel (New), 117
London, Alma, The, 118
London, Aragon House (New), 169
London, Artist Residence London, 119
London, Batty Langley's, 120
London, Beaufort, The, 121
London, Bedford, The (New), 122
London, Bingham Riverhouse, 123
London, Brama (New), 170
London, Capital, The, 124
London, Chiltern Firehouse, 26
London, Church Street Hotel, 125
London, Coach and Horses, Kew Green (New), 126
London, Colonnade, The, 127
London, Covent Garden Hotel, 128
London, Culpeper, The (New), 170
London, Fox and Grapes, 129
London, Franklin, The, 171
London, Georgian House Hotel, The (New), 130
London, Gore, The, 131
London, Hazlitts, 132
London, High Road House, 133
London, Hotel 55, 134
London, Laslett, The (New), 135
London, Lime Tree Hotel, 136
London, Mayflower Hotel, 171
London, Orange, The, 137
London, Prince Akatoki, The, 138
London, Princess Victoria, The (New), 139
London, Rookery, The, 140
London, Sydney House Chelsea, 141
London, Tommyfield, The, 142
London, Zetter, The, 143
Long Melford, Black Lion Hotel, 258
Longleat, Bath Arms, 59
Lower Bockhampton, Yalbury Cottage, 60
Lower Swell, Langford Fivehead, 26
Loweswater, Kirkstile Inn (New), 289
Lyme Regis, Alexandra, The (New), 94
Lymington, Stanwell House Hotel, 172

M

Magheralin, Newforge House, 374
Mallow, Longueville House Hotel, 395
Malpas, Cholmondeley Arms, 223
Malvern Wells, Cottage in The Wood, The, 224
Margate, Fort Road Hotel (New), 144
Margate, Reading Rooms, The, 145
Mawgan Porth, Scarlet, The, 26
Mells, The Talbot Inn, 61
Melrose*, Burts Hotel, 338
Melrose*, Town House Hotel, The, 338
Millgate, Millgate House, 319
Milton Abbot, Hotel Endsleigh, 62
Minster, Old Swan & Minster Mill, 177
Mistley, Mistley Thorn, The, 259
Morston, Morston Hall, 260
Mountrath, Roundwood House, 396
Mousehole, Old Coastguard, The, 63
Muir of Ord, Dower House, The, 369
Mulranny, Rosturk Woods, 373

N

Nant Gwynant, Pen Y Gwryd Hotel, 190
Narbeth, Grove of Narbeth, The, 191

Index – Hotel locations

Neenton, The Pheasant (New), 225
Nether Westcote, Feathered Nest Country Inn, The, 241
Nettleton, Fosse Farmhouse, 64
Newmarket-on-Fergus, Carrygerry House, 405
Newquay, Headland Cottages, The, 94
Northleach, Wheatsheaf Inn, The, 242
Norton, Hundred House, 226
Norwich, 38 St Giles St, 270
Nun Monkton, Alice Hawthorn, The (New), 320

O

Oakford Bridge, Bark House, The (New), 65
Oddington, Fox, The, 242
Old Radnor, Harp Inn, The (New), 192
Old Winsdor, Loch and Tyne (New), 146
Orford, Crown and Castle, The, 271
Oxford, Old Bank Hotel, 227
Oxford, Old Parsonage, The, 228

P

Padstow, Padstow Townhouse, 66
Padstow, Seafood Restaurant & St Petroc's Hotel, The, 67
Pangbourne, Elephant at Pangbourne, The (New), 172
Pateley Bridge, Sportsman's Arms, The, 321
Penally, Penally Abbey, 193
Penmaenpool, Penmaenuchaf Hall, 194
Penrith, Another Place Lakeside (New), 290
Penzance, Artist Residence Penzance, 68
Penzance, Chapel House, 69
Petworth, Old Railway Station, The, 173
Pitlochry, Knockendarroch House Hotel, 361
Port Appin, Airds Hotel, 362
Portpatrick, Knockingham Lodge, 339
Portree, Viewfield House, 363

R

Ramsden, Royal Oak Ramsden, The (New), 229
Ramsgill-in-Nidderdale, Burgoyne Hotel, 322
Rathmullan, Rathmullan House, 406
Rathnew, Hunter's Hotel, 397
Recess, Lough Inagh Lodge, 398
Repton, Boot, The (New), 230
Reynoldston, Fairyhill, 177
Rhydycroesau, Pen-y-Dyffryn, 231
Richmond, Easby Hall, 323
Ripley, Boars Head (New), 324
Riverstown, Rossnaree House, 399
Rock, St Enodoc, 70
Romaldkirk, Rose and Crown, The, 325
Rosevine, Driftwood Hotel, 71
Rowsley, Peacock at Rowsley, The, 232
Rye, George in Rye, The, 147
Rye, Jeake's House, 148
Rye, Mermaid Inn, The, 26

S

Sanquar, Blackaddie House, 340
Sawrey, Tower Bank Arms, 291
Scarista, Scarista House, 364
Sculthorpe, Sculthorpe Mill, The (New), 261
Seatoller, Seatoller House, 272
Seaview, Seaview Hotel, 173
Settle, Golden Lion (New), 304
Shanagarry, Ballymaloe House, 406
Sheffield, Brocco on the Park, 233
Shefford Woodlands, The Pheasant Inn, 149
Sheriff Hutton, Hall Farm B&B, 326
Shibden, Shibden Mill Inn (New), 292
Shipton-under-Wychwood, Shaven Crown Hotel, The, 243

Index – Hotel locations

Shrewsbury, Lion + Pheasant, 177
Sidlesham, Crab and Lobster, The, 150
Sissinghurst, Milk House, The, 151
Skenfrith, Bell at Skenfrith, The, 195
Sleat, Kinloch Lodge, 365
Sleat, Toravig House, 330
Snettishm, Rose and Crown, 262
South Dalton, Pipe and Glass, 327
South Leigh, Artist Residence Oxford, 234
Southampton, Pig in wall, The, 152
Southleigh, Glebe House (New), 77
Southwold, Swan Hotel, The, 271
Spean Bridge, Corriegour Lodge, 366
St Aubin, Clifden Yurts, 163
St Austell, Boscundle Manor Hotel, 72
St Brelade, Harbour View, 164
St Brelade, La Haule Manor, 165
St Hilary, Ennys, 73
St Leonards-on-Sea, Zanzibar International Hotel, 153
St Mary's, Star Castle Hotel, 88
St Mawes, Idle Rocks, 74
St Mawes, Tresanton, 75
St Minver, Trewornan Manor, 76
St Peter Port, Fermain Valley, 166
St Saviour, Longuevile Manor, 26
Stamford, Bull & Swan, The, 243
Stamford, William Cecil, The, 244
Stannersburn, Pheasant, The (New), 272
Stanstead, Linden House, 177
Stockbridge, Greyhound, The, 154
Stockbridge, Grosvenor, The (New), 155
Stockbridge, Peat Spade Inn, 156
Stoke by Nayland, Angel Inn, The, 263
Stoke-on-trent, Tawney, The, 177
Strachur, Creggans Inn, 370
Stratford-upon-Avon, Burnside, Stratford Upon Avon (New), 235
Strete, Strete Barton Guesthouse, 78
Strontian, KIlcamb Lodge, 367
Studland, Pig on the beach, The, 79
Sturminster Newton, Plumber Manor, 80
Swaffham, Strattons Hotel, 264
Swallowcliffe, Royal Oak, The, 81

T
Tal-y-llyn, Dolffanor Fawr, 196
Tarbert, Hotel Hebrides, 370
Tetbury, Calcot Manor Hotel, 236
Thorington, Husk (New), 265
Thorpe Market, Gunton Arms, The, 266
Three Cocks, Three Cocks, 197
Thurso, Forss House, 371
Tisbury, Pythouse Kitchen Garden, 82
Tollard Royal, King John Inn, 95
Totford, Woolpack Inn, The, 174
Tresco, Sea Garden Cottages, 89
Tunbridge Wells, Hotel du Vin, 26

U
Ullswater, Glenridding House, 293
Ullswater, Howtown House, 304
Urquhart, Old Church of Urquhart, The, 371

V
Ventnor, Hambrough, The, 174

W
Walberswick, Anchor, The, 267
Walls, Burrastow House, 372
Wareham, Priory Hotel and Restaurant, The, 83
Wasdale Head, Wasdale Head Inn, 294
Wedmore, Swan, The (New), 95
Wells-next-the-sea, Globe Inn, The (New), 268

Index – Hotel locations

West Hoathly, Cat Inn, The, 157
Whashton, Mount Pleasant Farm, 272
Whitby, White Horse and Griffin (New), 272
Whitewell, Inn at Whitewell, The, 295
Whitley, Pear Tree Inn, The, 26
Wickham, Old House Hotel, The, 175
Wilton, Pembroke Arms, The (New), 84
Winchester, Hotel du Vin, Winchester, 158
Winchester, Wykeham Arms, 175
Windermere, Cedar Manor, 296
Windermere, Gilpin Hotel and Lake House, 297
Windermere, Holbeck Ghyll, 298
Winkfield, Winning Post, The, 176
Winsford, Royal Oak, The, 85
Wiswell, Freemasons at Wiswell (New), 299
Woodstock, Feathers, The (New), 177
Woodstown, Gaultier Lodge, 407
Worfield, Old Vicarage, The, 237

Y
Yarmouth, George, The, 159
Yattendon, Royal Oak, Yattendon, 176
York, Bar Convent, 328
York, Grays Court, 329

Z
Zeals, Bell and Crown (New), 86
Zennor, Gurnards Head, The, 87

Other Duncan Petersen titles

Buy your *Charming Small Hotel Guide* or other titles by post or email directly from the publisher and you'll get a worthwhile discount. *

Titles:	Retail price	Discount price
Austria, Switzerland and the Alps	£14.99	£13.50
France	£14.99	£13.50
Germany	£14.99	£13.50
Italy	£16.99	£15.50
Spain	£14.99	£13.50

The *On Foot City Guides* are great companions for the *Charming Small Hotel Guides*. These books feature unique aerial-view maps, which show not only the city's street layout but the look of your surroundings too.

Titles:	Retail price	Discount price
London Walks	£10.99	£9.50
New York Walks	£10.99	£9.50
Paris Walks	£10.99	£9.50
Prague Walks	£10.99	£9.50
Rome Walks	£10.99	£9.50
Venice Walks	£10.99	£9.50
Florence Walks	£10.99	£9.50

We also publish an innovative series of country walking and cycling routes on cards in boxes, including *Walker's Britain in a Box* and *Walks For Mind and Spirit,* the perfect companions to *Charming Small Hotels Britain & Ireland*. All these guides are stocked by Amazon. You can also email us for more information on this series at duncan.petersen@zen.co.uk.

Please send orders to: Book Sales, Duncan Petersen Publishing Ltd, G9 82 Silverthorne Road, Battersea, London, SW8 3HE; or: duncan.petersen@zen.co.uk, giving: the title and number of copies; name and address; cheque made out to: Duncan Petersen Publishing Ltd, or card details.
*Offer applies to this edition and UK only.

Exchange rates
As we went to press, $1 bought 0.92 euros and £1 bought 1.17 euros